The Soviet Union and Eastern Europe

The Soviet Union and Eastern Europe:

A Bibliographic Guide to
Recommended Books for
Small and Medium-sized Libraries and
School Media Centers

Stephan M. Horak
Eastern Illinois University

1985
LIBRARIES UNLIMITED, INC.
Littleton, Colorado

LIBRARIES UNLIMITED, INC.
P.O. Box 263
Littleton, Colorado 80160-0263

Library of Congress Cataloging in Publication Data

Horak, Stephan M., 1920-
    The Soviet Union and Eastern Europe.

    Includes index.
    1. Soviet Union--Bibliography. 2. Europe, Eastern--
Bibliography. 3. Bibliography--Best books--Soviet
Union. 4. Bibliography--Best books--Europe, Eastern.
Z2491.H59   1985   [DK17]   016.947   84-25053
ISBN 0-87287-469-9

Libraries Unlimited books are bound with Type II nonwoven material that meets
and exceeds National Association of State Textbook Administrators' Type II
nonwoven material specifications Class A through E.

TABLE OF CONTENTS

PART 3
USSR—Non-Russian Republics, Jews, Other Peoples

PART 4
Eastern European Countries

ABBREVIATIONS OF PERIODICAL TITLES

AA	American Anthropology
AAPSS-A	American Academy of Political and Social Science, Annals
AER	American Economic Review
AHR	American Historical Review
APSR	American Political Science Review
ARBA	American Reference Books Annual
ASR	American Sociological Review
BHR	Business History Review
BL	Booklist
BRD	Book Review Digest
CASS	Canadian-American Slavic Studies
CH	Current History
Choice	Choice
CR	Contemporary Review
CRL	College and Research Libraries
CRSN	Canadian Review of Studies in Nationalism
CS	Contemporary Sociology
CSP	Canadian Slavonic Papers
EEQ	East European Quarterly
EG	Economic Geography
GJ	Geographical Journal
HE	Human Events
HRNB	History: Reviews of New Books
HT	History Today
ILR	International Labour Review
JAH	Journal of American History
JAS	Journal of Asian Studies

JBS	Journal of Baltic Studies
JC	Journal of Communication
JEH	Journal of Economic History
JEL	Journal of Economic Literature
JMH	Journal of Modern History
JP	Journal of Politics
LJ	Library Journal
LQ	Library Quarterly
MA	Modern Age
MQ	Musical Quarterly
NP	Nationalities Papers
NR	National Review
PR	Polish Review
PSQ	Political Science Quarterly
PW	Publishers Weekly
RP	Review of Politics
RQ	Reference Quarterly
RR	Russian Review
RSR	Reference Services Review
SEEJ	The Slavic and East European Journal
SEER	Slavonic and East European Review
SJA	Soviet Jewish Affairs
SR	Slavic Review
SRNB	Sociology: Review of New Books
SS	Soviet Studies
TLS	Times Literary Supplement
WLB	Wilson Library Bulletin
WLT	World Literature Today

INTRODUCTION

This selected, annotated bibliography on the Soviet Union and Eastern European countries is the first designed for use outside institutions specializing in that area of expertise. While it is true that the specialists are by now well educated and informed about the Soviet Union, Poland, Czechoslovakia, Hungary, Romania, Yugoslavia, Bulgaria, and Albania and have at their disposal a massive array of published reference sources, such is not yet the case for the much larger number of Americans as well as Canadians outside these institutions and special research centers.

For these reasons, and especially considering the urgent need for a democratic society to remain educated on worldwide issues and problems, the decision was made to provide the public at large as well as the younger generation at various educational levels with this reference tool offering works from the broadest possible list of subjects.

To this end, the bibliography offers 1,555 titles which should aid librarians in small and medium-sized public libraries and media centers and librarians of high schools, junior colleges, and four-year colleges in assisting students and especially teachers in the development of curricula, classroom instruction, and reading lists to enhance the learning process.

The selection of titles was made by targeting primarily the above-mentioned users and purpose. Priority was given to general studies, followed by special studies with a somewhat broader treatment in content and presentation. Also, special attention was given to encyclopedias, handbooks, and bibliographies for those seeking additional material in the areas of their special interest. Because of the physical limit on volume in the chapters on literature, works by individual authors have not been considered. They can be identified either in bibliographies or in anthologies listed here. On the other hand, dictionaries and grammars are provided, as well as histories of literatures of the respective nationalities.

Entries are grouped in four distinct parts: first, works on the Soviet Union and Eastern European countries; second, works on the Russian Empire prior to 1917 and the Soviet Union; third, books on the non-Russian Soviet republics, Jews, and other ethnic groups in the USSR; and fourth, books on Eastern European countries in alphabetical order. Each part subsequently is arranged by subjects, representing mainly social sciences and humanities.

To be most useful the bibliography lists mainly books published in the past four decades with emphasis on the most recent ones, which are considered to be the most up-to-date in knowledge and sources available to the respective authors, and either are still in print or directly accessible in most public and university libraries or indirectly accessible through the interlibrary loan system. Furthermore, for the users' convenience cited works are provided with a complete description and informative annotations which have been either abstracted from reviews published in professional journals or prepared by myself. For users who would like to be additionally informed on the substance and importance of the book, several review sources are given with the understanding that the first journal listed has been used for annotation. A list of abbreviations of the periodicals consulted is provided. Each source provides the title of the journal, volume, number or year, and pages.

The very process of selecting the titles from among some eight thousand books published in the English language in the past four decades had to be arbitrary and based on the judgment of the reviewers as well as the realization of the purpose and readership in mind. It is hoped that the volume will serve well the intended groups of users, and I shall be thankful for any comments concerning the extent of usefulness of this bibliography.

My personal thanks go to the publisher, Libraries Unlimited, for the suggestion that I prepare this reference tool and for its publication.

Stephan M. Horak

1

GENERAL AND INTERRELATED THEMES — UNION OF THE SOVIET SOCIALIST REPUBLICS AND EASTERN EUROPEAN COUNTRIES

1. **The American Bibliography of Slavic and East European Studies.** Published by Indiana University in "Slavic and East European Series" (1957-66); since 1967 under the sponsorship of the American Association for the Advancement of Slavic Studies; **for 1975** (1975) 224p.; **for 1976** (1976) 229p.; **for 1977** (1981) 272p.; **for 1978** (1982) 269p.; **for 1979** (1983) 291p. David H. Kraus, ed. $55.00 per vol. (Prepared at the Library of Congress for the American Association for the Advancement of Slavic Studies.)

This bibliography seeks to present (on an annual basis) as complete a record as possible of North American publications in Slavic and East European studies. It includes works, primarily in English but also in other languages, which are of research or information value and which were published in North America or, if published elsewhere, were written, edited, or compiled by North Americans. The average number of entries per issue is five thousand. An author index and a bibliographic index are provided. This is a basic tool for anyone involved in Soviet and East European studies.

2. Horak, Stephan M. **Russia, the USSR, and Eastern Europe: A Bibliographic Guide to English Language Publications, 1964-1974.** Edited by Rosemary Neiswender. Littleton, CO: Libraries Unlimited, 1978. xiv, 488p.

    Russia, the USSR, and Eastern Europe: A Bibliographic Guide to English Language Publications, 1975-1980. Littleton, CO: Libraries Unlimited, 1982. 279p. $30.00.

The entries are annotated with excerpts from or adaptations of reviews in British, Canadian, and American journals devoted to Slavic and East European studies. Included in the three parts of the book are works on Russia, the USSR, and Eastern Europe. Only monographic publications are listed. The first volume contains 1,611 entries; the supplement has 1,027 entries. Author-title and subject indexes are appended. College and university libraries, large public libraries, instructors, and students will find this annotated bibliography a most valuable resource.

ARBA, 10(1979):189; Choice, 15(1979):1642; Choice, 20(1982):53; WLB, 15(1982):702.

3.   Kanet, Roger E., comp. **Soviet and East European Foreign Policy: A Bibliography of English- and Russian-Language Publications, 1967-1971.** Santa Barbara, CA: ABC-Clio Press, 1974. 208p. $21.75.

Approximately thirty-two hundred items are listed, including journal articles as well as books. This increases the value of the bibliography enormously. The entries are arranged according to author, or by title if the author's name is not given. This means that the publications on any given subject are scattered throughout the volume instead of being conveniently grouped in one place. There is a long, detailed index, with many headings and subheadings.

   Choice, 11(1975):1608; CRL, 36(1975):314.

4.   Kerner, Robert Joseph. **Slavic Europe: A Selected Bibliography in the Western European Languages Comprising History, Languages and Literature.** New York: Russell & Russell, 1969. (Reprint of 1918 ed.) 402p. $11.50.

Originally published as volume 1 of the "Harvard Bibliographies, Library Series," this bibliography still retains its value, with forty-five hundred entries covering Russia and all other Slav peoples. Chapters on each nationality are divided by subjects, emphasizing historical and cultural topics.

5.   Kolarz, Walter, ed. **Books on Communism: A Bibliography.** 2d ed. New York: Oxford University Press, 1964. 568p. $4.80.

The first edition (1959) covered the years 1945-57, the present volume the years 1945-62. This new edition lists about twenty-five hundred items. The contents of this useful bibliography are divided into fifty-two "subject and country sections," of which the first five deal with Communism and the world Communist movement, the next twenty with the Soviet Union, the next twenty-five with Communism and related questions in other countries, and the last two with official publications on Communism and relations with the Soviet Union and the Communist bloc.

   SR, 24:2:363-64; LJ, 90(1965):1872.

6.   Schöpflin, George, ed. **The Soviet Union and Eastern Europe: A Handbook.** New York: Praeger, 1970. 614p. $25.00.

A team of contributors examine the political and economic systems of the Eastern European countries within the Soviet enclosure, the structure of their societies, and their cultural life. A brief introduction provides the historical background essential to an accurate understanding of the Soviet Union and Eastern Europe; it is followed by basic country-by-country information on the governments, economies, communications, and social structure of the Communist-ruled states in Central-Eastern-Balkan Europe.

   EEQ, 5:4:566-57; Choice, 7(1971):1646; LJ, 96(1971):64.

7.   Shoup, Paul S. **The East European and Soviet Data Handbook: Political, Social, and Developmental Indicators, 1945-1975.** New York: Columbia University Press, 1981; Stanford, CA: Hoover Institution Press, xv, 482p. $40.00

The *Handbook* is designed primarily to serve scholars and other researchers with basic social science data. Its major objective is to give an overview of social change and elite development in Eastern Europe and the Soviet Union since World War II with the data presented in such a way as to facilitate comparisons. The volume has eight main sections: population, party membership, national and religious affiliation, education attainment, classes, party leaders, occupations, developmental indicators, and standard of living. Appendixes offer additional data on education and party leadership. A lengthy general introduction as well as brief introductions to the individual sections are provided.

RQ, 21(1981):93; CRL, 43(1982):72.

ECONOMICS

8. Birkos, Alexander S., and Tambs, Lewis A., comps. **East European and Soviet Economic Affairs: A Bibliography (1965-1973).** Littleton, CO: Libraries Unlimited, 1975. 170p. $10.00.

A collection of English-language books and articles dealing with the economic affairs of Eastern Europe and the Soviet Union. The compilers present a broad, comprehensive bibliography of material available in most medium-sized and large libraries. The entries (1,168) are arranged geographically and subdivided by subjects. A list of publishing outlets for scholarly papers, and author, title, publisher, and periodical indexes are appended.

> ARBA, 7(1976):396.

9. Francisco, Ronald A.; Laird, Betty A., and Laird, Roy D., eds. **Agricultural Policies in the USSR and Eastern Europe.** Conclusion by Eugen Wädekin. Boulder, CO: Westview Press, 1980. xvii, 332p. Tables. $33.00.

Contributors to this volume see the agrarian problem in Communist systems as only the most conspicuous aspect of the more comprehensive problem of low efficiency—the price paid for the pursuit of ideological goals. The nations of Eastern Europe and the USSR seem destined to face, increasingly, a choice between satisfying citizen demand for improved diets and satisfying ideological imperatives. Between 1970 and 1979 enormous investments were made in the state and collective farms, but returns, especially in labor productivity, have been disappointing.

10. Holzman, Franklyn D. **International Trade under Communism—Politics and Economics.** New York: Basic Books, 1976. xvi, 239p. $15.00.

Holzman's arguments are so lucid and his explanations of institutional, political, and economic interactions so simple yet so complete that the complexities surrounding the Council for Mutual Economic Assistance (CMEA) are made accessible to the layperson. This book is a must reading for all students of socialist economies.

> Choice, 13(1977):1474; JEL, 15(1977):551.

11. Ingram, David. **The Communist Economic Challenge.** New York: Praeger, 1965. 168p.

As a calm and well-written study, touching selectively on the main weaknesses and strengths of Communist economies, this book should prove useful for a wide audience of nonspecialists. Communist economic trends since 1963 have certainly not made the book obsolete; they have, in fact, strengthened the author's judgments.

> SR, 25:4:708-9.

12.   Karcz, Jerzy F., ed. **Soviet and East European Agriculture.** Berkeley: University of California Press, 1967. 445p. $10.00.

This volume consists of fourteen papers presented at the Conference on Soviet Agricultural and Peasant Affairs held in Santa Barbara in August 1965. Eleven of them deal with Soviet agriculture, mostly during the Khrushchev era, and one each with Yugoslavian, Czechoslovakian, and Polish agriculture. The papers are well written and readily accessible to any student of the subject.

SR, 27:4:674-75; AER, 58(1968):293.

13.   Loeber, Dietrich André, comp. and ed. **East-West and Internationalist Trade: A Sourcebook on the International Economic Relations of Socialist Countries and Their Legal Aspects.** 4 vols. Dobbs Ferry, NY: Oceana Publications, 1976-77. xlix, 424p.; xviii, 578p.; xviii, 547p.; xviii, 647p. $45.00 each.

The book will be useful primarily to legal experts on East-West trade and to anyone interested in the organization of foreign trade systems in socialist countries. It concentrates on two principal subjects: the organizations of intrasocialist and East-West relations, and the equality and discrimination in East-West economic relations. It can be highly recommended as a basic reference.

SR, 36:2:328-30.

14.   Mellor, Roy E. H. **Comecon: Challenge to the West.** New York: Van Nostrand Reinhold Company, 1971. 152p. $3.50 pa. (Searchlight Book, no. 48.)

The purpose of this book is to provide "the layreader and those ... commercially involved in dealing with Comecon countries" with "a fund of basic information" about this Soviet bloc institution. Nearly half of this slender volume is devoted to a detailed, country-by-country account of the economic development patterns and present industrial potential of the individual Comecon members. The book contains a great deal of information of interest to general readers or businessmen as well as more serious students of economic relations in Eastern Europe.

SR, 32:1:179-80; GJ, 138(1972):260.

15.   Meznerics, Ivan. **Law of Banking in East-West Trade.** Translated by Emil Böszörményi Nagy. Budapest: Akademiai Kiado; Leiden: A. W. Sijthoff; Dobbs Ferry, NY: Oceana Publications, 1973. 427p. $25.00.

A Hungarian economist discusses various aspects of trade and commercial transactions between East European countries and the West; emphasis is placed on laws governing the operation of banks. The author not only provides relevant legal texts but also offers extensive commentaries on the various laws. The book will serve individuals and businesses involved in the growing East-West trade.

16.   Nayyar, Deepar, ed. **Economic Relations between Socialist Countries and the Third World.** Montclair, NJ: Allanheld, Osmun & Co., 1979. vii, 265p. $25.50.

This work consists of a collection of essays devoted to economic relations between the socialist countries of Eastern Europe and nonsocialist, less developed countries,

with a special chapter devoted to relations between the latter and China. An introductory article is followed by case studies of Tanzania, Egypt, Ghana, Nigeria, India, and Pakistan, in turn followed by an analysis of the impact of Soviet oil.
SEER, 58:4:628-29.

17.   Wilczynski, Jozef. **The Economics and Politics of East-West Trade.** New York: Praeger, 1969. 416p. $12.50 pa.
This book is a very competent introduction to East-West trade. The author analyzes the political and economic forces in trade since 1945 and finds trade increasingly conditioned by economic self-interest. The study is divided into three parts: (1) historical survey, (2) background on ideology, organization, exchange rates, and integration with central planning, and (3) analysis of trade issues—discrimination, dumping, bilateralism and settlements, gains from trade, and others.
Choice, 7(1970):269; LJ, 95(1970):491.

18.   Wilczynski, Jozef. **The Economics of Socialism: Principles Governing the Operation of the Centrally Planned Economies in the USSR and Eastern Europe under the New System.** Chicago: Aldine Publishing Co., 1970. 233p.; 4th ed. New York: Allen Unwin, 1982. 272p. $10.95 pa.
This survey brings together the elementary principles that govern the operation of the centrally planned economies of Eastern Europe and the USSR. The following topics are discussed: planning and the market, profit, production and growth, accumulation, consumption, labor, land, pricing, money and banking, fiscal policy and control, domestic trade, foreign trade, international economic cooperation, and socialism versus capitalism. Each chapter is followed by a list of suggested references available in English.
SR, 31:3:691.

19.   Wilczynski, Jozef. **Technology in COMECON: Acceleration of Technological Progress through Economic Planning and the Market.** New York: Praeger, 1974. 379p. $22.50.
This book is full of information, including fifty-nine tables and eight diagrams about technology in Comecon countries (excluding Cuba) as seen from the viewpoint of an economist. The book will be useful mainly for reference.
SR, 35:1:152; TLS, 14(1975):175.

20.   Zaleski, Eugen, and Wienert, Helgard. **Technology Transfer between East and West.** Paris: Organization for Economic Co-operation and Development, 1980. 435p. Tables. Paper.
Anyone interested in obtaining a clear and comprehensive overview of the development of East-West trade and of the role of technology transfer in that trade relationship will find this study a most valuable source of information. It provides as complete a picture as possible at present of the overall quantity and forms of technology transfer in East-West trade.
SR, 40:4:656.

21.   Bertsch, Gary K., and Ganschow, Thomas W., eds. **Comparative Communism: The Soviet, Chinese and Yugoslav Models.** San Francisco: W. H. Freeman, 1976. xi, 463p. $24.00 cl.; $10.95 pa.

The compilers of this volume have assembled a set of relevant readings intended primarily for undergraduate study. These are arranged in nine sections covering ideological and cultural background, historical development, the political system, the economy, and foreign relations. The readings are taken from published books and articles and include no primary material.

   SR, 36:1:124-25.

22.   Farrell, Robert Barry, ed. **Political Leadership in Eastern Europe and the Soviet Union.** Chicago: Aldine Publishing Co., 1970. 359p. $12.50 cl.; $4.95 pa.

This symposium comprises: A. G. Meyer, "Historical Development of the Communist Theory of Leadership"; Carl J. Friedrich, "The Theory of Political Leadership and the Issue of Totalitarianism"; Frederick C. Barghoorn, "Trends in Top Political Leadership"; plus five essays dealing with the theme "Leadership and Society."

23.   Gripp, Richard C. **The Political System of Communism.** New York: Dodd, Mead, 1973. 209p. $3.95 pa.

The author compares political structures and processes of fourteen Communist states, employing five hypotheses as organizing principles: intent to institute a Communist society, domination of the Communist party, introduction of public-socialist ownership, provision for popular participation, and establishment of foreign policies supporting Communist states and revolutionary movements in non-Communist countries.

   SR, 33:2:374; TLS, Feb. 8(1974):124.

24.   Hazard, John N. **Communists and Their Law: A Search for the Common Core of the Legal Systems of the Marxian Socialist States.** Chicago: University of Chicago Press, 1969. 560p. $17.50.

The author seeks to find the common core of all Marxian socialist legal systems. He mentions fourteen states: nine East European, four Asian, and one American— Cuba. He proceeds with an analysis of several chosen institutes or sectors of law, such as land utilization, property in the production enterprise, inheritance, family, contract law, state planning, torts, and correction of criminals. This is a most interesting study.

   CSP, 14:2:376-78; Choice, 7(1970):299.

25.   Rush, Myron. **How Communist States Change Their Rulers**. Ithaca, NY:
       Cornell University Press, 1974. 346p. $27.50.
In this book the concentration is on the Soviet Union and Soviet bloc countries
of Eastern Europe. It gives a reliable, factual account of the successions in six
countries, dealing with factional struggles, purges, and "plots against rulers." The
author sees Soviet intervention in Eastern Europe as an effort to remove individual
leaders rather than to inhibit or reverse unacceptable policies.
       SR, 34:4:840-41; Choice, 12(1975):290.

26.   Simons, William B., ed. **The Constitutions of the Communist World**. Ley-
       den, Holland: Sijthoff & Noordhoff, 1980. 662p. $92.50.
The volume presents translations into English of the texts of the current constitutions of all the Communist countries, including the USSR and Eastern Europe.
Each constitution is preceded by a brief introduction. This is an updated volume
to John Triska's *The Constitutions of the Communist-Party States* (1968).
       Choice, 18(1981):720.

27. Black, Cyril E., and Thornton, Thomas P., eds. **Communism and Revolution: The Strategic Uses of Political Violence.** Princeton: Princeton University Press, 1964. 467p. $34.00.

There is not a single statement by a prominent Communist to indicate that the objective of the world revolution has been changed or abandoned, or that faith in the ultimate outcome of the struggle has been lost. This text has the merit of combining history with analysis of current Communist activities. The book is a fountain of information, and it stimulates thinking. It is recommended to all students of Soviet strategy.

    SR, 24:2:335-36.

28. Bromke, Adam, and Rakowska-Harmstone, Teresa, eds. **The Communist States in Disarray, 1965-1971.** Minneapolis: University of Minnesota Press, 1972. 363p. $13.50 cl.; $4.95 pa. (The Carleton Series in Soviet and East European Studies.)

This work is devoted to the impact of the Sino-Soviet conflict on the world community of socialist states, together with the spread of nationalism and polycentrism. But the major concentration is on Eastern Europe; of the sixteen chapters, eight of the eleven on countries are devoted to particular East European countries and three of the other five concern the overall problems of the area.

    Choice, 9(1973):1503; JP, 35(1973):532.

29. Brown, Archie, and Gray, Jack, eds. **Political Culture and Political Change in Communist States.** 2d ed. New York: Holmes & Meier, 1979. xiv, 286p. $27.00.

This is a book about the intriguing question of why nations respond differently to similar challenges, in this case the Communist effort to create societies that conform to the presumed Marxist-Leninist ideal. The extremely uneven results of the bold experiment in social engineering is the problem to be analyzed. The authors focus on the examination of those aspects of political culture that are not readily susceptible to such explanations.

    SR, 37:4:681-82; CS, 9(1980):423.

30. Buzek, Antony. **How the Communist Press Works.** New York: Praeger, 1964. 287p. $7.50.

The book is unique in providing a fairly thorough survey of the workings of the Communist press. The author worked for the Czechoslovak news service in Prague and London from 1950 to 1961, when he severed the connection. This is a useful study of the ideology, structure, control, and functioning of the Soviet and East European press. It is focused on censorship and administrative manipulation and draws much of its material from the 1950s.

SR, 27:3:498.

31.　DeGeorge, Richard T. **The New Marxism: Soviet and East European Marxism since 1956.** New York: Pegasus, 1968. 170p.

The author surveys developments in Marxist philosophy from Khrushchev's devaluation of Stalin to the end of 1967. In the field of ethics, he finds, it follows that for the Soviet Marxist "the basic moral choice is not personal but social, the ultimate court of appeal is not one's conscience but society's decision." The implications of such thinking for established regimes are clear.

Choice, 6(1969):276; LJ, 94(1969):199.

32.　Degras, Jane, ed. **The Communist International, 1919-1943. Documents.** 3 vols. Vol. I: **1919-1922**; Vol. II: **1923-1928**; Vol. III: **1929-1943.** London: Oxford University Press for the Royal Institute of International Affairs, 1965-71. 494p. $47.50 each.

The third volume of documents of the Communist International completes a valuable series. Beginning with a rather heavy concentration in the early 1930s, the documents trail off after the Seventh World Congress, as the Comintern itself did, to the point where there is nothing at all in 1941, only a May Day manifesto in 1942, and the formal document of dissolution (1943) to open the archives.

RR, 25:3:317-18; Choice, 9(1972):564.

33.　Djilas, Milovan. **The New Class: An Analysis of the Communist System.** New York: Harcourt Brace Jovanovich, 1982. 224p. $4.95 pa.

The author, sentenced and resentenced to a Yugoslav prison, has given the world an illuminating and devastative treatise on the nature of Communist power. As a former believer in Marx and Lenin, Djilas reveals in his new credo against Communism a penetration and insight possible only to one who is an apostate. This book is highly recommended to all young people.

SR, 17:2:237-39.

34.　Hammond, Thomas T., and Farrell, Robert, eds. **The Anatomy of Communist Takeovers.** Foreword by Cyril E. Black. New Haven and London: Yale University Press, 1975 (1971). 664p. $22.00.

With contributions by thirty American and foreign experts, this is the most convenient and comprehensive analysis available of the ways and means by which Communists have come to power in various countries or parts of countries since 1917. Since 1917 there have been twenty-two successful Communist takeovers. A brief bibliography of basic books on international Communism is given at the end of the volume.

SR, 35:4:743-44; Choice, 12(1975):1348.

35.　Janos, Andrew C., ed. **Authoritarian Politics in Communist Europe: Uniformity and Diversity in One-Party States.** Berkeley: Institute of International Studies, University of California, Berkeley, 1976. xii, 196p. $3.95 pa.

The seven essays in this volume stress the factors of continuity as well as of change. The contributions attempt to introduce concepts that bring the discussion of Communist-governed societies closer to the general methods of social science. The opening essay offers an ambitious matrix of different types of authoritarian regimes. Among the contributors are T. H. Rigby, Robert C. Tucker, Alfred G. Meyer, and Zygmunt Baumann.

      SR, 37:4:682-83; JP, 40(1978):566.

36.   Kolarz, Walter. **Communism and Colonialism: Essays.** Edited by George Gretton. Introduction by Edward Crankshaw. New York: St. Martin's Press, 1964. 147p. $4.95.

Twelve penetrating essays discuss the impact of Communist tyranny on oppressed and captive nations and peoples and explain that the Communist threat is to mankind in its entirety. Kolarz devotes particular attention to the status of the nations and nationalities within the Soviet Union itself. He criticizes the "elder brother" theory and points out that the non-Russian ethnic groups are being Russified.

      SR, 24:1:137-38.

37.   Miller, Richard I. **Teaching about Communism.** New York: McGraw-Hill, 1966. 355p. $6.50.

This volume is intended as a handbook for teachers, school administrators, curriculum planners, and other educators. Its scope is broad, including a rationale for instruction, a survey of relevant curriculum practices, and suggestions for pedagogy, for pre- and in-service education of teachers, and for strategy and tactics in establishing courses relating to Communism. This is the only available book of its kind.

      SR, 26:3:523-24.

38.   Shapiro, Jane P., and Potichnyj, Peter J., eds. **Change and Adaptation in Soviet and East European Politics.** New York: Praeger, 1976. xii, 236p. Tables. $18.50.

This collection of papers is divided into sections on political culture, censorship, and nationalities. The "nationalities" section deals with the lessons to be drawn from Russian-Ukrainian-Byelorussian relations from historiography and with the involvement of Kazakhs in modernization in Central Asia.

      SEER, 56:1:158; Choice, 14(1977):264.

39.   Staar, Richard F. **Yearbook on International Communist Affairs 1982: Parties and Revolutionary Movements.** Preface by Robert Wesson. Stanford: Hoover Institution Press, 1982. xiv, 576p. $39.95; **1983.** Edited by Robert Wesson. Stanford: Hoover Institution Press, 1983. 534p. $44.95.

The latest editions of this important research source, published annually since 1966, feature a broader coverage of such countries as Afghanistan, Ethiopia, Angola, and South Yemen, in addition to the USSR and Eastern European countries. A major improvement over previous yearbooks concerns the focus of the analysis, which concentrates more on events occurring during 1981 and 1982.

40. Wolfe, Bertram D. **Marxism: One Hundred Years in the Life of a Doctrine.**
New York: Dial Press, 1965. 404p. $6.95.

The study deals exclusively with selected aspects of the part of Marx's heritage that reflects his determination to change the world by shaping the development of social and political events. The greatest single error of Marx was his belief that nationalism is not really an acting force in society. This is a useful study of Marx's pronouncements on contemporary international, political, and social events.

SR, 24:4:730-32; AHR, 71:4:905; APSR, 60(1966):126.

INTERNATIONAL RELATIONS

41. Anderson, M. S. **The Eastern Question, 1774-1923: A Study in International Relations.** New York: St. Martin's Press, 1966. 435p. $9.00.
This is a judicious and useful survey of the Eastern question from Kutchuk-Kainardji to the end of the Ottoman Empire. Twelve chapters, arranged chronologically, range from the Ottoman Empire and the Great Powers, 1774-98, to the Peace Settlement, 1918-23. It is a well-informed, integrative study based on mastery of the vast amount of monographic literature, both Western and Russian, that has appeared on this subject in recent decades.
AHR, 72:5:1345; Choice, 4(1967):738.

42. Bromke, Adam, and Uren, Philip E., eds. **The Communist States and the West.** New York: Praeger, 1967. 242p. $6.50.
In this symposium several experts discuss various aspects of the relations between the Communist countries and the West. The book successfully complements such works on related aspects of European Communism as *The Governments of Communist Europe* by Gordon Skilling and *Eastern European Governments and Politics* by Vaclav Beneš and associates. The various arguments and citations presented here clearly reflect the depth of study as well as the breadth of this book.
EEQ, 1:4:419-22; APSR, 62(1968):311.

HISTORY

43.   Adams, Arthur E.; Matley, Ian M.; and McCagg, William O. **An Atlas of Russian and East European History.** New York: Praeger, 1967. 204p. $6.00.

The authors survey the political, cultural, and economic development of the region, focusing especially on four themes: the impact of the acceptance of Christianity, the thirteenth-century calamities and their consequences, the continuous absorption of influences from both the East and the West, and the development of a distinct type of sociopolitical culture in recent decades. The book is an informative introduction to the history and historical geography of Eastern Europe.
    SR, 29:2:346-47.

44.   Gimbutas, Marija. **The Slavs.** London: Thames and Hudson; New York: Praeger, 1971. 240p. $10.00. (Ancient Peoples and Places, vol. 74.)

The author traces the history of the Slavs from their putative beginnings in the early second millennium B.C. to the rise of the Slavic states in the ninth and tenth centuries A.D. A true Slavic culture emerged about 500. The author deals admirably with the many controversies and problems of early Slavic culture.
    SR, 31:4:877-78.

45. De Bray, Reginald G. A. **Guide to the Slavonic Languages.** 3d ed., revised and expanded. 3 vols. Vol. 1: **Guide to the South Slavonic Languages.** Vol. 2: **Guide to the West Slavonic Languages.** Vol. 3: **Guide to the East Slavonic Languages.** Columbus, OH: Slavic Publishers, 1980. Vol. 1: 399p. $24.95; Vol. 2: 483p. $27.95; Vol. 3: 254p. $22.95.

In the recently published volume 3 the author has made substantial revisions to the sections on Russians and Ukrainians. The bibliography has also been brought up to date. In the Russian section, the introduction has been expanded to include an outline of the historical development of the language prior to the eighteenth century. The main changes in the Ukrainian section consist in substantial rewriting of the pronunciation, correction of some earlier errors, and complete rewriting of the dialects section in line with current thinking on their subdivision.

SEER, 59:4:589-90; Choice, 18(1981): 774.

46. Čiževskij, Dmitrij. **Comparative History of Slavic Literatures.** Edited by Serge A. Zenkovsky. Translated by Richard Noel Porter and Martin P. Rice. Nashville, TN: Vanderbilt University Press, 1971. 225p. $10.00.

The richness of the author's scholarly experience and his authority in the field of Slavic literatures and Slavic-Western cultural relations make this work a valuable contribution on the subject. The author points to the need for establishing connections between the Slavic East and the European and American West and provides an impressive repertoire of problems to be worked on, as well as several examples of effective methods for their scholarly treatment.

CSP, 15:3:419-20.

47. Mihailovich, Vasa D., et al., comps. and eds. **Modern Slavic Literatures.** 2 vols. Vol. 1: **Russian Literature**; Vol. 2: **Bulgarian, Czecho-Slovak, Polish, Ukrainian, and Yugoslav Literatures: A Library of Literary Criticism.** New York: Frederick Ungar, 1972-76. $100.00 set.

These volumes cover authors from the late nineteenth century to recent years. The chosen parts of literary criticisms deal with a particular writer's style, thematics, problematics, or ideology reflected or prominent in a given work. Comparative criticism is also included. In most cases, the earlier writers are provided with evaluations from their own times as well as from contemporary days.

NP, 6:2:214-15; Choice, 14(1977):180; LJ, 102(1977):386.

48. Terry, Garth M. **East European Languages and Literatures: A Subject and Name Index to Articles in English-Language Journals, 1900-1977.** Oxford and Santa Barbara, CA: Clio Press, 1978. xxvi, 276p. $47.50.

This reference work provides something of a key to the nonmonograph English-language and French-Canadian contributions to the study and appreciation of the Slavonic, Hungarian, Romanian, Baltic, and Finnish languages and literatures since the beginning of the present century. Over eight hundred titles have been consulted. A name index includes both authors and personalia not rating entries in the main text. The work includes over nine thousand references.

SEER, 58:3:471-72.

DISSENT, NATIONALISM, RELIGION

49. Bociurkiw, Bohdan R., and Strong, John W., eds. **Religion and Atheism in the U.S.S.R. and Eastern Europe.** Toronto and Buffalo: University of Toronto Press, 1975. xviii, 412p. $17.50.
The volume adds comparative dimensions to the existing literature by examining the status of religion in the Soviet Union and in all East European Communist countries, updated to 1974.
SR, 38:3:500; Choice, 12(1975):1321.

50. Simmonds, George W., ed. **Nationalism in the USSR and Eastern Europe in the Era of Brezhnev and Kosygin.** Detroit: University of Detroit Press, 1977. 534p. $12.00.
The contributions cover most of the major national minorities in the Soviet Union, four nationalities of Eastern Europe (Poles, Hungarians, Albanians, and Romanians), and two national minority groups (Slovaks and Croations). The volume demonstrates that little is still known about the national processes and their demographic, socioeconomic, and sociopscyhological underpinnings. All the contributors believe that nationalism has reemerged as one of the major forces shaping the history of Eastern Europe and the Soviet Union.
SR, 38:2:327-28.

SOCIOLOGY AND SOCIAL CONDITIONS

51. Connor, Walter D. **Socialism, Politics, and Equality: Hierarchy and Change in Eastern Europe and the USSR.** New York: Columbia University Press, 1979. x, 389p. $20.00.

The work's principal achievement is its presentation in reasonably systematic form of a considerable amount of data on prestige ratings, social mobility, income structure, and patterns of "cultural consumption" in Eastern Europe and the Soviet Union. It will be welcomed by all those interested in the nature and dimensions of inequality in existing socialist systems.

SR, 39:1:125-26; JP, 42(1980):577.

52. Connor, Walter D., and Gitelman, Zvi Y., et al. **Public Opinion in European Socialist Systems.** New York and London: Praeger Publishers, 1977. x, 197p. Tables. £12.50.

The authors analyze the ways in which existing social structures modify, constrain, and even affect the policies of ruling regimes. Most of the book is devoted to the nature and content of socialist opinion polling in particular and socialist research in general. The impact of opinion polling in Poland, Czechoslovakia, the USSR, and Hungary is discussed in greater detail.

SR, 37:4:690-91; Choice, 15(1978):298.

53. Jancar, Barbara Wolfe. **Women under Communism.** Baltimore and London: The Johns Hopkins University Press, 1978. xii, 291p. $16.00.

The book focuses on the multiple variables, nature, and texture of the environment as it affects the inability of women to achieve equality in Communist countries. Two important questions are raised: Why have women not moved into the higher reaches of society where policy is made? and why have women not risen to approximately the same status level in every Communist country? This is a valuable addition to the understanding of women in the Communist world.

SR, 39:1:128-29; Choice, 16(1979):922; JP, 41(1979):976.

54. Kaser, Michael. **Health Care in the Soviet Union and Eastern Europe.** Boulder, CO: Westview Press, 1976. vi, 278p. $30.00.

The study provides basic and indispensable information on the health care services available in Communist countries. It details the experience of Soviet "socialized medicine" and the 30 years of experience in Bulgaria, Czechoslovakia, the

German Democratic Republic, Hungary, Poland, and Romania. The book is valuable because the accumulation of statistical data permits the comparative focus to be carried out within the Comecon nations and between the Comecon and other nations.

SR, 37:1:143-45; Choice, 14(1977):1095.

MILITARY AFFAIRS

55. Adelman, Jonathan R., ed. **Communist Armies in Politics.** Boulder, CO: Westview Press, 1982. 226p. $25.00.

This book analyzes the historical and contemporary political roles of armies in the majority of the world's Communist countries, including the Soviet, Yugoslav, Czechoslovak, Romanian, and Polish armies. The authors emphasize such variables as the nature of revolution, the role of civil war, and the extent of external interference (particularly from the Soviet Union) and show how these variables are key factors in determining the path of army political development.

56. Nelson, Daniel N. **Soviet Allies: The Warsaw Pact and the Issue of Reliability.** Boulder, CO: Westview Press, 1983. 240p. $24.00.

Focusing on the degree to which Warsaw Treaty Organization (WTO) leaders can be assured of non-Soviet military support in hostile circumstances, this book provides empirical guidance for Western assessments of WTO "reliability." In six case studies the author assesses domestic-level variables such as party-military relations and material and manpower sources, and their relationship to the mobilization potential of Eastern Europe.

2

RUSSIAN EMPIRE PRIOR TO 1917 AND THE USSR

GENERAL REFERENCE WORKS

Bibliographies

57. Dossick, Jesse John. **Doctoral Research on Russia and the Soviet Union, 1960-1975: A Classified List of 3,150 American, Canadian, and British Dissertations, with Some Critical and Statistical Analysis.** New York: Garland Publishing, 1976. xxiv, 345p. $32.00. (Garland Reference Library of Social Science, vol. 7.)

This represents the continuation of Dossick's 1959 published bibliography covering the period from 1876 to 1959. The dissertations are arranged in twenty-one broad subject groups with subdivisions. Indexes include the names of authors and Russian and Soviet personal names.

58. Horecky, Paul L., ed. **Russia and the Soviet Union: A Bibliographic Guide to Western-Language Publications.** Chicago: University of Chicago Press, 1965. 473p. $8.95.

Horecky, Paul L., ed. **Basic Russian Publications: Annotated Bibliography on Russia and the Soviet Union.** Chicago: University of Chicago Press, 1962. 313p. $6.50.

The basic scheme of these two bibliographies is almost the same: General Reference Aids and Bibliographies; The Land; The People; History; The State; The Economic and Social Structure; The Intellectual (and Cultural) Life. The later volume also covers General and Descriptive Books; The Nations; Ukrainica; Baltica; and Other Nations.

SR, 25:2:370-72.

59. Maichel, Karol. **Guide to Russian Reference Books.** Vol. 1: **General Bibliographies and Reference Books.** Edited by J. S. G. Simmons. Stanford: Hoover Institution Press, 1962. 92p. $5.00. (Hoover Institution Bibliographical Series, X.) Vol. 2: **History, Auxiliary Historical Science, Ethnography, and Geography.** Edited by J. S. G. Simmons. Stanford: Hoover Institution Press, 1964. 297p. $12.00.

The volumes go beyond the listing of bibliographic reference works; they include other reference tools such as bibliographies, indexes, encyclopedias, chronologies, biographies, terminological dictionaries, atlases, gazetteers, handbooks, and dissertation abstracts.

SR, 25:2:370-72.

60. Thompson, Anthony. **Russia/U.S.S.R.: A Selective Annotated Bibliography of Books in English.** Oxford and Santa Barbara, CA: Clio Press, 1979. xiii, 287p. $21.00. (World Bibliographical Series, vol. 6.)

This bibliography is presented as " a selection of readable books on all aspects of a great federal country." Its 1,247 entries do not include periodical articles or works in languages other than English, and the emphasis is on more recent publications in all fields.

SEER, 59:1:158.

Biographies

61. Coolidge, Olivia. **Makers of the Red Revolution.** Boston: Houghton Mifflin, 1963. 240p. $3.75.

The author presents a series of seven brief and readable biographies on Marx, Lenin, Trotsky, Stalin, Tito, Khrushchev, and Mao Tse-Tung designed for the student and younger reader. In spite of some errors, this popular treatment serves its purpose well.

SR, 24:2:161-63; LJ, 90(1963):2780.

62. Crankshaw, Edward. **Khrushchev: A Career.** New York: Viking, 1966. 311p. $7.50.

This political biography of Khrushchev is broadly conceived, eminently readable, and should be welcomed by the general reader as well as the specialist. The Khrushchev that emerges from the record is clearly recognizable. All the essential traits of the politician the world came to know are there. The author's freshness of style and literary quality make the book enjoyable reading.

SR, 26:3:492-93; APSR, 61(1967):199; Choice, 3(1967):1067.

63. Crowley, Edward L., et al., eds. **Party and Government Officials of the Soviet Union, 1917-1967.** Metuchen, NJ: Scarecrow Press, 1969. 214p. $7.50.

This book traces the composition of Soviet officialdom, including government and party organs. Chronologically arranged, it begins with the first congress of the RSDRP and the governments starting with November 7, 1917. An extensive general index helps to identify individuals with either party or government position at a given time. A useful tool for students of Soviet affairs.

64. Crowley, Edward L, et al., eds. **Prominent Personalities in the USSR: A Biographic Directory Containing 6,015 Biographies of Prominent Personalities in the Soviet Union.** Munich: The Institute for the Study of the USSR; Metuchen, NJ: Scarecrow Press, 1968. 792p. $35.00.

This latest volume in the series of Soviet biographies is the most comprehensive to date. From the biographical material on 130,000 Soviet citizens assembled in the files of the Institute, the editorial staff of this reference tool culled data for 6,015 biographies, of which 4,300 represent updated entries and 1,715 are entirely new. The volume is organized under these main headings: education, career (positions), publications, awards. In addition to biographical data, the book contains a listing of names of key personnel of major party, government, military, scientific, and other organizations.

SR, 28:4:697-98; WLB, 43(1969):907.

65. Fischer, Louis. **The Life of Lenin.** New York: Harper & Row, 1964. 703p. $10.00.

The author brought many new advantages to his study of Lenin, not least of which was the fact that he knew Lenin and his retinue at first hand. He has not restricted his work to a personal memoir but has thoroughly researched his subject from logical sources. In no other work does Lenin emerge with such clarity as the leader of the Soviet state.

SR, 24:1:121-22; CH, 49(1965):235; JP, 27(1965):443.

66. Hare, Richard. **Portraits of Russian Personalities between Reform and Revolution.** New York and London: Oxford University Press, 1959. 360p. $6.75.

The book contains fifteen sketches of various lengths treating Turgenev, Dostoevsky, Tolstoy, and lesser known figures such as the *narodniks* N. Mikhailovsky, P. Lavrov, and L. Tikhomirov. The essays are informative and often stimulating because of a point of view that challenges more commonly accepted historical portraits.

AHR, 65:1:180-81; LJ, 84(1959):2181.

67. Haupt, Georges, and Marie, Jean-Jacques. **Makers of the Russian Revolution: Biographies of Bolshevik Leaders.** Translated from Russian by C. I. P. Ferdinand. Commentaries translated from French by D. M. Bellos. Ithaca, NY: Cornell University Press, 1974 (1969). 452p. $15.00.

The biographies are divided into two groups: "The Major Figures" (Bukharin, Kamenev, Lenin, Stalin, Sverdlov, Trotsky, and Zinoviev), and "Men of October," subdivided into three categories: early Bolsheviks, former dissidents, and recruits from other parties and other lands. Fifty-six brief autobiographies and biographies of the original guard of the Old Bolsheviks were first published in Moscow in 1927-29. The appended list of periodicals, abbreviations, acronyms, organizations, and a general and name index are complete and useful.

Choice, 11(1975):1606; LJ, 100(1975):51.

68. Hodnett, Grey, and Ogareff, Val. **Leaders of the Soviet Republics, 1955-1972: A Guide to Posts and Occupants.** Canberra: Department of Political Science, Research School of Social Sciences, Australian National University, 1973. 454p. $4.00pa.

This extensive and updated guide to the Soviet leadership in government and party covers all fifteen Soviet republics. The guide provides information on names and positions held on the regional and republic levels and other pertinent data. The book contains a name index. The broad coverage provides a valuable service for the student and specialist.

69. Lewytzkyj, Borys, and Stroynowski, Juliusz, eds. **Who's Who in the Socialist Countries: A Biographical Encyclopedia of 10,000 Leading Personalities in 16 Communist Countries.** Munich and New York: Verlag Dokumentation K. G. Saur, 1978. xi, 736p. DM198.00.

This monumental effort fills an existing void. The book lists over four thousand names for the Soviet Union alone, including all major changes in the Politburo and the Central Committee of the Communist party, along with changes in leadership that occurred in fifteen Union Republics as a result of the 25th Party Congress in February 1976. In addition to European Communist countries, the work covers Cambodia, China, Cuba, Korea, Laos, Mongolia, and Vietnam. The biographies contain information gathered as late as 1977.

     NP, 7:2:231-33.

70.   Morgan, Michael C. **Lenin**. Athens, OH: Ohio University Press, 1971. 236p. $8.75.

Although the title implies a biography, this study focuses on Lenin's ideology and politics. The narrative depicts the informal Lenin and provides a sketchy biographical framework. It is a skillful synthesis and useful reading for undergraduates.

     SR, 32:2:386; Choice, 9(1972):869.

71.   Payne, Robert. **The Life and Death of Lenin**. New York: Simon & Schuster, 1964. 672p. $8.50.

The author portrays Lenin as a compulsively destructive revolutionary, a product of Asiatic ancestry plus Nechaevism. This biography of Lenin is an exciting introduction for the casual reader.

     SR, 24:1:121-23; New Statesman, 69(1965):114.

72.   Payne, Robert. **The Rise and Fall of Stalin**. New York: Simon & Schuster, 1965. 767p. $10.00.

Payne uses a wide range of Russian and foreign materials on Stalin, including the documents and memoirs that have been published under Khrushchev. An attractive feature of the book is that several dozen of Stalin's letters and official documents are reproduced and translated in the text. The author is most interested in Stalin as a person and in the blood that he shed.

     SR, 25:2:343-44; Choice, 2(1966):899; New Statesman, 71(1966):474.

73.   Possony, Stefan T. **Lenin: The Compulsive Revolutionary**. Chicago: Henry Regnery, 1964. 418p. $7.95. (The Hoover Institution Series.)

The author concludes that Lenin was essentially a user, both of himself and of others. He destroyed in order to organize for destruction. The author establishes the case for Lenin's "compulsiveness." In an appended essay, Possony concludes that psychologically, Lenin was essentially his own master.

     SR, 24:1:121-23.

74.   Rush, Myron. **The Rise of Khrushchev**. Washington, DC: Public Affairs Press, 1958. 116p. $3.25.

This book deals with the question of how Khrushchev succeeded in ousting his rivals and becoming the ranking Soviet leader. It answers the question by showing that he did so through Stalin's method, namely by using the office of secretary of the Party as a jumping board. The book is suggestive as well as informative.

     SR, 17:3:359-61.

75.   Schultz, Heinrich E., and Andrew, Lebed I., eds. **Who's Who in the USSR, 1965-66 (A Biographical Directory)**. 2d ed. New York: Scarecrow Press, 1966. 1189p. $25.00.

This updated second edition of *Who's Who in the USSR* includes five thousand key figures from all fields of Soviet life. The book is an indispensable tool for libraries, journalists, politicians, historians, and students of Soviet affairs. Over a hundred researchers were involved in this monumental project, which is the only publication of its kind on the Soviet Union. It is not only used in the West but also kept in the archives of the CPSU for internal use.

76.   Simmonds, George W., ed. **Soviet Leaders.** New York: Thomas Y. Crowell, 1967. 405p. $10.00.
The present collection of biographical sketches represents the first substantial effort at individual assessment of the lesser Soviet leadership. The sketches include political figures, economic administrators, police leaders, military chiefs, diplomats, and leading literary figures.
    AHR, 74:5:1673-74; APSR, 63(1969):224.

77.   Tucker, Robert C. **Stalin as Revolutionary, 1879-1929: A Study in History and Personality.** New York: W. W. Norton, 1973. 519p. $12.95.
Against a multifaceted background, the author sketches the portrait of a tyrant who developed his dictatorial personality from his original servile obedience toward his master and prophet, Lenin. This is a most complete biography utilizing all essential material and presently available sources. It is written in superb and clear English. This fine biography should be read by the broadest public, especially those who are inclined to believe that Hitler and Stalin are singular experiences of the past.
    AHR, 79:3:820; Choice, 10(1974):1774.

78.   Ulam, Adam B. **Stalin: The Man and His Era.** New York: Viking Press, 1973. 760p. $12.95 cl.; $4.95 pa.
Within a conventional "life and times" framework, Ulam has produced a masterful portrait of Stalin. This is a thoroughly hostile biography of the great tyrant, and in view of the Pandora's box opened by Khrushchev's speech of 1956, no other sort is tenable. It is a fascinating biography written with authority and rare discernment.
    SR, 33:4:778-79; AHR, 79:2:820; Choice, 11(1974):316.

79.   Wolfe, Bertram D. **Three Who Made a Revolution: A Biographical History.** New York: Dial Press, 1948. 661p.; Boston: Beacon Press, 1959. 661p.
The author, the former director of TASS, presents a portrait of Lenin as a man of unswerving devotion to his cause, of Trotsky designed to restore Lenin as a man of great stature, and of Stalin as "the most striking example in all history of a man who has succeeded in inventing himself." The author's sympathies with Lenin do not reduce the value of this biographical study.
    SR, 8:3:227-29.

Encyclopedias and Handbooks

80.   **The Cambridge Encyclopedia of Russia and the Soviet Union.** Edited by Archie Brown et al. Cambridge: Cambridge University Press, 1982. 492p. $35.00.
This is a well-illustrated and attractively designed volume offering an impartial and balanced view of Soviet history. The text is broken up into units under a number of broad headings, rather than alphabetically arranged; it is very suitable for consecutive reading.

81.   Fitzsimmons, Thomas, ed. **USSR, Its People, Its Society, Its Culture.**
      New York: Taplinger Publishing Co. for the Human Relations Areas Files
      Press, 1960. 590p.
Broad in coverage, this volume treats geography, history, government, politics,
economics, and education, among other topics. An objective tone prevails throughout. It is useful for general reference and also for introduction to this particular
area of studies.
      SR, 22:2:349-50.

82.   Florinsky, Michael T., ed. **McGraw-Hill Encyclopedia of Russia and the
      Soviet Union.** New York: McGraw-Hill, 1961. 624p. $23.50.
The joint cooperative efforts of the editor and more than one hundred contributors
have yielded an excellent end product. It answers a number of questions that may
be asked by the specialist and student alike. This publication should prove a particularly sound investment for a library of any size.
      SR, 21:4:788-89.

83.   Kingsbury, Robert C., and Taafe, Robert N. **An Atlas of Soviet Affairs.**
      New York: Praeger, 1965. 153p. $4.00.
This handy atlas serves as an introduction to many aspects of Soviet life and is a
useful tool for general information. Short chapters on over sixty subjects will guide
the high school student into further and more comprehensive study of the Soviet
Union.

84.   Lensen, George Alexander. **The Soviet Union: An Introduction.** New
      York: Appleton-Century-Crofts, 1967. 181p.
This publication offers a handbook-like treatment of the Soviet Union, stressing
geography, history, economics, government, education, religion, and art. Numerous
photographs exemplify Soviet life. The narrow scope of discussion of various topics
is adaptable to high school rather than college use.

85.   Lewytzkyj, Borys, ed. **The Soviet Union: Figures—Facts—Data.** Munich,
      New York, London, and Paris: K. G. Saur, 1979. xxxvi, 614p. $49.00.
Utilizing Soviet sources as well as some Western ones, the volume covers such
diverse areas as size of the territories-republics, population, structure of administration, party and state apparatus, economy, science, and education.
      NP, 8:2:251-52.

86.   Maxwell, Robert, ed. and comp. **Information U.S.S.R.: An Authoritative
      Encyclopedia about the Union of Soviet Socialist Republics.** Oxford:
      Pergamon Press, 1962. 982p. $30.00.
Compiled in cooperation with the editors of the *Great Soviet Encyclopedia,* this
encyclopedia purports to make available the facts about the Soviet Union as seen
through the eyes of official institutions. The reader in search of objective information should keep this fact in mind.
      SR, 22:1:186-87.

87.   Mickiewicz, Ellen P., ed. **Handbook of Soviet Social Science Data.** Fore-
      word by Karl W. Deutsch. New York: Free Press; London: Collier-
      Macmillan, 1973. 225p. $30.00.

This is the first attempt in English to compile a comprehensive set of empirical data on the USSR. The handbook's nine chapters cover demography, agriculture, production, health, housing, education, elite recruitment and mobilization, communications, and international interactions. Each chapter begins with a brief headnote followed by numbered tables displayed in a readable manner, with source notes for each table at the end of the chapter. Tables are conveniently listed with page references at the front of the handbook.

SR, 34:1:162-63; LJ, 99(1974):126; Choice, 10(1974):1701.

88. Scherer, John L., ed. **USSR Facts and Figures Annual.** 6 vols. Gulf Breeze, FL: Academic International Press, 1977- . Vol. 1: **1977.** xii, 320p. $35.00; Vol. 2: **1978.** xv, 559p. $51.00; Vol. 3: **1979.** x, 308p. $38.50; Vol. 4: **1980.** x, 391p. $42.50; Vol. 5: **1981.** 350p. $43.00; Vol. 6: **1982.** 438p. $46.50.

Based on data drawn from official, private sector, and international sources as well as specialist literature in many fields, this annual statistical handbook presents information on contemporary Soviet life divided topically into fifteen sections. Volume 1 commences with information from the period 1974-76; volume 4 updates much of the previous data. Volume 6 features a table of contents for volumes 1 through 5. This is a formidable source of contemporary reference for students and specialists.

89. **The Soviet Union: An Introduction to the Geography, Peoples, History, and Political Structure of the USSR.** By the editors of Scholastic Book Services. New York: Scholastic Book Services, 1965. 160p. (Scholastic World Affairs Multi-Text, no. 2.)

This book is directed primarily at secondary school students. It is extremely brief and written in a simple, direct style. It provides sketches and basic information, as the subtitle explains.

SR, 24:1:161-62.

90. Utechin, Sergej V. **Everyman's Concise Encyclopedia of Russia.** London: Dent; New York: Dutton, 1961. 623p. $7.95.

This is a reference source of distinct usefulness. Some 2,050 articles range over Russian matters from Abkan to Zyryans, providing information of the kind that the general reader is most likely to seek and that the reference librarian is often hard-pressed to find. Students on all levels will use this book to advantage.

SR, 21:1:187-88.

91. Whiting, Kenneth R. **The Soviet Union Today: A Concise Handbook.** Rev. ed. New York: Praeger, 1966. 434p. $7.50.

This handbook of general information is suitable for any library to support effective teaching and reference services. A well-selected bibliography for suggested in-depth reading enhances the value of this work.

SR, 22:2:349-50; Choice, 3(1967):1170.

Description and Travel

92.   Adams, Charles Francis, ed. **John Quincy Adams in Russia: Comprising Portions of the Diary of John Quincy Adams from 1809 to 1814.** Introduction by Harry Schwartz, eng. ed. New York: Praeger, 1970 (1974). 622p. $25.00. (Praeger Scholarly Reprints, Source Books and Studies in Russian and Soviet History.)

John Quincy Adams served as the first U.S. emissary to the court in St. Petersburg after its recognition in 1809, and remained there until 1814. He enjoyed a close relationship with Alexander I. Thus his description of the Tsarist court and of the life in the capitol are particularly valuable to students of nineteenth-century Russian history.

93.   Baron, Samuel H., ed. and transl. **The Travels of Olearius in Seventeenth-Century Russia.** Stanford: Stanford University Press, 1967. 400p. $25.00.

This is a firsthand account of the travels of Adam Oelschlager, better known as Olearius, through Muscovy and Tartary from 1633 to 1636. Olearius, a young German, served as secretary to successive embassies sent by the Duke of Holstein to the Tsar of Russia and the Shah of Persia to negotiate trade agreements. The book includes sixteen pages of the original illustrations, which were based on Olearius' own drawings. This account is essential to the study of Russia's history.

94.   Berry, Lloyd E., and Crummey, Robert O., eds. **Rude and Barbarous Kingdom: Russia in the Accounts of Sixteenth-Century English Voyagers.** Milwaukee: University of Wisconsin Press, 1968. 391p. $7.50.

This is a good edition of valuable sources: a selection of the most important writings on Muscovy by Englishmen who came as traders and diplomats following the discovery of the White Sea route in 1553 and the establishment of the Russian Company a year later. Texts of the accounts are modernized but based on original manuscripts or first editions, with substantive variants recorded when they are not available elsewhere.

SR, 29:2:303-4; Choice, 5(1969):1490.

95.   Buchanan, Sir George W. **My Mission to Russia.** New York: Arno Press, 1970. (Reprint of 1923 edition.) 252p. $22.00.

The original 1923 edition appeared in two volumes under the title *My Mission to Russia and Other Diplomatic Memories.* Buchanan served as British ambassador to Russia from 1910 to 1918. His personal account of the events in Russia during the war and revolution of 1917 represents a significant contribution to the history of Russia. He describes the events in Petersburg on an almost day-to-day basis.

96.   Fletcher, Giles. **Of the Rus' Commonwealth.** Edited by Albert J. Schmidt. Ithaca, NY: Cornell University Press, 1966. 224p. $15.00. (Folger Documents of Tudor and Stuart Civilization.)

Originally published in 1591, this is a vivid discourse on the national resources, government, ecclesiastical and military organization, and class structure of Russian society as observed by a British traveler.

Choice, 3(1967):1166.

97. Herberstein, Sigmund von. **Description of Moscow and Muscovy.** Edited by Berthold Picard. Translated by J. B. C. Grundy. London: J. M. Dent, 1969. 105p. $8.50.

Sigmund von Herberstein (1488-1566) was a diplomatic envoy of the Habsburgs who journeyed to Moscow in 1516 and again in 1526. He published his memoirs in Latin in 1549. In this work he speaks of the Russians' fear that visitors to their country are really spies, of foul-ups in one's traveling plans in Russia, and of forced drinking at receptions.

SEEJ, 15:1:141-42.

98. Hollander, Paul. **Political Pilgrims: Travels of Western Intellectuals to the Soviet Union, China, and Cuba 1928-1978.** Toronto, New York, and Oxford: Oxford University Press, 1981. xvi, 516p. $34.95.

Hollander's analysis concentrates more on the American dimension of the subject and is generally more extensive and penetrating in its scope than other similar works. A prominent theme in his discussion is the Western intellectual's frequent estrangement from his own (capitalist) society. The fact that this led to the political myopia Hollander describes says more about the condition of Western societies than of Eastern ones. His work has an anti-utopian thrust. This is a substantial and provocative study on an important subject.

CSP, 25:2:318-19; Choice, 19(1982):1117; AHR, 87:3:751.

99. Kennan, George F. **The Marquis de Custine and His Russia in 1839.** London: Hutchinson, 1972; Princeton: Princeton University Press, 1971. 145p. $16.50.

The American ambassador to the Soviet Union in the period immediately after World War II, General Walter Bedell Smith, wrote in his introduction to translated excerpts from Custine: "I could have taken many pages verbatim from his journal and, after substituting present-day names and dates for those of a century ago, have sent them to the State Department as my own official reports." George Kennan took up his post as American ambassador to Moscow in 1952.

SEER, 51:1:313-15; AHR, 78:1:127.

100. Kohler, Phyllis Penn, ed. and transl. **Journey for Our Time: Selections from the Journals of the Marquis de Custine.** New York: Pellegrini & Cudahy, 1951. 338p. $8.95.

This is an account of the Russian autocracy of Nicholas I by a French aristocrat who came to the country as an admirer and left it as an enemy.

101. Smith, Hedrick. **The Russians.** New York: Quadrangle/The New York Times Book Company, 1976. xiv, 527p. $22.50.

Kaiser, Robert G. **Russia: The People and the Power.** New York: Atheneum, 1976. xiv, 499p. $12.95.

These two books by American reporters who spent several years in Moscow cover much the same ground but with differences in emphasis and style. Smith captures the look, sound, and mood of Russians with extraordinary immediacy. Kaiser occasionally touches on such issues as moral conduct and how it grows out of

social context. Both authors display admiration and sympathy for the Russian people and a sharp awareness of the controlling aspects of the Soviet system.
SR, 36:4:685-86.

102.   Staden, Heinrich von. **The Land and Government of Muscovy: A Sixteenth-Century Account.** Translated and edited by Thomas Esper. Stanford: Stanford University Press, 1967. 142p. $10.00.

This is a report by a German traveler who went to Russia in the 1560s and spent three years in the service of Ivan the Terrible's *Oprichnina.* The author had an eye for interesting details. His unique account has thus always attracted the attention of Western historians.

103.   Wilson, Francesca. **Muscovy: Russia through Foreign Eyes, 1553-1900.** New York: Praeger, 1971. 382p. $10.00.

In this book twenty-eight travelers are individually discussed. Within the chronological limits indicated in the title, most of the great names are included: Fletcher, Olearius, Collins, Custine. Hexthausen, Wallace. The documents chosen describe the Russian scene and the Russian people.
SR, 31:1:150-51.

ANTHROPOLOGY AND FOLKLORE

104. Alexander, Alex E. **Russian Folklore: An Anthology in English Translation.** Belmont, MA: Nordland, 1975. 400p. $16.95.
This anthology is ushered in with a foreword by William E. Harkins, followed by examples of the genres of Russian folklore such as wedding ceremonials and chants, funeral laments, proverbs, *byliny*, ballads, love lyrics, and the chastushki. Each group is preceded by a brief discussion of the genre. This impressive work is a must for students in the fields of folklore, literature, and Russian culture in general.
> RR, 35:2:220-21; Choice, 12(1976):1580.

105. Duddington, Natalie, trans. **Russian Folk Tales.** Illustrated by Dick Hart. New York: Funk & Wagnalls, 1969. 144p. $4.95.
This book, a selection of twenty-two tales taken from A. N. Afanasiev's classical collection (1855-63), represents a small segment of Russian folk tales—some animal tales and tales of magic ("fairy tales"). Both of these types are international. The only typically Russian tales—realistic tales and anecdotes—which constitute over half the Russian repertoire, have not been included in this collection.
> SR, 29:3:563-64.

106. Dunn, Stephen P., and Dunn, Ethel. **The Peasant of Central Russia.** New York: Holt, Rinehart & Winston, 1967. 139p. $1.95 pa. (Stanford University Case Studies in Cultural Anthropology.)
The Dunns have composed an ethnographic account of the peasants of Central Russia based on recent Soviet sources. The authors' objective is to describe broadly the life of the many million peasants who inhabit the region between the middle Volga and the Baltic and the changes being undergone.
> SR, 27:2:337-38.

107. Oinas, Felix J., and Soudakoff, Stephen, eds. and trans. **The Study of Russian Folklore.** The Hague: Mouton, 1976. x, 341p. Dfl 48. (Indiana University Folklore Institute, Monograph Series, vol. 25. Slavistic Printings and Reprintings, Textbook Series, 4.)
The editors present a readable introduction to the chief problems and genres of Russian folklore. The collection includes a number of key studies by leading Soviet specialists, past and present. Each article is preceded by an editorial commentary giving its background and placing it in context.
> SR, 36:1:161.

108.   Reeder, Roberta, ed. and trans. **Down along the Mother Volga: An Anthology of Russian Folk Lyrics**. Introduction by V. Ia. Propp. Philadelphia: University of Pennsylvania Press, 1975. xx, 246p. $14.00.

This publication consists of two separate parts: a translation of V. Ia. Propp's essay on Russian folk lyrics and a selection of translations of Russian folk lyrics, classified by subject matter and genre. A list of Propp's sources and a selected bibliography are included in the volume.

SR, 35:2:391-92.

109.   Warner, Elizabeth A. **The Russian Folk Theatre**. The Hague and Paris: Mouton, 1977. xviii, 257p. DM 75.00. (Slavistic Printings and Reprintings, 104.)

This is a well-documented presentation of an important topic derived from little-known primary and secondary sources. The book is divided into four parts: "Ritual Drama"; "The Puppet Theater"; "Non-Ritual Drama"; and the "Folk Actor and His Act." The study also provides an excellent model for future study of Russian folklore.

SR, 38:1:163-64.

THE ARTS, FINE ARTS, ARCHITECTURE

110. Birkos, Alexander S., comp. **Soviet Cinema: Directors and Films.** Hamden, CT: Archon Books, 1976. x, 344p. $19.50.

Over one hundred Soviet film directors and more than fifteen hundred of their films produced in the USSR from 1918 through 1975 are listed and described here. Although the book offers useful information, it is often incomplete.

ARBA, 8(1977):486.

111. Bowlt, John E., ed. and trans. **Russian Art of the Avant-Garde: Theory and Criticism, 1902-1934.** New York: Viking Press, 1976. xi, 360p. $20.00. Illus. (The Documents of 20th Century Art Series.)

This is not a history of the Russian avant-garde but a useful collection and translation of selected theoretical statements, written between 1902 and 1934 by Russian artists. Through the artists' words, the reader is able to witness the image of art change dramatically from a harbinger of a new religion to the revolutionary construction of a new society—the artist as priest giving way to the artist as engineer. The volume includes an introductory essay, biographical data, illustrations, and a bibliography of works in Russian and Western languages.

SR, 36:1:162-64; Choice, 13(1976):1285.

112. Frankel, Tobia. **The Russian Artist: The Creative Person in Russian Culture.** New York: Macmillan, 1972. 198p. $5.95. (Russia Old and New Series.)

This is a well-written, well-organized history of the arts in Russia from the earliest period to the present day. Although designed for students and others new to Russian culture, the book will encourage readers to plunge in more deeply. The arts surveyed include woodworking, icon-making, architecture, poetry, literary criticism, theatrical design and direction, music, ballet, and cinema.

SR, 33:3:612-13; LJ, 98(1973):176.

113. Kopp, Anatole. **Town and Revolution: Soviet Architecture and City Planning, 1917-1935.** Translated from the French by Thomas E. Burton. New York: George Braziller, 1970. 274p. $15.00.

Kopp, a practicing architect and urbanist, exploited the brilliant and largely untapped journals of the era. From these and other sources he culled over 200 photographs, plans, elevations, and sketches. These are presented in chapters divided between chronological and topical themes. The principal sections focus on

those areas in which the architects of the 1920s particularly distinguished themselves: public housing, workers' clubs, urban planning, and anti-urban schemes, including the pioneering linear cities.
SR, 29:4:744-45.

114.   Krebs, Stanley D. **Soviet Composers and the Development of Soviet Music**. New York: W. W. Norton, 1970. 364p. $11.50.
Part I of this book reviews Soviet cultural ideology in music, identifying its sources and tracing its development through the changing tensions generated whenever politics impinged on creative autonomy. Krebs's insight into cause and consequence clearly defines the methodology devised by the party to control creativity in music. A critical examination of the lives and works of some two dozen major Soviet composers occupies the bulk of the book.
SR, 30:3:699-700.

115.   Marshall, Herbert. **The Pictorial History of the Russian Theatre**. Introduction by Harold Clurman. New York: Crown Publishers, 1977. xvi, 208p. Photographs. $14.95.
This book adds valuable visual material to already known historical information as well as providing detailed descriptions of many theatrical troupes in existence in Moscow and Leningrad. The main part of the book discusses the histories of various historical endeavors in both cities. A short section summarizes the history of the theater up to the year 1900. The book contains over 500 black-and-white photographs and prints of stage sets, play scenes, graphic works, and portraits of personalities of the theatre. The book is intended for a general audience.
SR, 38:3:541; WLT, 52(1978):305.

116.   Schwarz, Boris. **Music and Musical Life in Soviet Russia, 1917-1970**. New York: W. W. Norton, 1972. 550p. $13.50.
This is a longish chronicle of Soviet musical life and the ways of the Soviet musical establishment; there is only cursory discussion of the music itself. There are five main parts: Experimentation, 1917-21; Consolidation, 1921-32; Regimentation, 1932-53; Liberalization, 1954-64; and Collective Leadership, 1964-70. The author apparently finds the twenties the most interesting of times in Soviet music.
SR, 32;1:204-5; MQ, 59(1973):134.

117.   Senkevitch, Anatole, Jr. **Soviet Architecture, 1917-1962: A Bibliographical Guide to Source Material**. Charlottesville: University Press of Virginia, 1974. 284p. $13.50.
The volume does not purport to be a comprehensive index. Rather, one thousand separate entries—including monographs and journal articles, both Russian and Western—have been selected "primarily to satisfy initial bibliographic enquiries into the history and theory of Soviet architecture." The brief summaries of entries are generally useful and the indexing unusually thorough.
SR, 34:2:444-45.

118.   Sjeklocha, Paul, and Mead, Igor. **Unofficial Art in the Soviet Union**. Berkeley: University of California Press, 1967. 213p. $42.50.

Following an impressively thorough introduction to the role of political influence on Russian and Soviet art in the past, the authors of this text have described and documented one of the most interesting phenomena in contemporary art: the appearance in the Soviet Union of a bona fide unofficial and underground art. This work is essential for any assessment of the place of the visual arts in Soviet life.

SR, 27:4:677-78; LJ, 93(1968):980.

119. Swift, Mary Grace. **The Art of the Dance in the U.S.S.R.** Notre Dame, IN: University of Notre Dame Press, 1968. 405p. $19.95.
The author endeavors to provide a broad outline of the evolution of ballet in Soviet Russia and some of the Soviet republics up to 1964. An attempt is made to describe the ideological principles underlying Soviet ballet, and there are numerous quotations from political literature and official pronouncements. The book is a mine of information, and there are some excellent illustrations.

SR, 29:2:356-57.

120. Taylor, Richard. **The Politics of the Soviet Cinema, 1917-1929.** New York and London: Cambridge University Press, 1979. xvi, 214p. $19.95.
Taylor focuses on the opportunities and problems confronting film industry executives, including intra-industry relations and dealings with other Soviet and Communist executives. His treatment of the material and organizational problems that beset the Soviet film industry at the beginning is particularly useful, and his examination of film revenues and taxes is enlightening.

SR, 39:2:360.

121. Vodarsky-Shiraeff, Alexandria. **Russian Composers and Musicians: A Biographical Dictionary.** New York: Greenwood Press, 1969 (1940). 158p. $12.50.
This useful reference aid offers brief sketches of eighty-two composers and musicians arranged in alphabetical order. Many of those whose names are included in this biography were victims of Stalin's purges, and despite limited de-Stalinization their complete biographical data have not yet been made available in Soviet publications. Therefore, this reprint represents the only guide to Russian musicians.

Choice, 7(1970):371.

ECONOMICS

Bibliographies

122. Kazmer, Daniel R., and Kazmer, Vera. **Russian Economic History: A Guide to Information Sources**. Detroit: Gale Research Company, 1977. x, 520p. $44.00.

This is an annotated bibliography of books, pamphlets, and articles in English on the Russian economy, covering both Imperial Russia and the Soviet Union. Each chapter is divided roughly into four sections. Three chronological sections, listing works covering periods up to 1860, 1860 to 1917, and since 1917, are preceded by a general section on the topic. Within each section, works are listed alphabetically by author.

BHR, 52(1978):289.

123. White, Paul M., comp. **Soviet Urban and Regional Planning: A Bibliography with Abstracts**. London: Mansell, 1979. ix, 276p. £12.95.

This is a classified bibliography of books and articles in English, French, and German, including both Soviet material published in English and Western translations of Russian material as well as Western studies. The compiler contributes an introduction on the theory and practice of Soviet planning.

SS, 32:4:613.

General Studies

124. Bergson, Abram. **Productivity and the Social System—the USSR and the West**. Cambridge, MA: Harvard University Press, 1978. xi, 256p. $18.50.

The author's ultimate concern is with economic merit, a major aspect of which is economic efficiency. The latter concept is not easily measurable operationally, though strong inferences about it can be drawn on the basis of what is measurable, i.e., productivity. Bergson approaches an evaluation of the performance of the Soviet economy by a variety of comparisons with nonsocialist economies.

SS, 31:4:600-1; Choice, 15(1979):1566.

125. Bornstein, Morris, and Fusfeld, Daniel R., eds. **The Soviet Economy: A Book of Readings**. 3d ed. Homewood, IL: Richard Irwin, 1970 (1962). 467p.; 4th ed., 1974. 543p.

This enlarged edition updates available material. The reader examines the three basic aspects of the Soviet economy: the fundamental strategy of planning, the role of Marxist ideology, and a summary view of the principles by which resources are allocated. Another part provides details about the operation of the Soviet planned economy, aspects of macroeconomics, and essays on the changing nature of the system.

JEL, 12(1974):1399.

126.   Campbell, Robert W. **Soviet-Type Economies: Performance and Evolution.** London: Macmillan, 1974. 259p. $14.50.
This book provides a general introduction to the working of the Soviet economic system. It is basically an extension of an earlier study, *Soviet Economic Power,* reappraising the economic development of the USSR in the light of recent research, and extending the work to include an assessment of managerial reforms in the Soviet Union and to discuss developments in Eastern Europe and, marginally, China and Cuba.

SEER, 53:132:470.

127.   Gregory, Paul R., and Stuart, Robert C. **Soviet Economic Structure and Performance.** New York: Harper & Row, 1974. 478p. $23.95.
The study is centered on four themes: (1) the evolution of the Soviet economic system, (2) the process of resource allocation in the Soviet economy, (3) reform of the Soviet command economy, and (4) the economic performance and development of the Soviet economy. The extensive bibliography, clear style, and objective presentation make this study a valuable source which can also be recommended as a textbook for classroom use.

JEL, 12(1974):1400.

128.   Holzman, Franklyn D., ed. **Readings on the Soviet Economy.** Chicago: Rand McNally, 1962. 763p.
This well-balanced collection of over forty articles and excerpts from books dealing with major aspects of the Soviet economy can serve as a supplementary reader with any textbook on the Soviet economy. Another useful volume of readings: Shaffer, Harry G. *The Soviet Economy.* New York: Appleton-Century-Crofts, 1963. 456p.

129.   Jasny, Naum. **Soviet Industrialization, 1928-1952.** Chicago: University of Chicago Press, 1961. 467p.
Jasny presents a comprehensive and systematic review of developments during Stalin's years in power. Major sectors of the economy such as industry, agriculture, retail trade, and consumption are dealt with. While the book was written by a specialist for students of Soviet affairs, it can be utilized by beginners because it offers basic information on the functioning of the economy under a totalitarian regime.

SR, 22:2:356-58.

130.   Kaser, Michael. **Soviet Economics.** New York: McGraw-Hill, 1970. 256p.
The book offers an original and imaginative treatment of the Soviet economy intended for the general reader as well as the college student. Instructors and specialists on the Soviet economy will benefit from many stimulating insights. Although the book includes some technical discussion of various points, non-economists will find it accessible and rewarding, particularly for its integration of ideological, historical, political, and social aspects with the economic analysis.

SR, 30:4:900-1.

131. Katsenelinboigen, Aron. **Soviet Economic Thought and Political Power in the USSR**. New York: Pergamon Press, 1980. xiv, 213p. $25.00.
This work describes the development of mathematical economics in the USSR. The author grew up in the movement and was himself a contributor to its progress prior to his emigration in 1973. He provides vivid sketches of the men and women involved in reviving economics in the USSR after Stalin died. The study can be recommended for all students of postwar Soviet economic thought.
RR, 40:2:209; PSQ, 96(1981):358.

132. Katz, Abraham. **The Politics of Economic Reform in the Soviet Union**. New York: Praeger, 1972. 242p. $15.00.
The author has produced a very useful book for all students of Soviet society. He focuses on the Kosygin economic reforms of September 1965, for the period of the Eighth Five-Year Plan. A careful documentation from primary Soviet sources provides a helpful reference source. A review of the Stalinist model for planning and management is provided as a frame of reference for assessing the nature of change implied by the proposed reform.
CSP, 16:2:301-2; Choice, 10(1973):661.

133. Kish, George. **Economic Atlas of the Soviet Union**. Ann Arbor: University of Michigan Press. 2d rev. ed., 1971. 90p.
This is the second edition of a work first published in 1960. Most of the changes deal with shifts in the structure of urban centers, the addition of new towns of importance, and the further diversification of industry in towns already in existence a decade ago. This volume will be useful for students and others seeking a quick guide to Soviet economic development.
Choice, 9(1972):492.

134. Nove, Alec. **The Soviet Economic System**. London: George Allen & Unwin, 1977. 399p. $23.25.
The author notes in his preface that the main difference between this and his earlier work is organizational. The present volume integrates the treatment of both structure and problems as each sector of the Soviet economy is discussed. It ends with a general assessment of the Soviet economy.
SR, 39:1:131-32.

135. Nove, Alec. **The Soviet Economy: An Introduction**. New York: Praeger, 1961. 328p.; rev. ed., 1965. 380p. $7.00.
Nove's book remains a landmark and standard work for the study of the Soviet economy. Undergraduates and general readers will appreciate the clarity of the text and the scope of material that it discusses. It also serves as an excellent reference tool.
LJ, 86(1961):4290.

136. Spulber, Nicholas. **The Soviet Economy: Structure, Principles, Problems**. New York: Norton, 1962. 311p.
The study examines the basic assumptions and working principles of the Soviet economy as viewed by Soviet economists themselves and contrasts Soviet with Western concepts. It serves as a handy summary of the intricacies of Soviet national

income accounting, choice of alternative investments, and a myriad of other Marxist measures.

SR, 22:1:167-68; LJ, 87(1962): 2542.

137. Sutton, Antony C. **Western Technology and Soviet Economic Development, 1917 to 1930.** Stanford: Hoover Institution Press, 1968. 318p. $10.00.

This book is the first detailed study of the large-scale infusion of Western technology and technical personnel into the Soviet economy during the 1920s. It contains a systematic review for each economic sector of the important commercial contracts concluded with Western firms during the 1920s, and an assessment of the overall effect of foreign concessions and technical assistance on Soviet economic development. The study shows that Soviet concessions involving foreign equity capital usually ended in expropriation or other failure. A great deal of interesting data and several insights into Soviet growth and the process of technology transfer make this a valuable source.

SR, 29:2:337-38.

138. Sutton, Antony C. **Western Technology and Soviet Economic Development, 1930 to 1945.** Second volume of a three-volume series. Stanford: Hoover Institution Press, 1971. 401p. $12.50.

This volume carefully documents the wide use and critical importance of Western technology and technical skills in the high-priority sectors during the early five-year plans and summarizes the major technology transfers occurring through the Lend Lease agreement. The study shows the great impact that blueprints and a dozen engineers can have on an industry.

SR, 31:4:904-5; LJ, 94(1969):988.

139. Sutton, Antony C. **Western Technology and Soviet Economic Development, 1945 to 1965.** Third volume of a three-volume series. Stanford: Hoover Institution Press, 1973. 482p. $15.00.

This third volume completes a comprehensive survey of the origins of applied technology transfer since 1917. The survey offers a comprehensive look at major technologies in use in all sectors. It shows that the USSR could concentrate its resources for high-priority sectors, having been supplied with Western technologies in other areas.

CSP, 17:2:536-37; Choice, 11(1974):645.

Economic History

140. Baykov, Alexander. **The Development of the Soviet Economic System.** Cambridge: Cambridge University Press, 1970 (1947). 514p. $15.00.

Baykov left Russia after the Bolshevik revolution. In this book he offers his personal assessment of the first three years of the new regime, followed by the history of economic changes and the development up to the Second World War. These periods are examined: (1) Transitional Period and Period of "War Communism," (2) Period of Restoration and Preparation for the Reconstruction of the National Economy, (3) Period of Extensive Industrialization, Collectivization of Agriculture, and Rationing, and (4) Period of Intensive Endeavour to Improve the Country's

Economy and Economic System. Not only the extensive bibliography, mainly of Russian titles, but also the author's qualifications justify the new edition of this valuable contribution.

141.   Carr, Edward Hallett. **A History of Soviet Russia: Foundation of a Planned Economy, 1926-1929**, vol. 3, parts 1 and 2. New York: Macmillan, 1976. Part 1: x, 313p.; Part 2: 330p. $17.50 each vol.

While volumes 1 and 2 of *Foundations of a Planned Economy, 1926-1929*, dealt in great detail with domestic matters, these two parts of volume 3 review Soviet relations with the capitalist world and developments within the Communist parties of seven capitalist countries. All libraries will want to have these volumes for use by all serious students.

142.   Davies, Robert W. **The Industrialization of Soviet Russia**. Vol. 1: **The Socialist Offensive: The Collectivization of Soviet Agriculture, 1929-1930**; Vol. 2: **The Soviet Collective Farm, 1929-1930**. Cambridge, MA: Harvard University Press, 1980. Vol. 1: xxii, 491p. Tables. $35.00; Vol. 2: x, 216p. Tables. $18.50.

This book deals essentially with economic problems. There is a thorough use of Soviet sources, and all sources are treated with appropriate caution. Many new points of detail in the collectivization emerge from the two volumes. This study is a worthy continuation of E. H. Carr's *Foundations of a Planned Economy*.

AHR, 86:2:625; Choice, 18(1981):712; BHR, 55(1981):272.

143.   McKay, John P. **Pioneers for Profit: Foreign Entrepreneurship and Russian Industrialization, 1885-1913**. Chicago: University of Chicago Press, 1970. 442p. $11.50.

According to McKay, profit could be made by the foreigner coming into partnership with Russian capital and a modus vivendi with the tsarist government—an arrangement mutually profitable for all concerned. The foreigner profited by selling his superior technology, which Russia could not duplicate. Advanced technology was worth money and it saved money in lower production costs. His materials enabled the author to study the operations of some two hundred foreign firms in Russia. He has made an original contribution and argued tellingly against some conventionally held interpretations. He has provided a mine of new facts and has described clearly for the first time how the foreign entrepreneur operated in Russia during the last years of tsarism. The book is clearly written and well organized. It must take its place as an essential monograph for the study of the economic history of Russia.

SR, 30:2:396-7; AHR, 76:4:1194; BHR, 45(1971):89.

144.   Nove, Alec. **An Economic History of the U.S.S.R.** Baltimore: Penguin Books, 1969. 416p. $10.00.

This valuable book is an extremely political economic history, for in the Soviet Union politics dominates economics. The author concentrates on economic policies, decisions, events, organizations, and conditions as they relate to the men, or man, at the top. He uses qualitative data—debates, literature, even jokes—which allows him to cut through the fog of propaganda and gives the reader a balanced view of Soviet economic experience.

SR, 29:1:713-14; LJ, 95(1970):152.

Special Studies—Theory and Planning

145. Bergson, Abram. **The Economics of Soviet Planning**. New Haven: Yale University Press, 1964. 394p. $7.50. (Studies in Comparative Economics, no. 5.)

Every English-speaking student of the Soviet economy has been partly molded by Bergson, the father of Soviet national product and income statistics. In approaching Soviet economic institutions he considers, one after the other, the principal components of the Soviet national income and product accounts. Each such component consists, basically, of a ruble value at any date; this value is the product of a physical quantity and a price. Hence, by systematically considering the administrative processes by which plans are drafted, physical quantities are produced or used, and prices are determined in the individual Soviet accounts, Bergson claims to have catalogued the entire set of economic institutions. His book is a useful, even important source of institutional detail, but is neither a satisfactory nor an unsatisfactory account of how the economic performance of Soviet institutions is to be appraised.

SR, 24:4:738-42.

146. Carr, Edward Hallett, and Davies, R. W. **Foundations of a Planned Economy, 1926-1929**. Volume 1, in two parts. London, 1969; New York: Macmillan, 1971. Part 1: pp. 1-542; Part 2: 453-1023. $12.50 ea.

These two volumes represent the first half of the final series in Carr's mammoth *A History of Soviet Russia.* With the aid of the economist Davis, Carr covers in exhaustive detail the economic institutions and development of the USSR during the three years just before the initiation of the First Five-Year Plan. The work is most useful in its specific descriptions of specific institutions: in agriculture, the details of land tenure, the development of the cooperatives, and the early Kolkhoz arrangements; in industry, the shifting relationships among ministries, syndicates, and trusts; the status of private enterprise and the treatment of managerial specialists; and the myriad of competing proposals and conflicting agency involvements that lay behind the ultimate formulation of the First Five-Year Plan.

SR, 31:2:428-29.

147. DiMaio, Alfred John, Jr. **Soviet Urban Housing: Problems and Policies**. New York: Praeger, 1974. 234p. $16.50. (Praeger Special Studies in International Economics.)

The study provides a critical analysis of the Soviet housing policy and cites experiences and problems stemming from a centralized and planned economy. It should prove of considerable interest to Western urbanologists facing and comparing modern urban problems.

148. Lewin, Moshe. **Political Undercurrents in Soviet Economic Debates: From Bukharin to the Modern Reformers**. Princeton, NJ: Princeton University Press, 1974. xix, 373p. $16.50.

This book focuses on the political aspects and ideas of the Soviet economic debates of the 1920s and 1960s. The author attempts to show the similarity of certain themes developed in the earlier period, notably by Bukharin, with those developed in the later period by the most representative modern Soviet economic reformers.

SR, 35:4:745-47; Choice, 12(1975):258; LJ, 100(1975):486.

149. Moorsteen, Richard, and Powell, Raymond P. **The Soviet Capital Stock, 1928-1962.** Homewood, IL: Richard D. Irwin, 1966. 671p.

The work contains two independent but related essays. In part 1 the authors set out to measure changes in the stock of Soviet capital and the annual flow of productive services to the Soviet economy of the capital stock. In part 2 they estimate the Soviet investment rate and the proportions of growth that can be attributed to growth of capital. This study has been extended by the essay published in 1968 by Abraham S. Becker, et al, *The Soviet Capital Stock: Revisions and Extensions, 1961-1967.*

SR, 28:3:508-10.

150. Richman, Barry M. **Management Development and Education in the Soviet Union.** East Lansing, MI: Bureau of Economic Research, Michigan State University, 1967. 308p.

According to the author, the present and future needs of the Soviet economy require industrial managers of a new type who can apply general managerial skills, who understand the use of quantitative techniques for planning and control, and who are also knowledgeable in areas such as marketing, cost accounting, and industrial psychology. This idea is no doubt correct, but Soviet engineering education (which trains most future managers) does not yet include these kinds of instruction. Despite certain deficiencies the book's publication is to be welcomed. It is the only monograph in English dealing with the education of Soviet managers.

SR, 28:1:165-66; AAA, 375(1968):211.

151. Ryavec, Karl W. **Implementation of Soviet Economic Reforms: Political Organizations, and Social Processes.** New York: Praeger, 1975. xiii, 360p.

This book explores what the process of economic reform tells us about the politics of the USSR and about the running of the world's largest hierarchical organization. The focus is on how change was initiated, implemented, amended, or held up by various groups. The work is also comprehensive in that it deals with all aspects of the Soviet manager's environment.

Choice, 13(1976):256.

152. Zauberman, Alfred. **The Mathematical Revolution in Soviet Economics.** London: Oxford University Press, 1975. xiv, 62p. $9.00.

Mathematical Theory in Soviet Planning: Concepts, Methods, Techniques. Toronto: Oxford University Press, 1976. xiv, 464p. $49.75.

The author argues that mathematical economics has influenced the theory of Soviet planning more than its practice. He has catalogued the very substantial contributions of Soviet mathematicians and economists to the theory of economic planning. He relates their work to that of Western counterparts. The studies have value as a reference tool for the mathematical economist interested in Soviet planning.

CSP, 19:4:518; SR, 35:2:355-56.

Agriculture

153. Hahn, Werner G. **The Politics of Soviet Agriculture, 1960-1970.** Baltimore: Johns Hopkins University Press, 1972. 311p. $12.50.

The study examines the agricultural issues over which the Soviet leaders have been divided during the decade 1960-70. It provides informative and readable accounts of the unfolding of some of the more important agricultural problems of the decade and the role played therein by certain Soviet officials.

SR, 33:3:547-48; Choice, 10(1973):682.

154. Laird, Roy D., and Crowley, Edward L., eds. **Soviet Agriculture: The Permanent Crisis.** New York: Praeger, 1965. 209p. $7.00.

This collection of papers presented at an international symposium on Soviet agriculture offers a rich store of statistical analysis of the "Ten Great Years" of the Khrushchev era. This volume is indispensable for those who want to know more about the Soviet Union as it really is, rather than the view one gets from the Intourist vehicle.

RR, 25:1:99-100; AER, 56(1966):279.

155. Lewin, Moshe. **Russian Peasants and Soviet Power: A Study of Collectivization.** Translated from the French by Irene Nove with John Biggart. Preface by Alec Nove. Evanston, IL: Northwestern University Press, 1968. 539p. $15.00.

No major event of Soviet history has been more thoroughly obscured by the official historiography than the collectivization of agriculture. One is therefore grateful for a knowledgeable, thorough, and fair-minded work of Lewin. The author finds the regime deficient not only in its understanding of peasant attitudes and aspirations but also in the development of its own programs and administrative structures. The primacy of considerations of power (being urban-oriented) and the tyranny of ideological abstractions over empirical economic data and analysis, which Lewin later describes as the essence of Stalin's agrarian policy, are an integral part of the same heritage. The most original and informative portions of the book are the chapters which detail the transition from NEP to general collectivization. Lewin's study adds a good deal to our specific understanding of the process of collectivization and its consequences.

SR, 31:2:429-31; Choice, 5(1969):1494.

156. McCauley, Martin. **Khrushchev and the Development of Soviet Agriculture: The Virgin Land Programme 1953-1964.** London: Macmillan, 1976. xiii, 232p. $30.00.

Although the main focus is on the virgin land program, the study does incorporate a review of Khrushchev's agricultural policies as a whole with their political implications. An introductory chapter traces the eastward expansion of the agricultural frontier during both tsarist and Soviet times, and the book concludes with a brief assessment of land productivity in the virgin land areas.

CSP, 20:4:577-78.

157. Shaffer, Harry G., ed. **Soviet Agriculture: An Assessment of Its Contribution to Economic Development.** New York and London: Praeger, 1977. xviii, 167p. Tables. $17.50.

This book comprises four pieces on Soviet agriculture by authors using widely differing ideological and analytical frames of reference. The objective is to offer readers a wide spectrum of views on Soviet agriculture based upon the supposition that Soviet agriculture is both important and controversial.

SR, 38:2:314-15.

158. Volin, Lazar. **A Century of Russian Agriculture: From Alexander II to Khrushchev.** Cambridge, MA: Harvard University Press, 1970. 644p. $18.50. (Russian Research Center Studies, 63.)

This volume of a detailed interpretive survey of Russian agriculture from the mid-nineteenth century through 1966 will be indispensable for both specialists and general readers interested in the Soviet area. Although the treatment is generally nontechnical, even the more specialized student of Soviet agriculture will find Volin's interpretations of specific policies and practices interesting and thought-provoking. The book is divided chronologically into three main sections: the reign of Alexander II through the October Revolution, "war Communism" through the Stalin era, and the Khrushchev era and beyond. The author has relied primarily on information from published Soviet and pre-Soviet sources. Fortunately for the reader, the writing style is lively, and complex technical questions are handled in a clear, comprehensible manner.

SR, 31:1:184-85; LJ, 96(1971):960.

159. Wädekin, Karl-Eugen. **The Private Sector in Soviet Agriculture.** Edited by George Karcz. Translated by Keith Bush. 2d rev. and enl. ed. Berkeley: University of California Press, 1973. 307p. $17.50.

To this translation of the German edition three chapters have been added to bring the historical account of Soviet policy toward "private" agriculture down to 1971. The study opens with the "ground rules" under which the private sector operates in the Soviet agricultural economy. It then assesses the performance of Soviet private agriculture and explains its connection with the rest of the economy.

SR, 33:2:356-57; APSR, 68(1974):1379.

Industry, Transportation

160. Athay, Robert E. **The Economics of Soviet Merchant-Shipping Policy.** Chapel Hill: University of North Carolina Press, 1971. 150p. $7.50.

This book sheds light on the motives, ways, and means underlying the development of the Soviet merchant fleet and its implications for capitalist countries. The study is based on primary sources and should have broad appeal to business-men, economists, and political scientists interested in East-West trade and shipping policies.

SR, 33:2:376-77; Choice, 9(1972):544.

161. Blackwell, William L. **The Industrialization of Russia: An Historical Perspective.** New York: Thomas Y. Crowell, 1970. 198p.

This historical survey of Russian economic development aims to provide students with "background usually lacking in more detailed and technical examinations of the contemporary economy of the USSR." The author has produced a manual that should prove useful in classroom teaching situations.

SR, 30:3:667.

162. Campbell, Robert W. **Trends in the Soviet Oil and Gas Industry**. Baltimore and London: Johns Hopkins University Press, 1976. xvi, 125p. Tables. Figures. $10.00.

This compact, succinct book is a useful companion to the author's *Economics of Soviet Oil and Gas* (1968); it updates the data base of the earlier work and reviews the most important developments since 1965. The study deals with Soviet energy policy and the related industry and with Soviet participation in world energy markets. This is a valuable book for both the serious student and the general reader.
SR, 36:4:696; Choice, 14(1977):424.

163. Conynghan, William J. **Industrial Management in the Soviet Union: The Role of the CPSU in Industrial Decision-Making, 1917-1970**. Stanford: Hoover Institution Press, 1973. 378p. $9.50.

This is a book with a broader horizon than its title suggests, and it should not be overlooked by students of Soviet politics or political scientists. It is a comprehensive evaluation of the record of the Soviet Communist Party's general political direction of the industrial and agricultural economy of the USSR. The study combines a well-drawn analytical perspective of party leadership of Soviet economic development from Lenin to Brezhnev with a perceptive case study of Khrushchev's ultimately abortive design for a major departure from past—principally Stalinist—direction of the economy.
SR, 33:3:543-44; Choice, 10(1973):1426.

164. Dewdney, John C. **The USSR**. Boulder, CO: Westview Press, 1976. xvi, 262p. Tables. $19.50. (Studies in Industrial Geography, vol. 3.)

The text contains a substantial amount of factual information in an encyclopedic manner and encompasses the environmental, resource, transport, and population factors related to industrialization in the USSR. The book also examines specific industrial sectors and regional contrasts in Soviet industry.
SR, 36:3:511; LJ, 101(1976):2567.

165. Goldman, Marshall I. **The Spoils of Progress: Environmental Pollution in the Soviet Union**. Cambridge, MA: MIT Press, 1972. 372p. $7.95.

The author finds that the Soviet Union has little to offer, either in theory or practice, that might lead to an improvement of environmental quality elsewhere. The study concludes that environmental disruption has been as extensive in the Soviet Union as anywhere.
SR, 32:3:629-30; LJ, 98(1973):1441; Choice, 10(1973):148.

166. Hunter, Holland. **Soviet Transport Experience: Its Lessons for Other Countries**. Washington, DC: The Brookings Institution, Transport Research Program, 1968. 194p. $6.00.

In this work the author continues his investigation of problems first explored in his previous monograph, *Soviet Transportation Policy* (1957). He offers a chapter and two appendixes on the commanding place of railroads in Soviet transportation, and he gives fine summaries of both the place of trucks in freight transport and the growth of passenger traffic, as Soviet planners enter the automobile age.
SR, 29:3:546-47; AAPSS-A, 381(1969):211.

167. Liberman, E. G. **Economic Methods and the Effectiveness of Production.** Translated by Arlo Schultz. Edited by Leonard J. Kirsch. White Plains, NY: International Arts and Sciences Press, 1971. 183p. $15.00.

This volume presents Liberman's proposals for reforms in the planning and management of the Soviet economy. While enterprise managers would have greater freedom in certain areas of production and in the use of inputs, they would still have to meet central fixed quotas, assortment and delivery assignments. Liberman hopes to achieve output while employing the initiative and knowledge available on the lower level of the Soviet economic structure.

   SR, 33:3:555-56.

168. North, Robert N. **Transport in Western Siberia: Tsarist and Soviet Development.** Vancouver: University of British Columbia Press and The Centre for Transportation Studies, 1979. viii, 364p. $22.00.

The author has not attempted to divorce transport from the rest of the economy with which it is so inextricably linked. The book is well-written and offers a penetrating analysis of Siberian development.

   SS, 32:2:313-14; JEH, 40(1980):416.

169. Stowell, Christopher E., assisted by Neal Weigel, with chapters by Edward Maguire and Erast Borisoff. **Soviet Industrial Import Priorities: With Marketing Considerations for Exporting to the USSR.** New York: Praeger, 1975. xxxii, 508p. Tables. Charts. Appendixes. $30.00.

The authors are all associated with WJS, Inc., a well-known export management and consulting firm dealing primarily in Soviet and Chinese markets, and this volume is directed at U.S. businessmen interested in the Soviet market. The businessman or scholar interested in description and analysis of selected facets of Soviet technology will find this handbook very valuable and useful.

   SR, 35:4:747-48.

170. Symons, Leslie, and White, Colin, eds. **Russian Transport: An Historical and Geographical Survey.** London: C. Bell & Sons, 1975. xxiv, 192p. Maps. Tables. £7.25.

Russian railways facilitated grain exports, encouraged regional specialization, and altered the domestic pattern of grain supply, according to an analysis of the first essay of this study. The second contribution is a history of railways and economic development in Turkestan before 1917.

   SR, 35:4:749.

171. Westwood, J. N. **A History of Russian Railways.** London: George Allen & Unwin, 1964. 326p.

The study reviews the growth of Russian railways up to World War I. Maps and photographs supplement a compact account of tsarist efforts, drawing on primarily Russian sources, including early ministerial documents. Four more chapters review Soviet developments through 1959. The bibliography and footnotes offer a rich variety of primary sources.

   SR, 24:1:147-48.

Labor, Trade Unions

172. Brodersen, Arvid. **The Soviet Worker: Labor and Government in Soviet Society.** New York: Random House (c. 1966). 278p.
The author offers a critical chronological survey of Soviet labor policies from 1917 to the early 1960s. Problems of ideology, economic policy, industrial development, education, and social stratification and mobility are raised. The study gives Western readers an introduction to the role of the working class in contemporary society.
SR, 26:4:688-89; ASR, 31(1966):888.

173. Dallin, David J., and Nicolaevsky, Boris I. **Forced Labor in Soviet Russia.** New Haven: Yale University, 1947. 331p.
The authors discuss the development of the forced labor phenomenon in Soviet Russia, basing their account on Soviet and émigré sources, showing terrorist practices during the Stalin era. This book offers informative reading for anyone interested in the Soviet Union, and the study has yet to be surpassed by a new version.
LJ, 72(1947):1102.

174. Kahan, Arcadius, and Ruble, Blair A. eds. **Industrial Labor in the USSR.** New York: Pergamon Press, 1979. xv, 421p. $32.50.
The essays are based on presentations at a conference on Soviet industrial labor. The topics discussed are characteristics of the industrial labor force, labor unions, standards of living, politics, and the worker as hero in Soviet literature.
RR, 39:3:378-79; Choice, 17(1980):118.

175. MacAuley, Mary. **Labour Disputes in Soviet Russia, 1957-1965.** Oxford, England: Clarendon Press, 1969. 269p. $6.75.
This book is restricted to the study of disputes in the industrial enterprise and is based primarily on the author's research in the Soviet Union. The bulk of the book is concerned with a discussion of disputes over the legal rights of the employee; for example, he may dispute his job classification, underpayment of overtime, or that his annual vacation may be given him in the summer. Wage rates, salaries, and hours of work are set by law and are not subject to dispute.
SR, 29:4:715-16; JLR, 102(1970):429.

176. Ruble, Blair A. **Soviet Trade Unions: Their Development in the 1970s.** Cambridge: Cambridge University Press, 1981. viii, 158p. Tables. $29.50.
The volume represents an attempt to write a reasonably popular book on Soviet trade unions. It could also be assigned for undergraduate reading. Ruble covers the history of Soviet trade union development at the national level from 1970 to 1980, discussing trade union activities at the enterprise level, and ends with a treatment of the international activities of the Soviet trade union movement. The book has a good set of footnotes and a useful classified bibliography.
SR, 42:1:125-26.

177. Shapiro, Leonard, and Godson, J., eds. **The Soviet Worker: Illusions and Realities.** London: Macmillan, 1981. xii, 291p. £15.00.

This collection of essays attempts to establish the extent to which the Soviet working class has been a beneficiary of the 1917 revolution by contrasting various aspects of the situation of the Soviet worker with official Soviet ideology. There is a supplement which compares retail prices and work-time equivalents of selected consumer goods and services in Moscow and four Western cities.

SS, 35:1:117-20.

178. Swianiewicz, S. **Forced Labour and Economic Development: An Enquiry into the Experience of Soviet Industrialization.** London: Oxford University Press, 1965. 321p. $7.20. (Issued under the auspices of the Royal Institute of International Affairs.)

The continued practice of forced labor camps in the Soviet Union is proven by the recurrent publicized sentencing of "guilty" persons to terms of forced labor. The institution of forced labor acquires for the author an aura of economic rationality from the point of view of the Stalinist development strategy.

SR, 26:3:505-6.

179. Zelnik, Reginald E. **Labor and Society in Tsarist Russia: The Factory Workers of St. Petersburg, 1855-1870.** Stanford: Stanford University Press, 1971. 450p. $15.00. (Sponsored by the Russian Institute, Columbia University.)

The work is one of the few on Russian history of European or American authorship that uses Soviet archives. The author also had at his disposal a rich fund of published sources. The book's aim is to "contribute to our ultimate understanding of the role of factory workers in the Russian revolutionary movement, and of the social and political repercussions of industrialization as it was carried out in the context of the Russian autocratic system." Zelnik's people function within a Russian context of autocracy and nationalism rather than acting out predetermined roles as a European bourgeois ruling class and proletariat, creating a kind of industrial populism.

SR, 31:3:665-67; Choice, 8(1972):1504.

Resources

180. Campbell, Robert W. **The Economics of Soviet Oil and Gas.** Baltimore: Johns Hopkins Press, 1968. 279p. $8.50.

The author assesses Soviet capabilities and intentions for exporting petroleum and the effectiveness of the Soviet system's arrangement for factory use. He asserts that underground gasification of solid fuels turned out to be a most unproductive venture. This is a most perceptive account on the issues arising in regard to Soviet international trade in petroleum and the economics of Soviet oil and gas.

SR, 28:3:510-11; Choice, 6(1969):547.

181. Conolly, Violet. **Beyond the Urals: Economic Development in Soviet Asia.** New York: Oxford University Press, 1967. 420p. $13.50.

The author deals with a wide range of questions, such as the progress of industrialization in the eastern part of the Soviet Union, population and migration problems, the Central Asian cotton industry, labor problems on Asian construction sites, and development aspects of the Soviet-Chinese dispute. She correctly assesses the new Soviet policy toward development of the eastern regions realizing that the government "now clearly tends to favor investment in the western regions where the best returns can be expected on capital, rather than, for example, developing new projects in the labor and capital intensive industries of east and west Siberia where returns on both capital and labor are below the Soviet average." The book contains new insights for the specialist.

SR, 28:2:346-47; Choice, 5(1968):227.

182. Conolly, Violet. **Siberia Today and Tomorrow: A Study of Economic Resources, Problems and Achievements.** New York: Taplinger Publishing Company, 1976. 248p. Illustrations. Maps. $20.50.

The author presents an account of the Siberian economy for readers unfamiliar with the Russian language. It tells of success and failure, of great hopes and grave problems, and draws upon journalistic accounts of local tribulations to enliven production statistics. The book is one of the best of its kind.

SR, 36:2:325-26.

183. Dienes, Leslie, and Shabad, Theodore. **The Soviet Energy System.** Washington, DC: V. H. Winston & Sons, 1979. Distributed by Halsted Press. vii, 298p. $19.95.

This study provides information on the energy industry, the production of oil, gas, solid fuels, and hydroelectric and nuclear power. There is a section on energy consumption. The authors claim that fuel usage is inefficient in the Soviet Union. The book draws together a mass of information in a well-written and easily readable form.

SS, 32:4:609-10.

184. Gerasimov, I. P.; Armand, D. L.; and Yefron, K. M., eds. **Natural Resources of the Soviet Union: Their Use and Renewal.** Translated by Jacek I. Romanowski. English edition edited by W. A. Douglas Jackson. San Francisco: W. H. Freeman, 1971. 349p. $12.50.

A translation of a Soviet collection of articles, primarily by geographers, pertaining to the use of water resources, climate, vegetation, agricultural land, and fish and game supplies. It provides an illuminating overview of Soviet resource problems and potentials.

SR, 31:3:695-96; Choice, 8(1972):1620.

185. Goldman, Marshall I. **The Enigma of Soviet Petroleum: Half-Full or Half-Empty?** London: George Allen & Unwin, 1980. 214p. $19.95.

The author discusses various aspects of the Soviet oil industry as it might affect Western economies. He argues in favor of supplying the Soviets with the new technology in order to keep Eastern Europe from competing in world oil markets, which could become detrimental for the economies of the Western industrialized states.

LJ, 106(1981):1235; Choice, 18(1981):996.

186. Shabad, Theodore. **Basic Industrial Resources of the USSR.** New York: Columbia University Press, 1969. 393p. $20.00.

This useful book sketches the trends of production in four groups of raw materials—fuels, electric power, metals, and chemicals—from 1940 to 1965. This review is reliable and judicious. In general, it combines discussions of resources, usually in qualitative terms, with those of location, technology, and markets. The regional statistics and the clear maps are systematically cross-indexed. The bulk of the work consists of a regional industrial gazetteer. The regional groupings— political, economical, and geological—are rather artificial. They include the European parts of the Russian SFSR, the Trans-Caucasus, the Ukraine and Moldavia, Belorussia, the Baltic, the Urals, Siberia, the Kazakh SSR, and Central Asia. The work can profitably be used in conjunction with Chauncy Harris's *Cities of the Soviet Union* (Chicago, 1970).

SR, 30:4:904-5; GJ, 136(1970):439.

187. Shabad, Theodore, and Mote, Victor L. **Gateway to Siberian Resources (the BAM).** Washington, DC: Scripta Publishing Co., Scripta Technica, 1977. viii, 189p.

The Baikal-Amur Mainline, or BAM, the prime physical project extending over 2,000 miles from the upper Lena River to the lower Amur and the Pacific, is the subject of this study. The author analyzes environmental, historical, and resource aspects, and describes how BAM fits into the wider context.

GJ, 144(1978):317.

188. Whiting, Allen S. **Siberian Development and East Asia: Threat or Promise?** Stanford: Stanford University Press, 1981. xvi, 276p. Maps. Tables. $22.50.

This study probes the implication of Siberian development as it pertains to East Asia and examines the associated policy issues for Japan, China, and the United States. The author shows that the formidable physical obstacles and Moscow's economic priorities combine to enhance the importance of external factors and relations for the large-scale exploitation of resources in Eastern Siberia.

SR, 41:3:552-53; AAPSS-A, 463(1982):162.

Credit and Finance

189. Garvy, George. **Money, Financial Flows and Credit in the Soviet Union.** Cambridge, MA: Ballinger Publishing Company, 1977. xii, 223p. $27.50. (National Bureau of Economic Research Studies in International Economic Relations, 7.)

The book describes in detail contemporary banking and financial institutions. The author notes that the system's inability to allocate resources efficiently, to provide incentives to increase productivity, and to respond to developments not anticipated in plans has been recognized.

SEER, 58:1:147-48; Choice, 15(1978):731.

Foreign Economic Policy

190. Carter, James Richard. **The Net Cost of Soviet Foreign Aid**. Foreword by Raymond F. Mikesell. New York: Praeger, 1971. 134p. $12.50.
Using methods developed for the analysis of Western aid programs, Carter finds that between 1955 and 1968 the USSR delivered $3.1 billion in goods and services to non-Communist underdeveloped countries. After deducting what they got back in repayment of the loan-aid, and the benefit from price discrimination, the net cost is estimated to be only $680 million.
SR, 32:1:177; APSR, 66(1972):1051.

191. Freedman, Robert Owen. **Economic Warfare in the Communist Block: A Study of Soviet Economic Pressure against Yugoslavia, Albania, and Communist China**. New York: Praeger, 1970. 192p. $14.00.
The volume contains detailed documentation of the chronology and extent of Soviet economic pressure against the three countries. We learn that the Soviet arsenal of measures ranges from delaying trade negotiations, refusal to ratify trade agreements, to complete embargo of trade with the "target" nation.
SR, 31:2:464-65; Choice, 8(1971):587.

192. Goldman, Marshall I. **Détente and Dollars: Doing Business with the Soviets**. New York: Basic Books, 1975. x, 337p. $15.00.
This book is intended to provide a perspective on the causes of the abrupt changes in U.S.-Soviet trade during the period 1971 to 1974. It raises issues for both the public and the behavior of American business firms through case studies of important examples of Soviet trading activities with the United States—grain purchases and efforts to purchase technical systems from U.S. firms.
SR, 35:3:539-40; Choice, 12(1976):1478; LJ, 100(1975):2254.

193. Hanson, Philip. **Trade and Technology in Soviet-Western Relations**. New York: Columbia University Press, 1981. xiv, 271p. Figures. Tables. $30.00.
Hanson surveys the issues involved in trade and technology between the USSR and the West. The book, for the most part, should be accessible to noneconomists and can be profitably consulted by everyone interested in this important subject.
SR, 41:2:344-45; AAPSS-A, 462(1982):157.

194. Holliday, George D. **Technology Transfer to the USSR, 1928-1937 and 1966-1975: The Role of Western Technology in Soviet Economic Development**. Boulder, CO: Westview Press, 1979. xiv, 225p. $18.50.
The author, an analyst of Soviet-bloc trade and finance for the Congressional Reference Service of the Library of Congress, argues that the current Soviet leadership has adopted a strategy of "technological interdependence" with the West. He provides the best description to date on the process of technology transfer in the Soviet motor vehicle industry.
SR, 39:4:679; Choice, 16(1980):1623.

195. Klinghoffer, Arthur Jay. **The Soviet Union and International Oil Products, 1977.** New York: Columbia University Press, 1977. ix, 389p. $16.50.

The central question in this volume is the interaction between the USSR's trade in oil and its general foreign policy operation. The author stipulates that the main objectives and criteria in oil trade are economic, that is, to earn foreign exchange, but goes on to illuminate the many cases in which the USSR has used oil trade to further political goals as well. The book reveals clearly what political leverage it gives the USSR in world affairs to have large oil exports.

CSP, 20:2:269-70; Choice, 15(1978):514.

196. Marer, Paul. **Soviet and East European Foreign Trade, 1946-1969: Statistical Compendium and Guide.** Computer programs by Gary J. Eubanks. Bloomington: Indiana University Press, 1972. 408p. $15.00. (International Development Research Center Studies in Development, no. 4.)

The book embodies a description and some rigorous analysis of the methods and practices underlying the organization and presentation of foreign trade statistics in the socialist countries. The book is divided into four parts. Part 1, "Introduction and Summary," provides a guide to the data presented in part 2, "Statistical Series." The methodology used in constructing the tables is considered in part 3, "Notes and Documentation." Part 4 consists of seven appendixes, dealing with the United Nations and Comecon trade classifications, the problems of reconciliation, valuation, definitions, and unspecified Soviet exports; the last two appendixes contain standardized statistics on trade with the United States, Canada, Japan, and Australia, and a description of the Soviet and East European Foreign Trade Data Bank developed at the International Research Center.

SR, 33:1:156-57; Choice, 10(1973):757.

197. Quigley, John. **The Soviet Foreign Trade Monopoly: Institutions and Laws.** Columbus: Ohio State University Press, 1974. 256p. $15.00.

The author analyzes the history, nature, and operation of the foreign trade monopoly in the Soviet Union. Much of the research for his book was done in the USSR. It copes with the subject in a competent, illuminating, and penetrating manner. It includes a number of documents. Most revealing are the "Conditions of Delivery of Goods for Export" of 1960. The reader is aided by a bibliography and an index. Quigley concludes that the "dismantling of the monopoly system seems unlikely in the foreseeable future."

RR, 34:2:220-1.

198. Sawyer, Carole A. **Communist Trade with Developing Countries: 1955-65.** New York: Praeger, 1966. 127p. $10.00.

In focusing on the market which the Communist countries offer for the goods of the Third World, the author has found little shift in the products that are purchased. Food products and raw material still make up more than 90 percent of all Communist imports, contrary to Communist claims that they are willing to purchase the manufactured goods of developing areas.

SR, 26:4:693-94; Choice, 4(1967):72.

199. Smith, Glen Alden. **Soviet Foreign Trade: Organization, Operations, and Policy, 1918-1971.** New York: Praeger, 1973. 370p. $21.00.

This book was written primarily for the use of businessmen interested in trade with the Soviet Union. Half of the text deals with the organizations involved in the conduct of foreign trade and the other half deals with Soviet trade policies and practices. A large part of the text is devoted to descriptions of the structure and functions of the various organizations that have been responsible for the conduct of trade at various periods.

SR, 33:1:155-56.

200. Stevens, Christopher. **The Soviet Union and Black Africa.** New York: Holmes & Meier, 1976. xiv, 236p. Tables. $24.00.

This study is noteworthy for its richness of detail. There are chapters describing trade and aid patterns, cost-benefit calculations, effectiveness of foreign aid, and adaptability of Soviet economic endeavors to conditions in technologically backward regions. Political objectives of economic pursuits receive only casual treatment in this book.

SR, 37:1:141-42.

201. Turpin, William Nelson. **Soviet Foreign Trade: Purpose and Performance.** Lexington, MA: Lexington Books, 1977. xi, 172p. $15.00.

The author examines the organizational structure of the foreign trade system and the reasons for the creation of its institutional peculiarities. He advocates the creation of a Western organization "to control and to perform trade with the Soviet Union in the interest of attaining political benefits."

SEER, 58:1:148-49; Choice, 14(1978):1689.

202. Wiles, P. J. D. **Communist International Economics.** New York: Praeger, 1969. 566p. $12.50.

This is probably the most important book to date in the burgeoning literature on the political economy of foreign trade of Soviet-type economies. In eighteen chapters and numerous quantitative examples, both empirical and theoretical, and stressing the USSR, Wiles covers all phases of the experience, including Marxist theory and Soviet institutions, balance of payments and exchange rates, efficiency criteria, trade structure and its terms, finance, international integration, and economic war. The book will be standard in the field for years to come.

SR, 32:1:177-78.

EDUCATION AND CULTURE

203.   Alston, Patrick L. **Education and the State in Tsarist Russia.** Stanford: Stanford University Press, 1969. 322p. $8.50.
This volume is a welcome addition to an all-too-brief list of modern works dealing primarily with education in the Russian empire. Among the positive aspects of the study are the translation and interpretation of hundreds of documentary sources unavailable to most students of the subject. A second value is the attractive literary style in which these elements are presented, and the excellent selection, organization, and arrangement of a stupendous quantity of material.
SR, 29:1:108-9; AAPSS-A, 389(1970):155.

204.   DeWitt, Nicholas. **Education and Professional Employment in the U.S.S.R.** Washington, DC: National Science Foundation, 1961. 856p.
This standard work on Soviet education gives an account in great detail of the entire program for the training of specialists at all occupational levels, from skilled worker to research scientist. The systems of the military and party schools are also examined. Superb primary sources were used to document this study, which is highly recommended for all types of libraries.
SR, 21:3:568-69.

205.   Dunstan, John. **Paths to Excellence and the Soviet School.** Windsor, England: NFER Publishing Company, 1978. Distributed by Humanities Press, Atlantic Highlands, NJ. 302p. $21.00.
Extensively researched and meticulously documented, this book provides the most complete coverage of educational opportunities provided for what may be called the "Soviet children of privilege." This work is essential to a full understanding of what is transpiring today in the USSR in the area of social values and organizational innovations in the mammoth Soviet school system.
SR, 39:1:137-39; Choice, 16(1979):272.

206.   Fitzpatrick, Sheila. **Education and Social Mobility in the Soviet Union, 1921-1934.** New York: Cambridge University Press, 1979. x, 355p. $32.50.
This monograph's important subject is the education and social mobility in the early 1930s of the new Soviet elite, which included Khrushchev, Brezhnev, and Kosygin. The author discusses the history of Soviet education in the 1920s, the cultural revolution of Stalin's First Five-Year Plan, with its attempt to mobilize

and educate workers and peasants for the new society, and the restoration of order in education 1932-1934.

SR, 39:3:500-1; Choice, 17(1980):578.

207. Gorokhoff, Boris I. **Publishing in the U.S.S.R.** Bloomington: Indiana University Publications, 1959. 306p. (Slavic and East European Series, vol. 29.)

All aspects of book printing are treated in this book. An impressive general survey of the publishing activities and their ramifications in the USSR is offered, supplemented by a profusion of charts, tables, and lists.

SEEJ, 7:4:432-33.

208. Grant, Nigel. **Soviet Education.** Baltimore: Penguin Books, 1964. 190p.; 3d ed. Harmondsworth, England: Penguin Books, 1972. $0.90 pa.

This paperback contains a useful account of the general features of the Soviet school system, updated to about 1963. It is also a good, brief account of the system for anyone not interested in pursuing the matter further. Recommended for high school teachers.

SR, 24:3:574-75.

209. Jacoby, Susan. **Inside Soviet Schools.** New York: Hill & Wang, 1974. 248p. $8.95.

The author visited several nursery schools, kindergartens, and elementary and secondary schools. She brings a fresh approach and accurate appraisal to the study of Soviet education. In contrast to American education, Soviet schools are oriented toward strict discipline. The administration of education is centralized in Moscow, and the objectives are unified in a comprehensive plan. The Soviet government has a strong commitment to education, and parents strive to obtain the best possible for their children.

RR, 34:2:219; Choice, 12(1975):122.

210. Korol, Alexander G. **Soviet Research and Development: Its Organization Personnel, and Funds.** Cambridge, MA: MIT Press, 1965. 375p. $11.00.

This volume surveys the background and development of the recent changes in the organizational structure of the Soviet research and development establishment. It analyzes Soviet published data on the scale and rate of growth of research, the number of institutions, the size and composition of the scientific labor force involved, and the research budget.

Choice, 2(1966):852; LQ, 36(1966):163.

211. Kreusler, Abraham A. **Contemporary Education and Moral Upbringing in the Soviet Union.** Ann Arbor, MI: University Microfilms International, 1976. viii, 243p.

The book deals with the structure and general features of the Soviet educational system and the main aspects of education. The focus is on the political and ideological aims and contents of the different forms of education, such as collective education within schools and youth organizations.

212. Matthews, Mervyn. **Education in the Soviet Union: Policies and Institutions since Stalin**. London: Allen & Unwin, 1982. xiv, 225p. $28.50.
The author provides an overview of changes in policy and practice which have occurred in the main sectors of the educational system from the death of Stalin to the late 1970s. General education in schools and higher education take up a third of the book each. Particular aspects of student life are given special consideration in a chapter of their own. The chapter on supplementary educational services surveys the less well-known facilities such as preschool provision, professional military education, the training of party and state officials, seminary courses, private tuition, and even job placement.
SS, 35:3:422-23.

213. Mickiewicz, Ellen Propper. **Soviet Political Schools: The Communist Party Adult Instruction System**. New Haven: Yale University Press, 1967. 190p. $6.50. (Yale Russian and East European Studies, 3.)
This study is essentially a description and analysis of adult education under Khrushchev. The author discusses the Evening University of Marxism-Leninism, the *politshkola*, and ways and means by which adult education is carried out. Independent study is highly organized and the most advanced form of adult instruction. It may serve purposes other than education.
SR, 29:1:135-36; APSR, 62(1968):276; Choice, 4(1967):1019.

214. Noah, Harold J., ed. and trans. **The Economics of Education in the U.S.S.R.** New York: Praeger, 1969. 227p. $16.50.
These are the papers of a conference on the economics of education. Three topics are considered: (1) general problems of the economics of education, (2) the impact of education on labor productivity, and (3) specific examples of educational planning. Some interesting light is shed on the economic consequences of the post-1958 policy of increasing the proportion of university students enrolled on a part-time basis.
SR, 29:1:141; Choice, 7(1970):730.

215. Riordan, James. **Sport in Soviet Society: Development of Sport and Physical Education in Russia and the USSR**. New York and London: Cambridge University Press, 1977. x, 435p. $21.50.
The study reflects the author's intimate knowledge of Soviet sports as it provides a wealth of factual information. The topic is modern sport—its organization, major periods, and influences in historical development. The author elaborates on the relationship of Soviet top sports to foreign policy.
SR, 39:2:324-25.

216. Rosen, Seymour M. **Higher Education in the USSR: Curriculum, Schools and Statistics**. Washington, DC: U.S. Office of Education, 1963. 195p.
This publication consists of an extensive, but nonanalytical compilation of basic information translated from Soviet sources. Statistical data on students, faculty, institutions, and enrollments are provided. For information on supervision and quantitative aspects of Soviet education, see the author's "Higher Education in the USSR," in *Dimension on Soviet Economic Power*, Washington, DC: Joint Committee of the U.S. Congress, 1962, pp. 269-304.

217.   Shimoniak, Wasyl. **Communist Education: Its History, Philosophy and Politics.** Chicago: Rand McNally, 1970. 506p. $4.50 pa.

The author's aims are not to analyze the process of narrow indoctrination in Communist ideology but rather "to present important Communist educational policies and practices and to analyze their role in social change." The author is able to use most of the languages of the countries he writes about, and he covers fourteen Communist nations, including Albania. However, the stress falls on the school in relation to society in the USSR. Shimoniak sketches the historical background of education in tsarist Russia, and then goes on to survey in historical context the aims, reforms, structure, administration, curriculum, and methodology of Soviet education. He pays particular attention to the influence of Communist policies on minority languages, chiefly in Ukraine and Central Asia, the struggle of atheism versus religion in school and life, and the role of women in society. In sum, the author presents a creditable analysis of the Communist impact on the school, society, and the individual in the Soviet Union.

   SR, 30:3:676-77.

218.   Shneidman, N. N. **Literatures and Ideology in Soviet Education.** Lexington, MA: D. C. Heath, for Centre for Russian and East European Studies, University of Toronto, 1973. 207p.

The volume offers a compact analytical treatment of such aspects as ideology in education; literature in primary, secondary, and tertiary education; basic concepts and their confused interrelation; the handling of Russian classics; and scholarship versus political needs. Another part of the study deals with curricula, programs, book lists, examination instructions, and other pertinent information on education.

219.   Walker, Gregory. **Soviet Book Publishing Policy.** New York and London: Cambridge University Press, 1978. xvi, 164p. $15.95.

Walker gives an overview of Soviet publishing, going beyond organizational description into detailed reporting of practices. The book contains fresh and valuable information on many aspects, including pricing, authors' fee scales, editorial procedure, management problems, and the book trade. It is made clear that Soviet publishing is a tool of political and ideological influence.

   SR, 38:3:506-7; Choice, 15(1979):1504; LR, 27(1978):257.

220.   Weaver, Kitty. **Russia's Future: The Communist Education of Soviet Youth.** New York: Praeger Publishers, 1981. 240p. $21.95.

Written in a lively and readable style, with a focus on the Young Pioneers, an organization to which nearly every Soviet child between the ages of 10 and 15 belongs, this book offers a comprehensive look at what it is like to be a youth in the Soviet Union today. Numerous illustrations and photographs contribute to the better understanding of the problems discussed.

GEOGRAPHY, DEMOGRAPHY, POPULATION

221. Bater, James H. **The Soviet City: Ideal and Reality**. London: Edward Arnold; Beverly Hills, CA: Sage Publications, 1980. 196p. $18.95.
Presenting, principally for students, an introduction to Soviet planning and its results in cities of the Soviet Union, the author concludes that many urban problems are rooted in inadequate financial resources of city governments and the inability of city Soviets and planners to overcome the very strong economic and political positions of ministries engaged in industrial production.
RR, 40:1:71-72; AHR, 86:2:625; GJ, 147(1981):89.

222. Besemeres, John F. **Socialist Population Politics: The Political Implications of Demographic Trends in the USSR and Eastern Europe**. White Plains, NY: M. E. Sharpe, 1980. 384p. $25.00.
The book deals with the current and pending shifts in the population of the USSR, Poland, and Yugoslavia. The author shows the growing political impact of Muslim demographic explosions in the USSR, manpower and migration problems, and differential demographic politics in their ethnic perspective as well as in relation to international politics.

223. Borisov, A. A. **Climates of the U.S.S.R.** Edited by Cyril A. Halstead; translated by R. A. Ledward; foreword by Chauncy D. Harris. Chicago: Aldine Publishing Co., 1966. 255p. $10.00.
This volume, translated from a second, revised edition that appeared in Moscow in 1959, has been widely used in the Soviet Union as a reference aid and as a university textbook. A brief introductory history of the study of climate in the USSR is followed by a discussion of climate-forming factors and climactic elements.
SR, 25:2:366-67.

224. Chinn, Jeff. **Manipulating Soviet Population Resources**. New York: Holmes & Meier, 1977. viii, 163p. Tables. $22.50.
The author's objective is to examine Soviet population policy under the assumption that, in a planned economy, population growth and distribution are elements of public policy and hence are subsumed within the overall framework of national economic planning. He focuses on population growth and population distribution. This study will be of interest to anyone working in the general area of Soviet population.
SR, 38:2:318-10; APSR, 73(1979):623.

225. Cole, John P., and German, F. C. **A Geography of the U.S.S.R.** Washington, DC: Butterworth, 1961. 290p. $8.95.

This book is the most balanced of numerous recent texts for teacher reference. It contains up-to-date surveys of branches of the economy and of economic planning regions at the beginning of the Seven-Year Plan (1959-65), with tables, bibliography, and index.

226. Cressey, George B. **Soviet Potentials: A Geographic Appraisal.** Syracuse, NY: Syracuse University Press, 1962. 232p. $5.75.

In this brief, readable survey of the natural conditions, resources, peoples, economy, and regions of the Soviet Union, the author attempts to take a critical look at a vast territory which claims to have potential for becoming the world's richest state. This lively book is rewarding reading to even the general reader.

SR, 21:4:764.

227. Gregory, James S. **Russian Land, Soviet People: A Geographical Approach to the U.S.S.R.** New York: Pegasus, 1968. 947p. $15.00.

The text is divided into two major parts: a general survey covering land forms, climate, vegetation, soils, agriculture, and industry, and a regional survey (approximately 500 pages) following a broad division into some thirteen regions. Although the author has visited the Soviet Union several times, he does not seem to have grasped the reality of Soviet life and experience and the nature of dissent that, in literary form or otherwise, has raised its head despite official efforts to suppress it. Does he really believe that the role British traditions and ideas play within the member nations of the Commonwealth is similar to that of "Russian ideology and technology," say in the Georgian SSR or in any of the Baltic republics?

SR, 29:2:6345-46; Choice, 5(1969):1625.

228. Harris, Chauncy D. **Cities of the Soviet Union: Studies in Their Functions, Size, Density, and Growth.** Chicago: Rand McNally, 1970. 484p. $9.95.

Over the last few decades the typical Russian—previously a peasant—has become an urbanite, and the metamorphosis continues. This process has created a significant geographic pattern, and this book presents an accurate analysis of that pattern. The bibliography of this work, running to over a thousand items, is a major achievement in itself, and there is a chapter that assesses postwar Soviet research on their own cities. This book is an invaluable reference on the phenomenon of urbanization.

SR, 30:2:431-32; GJ, 137(1971):227.

229. Harris, Chauncy D., comp. **Guide to Geographical Bibliographies and Reference Works in Russian or on the Soviet Union.** Chicago: University of Chicago, Department of Geography, 1975. xviii, 478p. Maps. $5.00 pa.

This work contains 2,660 bibliographies and reference materials, mainly maps, atlases, and encyclopedias, conveniently organized into seven parts. The first five parts cover Soviet publications. Part 6 lists reference works and bibliographies in Western languages, predominantly English. Also included are maps of administrative units of the USSR.

SR, 35:1:137-38; ARBA, 7(1976):274.

230. Hooson, David J. M. **The Soviet Union: People and Regions.** Belmont, CA: Wadsworth, 1966. 376p. $7.95.
This represents a notable attempt to understand the relationship between population and geographic factors. The first part of the volume is topically organized, containing chapters on the natural habitat, historical background, farming, industry, transport, and distribution of population. The second part includes a descriptive and analytical discussion of the regions.
SR, 26:2:331-32; GJ, 133(1967):76.

231. Leasure, J. William, and Lewis, Robert A. **Population Changes in Russia and the USSR: A Set of Comparable Territorial Units.** San Diego: San Diego State College Press, 1966. 43p. $2.50 pa. (Social Science Monograph Series, vol. 1, no. 2.)
This small volume provides data for 1851, 1897, 1926, 1939, and 1959 for regions in the Soviet Union with constant boundaries. The data include total population, urban population, average annual increase in the intercensal periods, labor force, literate population, and percentage of the population made up of Eastern Slavs.
SR, 26:1:501.

232. Lydolph, Paul E. **The Climate of the Soviet Union.** Amsterdam and New York: Elsevier Scientific Publishing Company, 1977. xii, 443p. Illus. $81.75. (World Survey of Climatology, vol. 7.)
Lydolph has compiled a comprehensive reference on climatic factors in the Soviet Union. Almost half of the book consists of maps and charts that cover a diverse range of subjects. Most of the figures are collected from a large number of Soviet sources. This book is worthwhile not only to climatologists but to economists, political scientists, and agronomists who deal with events controlled by and related to climate.
SR, 36:4:696-97.

233. Lydolph, Paul E. **Geography of the U.S.S.R.** New York: Wiley, 1964. 451p. $10.95.
This is a combination of a general regional geography and a systematic economic geography of the country as a whole, making it a versatile textbook on Soviet geography. Many excellent maps and illustrations add to its attractiveness. Recommended for undergraduate readers.

234. Lydolph, Paul E. **Geography of the USSR.** Elkhart Lake, WI: Misty Valley Publishing, 1979. ix, 522p. $17.95.
This is a companion volume to the author's previous book of the same title. This new volume treats the subject matter by topics, aiming to illustrate geographical principles with the USSR as an example and to analyze spatial distributions in the USSR with modern geographic methods.
SS, 31:4:622.

235. Mellor, R. E. H. **Geography of the U.S.S.R.** London: Macmillan; New York: St. Martin's Press, 1964. 403p. $12.00.
The study is a highly condensed survey of certain significant features of the Soviet Union. It treats physical features, historical development, agriculture, fuels and

minerals, industry and transport, and population and settlement forms for the Soviet Union as a whole. The general public will benefit from this introduction to that complex land.

SR, 25:2:365-66; Choice, 2(1965):186.

236. Shabad, Theodore. **Geography of the U.S.S.R.: A Regional Survey.** New York: Columbia University Press, 1951. 584p. $12.00.

Shabad surveys the Soviet Union by regions and oblasts. He has presented a valuable reference tool as it includes numerous maps, tables, bibliography, and an extensive index. Though dated, the book can be recommended for teaching.

SR, 10:4:320-24.

237. Taaffe, Robert, and Kingsbury, Robert. **An Atlas of Soviet Affairs.** New York: Praeger, 1965. 150p. $1.95 pa.

Small in format but rich in maps with useful commentary, this volume offers brief introductions and concise surveys of various aspects of Soviet history, geography, economy, population, and so on.

WLB, 41(1966): 99.

GOVERNMENT, STATE, AND POLITICS

Law

238. Barry, Donald D.; Ginsbury, George; and Maggs, Peter B., eds. **Soviet Law after Stalin**. Part 1: **The Citizen and the State in Contemporary Soviet Law**. Leyden, Holland: A. W. Sijthoff, 1977. xv, 303p. $36.00. Part 2: **Social Engineering through Law**. Alphen aan den Rijn, Holland: Sijthoff & Noordhoff, 1978. xiv, 335p. $48.00.

These books represent two parts of a planned three-volume series on legal developments in the USSR after 1953 to which more than a dozen prominent scholars have contributed. The volumes are the first comprehensive, systematic guides to Soviet law in English.

   RR, 40:2:211-14.

239. Berman, Harold J., and Quigley, John B., Jr., trans. and eds. **Basic Laws on the Structure of the Soviet State**. Cambridge, MA: Harvard University Press, 1969. 325p. $4.00 pa.

This collection comprises translations of the most important Soviet laws as of October 1968. The volume opens with helpful notes on the translation of Soviet legal terminology, sources of the documents translated, and territorial subdivisions of the Soviet Union. Part I includes the constitutions of the USSR and the RSFSR, statutes on elections to the Supreme Soviet, legislation on local soviets, and the statutes of the Committee on Party-State Control. Part II contains laws on the procuracy and the judiciary, military courts, conciliation courts, and statutes on state arbitration.

   CSP, 14:2:375-76.

240. Chenoweth, Don W. **Soviet Civil Procedure: History and Analysis**. Philadelphia: The American Philosophical Society, 1977. 55p. $6.00 pa. (Transactions of the American Philosophical Society, vol. 67, part 6, October 1977.)

The author reviews the salient features in the development and elaboration of Soviet theory and practice in the sphere of civil procedure, and assesses the highlights of the record to date. The study is well documented and good use is made of Soviet primary and secondary sources.

   SR, 38:2:313; AHR, 83:4:1063.

241. Feldbrugge, F. J. M., ed. **The Constitutions of the USSR and the Union Republics: Analysis, Texts, Reports.** Alphen aan den Rijn, Holland: Sijthoff & Noordhoff, 1979. xv, 366p. Dfl. 150.

This volume deals with the USSR constitution and fifteen union republic constitutions, offering an introductory profile, parallel texts of the 1936 and 1977 USSR constitutions so that changes and similarities may be directly compared, and translations of Brezhnev's speeches. The introductory profile explores the ideological policy, historical, and socialist community dimensions of the USSR.

SEER, 59:1:143-44.

242. Feldbrugge, F. J. M., ed. **Encyclopedia of Soviet Law.** 2 vols. Dobbs Ferry, NY: Oceana Publications; Leiden: A. W. Sijthoff, 1974. Vol. 1 (A-L), 429p.; Vol. 2 (M-Z), 431-774pp. $95.00 both vols.

The work consists of alphabetically arranged descriptions of the laws and customs of the Soviet legal system. The list of subject headings has been compiled on the basis of a corresponding list in the *Index to Foreign Legal Periodicals* and of the list contained in Soviet legal encyclopedias, so as to provide access of approach, as far as possible, through both Western and Soviet concepts and terms.

RQ, 14(1974):167.

243. Feldbrugge, F. J. M., and Szirmal, J., eds. **Soviet Criminal Law, General Part.** Leiden University, The Netherlands, 1964. 291p. Dglds. 32.50.

This volume contains a systematic description of the general part of Soviet criminal law from a lawyer's point of view. Readers interested in questions of criminal preparation and attempt, concepts of imputability and mental illness, and effects of mistake, drunkeness, or *concursus,* will find the answers here.

RR, 25:3:309-10.

244. Grzybowski, Kazimierz. **Soviet Public International Law: Doctrines and Diplomatic Practice.** Leiden, The Netherlands: A. W. Sijthoff; Durham, NC: Rule of Law Press, 1970. 544p. $18.00.

In a magisterial chronicle of a half century of development of Soviet doctrine and practice in public international law, the author has brought together an incredible amount of information in a small space. The "plus" of the book is in the lead provided to documentation, organized under a series of headings covering every aspect of the subject and even delving into broad fields of Soviet constitutional law. There is ample footnoting, bibliography, and quotation, not only from Soviet and Western sources but also from hard-to-use United Nations records. Other notable features are the discussions of the Soviet concept of *jus cogens,* the limits to application of the principles of self-determination, the legality of aid rendered to anticolonial movements, the recognition of government in exile and of incipient governments not yet in power in colonies, the attention to be given to the protection of individual foreigners in relation to the attention to be focused upon breaches of the "new" rules, the attitude toward application of Soviet law in annexed and even leased territories, and the law of the sea and space. As such it will find a place in foreign offices, embassies, and libraries, and on the desks of those concerned with international affairs.

SR, 30:2:428-29.

245. Hazard, John N.; Shapiro, Isaac; and Maggs, Peter B., eds. **The Soviet Legal System: Contemporary Documentation and Historical Commentary.** Rev. ed. Dobbs Ferry, NY: Oceana Publications, published for the Parker School of Foreign and Comparative Law, Columbia University, 1969. 687p. $17.50.

This book contains a collection of cases decided by Soviet courts and of excerpts from Soviet laws and from the writings of Soviet legal scholars. The book is divided into three parts: "The Soviet State and Its Citizens," "Administering Soviet Socialism," and "Private Legal Rights and Obligations of Soviet Citizens." There is a very useful bibliography of English-language writings on Soviet law.

SR, 29:3:544; Choice, 7(1970):299.

246. Johnson, E. L. **An Introduction to the Soviet Legal System.** London: Methuen, 1969; New York: Barnes & Noble, 1970. 248p. $10.50.

In this brief work the author attempts to introduce Soviet law and legal institutions to the educated layman. Its title notwithstanding, the book treats the law in much greater detail than it does the legal system. Brief attention is also given to contract and tort, labor law, and the Soviet equivalent of corporate law.

SR, 30:4:896.

247. Lapenna, Ivo. **Soviet Penal Policy. A Background Book.** Chester Springs, PA: Dufour Editions, 1968. 148p. $3.50.

About half of the book is devoted to a summary and evaluation of the main features of present-day Soviet criminal law and procedure, and about half to their historical and theoretical background in the period from 1917 to the death of Stalin. The author concludes that there is lacking in the Soviet Union a genuine system of law, a system that guarantees for the correct implementation of law, and the minimum legal standards recognized by civilized nations.

SR, 29:2:333; Choice, 6(1969):1116.

248. Ramundo, Bernard A. **Peaceful Coexistence: International Law in the Building of Communism.** Baltimore: Johns Hopkins Press, published in cooperation with the Institute for Sino-Soviet Studies, George Washington University, 1967. 262p. $6.95.

The book surveys Soviet legal literature and is particularly comprehensive in the range of Soviet institutional practice, providing a valuable compendium of Soviet law-in-action in the important field of international law.

SR, 29:4:705-6; APSR, 62(1968):312.

249. Newcity, Michael A. **Copyright Law in the Soviet Union.** New York and London: Praeger Publishers, 1978. x, 213p. $16.50.

The author begins with a historical survey of domestic copyright law from 1828 to 1973, when the USSR joined the Universal Copyright Convention. One of his interesting contributions is the account of how the Soviet Union joined. A concluding section reviews developments since accession to the copyright convention.

SR, 38:3:506-7.

250. Wortman, Richard S. **The Development of a Russian Legal Consciousness.** Chicago and London: University of Chicago Press, 1976. xii, 345p. $20.00.

Wortman explains how an entirely new legal ethos emerged in Russia during the first half of the nineteenth century. He provides a thought-provoking account of the Russian bureaucratic mind as it developed within the judicial and administrative agencies before the judicial reform of 1864.

SR, 36:2:296; LJ, 101(1976):2575.

Politics and Government

251. Anderson, Thornton. **Russian Political Thought: An Introduction.** Ithaca, NY: Cornell University Press, 1967. 432p. $9.75.

In this appraisal of Russian political theory and practice the author examines the present Soviet regime, not only in terms of its Marxist-Leninist concept, but as a development of traditional Russian political assumptions. Students of political science will find many answers in this penetrating study.

APSR, 62(1968):612; Choice, 4(1967):1032.

252. Armstrong, John A. **Ideology, Politics, and Government in the Soviet Union: An Introduction.** 3d rev. ed. New York: Praeger, 1974 (1962). 236p. $8.00.

Armstrong has brought up to date his introductory text on Soviet government. Many of the revisions amount to carrying the story from the Khrushchev era to the present. Some interpolations add clarity or rebut conflicting views. Others (*e.g.,* on nationalities and on Party membership) provide data which have only recently become available. Finally, a new chapter deals with "Interpretation of Domestic and Foreign Policy."

RR, 34:2:217-18.

253. Barghoorn, Frederick C. **Politics in the USSR.** Boston: Little, Brown, 1966; 2d ed., 1972. 418p.

The author has applied Gabriel Almond's structural-functional model of comparative politics to the Soviet polity with meritorious results. The chapter on "Implementing Public Policy" goes far in explaining what happens to policy when it is filtered through the labyrinthine channels of a highly bureaucratic system. In "Soviet Justice," Barghoorn's personal encounter with the KGB highlights an excellent treatment of a very complex subject.

SR, 27:1:159-60.

254. Barry, Donald D., and Barner-Barry, Carol. **Contemporary Soviet Politics: An Introduction.** Englewood Cliffs, NJ: Prentice-Hall, 1978. x, 406p. $8.95 pa.

The material in this textbook is condensed to a manageable 300 pages, with the narratives flowing smoothly and the major subject bases being touched. The book is aimed at the undergraduate student.

SR, 37:3:510-11.

255. Besançon, Alain. **The Soviet Syndrome.** New York: Harcourt Brace Jovanovich, 1978. 103p. $8.95.

The author of this thought-provoking publication warns that even after fifty years of economic difficulties and intellectual irresolution, the Soviet Union remains committed as ever to its ideology of Communist expansion. He offers an unfashionable and shocking overview of Soviet history, and he has provided a clear and pungent inquiry into the problems confronting the West in trying to understand Soviet thinking and actions.

    NP, 9:1:145-46.

256. Bialer, Seweryn. **Stalin's Successors: Leadership, Stability, and Change in the Soviet Union.** Cambridge: Cambridge University Press, 1980. v, 312p. $19.95.

This study offers a comprehensive and convincing account of the Soviet political system. The author is one of the most perceptive observers of Soviet politics, society, and foreign policy.

    APSR, 75(1981):793; Choice, 18(1981):850.

257. Bortoli, Georges. **The Death of Stalin.** Translated from the French by Raymond Rosenthal. New York: Praeger Publishers, 1975. vii, 214p. + 16pp. Photographs. $8.95.

This is an original and useful book that portrays Soviet life during the five months from the Nineteenth Party Congress to Stalin's death in March 1953. The book also reviews the condition of all classes of the population (peasants, workers, managers, government and party leaders), the economy, religious life, the status of national minorities, and special features of Stalinism.

    SR, 35:2:340.

258. Cohen, Stephen F.; Rabinowitch, Alexander; and Sharlet, Robert, eds. **The Soviet Union since Stalin.** Introduction by Alexander Rabinowitch. Bloomington: Indiana University Press, 1980. 342p. $22.50.

Topics in this compilation range from the development of pluralism within the Soviet party apparatus, to the problems of ethnicity, to foreign policy. Particularly refreshing is the treatment of emergent issues in the Soviet Union, such as feminism and environmental concerns. This volume can serve well as a supplementary text in undergraduate courses.

    APSR, 75(1981):228.

259. Conquest, Robert. **Russia after Khrushchev.** New York: Praeger, 1965. 267p. $5.95.

In the author's view of the USSR, "the political world is limited to a few thousand members of a self-perpetuating elite ... trained for decades with the purpose of enforcing its will against the tendencies of society as a whole."

    APSR, 361(1965):155; Choice, 2(1965):260.

260. Cornell, Richard, ed. **The Soviet Political System: A Book of Readings.** Englewood Cliffs, NJ: Prentice-Hall, 1970. 392p. $7.95.

The editor invited twenty-eight well-known specialists to contribute essays which explain and analyze the Soviet political system within six main themes: (1) "Understanding the Soviet Political System," (2) "The Environmental Influences," (3)

"The Party and Political Leadership," (4) "The Party and the Implementation of Decisions," (5) "The Party and Supervision of Society," and (6) "The Course of Change."

261. Dornberg, John. **The New Tsars: Russia under Stalin's Heirs**. Garden City, NY: Doubleday, 1972. 470p. $10.00.

The book is based on the author's observations as a correspondent in Moscow (1968-70), as well as on considerable historical research. The result is an up-to-date account of the USSR enriched by perspectives in the past. The author writes about the overbearing Russian "superiority complex" with regard to the non-Russian nations. This is a lively, persuasive, and informed work for the general reader and the student.

262. Gruber, Helmut. **Soviet Russia Masters the Comintern: International Communism in the Era of Stalin's Ascendancy**. Garden City, NY: Anchor Press/Doubleday, 1974. 544p.

This is a continuation of Gruber's earlier *International Communism in the Era of Lenin: A Documentary History* (1967). In the present volume the author treats the Comintern's "middle years," the 1924-31 period of Bolshevization, which coincided with Stalin's growing authority in the Party and, as the result of the international movement's increasing dependence on Moscow, in the Comintern itself.
RR, 34:1:98-99.

263. Hammer, Darrell P. **USSR: The Politics of Oligarchy**. Hinsdale, IL: Dryden Press, 1974. 452p. $6.50 pa.

Hammer has produced an unusual work of multiple value. It is a stimulating and original essay on the functioning of the Soviet political system and an update on a variety of points ranging from the role of Supreme Soviet committees to the experiment in "popular justice." Hammer views the Soviet top leadership as an oligarchy.
SR, 34:3:607.

264. Khrushchev, Nikita. **Khrushchev Remembers: The Last Testament**. Introduction and notes by Edward Crankshaw. Translated and edited by Strobe Talbott. Boston: Little, Brown, 1970. 639p. $12.95.

The publication of this unique book created worldwide interest and confusion. The book's essential importance centers around Khrushchev's bloody purges during the 1930s as an emissary of Stalin in the Ukraine, and especially since 1937, when Khrushchev liquidated the entire organization of the Communist party of Ukraine. Accusing Stalin of anti-Semitism, Khrushchev himself never missed an opportunity to make a disparaging remark about the Jews, insisting "that they be kept in their places."
LJ, 96(1971):952; Choice, 8(1971):461.

265. Laird, Roy D. **The Soviet Paradigm: An Experiment in Creating a Monohierarchical Polity**. New York: Free Press; London: Collier-Macmillan, 1970. 272p. $7.95.

In setting forth a "monohierarchical paradigm" of the Soviet polity the author aims to introduce upper level college students to the Soviet political system as it had evolved by 1970. He describes the various ideologies that have culminated in a new Soviet nationalism.
SR, 33:1:152-53; LJ, 96(1971):486.

266. Lyons, Eugene. **Workers Paradise Lost: Fifty Years of Soviet Communism: A Balance.** New York: Funk & Wagnalls, 1967. 387p.

This fact-filled work serves a constructive purpose. In recounting the history of the Soviet Union, the author provides a useful summary of the past fifty years. An easy narrative style and the exposure of numerous myths of Soviet origin promoted among the Western public unfamiliar with the realities existing in the USSR should invite the attention of the general reader.

Choice, 5(1968):114.

270. MacAuley, Mary. **Politics and the Soviet Union.** Harmondsworth, England, and New York: Penguin Books, 1977. 352p. $3.95 pa.

The book traces the evolution of the system to the late Stalin era and also describes and analyzes the contemporary political system, conveying a picture of both the flow of major events and the broad changes in the system over the past quarter-century. At each stage, the reader is invited to consider the central issues confronting the Soviet leadership and the alternatives available and visible to them. This is a fine introduction to Soviet politics.

SR, 37:3:509-10.

271. Marx, Karl, and Engels, Friedrich. **The Russian Menace to Europe.** Edited by Paul W. Blackstock and Bert F. Hoselitz. New York: The Free Press, 1952. 288p.

It is not surprising that both founding fathers of Marxism were extremely anti-Russian. Marx and Engels were well aware of Russian expansionism, as this collection of their writings amply proves. Reading of this unusual work will stimulate class discussion.

272. Matthews, Mervyn, comp. **Soviet Government: A Selection of Official Documents on Internal Policies.** New York: Taplinger, 1974. 472p. $30.00.

The official Soviet documents, dating from 1917 to the present, are divided into four main groups: state administration, law and the police, the peasantry, and workers' labor legislation. The selection reflects the compiler's own view of the importance of the various documents, which may not be shared by other specialists.

RSR, 2(1974):26.

273. Meyer, Alfred G. **The Soviet Political System: An Interpretation.** New York: Random House, 1964. 494p. $15.95.

Meyer sees in the Soviet Union many parallels with a giant Western business corporation. Both are bureaucracies, bureaucracy having been defined as "rational management on a comparatively large scale." The major difference between the "USSR, Inc." and a large Western corporation is that the former is bureaucracy-writ-large, the latter bureaucracy-simple.

RR, 25:4:429.

274. Nove, Alec. **Stalinism and After.** London: George Allen & Unwin, 1975. 205p. $7.50 pa.

This analysis of the origins of Stalinism emphasizes that the economic and political conditions created by the civil war and the early years of NEP seemed to favor the dominance of Stalin and his tough-minded cohorts over the more intellectual segments of the Bolshevik leadership. This survey includes the ideological and policy orientations of both the Khrushchev and Brezhnev regimes.

SR, 35:4:744-45; Choice, 12(1976):1491.

275. Odom, William E. **The Soviet Volunteers: Modernization and Bureaucracy in a Public Mass Organization.** Princeton, NJ: Princeton University Press, 1973. 360p. $14.50.

This work is a four-part treatment of the largest mass voluntary organization of the 1920s and 1930s, *Osoviakhim* (Society of Friends of Defense and Aviation-Chemical Construction), which was finally replaced in 1952 by the more familiar DOSAAF. The framework is an analysis of the organization as a modernizing agency; in addition, it is a study of Soviet administrative organization. The charts, tables, short chapters, and frequent summaries, as well as the bibliography and index, contribute to the book's value as a reference work. The study is highly recommended for the reader who is interested in enhancing his appreciation of the entire history of Soviet organizations and style in administration.

CSP, 17:1:157-58; LJ, 99(1974):1309; Choice, 10(1974):636.

276. Osborn, Robert J. **The Evolution of Soviet Politics.** Homewood, IL: Dorsey Press, 1974. 574p. $10.95.

Osborn combines a lucid writing style with a careful survey of Soviet political history, a summary of recent findings of social scientists specializing in the study of the USSR, and an eclectic methodological approach, to produce a volume of value not only for the undergraduate student of Soviet politics, but also for the scholar who specializes in the area. According to Osborn, there was nothing inevitable about the development of the Soviet Union. However, as important decisions were made in the years immediately following the Bolshevik Revolution, limits were placed on the options open to political leaders in future crisis situations. The author deals somewhat more fully with questions relating to social stratification, social welfare programs, and related matters than do most authors of introductory Soviet politics texts.

CSP, 17:1:158-60; Choice, 11(1975):1838.

277. Pinter, W. M., and Rowney, D. K., eds. **Russian Officialdom: The Bureaucratization of Russian Society from the Seventeenth to the Twentieth Century.** London: Macmillan, 1980. xvii, 396p. £20.00.

The collection of essays is arranged in chronological order and deals with such topics as "Administration for Development: The Emerging Bureaucratic Elite, 1920-1930" and "Evolution of Leadership Selection in the Central Committee, 1917-1927." The seventeenth to nineteenth centuries are also well covered, providing a comprehensive survey of the evolution of Russian and Soviet officialdom.

JMH, 54:3:638.

278. Raeff, Marc, ed. **Plans for Political Reform in Imperial Russa, 1730-1905.** Englewood Cliffs, NJ: Prentice-Hall, 1966. 159p. $4.95. (Russian Civilization Series, edited by Michael Cherniavsky and Ivo J. Lederer.)

This book consists of translated selected primary sources relating to a particular problem in Russian history. The documents are in unabridged form, wherever

feasible, and are succinctly annotated. Each volume of the Russian Civilization Series has a brief critical introductory essay by the compiler.
SR, 27:1:135-36.

279. Reshetar, John S., Jr. **The Soviet Polity: Government and Politics in the USSR.** 2d ed. New York: Harper & Row, 1978. xi, 413p. $4.50 pa.
This is an updated version of the first edition (1971). There is now a chapter devoted specifically to the economy and social services, one on law and the judiciary, and a separate chapter on political socialization and education. This is a text on Soviet government that can be recommended for its readable length, depth, and precision of preparation.
SR, 31:1:180-81.

280. Rush, Myron. **Political Succession in the USSR.** New York: Columbia University Press, 1965. 223p. $5.95. (A publication of the RAND Corporation and the Research Institute on Communist Affairs of Columbia University.)
The author's hypothesis is that Soviet politics always moves in a cyclical direction. There is a stable phase of one-man rule, Lenin (1917-21), Stalin (1929-53), and Khrushchev (1957-64). Each period of the transfer of power is an unstable phase of succession crisis. The crisis is resolved in a final phase, the emergence of a new sovereign.
SR, 28:3:499; LJ, 90:(1965):1334; Choice, 2(1965):433.

281. Szamuely, Tibor. **The Russian Tradition.** Edited with an introduction by Robert Conquest. New York: McGraw-Hill, 1975. xii, 443p. $12.50.
According to the author's view, the Russian political tradition had two mutually hostile but intimately related strands—the absolutist state brought to clear definition by Ivan IV, and the revolutionary movement created by the intelligentsia in the nineteenth century. Thus, after a period of gestation during the Mongol conquest, the Russian state emerged as a synthesis of oriental despotism, Muscovite patrimonialism (bondage of all classes), and Byzantine caesaropapism.
SR, 35:3:528-29.

282. Tatu, Michel. **Power in the Kremlin: From Khrushchev to Kosygin.** Translated by Helen Katel. New York: Viking Press, 1969. 570p. $10.00.
The work is divided into five parts, but the first four form a highly minute examination of the four crises that led to Khrushchev's downfall: the U-2 affair of 1960, the 21st Congress in 1961-62, the Cuban crisis in October 1962, and the crisis in 1964 that resulted in his ouster. The uninitiated reader will discover a wealth of reconstructed information shedding light on the political maneuverings in the Kremlin.

283. Tolstoy, Nikolai. **The Secret Betrayal: 1944-1947.** New York: Charles Scribner's Sons, 1978. 503p. $14.95.
This book tells of the forced repatriation by British and American authorities of several million Russians, Ukrainians, and Cossacks stranded in Western Europe in 1944-45. Some of these people had fought alongside the Axis powers in the hope of liberating their homelands from Soviet Communism. They were either summarily

shot, tortured and hanged, or sent to prison work camps in the Soviet Arctic, where few have survived. This study is an important contribution to the literature of "Big Three" diplomacy during World War II.

Choice, 16(1979):137; BL, 75(1979):905.

284. Tucker, Robert C. **The Soviet Political Mind: Stalinism and Post-Stalin Change.** Rev. ed. London: George Allen & Unwin, 1972. 306p. £3.50.
This new edition of the author's well-established work on Stalinism reopens old questions and reconsiders old answers in the light of new information that has come to light. The author stresses the continuities with the past, the Soviet political mind being a superposition upon what is in many respects merely the more traditional Russian political mind.

SEER, 53:130-35.

285. Walkin, Jacob. **The Rise of Democracy in Pre-Revolutionary Russia: Political and Social Institutions under the Last Three Czars.** New York: Praeger, 1962. 320p. $6.50. (Praeger Publications in Russian History and World Communism, no. 115.)
This informative and interesting treatment of prerevolutionary development in Russia is highly recommended to those specifically interested in its subject as well as to the general reader.

AHR, 68:4:1062-63.

286. Wesson, Robert G. **The Russian Dilemma: A Political and Geopolitical View.** New Brunswick, NJ: Rutgers University Press, 1974. 228p. $12.50.
This book is informed by the view that Soviet Russia may be regarded as basically a continuation of the tsarist state. Russians today face the same major political problems as they did before 1917—namely, to hold together and rule the huge multinational realm in the face of solvent forces of modernity, and to modernize economically (and militarily) without modernizing politically. The author's solution to the dilemma is for the Russians to shed their empire. They would then be free to develop their full potential. The Soviet political system is conservative and repressive. However, economic and/or military crises will force it to change radically.

SEER, 53:132:469; AAPSS-A, 417(1975):169; PSQ, 90(1975):384.

287. Wesson, Robert G. **The Soviet Russian State.** New York: John Wiley, 1972. 404p. $8.95.
This is a solid textbook written for the undergraduate course on Soviet politics. The unifying theme of the various chapters is that a strain toward autocratic structures of rule has existed in both the tsarist and Soviet periods, created by the functional need to prevent disintegration in a vast Russian-dominated multinational empire.

SR, 32:2:396-97.

288. Wesson, Robert G. **The Soviet State: An Aging Revolution.** New York: John Wiley, 1972. 222p. $3.95 pa.
This book is an abridged version of Wesson's other study, *The Soviet Russian State,* suitable for an introductory comparative government course. Wesson is

not impressed by recent attempts to reformulate the questions one should ask about Soviet politics. His approach is broadly historical-descriptive, stressing similarities between the Soviet and tsarist regimes, and between these and earlier "imperial orders." On this level of analysis his work ranks well above most other introductory texts.

    SR, 32:2:396-97.

289.   Wolfe, Bertram D. **Revolution and Reality: Essays on the Origin and Fate of the Soviet System.** Chapel Hill: University of North Carolina Press, 1981. xxi, 401p. Illustrated.

At the heart of Wolfe's analysis of the Soviet system lies the view that it has always been and will remain totalitarian, a single-centered, closed, highly centralized society run by a power that is both undivided and all-embracing. Lenin, who dreamed even in 1902 of a party that would hold all reins in its grasp, in practice turned the Communist party into a mere transmission belt for the will of the Central Committee, and Stalinism became an inevitable consolidation of the system inherent in the doctrine.

    AAPSS-A, 462(1982):178.

Communism and Communist Party

290.   **The Anti-Stalin Campaign and International Communism: A Selection of Documents.** Edited by the Russian Institute, Columbia University. New York: Columbia University Press, 1956. 338p.

The text of Nikita Khrushchev's "secret" speech, delivered on February 25, 1956, at the Twentieth Congress of the Communist party, is followed by shocked, semirebellious or semiapplauding statements by several Western Communist leaders, and by editorials from Western Communist newspapers. The collection furnishes a vast amount of important material for study.

291.   Armstrong, John A. **The Politics of Totalitarianism: The Communist Party of the Soviet Union from 1934 to the Present.** New York: Random House, 1961. 458p. $7.50.

The most crucial and decisive years of the history of the Communist party are examined in this account, although an unproportionate emphasis on power structures tends to lessen the importance of personal motives.

    SR, 21:3:555-57.

292.   Aspaturian, Vernon V. **The Soviet Union in the World Communist System.** Stanford, CA: Hoover Institution on War, Revolution and Peace, Stanford University, 1966. 96p. $2.50.

The imprint of the Soviet Union upon the Communist world is ineradicable. This study explores the relationship of the USSR to the Communist party states.

    Choice, 4(1967):90.

293.   Avtorkhanov, Abdurakham. **The Communist Party Apparatus.** Chicago: Regnery, 1966. 422p. $10.00.

Unlike any other book on this topic, this one offers firsthand experiences. Its author was a member of the Communist party of the Soviet Union from 1927 to

1937. His experiences on different levels and in many responsible positions equipped him with a unique insight. The book is packed with details of functional characteristics of the apparatus. The reader will find this story most revealing.

SR, 27:1:159-60; JP, 29(1967):669; Choice, 3(1966):956.

294. Dallin, Alexander, ed. **The Twenty-Fifth Congress of the CPSU: Assessment and Context**. Stanford, CA: Hoover Institution Press, 1977. xii, 127p. $5.95.

This volume resulted from a conference held at Stanford University to review the record of the Twenty-Fifth Congress. There are nine essays ranging from science policy to the economy and foreign policy. This is a useful summary that should stimulate readers to delve more deeply into some of the problems touched on at the conference.

SEER, 27:1:145-46; Choice, 15(1978):754.

295. Dan, Theodore. **The Origins of Bolshevism**. Translated by Joel Carmichael. Preface by Leonard Shapiro. New York: Harper & Row, 1965. 468p. $10.00.

The author, a long-time leader of the Mensheviks, analyzes the multiple elements in nineteenth- and early twentieth-century Russian socialism which constitute the background of the Russian revolution of 1917. Rare bibliographic references are of distinct value.

LJ, 90(1965):242; Choice, 2(1965):115.

296. Daniels, Robert V. **The Conscience of the Revolution: Communist Opposition in Soviet Russia**. Cambridge, MA: Harvard University Press, 1960. 256p. $10.00. (Russian Research Center Studies, no. 40.)

This work is a unique contribution to the understanding of Soviet Communism because it discusses the internal opposition that developed in the party at crucial stages in its history. Despite the complexity of the issues treated, this engaging study will make rewarding reading for the student.

SR, 21:1:162-63.

297. Djilas, Milovan. **Conversations with Stalin**. Translated by Michael B. Petrovich. New York: Harcourt, Brace & World, 1962. 214p. $3.95.

In this memoir the former vice-president of Yugoslavia describes three visits to Moscow and his encounters there with Stalin. This account should be recommended as required literature for students of Soviet studies.

LJ, 87(1962):2145.

298. Fisher, Ralph Talcott, Jr. **Pattern for Soviet Youth: A Study of the Congresses of the Komsomol, 1918-1954**. New York: Columbia University Press, 1959. 452p. $6.75. (Studies of the Russian Institute, Columbia University, no. 27.)

In this pioneering study of the All-Union Leninist Communist League of Youth, the Komsomol congresses, the author illustrates the pattern of attitudes and conduct that the Communist party sought to impose upon the Soviet youth numbering seventeen million members as of 1953.

AHR, 65:1:181.

299.   Hill, Ronald J., and Frank, Peter. **The Soviet Communist Party.** London and Boston: George Allen & Unwin, 1981. vii, 167p. Figures. Tables. $24.50.

This book deals respectively with membership, structure, institutions, and personnel; functions and performance; party-state relations; and the party's relationship with nonstate institutions. The book is useful for general information.

300.   Hudson, G. F. **Fifty Years of Communism: Theory and Practice.** New York: Basic Books, 1968. 234p. $5.95.

This survey by Hudson, addressed to the nonspecialist reader, is a straightforward, concise, chronological account of the evolution of Communism. It is clear, simply written, and generally accurate. Hudson brings out the important point of Soviet dissolution of the Polish Communist party in 1937, a prelude to the Nazi-Soviet Pact of 1939.

AHR, 75:2:547-50; LJ, 94(1969):1269; Choice, 6(1969):412.

302.   Lenin, V. I. **What Is To Be Done?** Translated by S. V. and Patricia Utechin. Edited, with an introduction and notes, by S. V. Utechin. Oxford: Oxford University; Clarendon Press, 1963. 213p. $4.00.

Still regarded in the Soviet Union as a work which "laid the foundations of the ideology of the Bolshevik Party," this discourse by Lenin is the master key to understanding Communist political action today. The editorial sketches of historical and party background add to the usefulness of the publication.

SR, 23:3:596.

303.   McNeal, Robert H. **Guide to the Decisions of the Communist Party of the Soviet Union, 1917-67.** Toronto: University of Toronto Press, 1974. 329p. $15.00.

This guide contains 3,265 entries, each representing a Party decision. The entries, which appear in chronological order, include the following descriptions: entry number, decision title, and bibliographic location—that is, the reference to a published source. A subject index based on Russian terms enables the reader to find a desired item.

CSP, 15:4:620.

304.   McNeal, Robert H., gen. ed. **Resolutions and Decisions of the Communist Party of the Soviet Union. Vol. 1: The Russian Social Democratic Labour Party, 1898-October 1917.** Edited by Ralph Carter Elwood. **Vol. 2: The Early Soviet Period, 1917-1929.** Edited by Richard Gregor. **Vol. 3: The Stalin Years, 1929-1953.** Edited by Robert H. McNeal. **Vol. 4: The Khrushchev Years, 1953-1964.** Edited by Grey Hodnett. Toronto: University of Toronto Press, 1974. Vol. 1: 306p.; Vol. 2: 382p.; Vol. 3: 280p.; Vol. 4: 328p. $75.00 set.

This set of four volumes is the indispensable reference work for the study of modern Russia in general and Soviet Communism in particular. It also amplifies the standard Soviet anthology in important respects and provides editorial explanation that is independent of Kremlin politics. The rich store of materials in these four volumes ranges from the formation of the party to the fall of Khrushchev, and it deals with a wide range of issues.

305. Meyer, Alfred G. **Leninism**. Cambridge, MA: Harvard University Press, 1957. 324p.

The author successfully answers the question: What is Leninism^ The book is thus not a full treatment of Leninism but a systematic exposition of Lenin's theory and practice, justified and limited by their survival value. Lenin's ideas are compared with those of Marx and other socialist thinkers.

JMH, 31:4:394-94; LJ, 82(1957):1892.

306. **The New Society: Final Text of the Program of the Communist Party of the Soviet Union**. With annotations and an introduction by Herbert Ritvo. New York: The New Leader, 1962. 251p.

The text of the program of the CPSU which was adopted by the Twenty-Second Party Congress in 1961.

307. Page, Stanley W. **The Geopolitics of Leninism**. Boulder, CO: *East European Quarterly*, 1982. xiii, 190p. $20.00. Distributed by Columbia University Press. (East European Monographs, no. 97.)

Page writes that all of Lenin's important ideas, especially regarding the peasantry, nationalities policy, and the definition of proletarian dictatorship, constituted an elaborate façade for the unavowed purpose of securing his position as head of the world revolution.

NP, 11:2:324-26; AHR, 88:1:76.

308. Page, Stanley W. **Lenin and World Revolution**. New York: New York University Press, 1959. 270p. $5.00.

This study of Lenin's concept of Communist revolution concentrates on the 1917-20 period. The account follows Lenin's changing views, which accommodated changing situations within and outside Soviet Russia. The student of political science may use this volume for helpful references.

LJ, 84(1959):1899.

309. Possony, Stefan T., ed. **Lenin Reader**. Chicago: Regnery, 1966. 528p. $10.00. (Hoover Institution Publications, no. 15.)

These are expertly selected, essential writings by Lenin, topically and chronologically arranged. They may serve as an introduction to Leninist philosophy.

310. Reshetar, John S., Jr. **A Concise History of the Communist Party of the Soviet Union**. Rev. ed. New York: Praeger, 1964. 381p. $2.50 pa.

This work is built on the theme that Lenin provided the presumptions that culminated in Stalin's great purge. Lenin was as ruthless, obsessed, headstrong, self-righteous, and confident as his successor, not the kindly humanitarian driven to severity by circumstances, as he is sometimes pictured. Stalin's difference lay in his creation of the apparatus of oppression, the organization. Khrushchev's regime is discussed in an added chapter.

AHR, 66:1:162-64.

311.   Rieber, Alfred J., and Nelson, Robert C. **A Study of the USSR and Communism: An Historical Approach.** Chicago: Scott-Foresman, 1962. 272p.; New York: Putnam's, 1964. 256p.
This volume is especially noteworthy for its attention to questions of cultural and intellectual history and to the cultural ferment that has been so prominent a part of Soviet life since 1953. It offers a very clear picture of the nature and extent of intellectual dissent in the Soviet Union and Eastern Europe during the past decade.
        SR, 23:1:161-62.

312.   Rieber, Alfred J., and Nelson, Robert C., eds. **The USSR and Communism: Source Readings and Interpretations.** Chicago: Scott-Foresman, 1964. 320p. $2.95 pa.
Selected readings on important issues. The material lends itself to high school use and should also be found in college libraries.

313.   Rigby, T. H. **Communist Party Membership in the U.S.S.R., 1917-1967.** Princeton, NJ: Princeton University Press, 1968. 573p. $15.00. (Studies of the Russian Institute, Columbia University.)
Rigby examines the general role of the party and summarizes in a most comprehensive manner all available statistical information about party membership over a fifty-year period. In fact, this is more an encyclopedia than a book to be read.
        SR, 33:1:150-52.

314.   Schapiro, Leonard. **The Communist Party of the Soviet Union.** 2d ed., rev. and enl. New York: Random House, 1971. 631p. $3.45 pa.
The author offers in this work the most comprehensive history of the Communist party in Russia ever written in English. The book offers an authoritative, comprehensive, and lively account of the origins, evolution, and thinking of the Soviet party leadership. Schapiro's personal experiences while living in Russia enhance his critical analysis. Getting familiar with this publication should be in the interest of any responsible citizen and inquiring young student.
        LJ, 85(1960):2602.

315.   Schapiro, Leonard. **The Origin of the Communist Autocracy. Political Opposition in the Soviet State: First Phase 1917-1922.** London: Bell, for London School of Economics and Political Science, 1955. 397p. Cambridge, MA: Harvard University Press; New York: Praeger, 1965. 416p. $2.95 pa.
This first-rate contribution to the literature on the Russian revolution, better than any other, explains how and why Lenin defeated his rivals and seized power within the Russian Communist party. It is a carefully documented analysis of the emergence of dictatorship in the Soviet Union.

316.   Service, Robert. **The Bolshevik Party in Revolution: A Study in Organizational Change 1917-1923.** New York: Barnes & Noble, 1979. 246p. Maps. $24.50.
The author provides a comprehensive answer to the question: How did the Bolshevik party emerge in the period 1917-23 to dominate state administration? In this analysis, a Stalinist party is shown to have developed as much or more from local

pressures after 1917 as from pressures from above. The creation of the Orgburo and the burgeoning Secretariat were responses to practical needs.

RR, 39:1:84-86; JMH, 52:2:366; Choice, 16(1980):1496.

317.   Swearer, Howard R., and Longaker, Richard P., eds. **Contemporary Communism: Theory and Practice.** Belmont, CA: Wadsworth, 1963. 405p. $3.95 pa.

This selection of readings for use by students of high school and college age contains excerpts ranging from the classics of Marxism-Leninism and the 1961 Program of the Communist Party of the Soviet Union to studies by Western specialists, offering a comprehensive picture of the role and appeal of Communist ideology and of major facets of the Soviet system.

SR, 24:1:161-62.

318.   Tompkins, Stuart Ramsey. **The Triumph of Bolshevism: Revolution or Reaction?** Norman: University of Oklahoma Press, 1967. 331p. $5.95.

This volume completes the author's trilogy on Russian thought and character. The book examines the heritage of bolshevism and its features as revealed by social, ideological, political, and economic policies. Bolshevism in action does not perform identically with the aims set up by Marxism.

AHR, 73:2:543; JP, 30(1968):248.

319.   Tucker, Robert C., ed. **The Lenin Anthology.** New York: W. W. Norton & Co., 1974. 764p. $4.95 pa.

This comprehensive volume includes essential writings of Lenin, each of them introduced with a brief interpretive commentary by the editor. A general introduction to the volume traces Lenin's career as a revolutionary, both in writings and in actions. Also included are a chronology, a bibliographic note, and an index.

320.   Unger, Aryeh L. **The Totalitarian Party: Party and People in Nazi Germany and Soviet Russia.** London: Cambridge University Press, 1974. 286p. $13.95.

This comparative study of totalitarianism in Germany and Russia largely concentrates on the propaganda put out by the two regimes and on the aims and claims of the two ruling parties. Throughout, and especially in the conclusions at the end, the similarities between the two regimes are emphasized.

SEER, 53:3:623-24.

321.   Wesson, Robert G. **Lenin's Legacy: The Story of the CPSU.** Stanford, CA: Hoover Institution Press, 1978. xviii, 318p. Appendixes. $7.50 pa. (Histories of Ruling Communist Parties series.)

Wesson uses the supreme leadership of the party as the main theme of his book, which is basically divided into four sections, devoted respectively to Lenin, Stalin, Khrushchev, and Brezhnev. The book contains tables showing Politburo and Secretariat membership in 1977, party membership since 1905, ethnic composition, percent of female membership, age distribution, and other pertinent information.

SR, 38:2:306; Choice, 15(1979):1723.

322. Wolfe, Bertram D., ed. **Khrushchev and Stalin's Ghost: Text, Background and Meaning of Khrushchev's Secret Report to the Twentieth Congress on the Night of February 24, 1956.** New York: Praeger, 1957. 322p. $3.95.
The author attempts to analyze what he calls "the most important document ever to have come from the Communist movement" and "the most damning indictment of the Soviet system ever to have been made by a Soviet leader." This publication should be required reading on all levels of teaching.
JMH, 29:3:303-4.

323. Zemtsov, Ilya. **Andropov: Policy Dilemmas and the Struggle for Power.** Jerusalem: IRICS, 1983. 252p. $19.00.
The monograph focuses on the vicissitudes of the careers of two generals: Yuriy Andropov and Gaidar Aliev, the former head of the secret police in the USSR, and the latter in the republic of Azerbaijan. Andropov finds himself in a precarious position between two opposing factions in the Politburo: the one which brought him to power and on which he now depends, and the one which opposed his appointment as General Secretary and which now depends on him. This system of dual dependence leaves Andropov with little room for carrying out policies that would fit his ambitions or correspond to his inner convictions.
NP, 12:1:163-64.

Police Terror, Espionage, Propaganda, Censorship

324. Andres, Karl. **Murder to Order.** New York: Devin-Adair, 1967. 127p. $3.95.
The author describes two case histories of political assassination ordered by a top Kremlin official. On October 12, 1957, a Soviet agent discharged a poison gas pistol at Dr. Lev Rebet. In 1959 Shelepin ordered the agent Stashynsky to murder Stepan Bandera, leader of the Organization of Ukrainian Nationalists. The murder was carried out on October 15, 1959, in Munich. The agent later defected to the West, where, in a sensational trial, the Soviet policy of political assassinations was exposed.

325. Barghoorn, Frederick C. **Soviet Foreign Propaganda.** Princeton, NJ: Princeton University Press, 1964. 329p. $6.00.
Barghoorn attempts to show how the Communists try to use cultural diplomacy as an instrument of foreign policy. He speaks of "the manipulation of cultural materials and personnel for propaganda purposes," and accurately describes this special and significant branch of intergovernmental propaganda as one much more highly developed by Communist states than by non-Communist countries. He finds that Soviet foreign cultural policy is a crucial Soviet instrument of power.
SR, 23:4:764-65; LJ, 89(1964):1970.

326. Barghoorn, Frederick C. **The Soviet Image of the United States: A Study in Distortion.** New York: Harcourt, Brace, for Yale Institute of International Studies, 1950. 297p. $4.00.
This is an interesting account, surveying the Soviet propaganda picture of American wickedness from the early years to the Korean war. The book is not an analysis of propaganda techniques but rather a description of content, with excerpts and anecdotes.
SR, 10:3:231-32; LJ, 75(1950):2072.

327. Barron, John. **KGB: The Secret Work of Soviet Secret Agents**. London: Hodder & Stoughton, 1974. 460p.; New York: Reader's Digest Press, 1974. 462p. $10.95.

The work consists of a series of case studies of KGB actions, with summaries setting forth the historical background and nature of KGB operations in the Soviet Union itself. It contains vivid details and is written in a lively style, offering much that should be new to most readers. Barron has been careful to cross-check his facts, and his accounts of KGB skulduggery in the Middle East, the United States, France, and Mexico carry an air of conviction.

  RR, 33:4:437-38; CH, 69(1975):142.

328. Carmichael, Joel. **Stalin's Masterpiece: The "Show Trials" and Purges of the Thirties—the Consolidation of the Bolshevik Dictatorship**. London: Weidenfield & Nicolson, 1976. viii, 238p. £6.95.

Between August 1936 and the end of 1938, literally all of the old Bolshevik leaders were brought before the court and accused of treason and espionage, to which they ardently confessed and were sentenced and immediately executed or else perished in camps. This book is full of plausible assumptions and intelligent questions.

  CSP, 19:3:377-78.

329. Clews, John C. **Communist Propaganda Techniques**. Foreword by G. F. Hudson. New York: Praeger, 1964. 326p. $8.50.

The author discusses the ideological and political context of Communist propaganda, with emphasis on an historical presentation. He examines the Leninist doctrine of propaganda, relating it to general discussions of the nature and development of modern uses of mass communication, and he describes Soviet propaganda during the Stalinist and post-Stalinist periods as well as propaganda as an instrument of Soviet foreign policy.

  SR, 25:1:167-68; JP, 27(1965):442.

330. Conquest, Robert. **The Great Terror: Stalin's Purge of the Thirties**. New York: Macmillan, 1968. 633p. $9.95.

To read this book is unbearably painful and profoundly illuminating. Every chapter, almost every page, has its separate shock. We witness the tortures of the men who were brought to confess, and examine the self-refuting nature of their confessions. A minimum of twenty million lives are attributable to Stalin's peacetime measures from 1930 to 1953.

  SR, 28:2:335-36; CH, 56(1969):233; AAPSS-A, 383(1969):178.

331. Conquest, Robert. **Kolyma—the Arctic Death Camps**. London: Macmillan, 1978. 256p. £6.95.

This book is concerned with the forced labor camps in the basin of the rivers Kolyma and Indigirka, northeastern Siberia, in the period of Stalinism, roughly from 1930 to 1954. A considerable part of the book is devoted to the presentation of the conditions of work and death in the Kolyma camps. During the quarter of a century of Stalinist industrialization, probably about three million people lost their lives in the Kolyma slave camps.

  HE, 39(July 1979):15.

332.   Conquest, Robert, ed. **The Soviet Police System**. New York: Praeger, 1968. 103p. $5.00.
Not formally a history of the police but rather a systematic survey of its development, organization, and functions, the volume edited by Conquest is an attempt to provide in concise form the basic data needed for an understanding of the police's role in Soviet history and the functioning of the Soviet political system. The book's principal value lies in its documentation.
        SR, 32:4:825-27; JP, 31(1969):589.

333.   Crowl, James William. **Angels in Stalin's Paradise: Western Reporters in Soviet Russia, 1917 to 1937. A Case Study of Louis Fischer and Walter Duranty**. Washington, DC: University Press of America, 1982. viii, 224p. $20.25.
This book shows how the Soviet regime manipulated key Western reporters from 1917 to 1937 in an effort to influence American public opinion about Soviet Russia. The author focuses on two American correspondents in Moscow who stand out both for the impact they had on the American public and for the distorted views they offered their readers. Walter Duranty of the *New York Times* was the dean of the Western press in Moscow, while Louis Fischer of the *Nation* was a favorite reporter of American liberals.
        HRNB, 10(Aug. 1982):243.

334.   Dallin, Alexander, and Breslauer, George W. **Political Terror in Communist Systems**. Stanford, CA: Stanford University Press, 1970. 172p. $5.95.
The authors have tried in their book to view the secret police's operations in the context of comparative Communist studies, a new and still exploratory field.
        SR, 32:4:828; AAPSS-A, 395(1971):245.

335.   Dallin, David J. **Soviet Espionage**. New Haven: Yale University Press, 1955. 558p. $5.75.
This is still a most complete and detailed account of Soviet espionage told in a single volume. It centers on the Soviet spy network in Europe and the Western hemisphere. The reader will be introduced to the importance of Soviet espionage, its working system, and the dangers the free world is still facing. The general reader will benefit from this account.
        SR, 16:3:423-25.

336.   Deacon, Richard. **A History of the Russian Secret Service**. London: Frederick Muller, 1972; New York: Taplinger, 1972. 568p. £5.80.
Deacon focuses on the secret police's operations, especially espionage. He begins his account in remote pre-Soviet times, finding the origin of the attitudes that underlie the centuries-long history of Russian secret police in the period of the Mongol yoke.
        SR, 32:4:825-27.

337.   Deriabin, Peter. **Watchdogs of Terror: Russian Bodyguards from the Tsars to the Commissars**. New Rochelle, NY: Arlington House, 1972. 448p. $11.95.
A former Soviet counterintelligence officer who escaped in 1954, Deriabin offers a history of Tsarist and Soviet "bodyguards" (security police and agents) from

oprichnina to the KGB. The book is not based on sources but rather a popular account aimed at the general reader, providing details unknown heretofore and an extensive bibliography for further study.
>Choice, 10(1973):516.

338. Dewhirst, Martin, and Farrell, Robert, eds. **The Soviet Censorship.** Metuchen, NJ: Scarecrow Press, published in cooperation with Radio Liberty Committee, New York, and the Institute for the Study of the USSR, Munich, 1973. 170p. $7.50.

This collection is the result of a symposium on Soviet censorship in which a group of Soviet intellectuals, who settled in the West since 1966, participated together with Western scholars. The discussions center around various forms of censorship as practiced in the Soviet Union.
>LJ, 99(1974):349; Choice, 11(1974):242.

339. Dolgun, Alexander, with Patrick Watson. **Alexander Dolgun's Story: An American in the Gulag.** New York: Alfred A. Knopf, 1975. viii, 370p. $10.00.

Dolgun—an American citizen and clerk in the American embassy in Moscow, who was arrested in 1948, released from Gulag in 1956, and allowed to leave the USSR in 1971—survived the worst of Stalin's prisons, in part by playing teasing games with the interrogators. His story is the implicit lesson to be learned from the volume—that Stalinism is farce as well as tragedy.
>SR, 35:2:340-41.

340. Gerson, Lennard D. **The Secret Police in Lenin's Russia.** Philadelphia: Temple University Press, 1976. xvi, 332p. + 8pp. photographs. $15.00.

This clearly written book emphasizes Lenin's personal role in sponsoring and encouraging the Cheka, particularly in its ruthless disregard for procedure or, precisely, for everything we associate with the rule of law.
>SR, 36:2:302-4; Choice, 14(1977):113; LJ, 101(1976):2484.

341. Glaser, Kurt, and Possony, Stefan T. **Victims of Politics: The State of Human Rights.** New York: Columbia University Press, 1979. xvi, 614p. Illustrated. $35.00.

This book recounts instances of human rights violations under such rubrics as racial discrimination; class, caste, and sex discrimination; discrimination against entire cultures, languages, religions; mass expulsions; slavery; forced labor; torture; and genocide. The authors draw on examples from a variety of countries but focus heavily on the USSR.
>APSR, 73(1979):1213.

342. Hingley, Ronald. **The Russian Secret Police: Muscovite, Imperial Russian and Soviet Political Security Operations.** New York: Simon & Schuster, 1970. 313p. $7.50.

The question of continuity between tsarist and Soviet Russia underlies the whole book. The author notes that one of the links between the old and the new political police is the lesson that Lenin and Dzerzhinsky, as experienced quarries of the Okhrana, passed on to the Cheka. He shows how much more limited, and often humane, tsarist political police action was, compared to Soviet.
>SR, 31:1:152-53; LJ, 96(1971):1264; Choice, 8(1971):1238.

343.   Hopkins, Mark W. **Mass Media in the Soviet Union.** New York: Pegasus, 1970. 384p. Tables. Charts. Maps. Photographs. $8.95.

This is a useful survey, covering the growth of the media, their structure, controls, functions, and practices. Students setting out to deal with baffling source materials from the Soviet media will find this book a helpful introduction to their work. The solid factual data incorporated in the book give it reference value, and the author's firsthand inquiries during his study and travels in the Soviet Union contribute much new and lively detail.

   SR, 30:2:434.

344.   Hutton, J. Bernard. **School for Spies: The ABC of How Russia's Secret Service Operates.** New York: Coward-McCann, 1962. 222p. $3.95.

This book is particularly useful in enlightening people who believe that Communism is on its way out. It reads like a science fiction mystery, and if even part of it is true, the reader will be disturbed and alerted, for we have nothing to compare with the Russian spy system; it cannot exist in a democracy.

   SR, 22:2:351-53.

345.   Inkeles, Alex. **Public Opinion in Soviet Russia: A Study in Mass Persuasion.** Cambridge, MA: Harvard University Press, 1950. 379p. 2d ed., 1958. 393p. $7.50.

In this pioneering study of the methods of Soviet propaganda the author places particular emphasis on communication media since 1917 and their influence on Soviet social life, telling us how Russians behave and why they behave as they do.

   SR, 10:2:146-47.

346.   Leggett, George. **The Cheka: Lenin's Political Police. The All-Russian Extraordinary Commission for Combatting Counterrevolution and Sabotage (December 1917 to February 1922).** New York and Oxford: Clarendon Press, Oxford University Press, 1981. ix, 514p. Tables. $29.95.

Leggett's explanations of why the Cheka grew to be such a formidable organization and why the Red Terror erupted strongly emphasize Lenin's personal contribution. Lenin is credited with opening and deepening internal strife, and the author suggests that Lenin must bear responsibility for provoking foreign intervention. The Red Terror itself undoubtedly sprang from Lenin's doctrine of terror, preached and practiced as an integral part of his unrelenting pursuit of power.

   Choice, 19(1982):676.

347.   Levytsky, Boris, comp. **The Stalinist Terror in the Thirties: Documentation from the Soviet Press.** Stanford, CA: Hoover Institution Press, 1974. 525p. $14.50.

The core of the book is 234 biographical entries concerning purge victims, each entry consisting of one or more excerpts from Soviet publications during the period of the anti-Stalin campaign and rehabilitation of its victims. In addition, more general surveys of the impact of the purge are provided.

   CSP, 17:1:155-57.

348. Levytsky, Boris. **The Uses of Terror: The Soviet Secret Police, 1917-1970**. Translated by H. A. Piehler. New York: Coward, McCann & Geoghegan, 1972. 349p. $7.95.

A notable feature of this book is the extensive use the author makes of émigré publications, which provide detailed information on such matters as the struggle against nationalist guerrillas in the Ukraine and elsewhere in the period after 1945.

SR, 32:4:825-27.

349. Marchenko, Anatoly. **My Testimony**. Translated by Michael Scammell. Introduction by Max Hayward. New York: E. P. Dutton, 1969. 415p. $8.95.

This is an eyewitness account of prison life in the USSR. There now appear to be four categories of prisoners in the USSR: (1) intellectuals arrested for "anti-Soviet activities and propaganda," (2) "nationalists" from various non-Russian nationalities in the Soviet Union, (3) members of the many persecuted religious denominations, and (4) common criminals. After publication of this book in England in 1968 Marchenko was again arrested, and he is now probably back in those Siberian prison camps that he so vividly describes in his book.

LJ, 95(1970):891; BL, 66(1970):867.

350. Mickiewicz, Ellen Propper. **Media and the Russian Public**. New York: Praeger, 1981. xii, 156p. $9.95 pa.

This survey provides one of the few prisms available to Western readers looking at the public opinion of average Soviet citizens. It also provides a sharp look at Soviet sociological research, its concerns and methods. In the Soviet Union, the media are the prime link between the political leadership and the citizens.

SR, 41:4:731-32; JC, 32(1982):234.

351. Powell, David E. **Antireligious Propaganda in the Soviet Union**. Cambridge, MA: MIT Press, 1975. x, 206p. $25.00.

A large number of tables, graphs, and maps aid in analyzing the ideological warfare waged by the Soviet regime against religious believers. Enormous resources are expended in this effort: tens of thousands of propagandists, reams of literature, stocks of films, and museum displays. Yet the data also support the ironic conclusion by Powell that antireligious propaganda reinforces the religious convictions it aims to destroy.

CSP, 18:1:103-4; AAPSS-A, 422(1975):171; Choice, 12(1975):1323.

352. Seth, Ronald. **The Executioners: The Story of Smersh**. New York: Hawthorn Books, 1968. 199p. $5.95.

Seth's study of the Soviet security services in World War II centers on the counterespionage agency known as "Smersh" ("Death to Spies"). Since the author tends to equate Smersh with the secret police itself, his book includes a much broader treatment of the subject than one might infer. Seth apparently enjoyed good contacts in Western counterespionage circles.

SR, 32:4:825-27; LJ, 94(1969):73.

353. **Soviet Intelligence and Security Services, 1964-70: A Selected Bibliography of Soviet Publications, with Some Additional Titles from Other Sources.** U.S. Senate, Committee on the Judiciary, 92d Congress, 1st Session. Washington, DC: Government Printing Office, 1972. 289p. $1.25 pa.

This bibliography is far more than a mere listing of titles; it includes concise analytical comments on many works, and thereby facilitates research on a multitude of fascinating and important topics.

SR, 32:4:825-26.

354. Tucker, Robert C., and Cohen, Stephen F., eds. **The Great Purge Trial.** Introduction by Robert C. Tucker. New York: Grosset & Dunlap, 1965. 725p. $5.95 pa.

The trial of March 1938, in which the principal surviving figures of the "Right Opposition," N. I. Bukharin and A. I. Rykov, together with a number of lesser figures, were tried and condemned, has been examined in this volume. Tucker regards Stalin and Bukharin as the principal antagonists in the 1938 trial.

SR, 25:2:353-55; JP, 28(1966):250; Choice, 3(1966):161.

355. Wittlin, Thaddeus. **Commissar: The Life and Death of Lavrenty Pavlovich Beria.** New York: Macmillan, 1972. 566p. $12.95.

This first full-length biography of Beria, Soviet secret police chief from 1938 to 1953, has been written by a Polish-born writer who earlier published an absorbing account of his imprisonment in Soviet concentration camps during World War II (*Reluctant Traveler in Russia,* 1952). The value of his book is enhanced by rare photographs.

SR, 32:4:828; Choice, 9(1973):1498.

Dissent and National Movement

356. Amalrik, Andrei. **Involuntary Journey to Siberia.** Translated by Manya Harari and Max Hayward. Introduction by Max Hayward. New York: Harcourt Brace Jovanovich, 1970. 297p. $6.95.

In this work Amalrik narrates his earlier encounters with the Soviet repression system. Most revealing, perhaps, is Amalrik's account of the real extent of punishment resulting from a Soviet conviction.

RR, 30:2:188-89.

357. Barghoorn, Frederick C. **Détente and the Democratic Movement in the USSR.** New York and London: The Free Press and Collier Macmillan, 1976. x, 229p. $12.95.

The author examines post-Khrushchev foreign policy from the new and unique perspective provided by the critical voices of dissent. His sources are the part of the broad spectrum of dissent that has articulated demands for greater civil liberties and human rights. He recommends continued pressure by individuals and groups in America on behalf of those struggling for human rights in the USSR.

SR, 36:2:310-11; LJ, 101(1976):1613.

358. Brumberg, Abraham, ed. **In Quest of Justice: Protest and Dissent in the Soviet Union Today.** New York: Praeger, 1970. 477p. $10.95.

The heart of the book contains documents prepared by Soviet citizens, signed with names and addresses, and usually sent to appropriate "instances" in the Soviet government or the United Nations. Most of the documents are links in the chain of repression, protest, secondary repression, and secondary protest in such areas as literature, nationalities, religion, self-expression, and intervention in Czechoslovakia.

SR, 30:4:897-98.

359. Chalidze, Valery. **To Defend These Rights: Human Rights and the Soviet Union.** Translated by Guy Daniels. New York: Random House, 1974. 340p. $10.00.

Chalidze offers, in the opening chapters, features of Soviet law and the Soviet Union's position with respect to international conventions on human rights. Then he analyzes and exposes all the restrictions on basic human rights and freedom as related to social, religious, and national minority aspects. Also, the treatment of prisoners and their prospects for the future are subjects of his concern. The author was a member of the USSR human rights movement but is now—since 1972—a U.S. citizen. His moving account deserves a special place in college and public libraries.

LJ, 99(1974):3191; Choice, 12(1975):595.

360. Cohen, Stephen F., ed. **An End to Silence: Uncensored Opinion in the Soviet Union. From Roy Medvedev's Underground Magazine** *Political Diary.* Translated by George Saunders. New York and London: W. W. Norton, 1982. xiv, 361p. $19.95.

Cohen presents selected materials published by Roy Medvedev in his *samizdat* journal *Political Diary* from October 1964 to March 1971. In this journal, the most important critics in the country spoke out against Stalin's crimes, the Brezhnev regime's hesitation to root out evil vestiges of Stalinism, and its subsequent revival of approval for Stalin and his accomplishments. The writers pleaded for civil rights, justice, and democratic reform.

SR, 41:4:731.

361. Dunlop, John B. **The New Russian Revolutionaries.** Belmont, MA: Nordland Publishing Company, 1976. 344p. $18.50.

In early 1967, the KGB uncovered an oppositionist organization consisting of barely a score of members, who were arrested and brought to trial. The author has reconstructed the biographies of the main leaders, chronicled the life and collapse of the organization, and provided a summary of the main programmatic tenets and of their intellectual sources.

SR, 39:1:124-25; Choice, 13(1977):1483.

362. Fireside, Harvey. **Soviet Psychoprisons.** Foreword by Zhores Medvedev. New York: Norton, 1979. 201p. $11.95.

This volume adds much recent useful information on the subject of Soviet psychoprisons. The author offers a historical background of psychiatric internment of dissidents, the internal politics of the Soviet psychiatric profession, and recent organized dissident efforts to stop the practice.

NP, 9:1:144-45; LJ, 105(1980):108; Choice, 17(1980):424.

363. Gaucher, Roland. **Opposition in the U.S.S.R., 1917-1967.** Translated by Charles Lam Markman. New York: Funk & Wagnalls, 1969. 547p. $10.00.

This volume consists of the writings of anti-Bolshevik opposition groups from 1917 to 1967. It includes Whites, anarchists, social-revolutionaries from the period of the Civil War, opposition during the 1920s and 1930s, national and religious forces. It is an anthology of the resistance to the Soviet system.

LJ, 95(1970):66; Choice, 7(1970):284.

364. Gerstenmaier, Cornelia. **The Voices of the Silent.** Translated by Susan Hecker. New York: Hart Publishing Co., 1972. 587p. $10.00.

Gerstenmeier, the former editor of *Ost-Probleme,* has made the personal acquaintance of many of the better-known figures involved in the Democratic Movement. This volume serves as a general introduction to the problems of dissent and also fills in much information on the fate of those whose names have flashed briefly in the Western consciousness and then disappeared.

SR, 32:3:623-24; Choice, 10(1973):629.

365. Grigorenko, Peter G. **The Grigorenko Papers: Writings by General P. G. Grigorenko and Documents on His Case.** Introduction by Edward Crankshaw. Boulder, CO: Westview Press, 1976; Amsterdam: Alexander Herzen Foundation, 1973. viii, 187p. $12.50.

The life of Peter Grigorenko is similar to the kind of model life that Soviet journalists love to feature under a heading like "From a Farm Laborer to a General." Just when Grigorenko's career had progressed to its logical end—retirement—a new life began for him: arrest, reduction to the ranks and declaration of insanity, almost five years in KGB prisons and prison psychiatric hospitals. At the age of seventy he became one of the founders of the Helsinki Group.

SR, 37:2:316-17.

366. Harasowska, Marta, and Olhovych, Orest, eds. **The International Sakharov Hearing.** Baltimore: Smoloskyp Publishers, 1977. 335p. $8.95.

The Common Committee of East European Exiles in Denmark sponsored a public hearing in Copenhagen in October 1975 on human rights in the USSR. The oral testimony of twenty-four Soviet émigrés who testified at the hearing is reproduced in this volume. The testimony, focusing on the period 1965 to 1975, is grouped under four headings: "Political Oppression and the Persecution of Dissidents," "The Fight against Religion," "The Abuse of Psychiatry," and "The Oppression of Non-Russian Nationalities."

SR, 38:4:689-90.

367. Haynes, Victor, and Semyonova, Olga, eds. **Workers against the Gulag: The New Opposition in the Soviet Union.** London: Pluto Press, 1979. 129p. £1.95.

The editors document case after case of illegal dismissal, discrimination, victimization, and imprisonment in the Soviet Union. A considerable amount of documentation is provided on the Free Trade Union Association of Soviet Working People, which came into being in late 1977.

SEER, 58:3:478.

368. Hayward, Max, ed. **On Trial: The Soviet State versus "Abram Tertz" and "Nikolai Arzhak."** Translated, edited, and with an introduction by Max Hayward. New York: Harper & Row, 1966. 183p. $4.95.

This is a disturbing book. It is a reminder that the Soviet Union, despite its obvious industrial and technological accomplishments, has yet to guarantee to its intellectuals that measure of freedom of expression which affords them the right to publish social and political criticism in a nonconforming, unorthodox literary style. In 1965, Siniavski and Daniel, Soviet citizens who published abroad under the pseudonyms Tertz and Arzhak, were tried and convicted for anti-Soviet agitation.

SR, 27:1:157-58; Choice, 4(1967):538.

369. Litvinov, Pavel. **The Demonstration in Pushkin Square: The Trial Records with Commentary and an Open Letter.** Translated by Manya Harari. Boston: Gambit, 1969. 176p. $4.95.

The main and central part of this book is a faithful account of two trials that took place in the Moscow City Court in February and September 1967 and that are somewhere in the middle of a chain of dramatic events, all connected with the struggle for freedom of expression, freedom of peaceful assembly, and other fundamental rights and freedoms contained in the Universal Declaration of Human Rights of 1948. This documentary book should be read by all.

SR, 30:1:161-62; BL, 66(1970):809.

370. Litvinov, Pavel, comp. **The Trial of the Four: A Collection of Materials on the Case of Galanskov, Ginzburg, Dobrovolsky and Lashkova, 1967-68.** English text edited and annotated by Peter Reddaway. Translated by Janis Sapiets, Hilary Sternberg, and Daniel Weissbort. Foreword by Leonard Schapiro. New York: Viking Press, 1972. 434p. $10.00.

This trial of January 1968 elicited so powerful a response among Soviet intellectuals that it may be said to have sparked the Soviet human rights movement. The protests which it generated exceeded in scope those following the 1966 trial of writers Andrei Siniavsky and Iulii Daniel. This book should be required reading for any serious student of the contemporary Soviet scene.

SR, 32:3:622-23; Choice, 10(1973):182.

371. Medvedev, Roy A. **Let History Judge: The Origins and Consequences of Stalinism.** Translated by Colleen Taylor. Edited by David Joravsky and Georges Haupt. New York: Knopf, 1971. 566p. $12.50.

In the environment of the Soviet critical intelligentsia in which this was written, it is a wonder. Not only does it represent the first foray of the unofficial writers into the mainstream of Soviet history, it is a triumph of judicious scholarship over persecution, isolation, and taboo. It demolishes official Soviet historiography and courageously raises basic questions defying the KGB and the fundamental structure of the system. This book should be a must not only for all students of Soviet and East European affairs, but also for the Western intellectual who is still confused about the real nature of the Soviet system.

RR, 31:2:179-81; LJ, 97(1972):373; Choice, 9(1972):270.

372. Medvedev, Zhores A. **The Medvedev Papers: "Fruitful Meetings between Scientists of the World" [and] "Secrecy of Correspondence is Guaranteed by Law."** Translated by Vera Richa. Foreword by John Ziman. London: Macmillan; New York: St. Martin's Press, 1971. 471p. $11.95.

In 1962 Medvedev's manuscript (later published in the United States as *The Rise and Fall of T. D. Lysenko*) began to circulate in *samizdat,* and indeed by 1965 Lysenko's power had dwindled. His punishment for publishing the *Papers* was two weeks of "psychiatric detention" in May 1970 (described by Medvedev and his brother Roy in *A Question of Madness,* 1971). Many important topics are examined by Medvedev in the *Papers*: the internal and external passport system in the Soviet Union, the trials of publishing, the process of election to the Academy of Sciences, and the post office system. Fascinating as these insights are, the author's main emphasis is on two other themes—the obstacles to international travel, and the censorship of mail.

SR, 31:3:697-98; LJ, 97(1972):881; Choice, 9(1972):832.

373. Medvedev, Zhores A. **Ten Years after Ivan Denisovich.** Translated by Hilary Sternberg. New York: Knopf, 1973. 202p. $6.95.

Medvedev traces the gradual emergence of criticism hostile to Solzhenitsyn, the refusal to award him a Lenin Prize or to publish his later works, the appearance of his books abroad, his expulsion from the Soviet Writers' Union, and the reaction to his Nobel award. The reader is also provided with fascinating glimpses of such prominent representatives of the Soviet intelligentsia as Tvardovsky, physicist Kapitsa, cellist Rostropovich, all of whose paths crossed Solzhenitsyn's. Yet the most arresting aspect of this work is not its explicit informational content, but what it reveals about perceptions by Soviet intellectuals of the proper boundaries between freedom and order.

RR, 33:4:446-48; LR, 24(Winter 1973-74):182; Choice, 11(1974):444.

374. Meerson-Aksenov, Michael, and Shragin, Boris, eds. **The Political, Social and Religious Thought of Russian "Samizdat": An Anthology.** Translated by Nicholas Lupinin. Belmont, MA: Nordland Publishing Company, 1977. 624p. $29.50.

This anthology consists of essays by men who are recognized as professional intellectuals, that is, as men of thought, many of whom have academic training in philosophy and other humanities. This book should be on the list of required reading for teachers dealing with the Soviet Union.

NP, 7:2:226-27; Choice, 15(1978):288.

375. Podrabinek, Alexander. **Punitive Medicine.** Ann Arbor, MI: Karoma Publishers, 1980. 237p. $12.95.

Podrabinek discusses material available to him at the time of writing (1976-77), examining the historical, legal, and medical aspects of incarceration in general and special psychiatric hospitals, with numerous references to individual cases and personal reports.

RP, 43(Aug. 1981):310.

376. Reddaway, Peter, and Kline, Edward, eds. **A Chronicle of Human Rights in the USSR.** New York: Khronika Press, 1973. No. 1: November 1972-March 1973. 80p.; No. 2: April-May 1973. 77p.; No. 3: July-August 1973. 78p. $3.00 pa.

The editors have translated material that was published in the Soviet Union by the Russian Democratic Movement and appeared in either the *Chronicle of Current Events* or in other underground *samizdat* publications. Through these translations, the West is slowly seeing the true picture of Soviet life and the fate of the intellectuals who have the courage to oppose an oppressive system.

377. Reddaway, Peter, ed. and trans. **Uncensored Russia: Protest and Dissent in the Soviet Union: The Unofficial Moscow Journal. A Chronicle of Current Events.** Foreword by Julius Telesin. New York: American Heritage Press, 1972. 499p. $10.00.

Reddaway has translated the first eleven issues of the *Chronicle of Current Events,* dating from April 1968 to December 1969. Instead of presenting the issues *ad seriatim,* the editor arranged the materials topically into seven parts. The introduction is informative, concise, and sober.

SR, 32:3:595-600; APSR, 67(1973):1086.

378. Reve, Karel van het, ed. **Dear Comrade: Pavel Litvinov and the Voices of Soviet Citizens in Dissent.** New York: Pitman Publishing Corp., 1969. 199p. $4.95.

Dear Comrade is a significant document of political dissent in the USSR, directed against the portents of neo-Stalinism. It contains two important protest letters written by Pavel Litvinov, the grandson of the late people's commissar of foreign affairs, and letters and telegrams sent to Litvinov between December 1967 and May 1968.

SR, 29:2:343-44.

379. Rothberg, Abraham. **The Heirs of Stalin: Dissidence and the Soviet Regime, 1953-1970.** Ithaca, NY: Cornell University Press, 1970. 450p. $14.50.

The author has provided a far-ranging chronicle of the conflict between Soviet intellectuals and their government from the time of Stalin's death until the present day. The book contains a readable and comprehensive glimpse into one aspect of recent Soviet history. It contains a wealth of information that will be of great interest to everyone who follows Soviet affairs.

SR, 32:1:212-13; AAPSS-A, 403(1972):193; LJ, 97(1972):70.

380. Rubenstein, Joshua. **Soviet Dissidents: Their Struggle for Human Rights.** Beacon, NY: Beacon House, 1980. 288p. $12.95.

This study provides a good history of the Soviet dissident movement from its roots in the Khrushchev years to Andrei Sakharov's exile from Moscow. The author describes the variety of groups criticizing the Soviet regime and its policies. The book is especially valuable for the layperson concerned with human rights or current affairs.

LJBR, (1980):368; Choice, 18(1981):1163.

381. Sakharov, Andrei D. **My Country and the World**. Translated by Guy V. Daniels. New York: Alfred A. Knopf, 1975. xvi, 109p. $5.95.

Sakharov is convinced that the political rulers of the Soviet Union are extremely sensitive to public opinion in the West and to the policies of the nations in NATO. He deplores the absence of unity among the Western countries in their attitudes toward the Soviet Union.

RR, 35:4:486-87; LJ, 101(1976):623; Choice, 13(1976):588.

382. Sakharov, Andrei D. **Progress, Coexistence, and Intellectual Freedom**. Translated from the Russian by the *New York Times*, with introduction, afterword, and notes by H. E. Salisbury. New York: Norton, 1968. 158p. $2.50 pa.

Sakharov expresses his views on the democratization of the Soviet system. He takes a critical stand on the policy of coexistence, which, according to him, serves Soviet needs only.

Choice, 6(1969):142; BL, 65(1969):940.

383. Sakharov, Andrei D. **Sakharov Speaks**. Edited by Harrison E. Salisbury. New York: Knopf, 1974. 245p. $6.95.

These are the translations of a wide range of material—memoranda, statements, interviews, letters—dealing essentially with the human rights issue. This work represents a refreshing source of humanistic ideas and thoughts. The author also shows a considerable awareness of what is going on in the various non-Russian republics.

Choice, 11(1974):1463.

384. Sakharov, Vladimir, and Tosi, Umberto. **High Treason**. New York: G. P. Putnam's Sons, 1980. 318p. $11.95.

Sakharov writes of his privileged youth among the elite of Soviet Russia, his exclusive education, and his promising career as a Soviet foreign service officer and part-time KGB agent. This autobiography offers a glimpse of the new Communist elite and presents the argument that a principal Soviet goal is to strangle the West by controlling the Middle East and its oil. The book is suited more for the general reader than the expert.

LJBR, (1980):125; PW, 220(Jl. 1981):93.

385. Shatz, Marshall S. **Soviet Dissent in Historical Perspective**. Cambridge and New York: Cambridge University Press, 1981. x, 214p. $19.95.

This useful and timely book on dissent in the Soviet Union is designed for the layman. Shatz attempts to place Soviet dissent in a historical framework stretching back to the prerevolutionary era. He believes that the current cycle of dissent is part of a recurring tendency that has influenced Russia for at least two centuries, rather than one unique or endemic to the Soviet system itself.

AHR, 87:1:224.

386. Siniavskii, Andrei. **For Freedom of Imagination**. Translated by Laszlo Tikos and Murray Peppard. New York: Holt, Rinehart & Winston, 1971. 212p. $6.95.

This is a collection of well-chosen literary pieces, most of which are available only in the West. The book is a small tribute to the man who, despite imprisonment and endless persecution, has the courage to express ideas that challenge the whole Soviet totalitarian system.

387. Solzhenitsyn, Alexander, et al. **From Under the Ruble.** Translated by A. M. Brock. Introduction by Max Hayward. Boston and Toronto: Little, Brown & Company, 1975. xii, 308p. $8.95.

The essays in this volume are rooted in a nationally Russian and spiritually Christian outlook. They express the views of what has emerged as the conservative and nationalist wing of the dissident movement in the USSR, and were written between 1971 and 1974, when all the authors were still in Russia.

SR, 35:3:544.

388. Tökés, Rudolf L., ed. **Dissent in the USSR : Politics, Ideology, and People.** Baltimore and London: The Johns Hopkins University Press, 1975. xvi, 453p. $15.00.

This book raises some key issues: the political significance of dissent; the range of ideas, beliefs, and convictions that motivate dissident activities; the methods of communication; and what is being accomplished through dissent. Most of the prominent Soviet dissidents who appear in this volume now live in the West.

SR, 37:4:683-85; Choice, 12(1975):1366.

389. Yakir, Pyotr. **A Childhood in Prison.** Edited with an introduction by Robert Conquest. New York: Coward, McCann & Geoghegan, 1973. 155p. $5.95.

This volume consists of Yakir's moving account of his coming-of-age in the jungle of Stalin-era concentration camps. Laconic, terse, and matter-of-fact, Yakir's story is a classic which should be read by everyone concerned with modern Russian and Soviet history and politics.

SR, 32:4:828.

DIPLOMACY AND FOREIGN RELATIONS

Reference Works

390. Clemens, Walter C., Jr. **Soviet Disarmament Policy 1917-1963: An Annotated Bibliography.** Stanford, CA: The Hoover Institution, 1965. 151p. $4.00 pa.

This bibliography lists the most important primary and secondary material that has appeared in Russia, Europe, and North America.

391. Crowley, Edward L., ed. **The Soviet Diplomatic Corps, 1917-1967.** Metuchen, NJ: Scarecrow Press, 1970. 426p. $7.50.

This volume will be most useful both to the historian of Soviet foreign affairs and to the practitioner of diplomacy with an interest in the USSR. It contains lists of past and present ministers of foreign affairs and their deputies of personnel in the ministry's various functional and geographic divisions, and of heads of foreign missions. It also provides a list of Soviet vetoes in the United Nations.

392. Dallin, Alexander, ed. **Soviet Conduct in World Affairs: A Selection of Readings.** New York: Columbia University Press, 1960. 318p. $4.50.

Perceptive, challenging, and skillfully written articles on Soviet foreign relations were selected for this reader. This well-balanced material lends itself to be used by undergraduates and in class discussions.

SR, 20:1:134-35.

393. Hammond, Thomas T., comp. and ed. **Soviet Foreign Relations and World Communism: A Selected, Annotated Bibliography of 7,000 Books in 30 Languages.** Princeton, NJ: Princeton University Press, 1965. 1240p. $25.00.

This handy reference tool is broken down in four subject areas: (1) Soviet foreign relations, economic as well as political with all countries since 1917; (2) Communist movement outside Russia since 1917; (3) certain specific aspects of Soviet foreign policy, such as ideology, propaganda, strategy and tactics, and espionage; and (4) internal developments in all Communist countries except Russia.

RR, 25:2:199-201.

General Works

394. Beloff, Max. **Foreign Policy of Soviet Russia, 1929-1936**; Vol. 2: **1936-1941**. London and New York: Oxford University Press, issued under the auspices of the Royal Institute of International Affairs, 1947-49. 2 vols.
This collection contains the record of Soviet diplomatic actions that followed the Locarno Pact.
SR, 7:1:95-97.

395. Berzins, Alfred. **The Two Faces of Co-existence**. New York: Robert Speller, 1967. 355p. $6.95.
The author of this interesting book discusses Lenin's attitude toward capitalism and democracies, explains the use of peace, friendship, and nonaggression pacts as the tools of Soviet expansionist policy, and pays particular attention to the Soviet policy toward Poland, Finland, Hungary, and the Baltic and Balkan states, as examples. The author ridicules the new breed of scientists, the so-called Kremlinologists, whom he compares to the latter-day soothsayers.
AHR, 73:2:550-51; Choice, 5(1968):406.

396. Bialer, Seweryn, ed. **The Domestic Context of Soviet Foreign Policy**. Boulder, CO, and London: Westview Press and Croom Helm, 1981. xviii, 441p. Figures.Tables. $35.00.
In the author's words, this is an attempt "to understand some of the sources of the conduct of Soviet foreign policy and the contradictory pressures that shape its formation." The essays as a whole strike an excellent balance between theoretical and empirical perspectives. They include the role of culture, ideology, political and social factors, and economics.
SR, 41:4:724-25; APSR, 75(1981):1066.

397. Byrnes, Robert F., ed. **After Brezhnev: Sources of Soviet Conduct in the 1980s**. Bloomington, IN: Indiana University Press, 1983. 480p. $25.00.
This essential book will help the interested general reader, as well as the policymaker, analyze and understand the Soviet Union and the elements that will most affect its policies in the 1980s. A distinguished group of American specialists focus on the Soviet system and society within the context of international politics.

398. Dallin, David J. **Soviet Foreign Policy after Stalin**. Philadelphia: Lippincott, 1961. 543p. $7.95.
In this thoroughly documented general survey of Soviet foreign policy since Stalin's death, the author demonstrates intimate knowledge of the Soviet system. Thus his explanation of methods and aims appears to be more reliable than similar accounts on this topic.

399. Debo, Richard K. **Revolution and Survival: The Foreign Policy of Soviet Russia, 1917-18**. Toronto and Buffalo: University of Toronto Press, 1979. xiv, 462p. $25.00.
Debo's Lenin is the theorist-cum-pragmatist who never gave up his dedication to revolution, but who, almost without ever having intended to do so, found himself

defending a nation and his right to rule it. Rejecting Trotsky's dream of immediate and permanent revolution, Lenin sought realistic ways to maintain Bolshevik power.

SR, 39:2:307-8; AHR, 85:1:178.

400. Degras, Jane T., comp. **Calendar of Soviet Documents on Foreign Policy, 1917-1941.** London and New York, Royal Institute of International Affairs, 1948. 248p.

Arranged chronologically and by countries, this collection lists a great number of Soviet treaties and agreements together with important documents, speeches, interviews, and newspaper articles.

401. Edmonds, Robin. **Soviet Foreign Policy, 1962-73: The Paradox of Super Power.** New York: Oxford University Press, 1975. xiv, 197p. $12.00.

The author, a senior British diplomat who was minister in Moscow in 1969 to 1972, describes Soviet policy decisions step by step, relating them to each other and to the Soviet internal situation. The period covered here begins with the nuclear war scare of October 1962 and ends with the global nuclear alert of October 1973.

RR, 35:2:215-16; AAPSS-A, 424(1976):121; Choice, 12(1976):1490.

402. Eudin, Xenia Joukoff, and Slusser, Robert M., eds. **Soviet Foreign Policy, 1928-1934: Documents and Materials.** 2 vols. University Park, PA: Pennsylvania State University Press, 1966, Vol. 1: 353p.; 1967, Vol. 2: 423p. $9.50 each. (Publication of the Hoover Institution on War, Revolution and Peace.)

These two volumes present in the words of the Soviet leaders themselves the most important points of Soviet foreign policy. Volume 1 covers the period 1928-31 and volume 2, 1932-34. A narrative summary introduces documents selected from Soviet newspapers, periodicals, and Comintern reports.

SR, 28:1:194.

403. Fischer, Louis. **Russia's Road from Peace to War: Soviet Foreign Relations, 1917-1941.** New York: Harper & Row, 1969. 499p. $12.50.

Fischer is at his best in the analysis of Soviet foreign policy in the period he witnessed in Russia in the 1920s, when he had access to documents that probably no other Western author was permitted to see. He attempts to interpret Soviet behavior as a mixture of internal and external exigencies, of ideological commitments and hard realities, and of the Soviet leaders' own structures.

SR, 29:3:535-36.

404. Fischer, Louis. **The Soviets in World Affairs: A History of Relations between the Soviet Union and the Rest of the World, 1917-1929.** London and New York: Cape & Smith, 1930. 2 vols.; New York: Vintage Books, 1960. 616p.

This classic study of the international relations of the Soviet Union, from the Treaty of Brest-Litovsk down to the resumption of diplomatic relations with Great Britain in 1929, represents a thorough work of investigation. The author's personal acquaintance with leading Soviet personalities of that time lends even greater value to his interpretation.

405. Gehlen, Michael P. **The Politics of Coexistence: Soviet Methods and Motives.** Bloomington, IN: Indiana University Press, 1967. 334p. $6.75.

This is a highly readable survey of recent Soviet foreign policies. While it does not take the reader far into the politics of coexistence, this survey is a discriminating piece of work and should prove useful as an introductory text to the study of Soviet foreign policy.

SR, 28:1:155-56; JP, 30(1968):551.

406. Goldman, Marshall I. **Soviet Foreign Aid.** New York: Praeger, 1967. 265p.

The informed layman will profit from this thoroughly documented study of Soviet foreign aid. The historical account also treats the satellite aid programs in conjunction with Soviet efforts.

APSR, 62(1968):689; JP, 30(1968):867.

407. Goodman, Elliot R. **The Soviet Design for a World State.** Foreword by Philip E. Mosely. New York: Columbia University Press, 1960. 512p.

The author argues that the Soviet government is, and always has been, dedicated to the long-range goal of a worldwide socialist state in which the Russians will play the dominant role. He demonstrates his point partly by generous quotations from the writings of Communist leaders, and partly by surveying the record of Soviet history since 1917.

AHR, 68:1:136-37.

408. Harvey, Mose L., et al. **Science and Technology as an Instrument of Soviet Policy.** Foreword by Ambassador Foy D. Kohler. Coral Gables, FL: Center for Advanced International Studies, University of Miami, 1972. 219p. $5.95.

In the first part, this book presents translated extracts from Soviet articles and official documents on science and technology. In the second part, several authors analyze the relationship between science and technology and Soviet foreign policy. The study offers an insight into Soviet technological potential.

AAPSS-A, 408(Jl. 1973):147; Choice, 10(1973):1075.

409. Hoffman, Eric P., and Fleron, Frederic J., Jr., eds. **The Conduct of Soviet Foreign Policy.** Chicago: Aldine-Atherton, 1971. 478p. $12.00.

The editors rely on the efforts of other social scientists to illuminate the problems posed by Soviet external behavior, modestly staying in the background and being content with supplying needed introductory remarks. Their work brings together most of the great articles written during the past fifteen years. Most of these articles have survived the test of time. The book is divided into seven parts, each dealing with a different basic topic: The Study of Soviet Foreign Policy; Domestic Politics and the Formation of Soviet Foreign Policy; Communist Ideology, Belief Systems and Soviet Foreign Policy; The Origins of the Cold War; Western Diplomacy and Soviet Foreign Policy; Competitive Coexistence and the Cold War; The Third World and Soviet Foreign Policy; and Retrospect and Prospect. This volume will remain constantly in demand as one of the finest sourcebooks for professors of political science specializing in the analysis of "the conduct of Soviet foreign policy."

CSP, 15:3:412-14; Choice, 9(1972):131.

410.   Jacobsen, C. G. **Soviet Strategy—Soviet Foreign Policy: Military Considerations Affecting Soviet Policy-making.** Glasgow: Glasgow University Press, 1972. 236p.
The author, who has researched relevant Soviet and Western publications, presents an analysis of Soviet military debates, Soviet strategic capabilities, strategic hardware, and the practical and psychological implications of different weapons systems. The book deals mainly with the post-Khrushchev period.
   CH, 65(1973):178.

411.   Jelavich, Charles. **Tsarist Russia and Balkan Nationalism: Russian Influence in the International Affairs of Bulgaria and Serbia, 1879-1886.** Berkeley: University of California Press, 1958. 304p. $6.50.
The author discusses the influence of military consideration on the formulation of Russian policy. The study sheds light on the motives of Russian engagement in Bulgaria and Serbia.
   SEER, 39:92:263-65.

412.   Kanet, Roger, ed. **Soviet Foreign Policy in the 1980s.** New York: Praeger Publishers, 1982. 300p. $28.95.
After an introduction on the Soviet Union as a global power, the reader is guided through the domestic-foreign linkages in Soviet foreign policy: the economic factors, the implications of nationalities policy, the military influences, and domestic dissent. The volume also covers the Soviet Union and the Communist world, including Eastern Europe, China and Southeast Asia, Cuba, and the West European Communist challenge.

413.   Kaplan, Stephen S. **Diplomacy of Power: Soviet Armed Forces as a Political Instrument.** With ten case studies. Foreword by Bruce K. Mac-Laury. Washington, DC: The Brookings Institution, 1981. xvi, 733p. Figures. Tables. $29.95.
This work attempts to discuss Soviet military behavior in the aggregate while providing the reader with informative case studies. The book focuses on the investigation of the Soviet armed forces as a "political instrument." Thus Kaplan analyzes 190 separate political uses of the Soviet armed forces between June 1944 and August 1979.
   APSR, 76(1982):450; Choice, 19(1982):1134.

414.   Kennan, George F. **The Decline of Bismarck's European Order: Franco-Russian Relations, 1875-1890.** Princeton, NJ: Princeton University Press, 1979. xii, 466p. $25.00.
Kennan's central interest is Russian foreign policy—the men who made it, the interests it served, the schemers who sought to influence it, and the view of Europe as seen from St. Petersburg. Kennan believes, despite the prevailing mood of historians these days, that individuals can and do play important roles in history.
   RR, 39:4:449-500; Choice, 10(1980):277.

415.   Kennan, George F. **Russia and the West under Lenin and Stalin.** Boston: Little, Brown, 1961. 411p.; New York: Mentor, 1962. 384p.

A series of lectures of Ambassador Kennan are presented in a charming form of communication with the reader. The author's experiences and scholarship give considerable value to his views and interpretations. Though personal political motivations are exposed here to a point of debate, the keen insight into Soviet behavior is challenging to both scholar and layman.
AHR, 67:1:87-88.

416.   Kohler, Foy D., et al. **Soviet Strategy for the Seventies: From Cold War to Peaceful Coexistence.** Miami: University of Miami Press, 1977. v, 241p. $5.95.
The authors trace the evolution of the concept and policy of "peaceful coexistence" from its initial formulation by Lenin in 1921 to its role in Soviet foreign policy under Brezhnev. Considering that this book was written well before active Soviet involvement in the struggles in Africa and the invasion of Afghanistan (it was first published in 1969), it can be regarded as truly prophetic.
NR, 31(1979):1248.

417.   Kovner, Milton. **The Challenge of Coexistence.** Washington, DC: Public Affairs Press, 1961. 130p.
The author believes that the Soviet Union plans to implement "peaceful coexistence" through an aggressive economic policy, particularly in the underdeveloped areas. The benefits of this policy will be employed by the Soviets in their economic penetration of underdeveloped countries.

418.   Kulski, W. W. **The Soviet Union in World Affairs: A Documented Analysis, 1964-1972.** Syracuse, NY: Syracuse University Press, 1973. 526p. $17.50.
Kulski demonstrates that Soviet specialists have a much more sophisticated, hardheaded, and nonideological attitude in their perspective on international affairs than is commonly felt to be the case. The author is particularly strong in his discussion of the limited influence of ideological beliefs on definitions of Soviet national interest.
AHR, 79:1:201; JP, 36(1974):267.

419.   Kulski, Wladyslaw W. **Peaceful Coexistence: An Analysis of Soviet Foreign Policy.** Chicago: Regnery, 1959. 661p.
The author concentrates on two motives of Soviet foreign policy: the mission to communize the world, and the desire to preserve the Soviet state through Russian national interests as the center of world revolution. The author's presentation requires of the reader some background knowledge on the subject.
JMH, 32:4:416-17.

420.   Lederer, Ivo J., ed. **Russian Foreign Policy: Essays in Historical Perspective.** New Haven, CT: Yale University Press, 1962. 620p.
This collection of essays examines Russian foreign relations over the past century and gives special consideration to the elements of continuity and change in major aspects of that subject. This volume provides rich material for discussion and study.
SR, 22:1:149-50.

421.   Librach, Jan. **The Rise of the Soviet Empire: A Study of Soviet Foreign Policy.** New York: Praeger, 1964. 382p.

The volume provides the reader with a good synthesis of Soviet foreign policy by emphasizing the basic assumptions underlying this policy. The author is at his best when relating Communist theory to practice and when defining such concepts as "peace," "peaceful coexistence," and "national self-determination."

    JMH, 37:2:284.

422.   London, Kurt L., ed. **The Soviet Impact on World Politics.** New York: Hawthorn Books, 1974. 312p. $13.95.

This collection of essays by well-known specialists sets out to assess the Soviet impact on world politics and to warn the reader of the unrelievedly bleak record. It is evident that while the rest of the world changes, Soviet nature and purpose remain constant.

    RR, 34:3:340-41.

423.   London, Kurt, ed. **The Soviet Union in World Politics.** Boulder, CO: Westview Press, 1980. xiv, 380p. $27.50.

This is an updated and revised edition of *The Soviet Impact on World Politics* (see entry 422). Taken together, the two editions record a somber period in the world's history during which Soviet military power and diplomatic influence increased at a steady rate and on a global scale.

    SR, 41:3:554-55.

424.   Mastny, Vojtech. **Russia's Road to the Cold War: Diplomacy, Warfare, and the Politics of Communism, 1941-1945.** New York: Columbia University, 1979. xxii, 409p. $16.95.

This is a book that should be read and pondered by everyone concerned with the foreign policy of the Soviet Union as it was shaped by the conflicts of World War II. The author masters formidable, diverse, and controversial literature on Soviet actions and interactions and candidly states his conclusions.

    SR, 39:1:122-23; AHR, 85:2:438; JP, 42(1980):908.

425.   Mosely, Philip E. **The Kremlin and World Politics: Studies in Soviet Policy and Action.** New York: Random House, 1960. 557p.

The author, an eminent student of Soviet affairs, presents in this volume a selection of articles which he wrote in the past quarter-century to aid in the understanding of the "Russian problem." The effort illustrates the American viewpoint over an extended period of time, offering the student of Soviet foreign policies challenging and interesting reading.

426.   Nogee, Joseph L., and Donaldson, Robert H. **Soviet Foreign Policy since World War II.** New York: Pergamon Press, 1981. viii, 320p. $35.00.

This book meets the need for an up-to-date discussion of Soviet foreign policy since 1945. The authors allocate adequate space to Khrushchev, and their treatment of the Brezhnev period is extensive. Interested students from many disciplines will find this study helpful.

    SS, 34:1:126-28; AAPSS-A, 459(Ja. 1982): 178.

427.   Oliva, L. Jay, ed. **Russia and the West: From Peter to Khrushchev.** Boston: Heath, 1965. 289p. $5.95.

A collection of excerpts from the writings of those who have described important aspects of the process of Russia's Westernization, or interpreted its manifestations. Included in this book are observations of ministers of state, foreign ambassadors and historians. The political and diplomatic relations of Russia and the West are given equal weight with the cultural and the intellectual. This is a very useful volume for students lacking knowledge of Russian.

SR, 29:3:505-6; Choice, 3(1966):249.

428.   Ramundo, Bernard A. **Peaceful Coexistence: International Law in the Building of Communism.** Baltimore: Johns Hopkins Press, 1967. 262p. $11.95.

The bulk of the volume consists of a translation of the text of the latest RSFSR Criminal Code, Code of Criminal Procedure, and Law on Court Organization, as amended to July 1965. It is preceded by a 139-page introduction in which Harold J. Berman analyzes and comments on the significance of the new legislation, its place in the history of Soviet legal development to date, and the technical impact on the average Soviet citizen of these major reforms in the administration of justice in the USSR. The result is a handy, highly condensed survey of the progression of Soviet offical behavior up till now in this crucial area of social regulation and control.

SR, 25:3:542-43; JP, 30(1968):597.

429.   Rosser, Richard F. **An Introduction to Soviet Foreign Policy.** Englewood Cliffs, NJ: Prentice-Hall, 1969. 391p. $8.50.

The author proceeds methodically to acquaint his reader with the principal moves of the Soviet policy-makers in the international arena. His discussion incorporates relevant matters of interest, such as geopolitics, the balance of power, and the Russian heritage, as well as Communist ideology. The study covers the entire period of the Soviet government's existence and all areas of the world in which it has been involved.

SR, 29:3:535.

430.   Rubinstein, Alvin Z., ed. **The Foreign Policy of the Soviet Union.** 3d ed. New York: Random House, 1972 (1960). 474p. $6.50 pa.

Rubinstein provides a series of excerpts from Soviet documents together with his notes. In addition, five Western authors contribute to this still useful though somewhat dated work. This collection has by now more historical value than value as a study of contemporary Soviet diplomacy.

CH, 64(1973):225.

431.   Rush, Myron, ed. **The International Situation and Soviet Foreign Policy: Key Reports by Soviet Leaders from the Revolution to the Present.** Columbus, OH: C. E. Merrill Publishers, 1969. 358p. $4.95.

Rush, the author of several books on the Soviet Union, collected relevant documents that are judged basic to the process of the formulation of Soviet foreign policy. Many documents are translated into English for the first time, thus increasing the number of essential Soviet sources to which the non-Russian-speaking reader has access.

Choice, 7(1970):1138.

432. Shapiro, Leonard, ed. **Soviet Treaty Series: A Collection of Bilateral Agreements and Conventions, etc., Concluded between the Soviet Union and Foreign Powers.** Washington, DC: Georgetown University Press, 1950-55. Vol. I: 1917-1928. 237p.; Vol. II: 1929-1939. 425p.

This collection is of unsurpassed value for the study of international affairs of the Soviet Union. It offers excerpts of all significant treaties.

433. Slusser, Robert M., and Triska, Jan F. **A Calendar of Soviet Treaties 1917-57.** Stanford, CA: Stanford University Press; London: Oxford University Press, 1959. 530p. $15.00.

An invaluable source for all students of Soviet affairs, this book consists of an elaborate calendar, not only of the treaties entered into by the Soviet regime, but of all other traceable international agreements to which the Soviet Union has been a party. References to the full text of treaties are indicated.
    SEER, 39:93:571.

434. Smith, C. Jay, Jr. **The Russian Struggle for Power, 1914-1917: A Study of Russian Foreign Policy during the First World War.** New York: Greenwood Press, 1969 (1956). 553p. $17.00.

Drawing extensively on a large number of documents from the Imperial Foreign Office, Smith has produced the first detailed account of Russia's diplomacy during 1914-17. He concentrates mainly on political issues, which reveal Russian aggressive aspirations. With its unsurpassed documentation, this book serves as a basic study of Russian wartime diplomacy.

435. Solzhenitsyn, Aleksandr I. **East and West: The Nobel Lecture on Literature, a World Split Apart, Letter to the Soviet Leaders, and an Interview with Aleksandr Solzhenitsyn by Janis Sapiets.** New York: Harper & Row, 1980. 182p. $1.95 pa.

This is a useful collection of public statements by Solzhenitsyn. The translations are accurate and readable and his pronouncements are directed at a mass audience.

436. Ulam, Adam B. **Expansion and Coexistence: The History of Soviet Foreign Policy, 1917-67.** New York: Praeger, 1968. 755p. 2d rev. and updated ed., 1974. $15.95.

Ulam has written an interpretive history, one in which the emphasis is on specific events, trends, external and internal circumstances, and the leaders who have made policy. Largely chronological in its basic organization, this study is a thorough and judicious presentation of information and an intelligible interpretation of Soviet foreign policy.
    SR, 29:4:482-83; PSQ, 90(1970):187.

437. Warth, Robert D. **Soviet Russia in World Politics.** New York: Twayne, 1963. 544p.

This work fills a gap in the literature on Soviet affairs with a running chronological narrative of Soviet Russia's foreign relations from the Revolution to 1962. The book is well suited for quick reference.
    AHR, 69:2:461-62.

438. Wesson, Robert G. **Soviet Foreign Policy in Perspective.** Homewood, IL: Dorsey Press; Georgetown, Ontario: Irwin-Dorsey Ltd., 1969. 472p. $9.50.

The discrepancy between ideology and practical foreign policy "outputs" in Soviet relations with the rest of the world is a major theme in this work. The resulting difficulties for Soviet foreign policy in many areas have been well documented by the author. The book attempts to deal with Soviet approaches to the world in terms of state interests. Its chief virtue is that it gives the broad lines of development of Soviet foreign policy.

SR, 30:1:157-59; Choice, 7(1970):607.

With the United States

439. Anderson, Terry H. **The United States, Great Britain, and the Cold War, 1944-1947.** Columbia, MO: University of Missouri Press, 1981. xiv, 256p. $18.00.

This is a novel approach to the discussion of the origins of the Cold War. While most historians focus on the Soviet Union and the United States to explain the evolving East-West conflict, Anderson concentrates on the role the British played to generate a joint British-American policy vis-à-vis the Soviet Union during the crucial 1944-47 era. He draws on British Foreign Office records and Cabinet papers that have recently been opened to the researcher.

NP, 10:2:260-61; AHR, 87:2:558.

440. Bennett, Edward M. **Recognition of Russia: An American Foreign Policy Dilemma.** Waltham, MA: Blaisdell Publishing Co., 1970. 232p. $2.95 pa.

Making excellent use of newly available source material, Bennett has retold the story with new insights and broad strokes of perceptive interpretation. Recognition of the USSR was necessary and beneficial. Its tragedy lay in the unfounded optimism that motivated many of the American negotiators—the folly of utopian hopes in dealing with the USSR.

SR, 30:2:400-1; AAPSS-A, 393(1971):132.

441. Bishop, Donald G. **The Roosevelt-Litvinov Agreements: The American View.** Syracuse, NY: Syracuse University Press, 1965. 297p. $7.50.

The author sets out to examine the extent to which the promises that Litvinov made to the United States at the time of recognition in November 1933 were implemented. Not surprisingly, he finds that "in the cases of the agreements on interference in internal affairs, legal rights of [American] nationals in the Soviet Union, and payment of the Soviet debts," the Soviets conspicuously failed to live up to their promises.

SR, 27:1:151-53; AHR, 71:2:518.

442. Bohlen, Charles E. **Witness to History, 1929-1969.** New York: W. W. Norton, 1973. 562p. $12.50.

This autobiographical account contains a wealth of incidents, details, and observations that contribute to the understanding of American-Soviet relations. The author also argues that a more realistic assessment of the Soviet Union by American policymakers, such as urged by himself, could not have made a great deal of difference whether in 1944-45 or in the late 1950s.

SR, 33:3:546-47.

443. Brzezinski, Zbigniew, and Huntington, Samuel P. **Political Power: USA/USSR.** New York: Viking Press, 1964. 461p. $7.50.

The authors answer three broad questions: (1) What are the principal similarities and differences between the Soviet and American political systems? (2) Are the two systems becoming more alike or less so? and (3) What are the strengths and weaknesses of each system? The authors conclude: "the Soviet and American systems are effective, authoritative, and stable, each in its own way." This is a pioneering work in comparative political analysis.

SR, 24:1:134-36; CH, 48(March 1965):175.

444.   Cate, Curtis. **The Ides of August: The Berlin Wall Crisis, 1961.** New York: M. Evans & Co., 1978. x, 534p. + 16pp. plates. Maps. $15.00.

Encouraged by the Bay of Pigs debacle, Khrushchev decided to end the unacceptable drain on East Germany's manpower, to end the exodus, and eventually to evict the Western powers from Berlin. While the Berlin wall was built, Western leaders remained unsure of what to do. The book deserves a wide readership, especially among young Americans, who do not know enough about the history of their country.

SR, 39:2:318-19; Choice, 16(1979):438.

445.   Davis, Lynn Etheridge. **The Cold War Begins: Soviet-American Conflicts over Eastern Europe.** Princeton, NJ: Princeton University Press, 1974. 427p. $15.00.

The slow but gradual erosion of U.S. influence in central-eastern Europe since 1945 is brilliantly described in this competent study of the tragic series of steps undertaken by the U.S. decision-makers, "utterly ignorant of Mackinder's classical dictum: "Who rules East Europe commands the Heartland; Who rules the Heartland commands the World Island; Who rules the World Island commands the World."

LJ, 100(1975):675; Choice, 12(1975):124.

446.   Deane, John R. **The Strange Alliance: The Story of Our Efforts at Wartime Co-operation with Russia.** Bloomington, IN: Indiana University Press, 1973. 344p. $3.50 pa.

General Deane served as head of the U.S. Military Mission to the USSR, and his account was published as long ago as 1946. The book shows the difficulty of any negotiation with the Soviet Union. Deane realized that concessions made to the Soviets did not earn gratefulness. On the contrary, they were to the Soviets a sign of weakness and resulted in demands for even more concessions. But a determined stand often resulted in a Soviet climb-down.

SEER, 53:132:467-68.

447.   Dinerstein, Herbert S. **The Making of a Missile Crisis: October 1962.** Baltimore and London: The Johns Hopkins University Press, 1976. xiv, 302p. $14.95.

According to Dinerstein, faulty perceptions, miscalculations, and varying theories within and among the three involved nations (USSR, Cuba, the United States) led to a situation that none of these three desired and all could have avoided. This book should be required reading for the student of world diplomacy and Russian, Latin American, and U.S. foreign policy.

SR, 36:1:109-10; AHR, 82:1:65.

448. Dobriansky, Lev E. **U.S.A. and the Soviet Myth**. Introduction by William G. Bray. Old Greenwich, CT: Devin-Adair, 1971. 274p. $6.50.
The main part of this work deals with the Soviet captive nations, with emphasis on Ukraine. Two chapters focus on the Captive Nations program in the United States; the next two analyze diplomatic traps dealing with Moscow; and the last chapter outlines the objectives and achievements of the Ukrainian Congress Committee of America. The author cites examples of shocking lack of knowledge in high circles about the nationality problem of the USSR.
    MA, 16:(Spring 1972):209.

449. Eidelberg, Paul. **Beyond Détente: Toward an American Foreign Policy**. La Salle, IL: Sherwood Sugden & Company, 1977. xvi, 255p. $12.95.
The author of this book is convinced that America's drift toward military weakness has destroyed U.S. will and reduced its interest in confronting the expansion of Soviet influence around the globe. He asserts that détente has destroyed the will of the United States to protect the world against Soviet encroachments.
    SR, 38:2:308-9; JP, 39(1977):1147.

450. Elliot, Mark R. **Pawns of Yalta: Soviet Refugees and America's Role in Their Repatriation**. Urbana, IL, Chicago, and London: University of Illinois Press, 1982. xiii, 287p. Illustrations. Tables. $17.95.
It is seldom realized that the American government, by agreement at Yalta, helped to condemn millions of Soviet refugees to imprisonment or death by forcibly returning them to Soviet Russia after World War II. Primarily out of fear for the safety of twenty-four thousand American servicemen in Soviet-controlled territory, Roosevelt agreed to repatriate the more than two million Soviet refugees behind American lines. Elliot has drawn on declassified sources in documenting the American involvement in Soviet repatriation.
    SS, 35:2:251-53; NP, 11:2:334.

451. Epstein, Julius. **Operation Keelhaul: The Story of Forced Repatriation from 1944 to the Present**. Introduction by Bertram D. Wolfe. Old Greenwich, CT: Devin-Adair, 1973. 255p. $8.95.
The book begins with the story of a Lithuanian seaman, Simas Kudirka, who in 1970 made a dramatic leap to freedom from a Soviet ship onto the deck of a U.S. Coast Guard cutter in American waters. The bulk of the volume treats the forcible repatriation by British, American, and French armies of hundreds of thousands of refugees from the occupied zones of Germany and Austria, a shameful sequel to and by-product of the alliance between the Western democracies and the Soviet totalitarian regime.
    BS, 33(Feb. 1974):499.

452. Farnsworth, Beatrice. **William C. Bullitt and the Soviet Union**. Bloomington, IN: Indiana University Press, 1967. 244p. $7.50.
At the age of twenty-eight, the late W. C. Bullitt obtained a place on the American delegation to the Paris Peace Conference, where he maneuvered a mission to interview the new leaders of Soviet Russia. In the FDR administration he helped arrange the recognition of Russia in 1933, and was rewarded with the ambassadorship to the Soviet Union.
    SR, 27:4:657; Choice, 4(1967):1164.

453. Friedland, Edward; Seabury, Paul; and Wildavsky, Aaron. **The Great Détente: Oil and the Decline of American Foreign Policy.** New York: Basic Books, 1975. x, 210p. $7.95.

The three authors are upset about the position of the United States in the world as a result of U.S.-Soviet détente and the oil crisis of 1973-74. They conclude that the Soviet Union, taking advantage of the West's myopia about détente and inability to define and defend its own vital interests, is making uncontested gains so that the choice must now be made between defense and surrender, between order and disorder.

SR, 35:3:536-37; JP, 38(1976):508.

454. Gaddis, John Lewis. **Russia, the Soviet Union and the United States: An Interpretive History.** New York, Santa Barbara, CA, Toronto: John Wiley & Sons, 1978. xiii, 309p.

This well-informed account of the relations between two powers from the time of the American Revolution contains two main themes: (1) that the relations of the powers have been far better than is generally believed, and (2) that conflict arose only when an ideological factor was imposed upon these relations.

AHR, 83:5:1364.

455. Gaddis, John Lewis. **The United States and the Origins of the Cold War, 1941-47.** New York: Columbia University Press, 1972. 396p. £9.20. (Contemporary American History Series.)

The strength of this most interesting work on the origins of the Cold War lies in careful research, superb organization, and good writing. The book offers both the student and the layman a wealth of clearly presented information. The author claims that economics played only a minimal role and that American public opinion was the key determinant in American policy toward the Soviets.

SEER, 58:3:450-51; JP, 35(1973):785.

456. Harriman, W. Averell. **America and Russia in a Changing World: Half a Century of Personal Observation.** Introduction by Arthur M. Schlesinger, Jr. Garden City, NY: Doubleday, 1971. 218p. $5.95.

This volume includes Harriman's three lectures delivered at Lehigh University in 1970 and focuses mainly on the past fifty years of Soviet-American relations as seen by a statesman who himself was actively involved in the formulation and execution of U.S. policy.

APSR, 66(Dec. 1972):407.

457. Harriman, W. Averell, and Abel, Elie. **Special Envoy to Churchill and Stalin, 1941-1946.** New York: Random House, 1975. xii, 595p. + 16pp. photographs. $15.00.

This is a well-written, familiar story of the Big Three relationships during World War II, told from Harriman's angle of vision. What is new in this book is the insight into Harriman's own character and the tart judgments he makes of the men with whom he worked. He presents himself as a vigorous man of action and sound judgment, skilled in diplomacy. Of Stalin he says: "I found him better informed than

Roosevelt, more realistic than Churchill, in some ways the most effective of the war leaders."

SR, 36:2:307-8; AHR, 81:3:999; Choice, 13(1978):260.

458.   Herring, George C., Jr. **Aid to Russia, 1941-46: Strategy, Diplomacy, the Origins of the Cold War.** New York: Columbia University Press, 1973. 365p. $15.00. (Contemporary American History Series.)

The author presents a realistic picture of the place of lend-lease aid to the USSR in the policy of the United States. His fundamental thesis is that lend-lease for the USSR and Britain was intended mainly to facilitate the victory over Germany and was to terminate with the end of hostilities. Herring maintains that no amount of American aid to the Soviet Union could have brought about major Soviet concessions, particularly in east-central Europe.

SR, 33:2:364-65; AAPSS-A, 413(May 1974):178.

459.   Horelik, Arnold L., and Rush, Myron. **Strategic Power and Soviet Foreign Policy.** Chicago: University of Chicago Press, 1966. 255p. $5.95.

The authors hold it to be crucial for the United States to maintain a margin of superiority large enough to offer hope of deterring not only war, but also "the dangerous employment of Soviet strategic power for political ends." The result of their study is well worth equally careful consideration.

RR, 26:1:93-94; APSR, 61(1967):836; Choice, 3(1966):959.

460.   Hurewitz, J. C., ed. **Soviet-American Rivalry in the Middle East.** New York: Praeger, 1969. 250p. $7.00.

This collection of essays by prominent specialists in Soviet and Middle Eastern affairs is divided into four parts dealing with the topics "Struggle for Military Supremacy," "Economic Competition in the 1970s," "Cultural Contest," and "Quest for Stability." Most of the contributors take a pessimistic view of the possibility of a superpower détente in the Middle East and, by implication, in the rest of the world as well.

SR, 29:3:536-37; RQ, 10(Fall 1970):87.

461.   Jones, Robert Huhn. **The Roads to Russia: United States Lend-Lease to the Soviet Union.** Foreword by Edgar L. Erickson. Norman: University of Oklahoma Press, 1969. 326p. $6.95.

This is a documented account of U.S. lend-lease to Russia. The study uses U.S. presidential papers, government reports, memoirs, and press accounts, with occasional references to a few standard official Soviet sources, to compile a narrative of U.S. efforts to aid a suspicious and ungrateful ally.

SR, 29:2:327-28.

462.   Kennan, George F. **Soviet-American Relations, 1917-1920.** Vol. I: **Russia Leaves the War.** Vol. II: **The Decision to Intervene.** Princeton, NJ: Princeton University Press, 1956-1958; New York: Atheneum, 1967. Vol. I: 544p.; Vol. II: 513p. Paper $3.95 each.

These two volumes, along with the author's numerous other contributions, are among the finest works on the study of American policy toward Soviet Russia. All students of Soviet affairs and those in international diplomacy should be familiar with Kennan's works.

BRD, May 1958.

463. Larson, Thomas B. **Soviet-American Rivalry.** New York and Toronto: W. W. Norton and George J. McLeod, 1978. xii, 308p. $13.95.
Larson, a veteran State Department official, has written an excellent study of the complex relationship between Moscow and Washington. It is a sophisticated investigation of their interactions in the economic, ideological, military, political, and diplomatic arenas. The information on a wide range of topics contained in his book will be useful to students, businessmen, and political leaders.

SR, 38:3:497-98; Choice, 15(1979):1588.

464. Lenczowski, John. **Soviet Perception of U.S. Foreign Policy: A Study of Ideology, Power, and Consensus.** Ithaca, NY, and London: Cornell University Press, 1982. 318p. $25.00.
This volume includes an imposing array of Soviet monographic literature, particularly the considerable output of the Institute of the USA and Canada. The author casts a new light on the "realist-traditionalist" dichotomy in Soviet writing on the United States. The study is useful as a remedy for excessive "mirror imaging," or the derivation of Soviet views from the American experience.

465. Libbey, James K. **Alexander Gumberg and Soviet-American Relations, 1917-1933.** Lexington: The University Press of Kentucky, 1977. xii, 229p. $13.50.
Alexander Gumberg was closely associated with the well-known group of colorful Americans in Russia during 1917 to 1918, and also with Americans prominent in business and politics during 1921 to 1933. The author has consulted Gumberg's and other private papers for further information on the role played by Gumberg. He was born in Russia and immigrated to the United States in 1902. His two brothers were Bolsheviks and occupied high positions in Soviet Russia.

SR, 37:2:299; Choice, 15(1978):935.

466. Lukas, Richard C. **Eagles East: The Army Air Forces and the Soviet Union, 1941-45.** Tallahassee: Florida State University, 1970. 256p. $10.00.
This study sketches the story of American supply of military aircraft to the Soviet Union under lend-lease, and the use of Soviet bases by American bombers. The study illustrates in many specific ways how American military assistance to the Soviet Union for political and military reasons interacted with other military and a variety of bureaucratic and political problems.

SR, 30:4:895-96; Choice, 8(1971):1370.

467. Maddux, Thomas R. **Years of Estrangement: American Relations with the Soviet Union, 1933-1941.** Tallahassee: Florida State University, 1980. ix, 238p. $15.00.

This account of U.S.-Soviet relations during the "years of estrangement" effectively captures the conflict between the two governments, along with the inconsistent policies that resulted from the fact that neither country's wartime approach succeeded in fully displacing the other. The result: a set of wartime agreements, concluded by Roosevelt, that Moscow would be very unlikely to keep.

 RR, 40:1:65-66; JAH, 67:3:961.

468. Mayer, Arno J. **Wilson vs. Lenin: Political Origins of the New Diplomacy, 1917-1918.** Cleveland, OH: World Publishing Co., 1964. 435p.

Mayer's study provides, for the Soviet specialist, a broader perspective in which to place Lenin's early diplomatic moves. He suggests that a full-length parallel biographical work on Wilson and Lenin might be enlightening.

 SR, 24:1:121-23.

469. Paterson, Thomas G. **Soviet-American Confrontation: Postwar Reconstruction and the Origins of the Cold War.** Baltimore: Johns Hopkins University Press, 1973. 287p. $12.00.

The book is based on an exhaustive research of sources and unpublished manuscripts, but without the benefit of Soviet material. The author's political credo is manifest in the study. The book deserves the attention of the student and lay reader alike for its excellent bibliographic essay on unpublished manuscripts and as an example of an ideologically confused interpretation of events.

 JAH, 61:3:636; LJ, 99(1974):60; Choice, 11(1974):1208.

470. Pipes, Richard. **U.S.-Soviet Relations in the Era of Détente.** Boulder, CO: Westview Press, 1981. 228p. $25.00.

Pipes offers eight of his most important papers in this collection. He concentrates on the constants that form the bedrock of Soviet policy, its psychological, historical, and cultural foundations, its techniques, and the Soviet variant of a policy of détente. Pipes argues that the underlying strategy of Soviet foreign and military policy is deeply rooted in Russian history. The tactics of Soviet détente is to undertake a major rearmament program and, at the same time, to seek nuclear superiority to obtain Western compliance.

 AAPSS-A, 462(1982):159.

471. Roberts, Henry L. **Russia and America.** New York: Harper, 1956. 251p.

The theme of the book is the question, What policy should the United States pursue regarding Communist totalitarianism in the nuclear age? The author has no doubt that even in this age America must, if necessary, be prepared to accept general war to prevent the worldwide establishment of Communism. This stimulating and expert presentation of a timely topic is well suited for classroom discussion.

 SR, 16:1:82-83.

472. Rummel, R.J. **Peace Endangered: The Reality of Détente.** Beverly Hills, CA, and London: Sage, 1976. x, 189p. $10.00.

This study focuses on the U.S.-Soviet military balance and its effect on American interests and will. For Rummel, a successful deterrent requires the prevention of Soviet first-strike capability, power to cover all danger spots, and conventional forces of sufficient strength to deter or win a local war without resorting to nuclear weapons. He believes that détente was based on false assumptions, and it placed the United States in a position of military inferiority.

> SR, 38:2:308-9; Choice, 14(1977):267.

473. Slusser, Robert M. **The Berlin Crisis of 1961: Soviet-American Relations and the Struggle for Power in the Kremlin, June-November 1961.** Baltimore: Johns Hopkins University Press, 1973. 509p. $17.50.

Slusser has written a detailed, closely argued, day-to-day monograph on the 1961 stage of the Berlin crisis. He concentrates on continuing factional divisions in the Soviet leadership with respect to the Soviet handling of the crisis, centering on the rivalry between Khrushchev and Kozlov, who took a more hostile line toward the West. The book is of interest to students of the Khrushchev and Kennedy era.

> JP, 36(1974):233; APSR, 68(1974):1410.

474. Taubman, William. **Stalin's American Policy: From Entente to Détente to Cold War.** New York and London: W. W. Norton, 1982. xii, 291p. $18.95.

The narrative spans the period from the German invasion of the USSR in 1941 to Stalin's death in 1953. Taubman states the thesis that, to Stalin and also to his predecessors and successors, "détente was a recurring aspiration of Soviet diplomacy." He emphasizes the continuity of Stalin's policies with those of Lenin and Brezhnev and stresses that the Soviet leaders are taking economic and political advantage of the conflicts within and among capitalist countries, as well as of the sheer ignorance and ineptitude of their adversaries.

> SR, 42:2:292-93.

475. Ulam, Adam B. **The Rivals: America and Russia since World War II.** New York: Viking Press, 1971. 405p. $10.95.

In this volume the author elaborates an approach voiced earlier in his *Expansion and Coexistence,* with greater stress on the American side. It is a personal narrative—always informed, often clever, sometimes elegant—somewhat condescending, barely tolerant of human foibles. It is much like a series of lectures to Harvard undergraduates. It will provoke both approval and annoyance, which is a good test of a fine book. Ulam is best in laying bare the American misjudgment of Soviet intentions and capabilities. He is concerned primarily with power and politics. He recognizes but slights the strategic and economic factors, and he ignores ideology altogether. And he fails to explore alternative Soviet and American conceptions of the outside world—their roots and implications.

> SR, 31:2:434-35; Choice, 8(1972):1626.

476. Weeks, Albert L. **The Troubled Détente.** Introduction by Gene Sosin. New York: New York University Press, 1976. xxiv, 190p. $10.00.

The author traces, from Lenin to the mid-1970s, largely familiar aspects of Soviet doctrine on relations with capitalist countries. His emphasis is on continuing, underlying elements, though he notes fluctuations in operational Soviet policies over the decades. He provides a useful updating through the Twenty-Fifth Party Congress.

SR, 37:2:303-4; LJ, 102(1977):1024; Choice, 14(1977):1281.

477. Wildavsky, Aaron, ed. **Beyond Containment: Alternative American Policies toward the Soviet Union.** San Francisco, CA: ICS Press, 1983. 270p.
This study provides a comprehensive view of containment and its major alternatives. Each contributor proposes a somewhat different strategy, and their prescriptions range from the status quo to more "activist" alternatives, such as providing U.S. support for anti-Communist insurgent movements, refusing to subsidize the Soviet economy, and attempting to "pluralize" the Soviet empire.

478. Wilson, Joan Hoff. **Ideology and Economics: U.S. Relations with the Soviet Union, 1918-1933.** Columbia, MO: University of Missouri Press, 1974. 192p. $10.00.
This study provides a solid background for the understanding of FDR's decision to extend diplomatic recognition to the USSR. The author discusses the attitudes prevalent within the American government and business circles toward trade with the Soviet Union. She concludes that on this issue the business community was rather divided and there was no coordination between economic and foreign policy, a fact that remains an endemic weakness of U.S. policy toward the USSR.

AHR, 80:4:1056; JAH, 62(1975):453.

479. Yergin, Daniel. **Shattered Peace: The Origins of the Cold War and the Security State.** Boston: Houghton Mifflin, 1977. xii, 526p. $15.00.
This thoroughly researched book covers the years between the Yalta conference and the Berlin blockade that marked the end of the wartime alliance. It contains dozens of interviews and unpublished private papers, many of which provide new information. Yergin believes the Soviet Union should be seen as a revolutionary state that denies the possibility of coexistence and aims at world mastery.

SR, 38:1:117-18; AHR, 83:1:297.

With Western and Third World Countries

480. Albright, David E., ed. **Communism in Africa.** Bloomington and London: Indiana University Press, 1980. vii, 278p. $12.95.
The marked intensification of Moscow's intrusion into Africa during the 1970s has revived interest in the role the Soviet Union is playing on that continent. This collection of essays by American rather than African authors is a product of this renewed concern. The book focuses on "the dynamics of Soviet-African relations" and particularly on the USSR's priorities, objectives, and strategy in Africa.

CSP, 23:3:362-63; APSR, 75:1:259.

481. Arnold, Anthony. **Afghanistan: The Soviet Invasion in Perspective.** Stanford, CA: Hoover Institution Press, 1981. 126p. $9.95.
Arnold pieces together the fragments of information in a convincing and subtle fashion and argues the case for Soviet complicity in the Communist coup in Kabul in April 1978. The book briefly examines the relationship between Russia and

Afghanistan in the nineteenth century and the first half of the twentieth century, and then focuses on the economic and military relationship from 1953 onward.
SS, 34:3:454-55.

482.   Atkin, Muriel. **Russia and Iran, 1780-1828.** Minneapolis, University of Minnesota Press, 1980. xvi, 216p. Maps. $20.00.
The author presents a detailed discussion of Russian policy-making and military activities, along with the situation of the Iranian monarchy and the work of British and French military and diplomatic missions in Iran. This work breaks new ground as a useful contribution to the history of Russia's frontiers in Asia.
LJBR(1980):178; Choice, 19(1981):548.

483.   Carr, Edward Hallet. **German-Soviet Relations between the Two World Wars, 1919-1939.** New York: Harper & Row, c. 1951. 146p.
The British historian presents his view on German-Soviet relations in a lucid and altogether excellent survey. The lay reader and college student will be especially rewarded by this narrative.

484.   Clissold, Stephen, ed. **Soviet Relations with Latin America, 1918-1968: A Documentary Survey.** Issued under the auspices of the Royal Institute of International Affairs. London: Oxford University Press, 1970. 313p. $12.00.
The purpose of this collection of documents is to assist experts investigating Soviet foreign policy toward Latin American countries. As stated in the introduction, "the documents included in this volume have been drawn from a wide range of Soviet and Latin American sources, some of them readily accessible, others—from the Comintern and Latin American Communist sources—less so."
APSR, 65(1971):581; Choice, 7(1971):1558.

485.   Cohn, Helen Desfosses. **Soviet Policy toward Black Africa: The Focus on National Integration.** Foreword by John N. Hazard. New York: Praeger, 1972. 316p. $17.50. (Praeger Special Studies in International Politics and Public Affairs.)
The study is one of a number of bibliographic essays analyzing Soviet works on Africa. The emphasis is on the Brezhnev period and usefully brings some of the earlier studies up to date. The author has thoroughly documented her basic thesis that pragmatism has replaced ideological considerations and that Soviet writers are increasingly less optimistic about the immediate future of Africa.
SR, 32:4:824; Choice, 10(1973):178.

486.   Confino, Michael, and Shamir, Shimon, eds. **The U.S.S.R. and the Middle East.** New York: John Wiley; Jerusalem: Israel University Press, 1973. 441p.
This collection of twenty papers, presented at an international symposium in Tel Aviv in 1971, is devoted to an examination of the Soviet presence in the Middle East. The book is significant not only for its contents but also as an illustration of the limits of our understanding of Soviet motives and objectives after almost twenty years of Moscow's active involvement in the region.
SR, 33:2:371-72; Choice, 10(1973):1631.

487.   Dallin, David J. **Soviet Russia and the Far East.** Hamden, CT: Archon Books, 1972 (1948). 398p. $12.25.

Dallin sees Soviet policy toward China, Japan, and Korea during the years 1931-47 as a pattern of Communist imperialism resulting from its long-range planning, fifth-column infiltration, and ruthless suppression of any opposition in its march toward world domination. In this regard, little has changed since 1948, and Dallin's perceptive view is valid today as well. The author regards U.S. diplomacy and foreign policy as lacking in ability to comprehend the complexities involved.

488.   Darch, Colin. **A Soviet View of Africa: An Annotated Bibliography on Ethiopia, Somalia and Djibouti.** Boston: G. K. Hall, 1980. xxxvi, 200p. $30.00.

This excellent bibliography deals with the Soviet Union's African policy. The emphasis is on original materials in print. In his introduction the author summarizes with critical sympathy the contributions of Soviet observers and their forerunners under the tsars. The bulk of the material refers to Ethiopia proper, although some interesting items are recorded for Somalia.
    SR, 40:4:654; BL, 77(1981):770.

489.   Dawisha, Karen. **Soviet Foreign Policy towards Egypt.** London: Macmillan, 1979. 271p. £12.00.

The author first describes and then analyzes Soviet-Egyptian relations with painstaking thoroughness. A detailed chronology of Soviet-Egyptian relations presents an accurate account of the arduous course of Soviet foreign policy with respect to Egypt. This work is replete with illuminating tables and figures, well placed to help the reader through the complex economic and military data.
    SS, 32:3:434-35; Choice, 16(1979):1352.

490.   DePorte, A. W. **Europe between the Superpowers: The Enduring Balance.** New Haven and London: Yale University Press, 1979. xvi, 256p. $18.50.

This is an excellent work, tightly argued and written in a lively style. It provides the best exposition of how the Euratlantik system came into being after World War II, why it appears strong, and why it apparently continues to grow. This is a timely contribution to the debate over the Western response to Soviet expansion in the Third World.
    SR, 39:4:688-89; APSR, 74(1980):580.

491.   Donaldson, Robert H. **Soviet Policy toward India: Ideology and Strategy.** Cambridge, MA: Harvard University Press, 1974. xiv, 338p. $15.00.

The study focuses on Soviet efforts to bring about changes in Marxist-Leninist doctrine to suit their changing postures toward India. The author believes that considerations of Soviet national interests, rather than those of ideology, have determined Moscow's policy toward India. The book adds immensely to the understanding of Moscow's efforts to reinterpret Marxism-Leninism in order to justify or support changes in foreign policy.
    SR, 36:2:316; Choice, 12(1975):596.

492.   Donaldson, Robert H., ed. **The Soviet Union in the Third World: Successes and Failures.** Boulder, CO: Westview Press; London: Croom Helm, 1981. xiv, 458p. $25.00.

The volume stems from a conference at which twenty specialists contributed papers covering Latin America to Asia and considering issues from the political and economic to the purely military. Some chapters contain interesting tables on the economic and military instruments of Soviet policy. Soviet military aid and trade is now taking over from economic, with arms sales bringing in hard currency or scarce products.

SS, 34:1:128-30; APSR, 75(1981):1103.

493. Dyck, Harvey L. **Weimar Germany and Soviet Russia, 1926-1933: A Study in Diplomatic Instability**. New York: Columbia University Press, 1966. 279p. $6.75.

The two countries were tied together by their hostility toward the order established by the Versailles Treaty; their economic needs were satisfied to a considerable extent by mutual trade; their security interests were to be met by secret military cooperation; and their designs against Poland were only an outgrowth of the Romanov-Hohenzollern policy of Poland's partition.

RR, 26:3:302-3; AHR, 72:3:964; Choice, 4(1967):894.

494. Freund, Gerald. **Unholy Alliance**. New York: Harcourt, Brace, 1957. 283p. $6.00.

This study provides the fullest account to date of German-Russian relations in the period from the Treaty of Brest-Litovsk to the Treaty of Berlin, 1918-26. The author throws new light on these relations. Students of international affairs should not overlook this title.

JMH, 30:4:378-79.

495. Ginsburgs, George, and Rubinstein, Alvin Z., eds. **Soviet Foreign Policy toward Western Europe**. New York and London: Praeger Publishers, 1978. viii, 295p. $20.00. (Praeger Special Studies.)

This book is divided into four sections. The first is the editors' introduction. The second examines the nations of Western Europe individually and by regions in order to assess the extent to which "Finlandization" is present. The third section addresses the basic functional relationship affecting Soviet-West European relations, and the final section addresses the implications for U.S. foreign policy.

SR, 39:4:690-91; Choice, 16(1979):144.

496. Glassman, Jon D. **Arms for the Arabs: The Soviet Union and War in the Middle East**. Baltimore and London: The Johns Hopkins University Press, 1975. x, 243p. $12.50.

The author examines the strategy behind, and the motivation for, the Soviet arms shipment to the Middle East. He traces involvement through the Arab-Israeli wars, cataloging all known information on this matter. His comment that "Moscow will continue to play an   important political-military role in the region" is borne out by recent developments.

SR, 35:4:739-40; LJ, 101(1976):820; Choice, 13(1976):717.

497. Golan, Galia. **Yom Kippur and After: The Soviet Union and the Middle East Crisis**. New York and London: Cambridge University Press, 1977. ix, 350p. $18.95.

Golan has produced a detailed and interesting survey of many of the factors leading to the October 1973 Yom Kippur war. She places the Middle East developments in the perspective of Soviet global economic, strategic, ideological, and political interests. Golan does very well in developing the factors that tend to negate Soviet foreign policy objectives in the Middle East. Anyone interested in world events should read her book.

 CSP, 20:2:265-66; JP, 40(1978):563.

498. Hammond, Thomas T. **Red Flag over Afghanistan: The Communist Coup, the Soviet Invasion, and the Consequences.** Boulder, CO: Westview Press, 1983. 250p. $25.00.

Hammond focuses on the Communist seizure of power in Afghanistan, the disastrous policies of the various Communist leaders, and Soviet tactics and strategy in Afghanistan and the Gulf. He makes extensive use of previously classified documents that not only provide facts about events in Afghanistan, but also trace the development of U.S. policy toward the country. The book benefits from the author's interviews with former U.S. officials who helped to formulate policy toward Afghanistan and the USSR.

499. Horn, Robert C. **Soviet-Indian Relations.** New York: Praeger Publishers, 1983. 254p. $25.95.

This chronologically organized study begins with the year 1969 and brings the analysis of the influence relationship up to the present. Drawing extensively on numerous sources, Horn launches a thorough investigation to identify the crucial issue areas in Soviet-Indian relations. Throughout, the internal developments and foreign policy of each country are used as a backdrop.

500. Jain, R. K. **Soviet South Asian Relations, 1947-1978. Vol. 1: The Kashmir Question, 1952-1964. The Kutch Conflict of 1965. Bangladesh Crisis and Indo-Pak War of 1971. India.** Vol. 2: **Pakistan, Bangladesh, Nepal, Sri Lanka.** Atlantic Highlands, NJ, and Boston: Humanities Press, 1979. Vol. 1: xx, 602p.; Vol. 2: xx, 459p. $20.00 each.

This is a unique and valuable collection of documents and other data essential to the understanding of recent diplomacy in South Asia. Originally published in India, it is now available in this American edition.

 Choice, 16(1979):1353.

501. Joshi, Nirmala. **Foundations of Indo-Soviet Relations: A Study of Non-Official Attitudes and Contacts, 1917-1947.** Foreword by Y. B. Chavan. New Delhi: Radiant Publishers, 1975. xiv, 204p. Rs. 30.00.

The "Russian menace" was never taken seriously by Indian nationalists, who viewed it as a British ploy to preserve hegemony in India. The Indian image of the Soviet Union was not, however, entirely an uncritical one. The major leaders of the Indian Left were democrats who were repelled by the suppression of civil liberties, and they became progressively disillusioned with Soviet foreign policy after the signing of the 1939 Nazi-Soviet pact.

 SR, 36:1:125-26.

502. Jukes, Geoffrey. **The Soviet Union in Asia**. Berkeley: University of California Press, 1973. 304p. $8.75.

The book consists of a general study of Soviet interests in the Asian area on a broad basis, both inside and outside the Soviet borders. Recommended for the general reader and public at large.

SR, 33:2:368-69; CH, 67(Oct. 1974):177.

503. Kanet, Roger E., ed. **The Soviet Union and the Developing Nations**. Baltimore: Johns Hopkins University Press, 1974. 302p. $12.50.

This collection of ten articles, written by various authors specializing in Soviet foreign policy, surveys the Soviet Union's current policies toward the Third World. The result is a loosely organized summary of Soviet attitudes and policies toward the Third World, useful primarily for the classroom.

SR, 34:1:163-64; JP, 37(1975):325.

504. Kapur, Harish. **Soviet Russia and Asia 1917-1927: A Study of Soviet Policy toward Turkey, Iran and Afghanistan**. New York: Humanities Press, 1967. 266p. $8.50.

The study covers the first decade of Soviet Russian relations with the three border states of the non-Arabic Middle East. The bulk of the work deals with Soviet-Turkish relations. Another part is devoted to Soviet-Iranian relations, and a small chapter to Soviet-Afghanistan affairs.

SR, 27:1:152-53; AHR, 73:5:1480.

505. Kapur, Harish. **The Soviet Union and the Emerging Nations: A Case Study of Soviet Policy towards India**. London: Michael Joseph, for the Graduate Institute of International Studies, Geneva, 1972. Distributed by Humanities Press, New York. 124p. $10.50.

The study does not provide a detailed analysis of Soviet policy toward India; rather, the author pinpoints certain aspects of Soviet and Indian policies often neglected by other scholars and offers some interesting and provocative interpretations. Soviet policy toward India was an effort to prevent the Communist leadership in Asia from passing into Chinese hands.

SR, 33:2:369-70; Choice, 10:(1973):184.

506. Klinghoffer, Arthur Jay. **The Angolan War: A Study in Soviet Policy in the Third World**. Boulder, CO: Westview Press, 1980. 231p. $23.75.

This first study discusses both the Soviet and the Cuban involvement in Angola and assesses the decisive change in Soviet foreign policy that contributed to the reevaluation of détente by the United States. The author addresses key questions in regard to Soviet involvement in Angola and its relationship to U.S. policy in Africa.

JP, 44(1982):303.

507. Klinghoffer, Arthur Jay. **Soviet Perspectives on African Socialism**. Rutherford, NJ: Fairleigh Dickinson University Press, 1969. 276p. $8.00.

This is a study in detail of the Soviet attitude toward the various strains of African socialism and Soviet interpretations of developments in Africa from 1955 to 1964.

The guidelines for the Soviet line on Africa were set by Khrushchev, and it was left to the African Institute of the Soviet Academy of Science to justify and explain Khrushchev's pronouncements in the light of Marxism-Leninism and to adapt them to African developments.

SR, 29:1:142-43; APSR, 64(1970):212.

508. Kochan, Lionel E. **Russia and the Weimar Republic.** Cambridge, England: Bowes & Bowes, 1954; New York: Praeger, 1955. 190p.

The book deals with diplomatic and military relations as well as with the relations between the Communist International and the Communist Party of Germany (KPD). An excellent bibliography is included.

509. Kohler, Foy D., et al. **The Soviet Union and the October 1973 Middle East War: The Implications for Détente.** Coral Gables, FL: Center for Advanced International Studies, University of Miami, 1974. 131p.

Kohler, Leon Goure, and Mose L. Harvey discuss the tough policy pursued by the USSR in the Middle East crisis, which, perhaps for the first time, revealed to the world how Moscow sees the meaning of détente. This case study should receive close attention from politicians and interested lay readers for its relevance to contemporary Soviet strategy.

Choice, 12(1975):143.

510. Korbel, Joseph. **Détente in Europe: Real or Imaginary?** Princeton, NJ: Princeton University Press, 1972. 302p. $10.00.

The author examines the underlying question of East-West relations, the meaning of détente. Although the book is by intent an essay, it is substantially a review of the European scene in the 1960s. Korbel concludes that either détente will be successful in breaking down the secretiveness of the East or it will lull the West into a potentially catastrophic complacency.

CSP, 26:4:660-61; LJ, 98(1973):1594; Choice, 9(1972):1355.

511. Landis, Lincoln. **Politics and Oil: Moscow in the Middle East.** New York: Dunellen Publishing Co., 1973. 201p. $12.95.

Landis sees Russian barter arrangements for the importation of Iraqui petroleum and Iranian natural gas as ominous portents of a dark future for the West. He asserts that these economic arrangements are but an interim stage in Moscow's long-range design for domination of the Middle East. If successful, "Moscow would expect eventually to achieve a position of strategic economic dominance over the Middle East" and a "level of political authority as predominant power" in the region.

SR, 33:4:783-84; Choice, 11(1974):510.

512. Laquer, Walter. **Russia and Germany: A Century of Conflict.** Boston: Little, Brown, 1965. 367p. $6.75.

This volume consists of a series of papers dealing with key episodes and problems. The book's emphasis centers around "a study in mutual misunderstanding," and while this phrase may apply to the years before the First World War and to those following the Second, it is to the interwar period that the author devotes major attention.

RR, 25:4:413-14; AHR, 71:4:1323.

513.   Legvold, Robert. **Soviet Policy in West Africa.** Cambridge, MA: Harvard University Press, 1970. 372p. $13.00.

This study analyzes the evolution and shifts in the USSR's relations with six West African states–Ghana, Guinea, the Ivory Coast, Mali, Nigeria, and Senegal–between 1957 and 1968. The author points out the initial unfounded optimism of the Soviets about their opportunities in such "radical" states as Guinea, Ghana, and Mali. This book deserves wide circulation in public libraries and government offices, and among students and teachers.

      SR, 30:3:674; APSR, 65(1971):877.

514.   Lensen, George Alexander. **Japanese Recognition of the U.S.S.R.: Soviet–Japanese Relations, 1921-1930.** Tokyo: Sophia University, in cooperation with The Diplomatic Press, Tallahassee, FL, 1970. 419p. $15.00.

The author painstakingly traces a series of attempts by the Japanese and Soviet governments to resume diplomatic relations following the Japanese intervention in Siberia. These efforts finally resulted in Japanese recognition of the Soviet Union in 1925. Suspicion and mistrust rather than friendship characterized Japanese-Soviet relations for the remainder of the decade. Strictly speaking, this book is a history of Japanese-Soviet negotiations; the author chose to limit himself to describing the events in the conference rooms.

      SR, 30:2:399-400; Choice, 7(1971):1716.

515.   Lensen, George Alexander. **The Strange Neutrality: Soviet-Japanese Relations during the Second World War, 1941-1945.** Tallahassee, FL: The Diplomatic Press, 1972. 332p. $15.00.

Lensen's use of both the principal languages of his subject and his fondness for finding new sources have enabled him to include sources not yet available for general circulation, which the Japanese Foreign Office has permitted him to use without specific citation and which appear in footnotes only as "classified." The narrative is, to a great extent, an analysis of these sources, reinforced by a variety of secondary accounts.

      SR, 32:2:391-92; Choice, 9(1973):1488.

516.   Maude, George. **The Finnish Dilemma: Neutrality in the Shadow of Power.** London: Oxford University Press, published for the Institute of International Affairs, 1976. vi, 153p. $13.25.

This well-written and instructive book deals with Finland's intricate connections with her neighbor, the Soviet Union. Maude presents Finnish neutrality against the background of a brief outline of Finland's modern history and concentrates on Soviet-Finnish relations.

      SR, 36:2:304; Choice, 14(1977):928.

517.   Morley, James William, ed. **Deterrent Diplomacy: Japan, Germany, and the USSR, 1935-1940.** Selected translations from *Taiheiyō sensō e no Michi: Kaisen Gaikō Shi.* New York: Columbia University Press, 1976. xii, 363p. $17.50. (Japan's Road to Pacific War Series, vol. 1.)

Three essays by distinguished Japanese scholars are assembled in this study. "The Anti-Comintern Pact, 1935-1939," "The Japanese-Soviet Confrontation, 1935-1939," and "The Tripartite Pact, 1939-1940" are based on published and unpublished Japanese sources, and their publication makes valuable information available to Western students of this period.

SR, 37:3:501-2; Choice, 14(1977):730.

518. Pennar, Jaan. **The U.S.S.R. and the Arabs: The Ideological Dimension.** New York: Crane, Russak, 1973. 180p. $9.75.

Proceeding from the assumption that ideology is an "indivisible component of the power struggle" in the international system, Pennar sets out to illustrate its significance in a case study devoted to Soviet-Arab relations. The various chapters trace the evolution of Communist theories on "national liberation" and the "noncapitalist path" of development, supplemented by a discussion of the ideological interaction between Moscow and Nasser, the Ba'th, and the Algerian FLN. In emphasizing the basic long-range incompatibility of Soviet and Arab nationalist interests—incompatibility which emerges particularly clearly in their ideological controversies—the author has performed a valuable service.

SR, 33:4:783; Choice, 11(1974):163.

519. Ra'anan, Uri. **The USSR Arms the Third World: Case Studies in Soviet Foreign Policy.** Cambridge, MA: MIT Press, 1969. 256p. $10.00.

Two case studies from the middle 1950s make up this book. One is the famous arms deal involving the Soviet Union, Czechoslovakia, and Egypt; the other is the Soviet decision to arm Indonesia, a move that had certain parallels with the Egyptian case but not such durable results. Both studies are most helpful in increasing our knowledge of what really happened at this time of a major shift in Soviet policy toward the Third World.

SR, 29:1:702-3; LJ, 95(1970):673; Choice, 7(1970):301.

520. Ro'i, Yaakov. **From Encroachment to Involvement: A Documentary Study of Soviet Policy in the Middle East, 1945-1973.** New York and Toronto: Halsted Press, a division of John Wiley & Sons; Jerusalem: Israel Universities Press, 1974. xi, 616p. $26.75.

The author has brought together 116 documents, speeches, communiques, and commentaries that touch on all the key crises and developments of the 1945-73 period. The usefulness of the materials, most of which are Russian and Arabic in origin, is greatly enhanced by the author's background essays.

SR, 35:3:535-36; Choice, 12(1975):730.

521. Rosenbaum, Kurt. **Community of Fate: German-Soviet Diplomatic Relations 1922-1928.** Syracuse, NY: Syracuse University Press, 1965. 325p. $6.75.

The author made extensive use of the captured files of the German Foreign Office for this well-written retelling of German-Soviet relations during the Weimar period. He concentrated mainly on the papers of Count Ulrich von Brockdorff-Rantzau, German ambassador in Moscow for most of the period.

SR, 25:1:165-66; JMH, 38:1:115.

522.   Rothenberg, Morris. **The USSR and Africa: New Dimensions of Soviet Global Power.** Foreword by Mose L. Harvey. Coral Gables, FL: Advanced International Studies Institute, in association with the University of Miami, 1980. xii, 280p. $12.95. (Monographs in International Affairs.)

Coupled with growing Soviet logistics capabilities, the availability of large Cuban expeditionary forces gives the USSR a potent new instrumentality for extending its influence in Africa. The Soviet aim is to force Western powers out of Africa in order to break the back of the world system headed by the United States.

Choice, 18(1980):457.

523.   Rubinstein, Alvin Z. **Red Star on the Nile: The Soviet-Egyptian Influence Relationship since the June War.** Princeton, NJ: Princeton University Press, 1977. xxiv, 383p. $25.00.

The book, written in a lively and engaging style, traces the ups and downs of Soviet-Egyptian relations in an intrigue-by-intrigue account of persistent Soviet attempts to gain commanding influence over Egypt and of Egypt's largely successful parries of these attempts while making full use of desperately needed Soviet aid and diplomatic support.

CSP, 20:2:264; JP, 40(1978):575.

524.   Rubinstein, Alvin Z. **Soviet Foreign Policy since World War II: Imperial and Global.** Cambridge, MA: Winthrop Publishers, 1981. vii, 295p. $15.00.

The author chose a regional approach to this survey of recent Soviet foreign policy. He has brought together a wealth of information, a mass of factual data from the many specialized areas with which the book deals, and he has provided authoritative pronouncements on the significance of the evidence. The general reader will find this book highly informative.

AAPSS-A, 459(1982):178.

525.   Rubinstein, Alvin Z. **Soviet Policy toward Turkey, Iran, and Afghanistan.** New York: Praeger Publishers, 1983. 218p. $25.95.

Rubinstein analyzes the relationship between the "southern tier" countries within the framework of his influence theory. He discusses such recent political and strategic changes as the coup in Afghanistan, the political revolution in Iran, and Turkey's altered NATO position in the eastern Mediterranean, which will make future relations with the USSR even more interesting.

Choice, 20(1983):1060.

526.   Rubinstein, Alvin Z. **The Soviets in International Organizations: Changing Policy toward Developing Countries, 1953-1963.** Princeton, NJ: Princeton University Press, 1964. 380p. $7.50.

Soviet policy toward developing countries can be studied in the context of the United Nations. As Rubinstein makes abundantly clear, Soviet participation in the functional agencies of the United Nations has the purpose of political propaganda. He points out how successful such a policy has been in the various agencies and branches of the United Nations.

SEER, 44:102:255-56; APSR, 59(1965):221; CH, 48(1965):304.

527. Scott, William E. **Alliance against Hitler: The Origins of the Franco-Soviet Pact.** Durham, NC: Duke University Press, 1962. 296p.
This excellent volume treats the labyrinth of European politics in the early 1930s. The author concentrates on the internal and external pressures on France which culminated in the signing of the pact on May 2, 1935.
    LJ, 87(1962):4536.

528. Sen Gupta, Bhabani. **The Fulcrum of Asia: Relations among China, India, Pakistan, and the USSR.** Prepared under the auspices of the Research Institute on Communist Affairs and the East Asian Institute, Columbia University. New York: Pegasus, 1970. 383p. $8.95.
This study involves several Asian states in their relations with the USSR and with each other. Since the foreign policy of each state is closely linked with its domestic affairs, the international relations between China, India, Pakistan, and the USSR must also be viewed in the context of the internal situations in all respective countries as well as in the context of the global strategy of those countries. Extensive notes provide the reader with essential information concerning persons, events, and bibliographic material.
    JAS, 30(1971):473.

529. Senn, Alfred Erich. **Diplomacy and Revolution: The Soviet Mission to Switzerland, 1918.** Notre Dame, IN: University of Notre Dame Press, 1974. 221p. $9.95.
Senn describes the tangled web of events that led to the establishment and expulsion of the first Soviet mission to Switzerland in 1918. The Bolshevik efforts in Zurich and Bern during the last year of World War I assumed unusual significance, because Switzerland was one of the few places on the Continent where plans for the international Communist revolution could be prepared more openly.
    SR, 34:3:395.

530. Smolansky, Oles M. **The Soviet Union and the Arab East under Khrushchev.** Lewisburg, PA: Bucknell University Press, 1974. 326p. $15.00.
The author focuses on nine years of the relationship between the Soviet Union and the Arab states, beginning with the arms deal of 1955. The 1955-64 era is a crucial one, especially in the troubled emergence of Arab unity, and is punctuated by heroic episodes. The Soviet Union's part in these events and reaction to them are dealt with in extensive detail. The central conclusion is that Khrushchev failed.
    CSP, 27:1:160-61; PSQ, 89(Winter 1974-75):890.

531. Solzhenitsyn, Alexander. **Warning to the West.** Introduction by George Meany. New York: Farrar, Straus & Giroux, 1976. viii, 146p. $7.95.
Solzhenitsyn submits that a system [Soviet] so corrupt and abusive to its own people cannot be trusted in its dealings with foreign powers, especially if the latter manifests little stomach for long-term struggle. Apart from the author's oversimplifications, his views deserve attention now more than ever.
    BS, 37(April 1977):17.

532.   Tarulis, Albert N. **Soviet Policy toward the Baltic States, 1918-1940.** Notre Dame, IN: University of Notre Dame Press, 1959. 276p.
The book centers on the events of 1918-19 and 1939-40. The author's main objective is to examine the theory and practice of Soviet national and diplomatic policy, and in so doing he points up very sharply the double standard that permeates the Soviet attitude. The study is a rare contribution to a neglected area of scholarship.
        SR, 19:4:597-98.

533.   Thompson, John M. **Russia, Bolshevism, and the Versailles Peace.** Princeton, NJ: Princeton University Press, 1967. 429p. $11.50.
This work deals in the main with two political questions: power within Russia itself, that is, the case for and against Allied intervention once Germany was no longer valid, and what was to be done to meet the challenges and dangers of Bolshevism in a world exhausted and embittered by war.
        SR, 27:1:149-50; AHR, 73:2:549.

534.   Ullman, Richard H. **Anglo-Soviet Relations, 1917-1921.** Vol. 1: **Intervention and the War.** Princeton, Princeton University Press, 1961. 360p. $7.50. Vol. 2: **Britain and the Russian Civil War: November 1918-February 1920.** Princeton, Princeton University Press, 1968. 395p. $10.00. Vol. 3: **The Anglo-Soviet Accord.** Princeton, Princeton University Press, 1972. 509p. (Published for the Center of International Studies.) $17.50 cl.; $9.50 pa.
This first exhaustive study in English on Anglo-Soviet relations covers the period from the Bolshevik revolution to the Compiègne Armistice in November 1918. The author elaborates with marked success on British policy, which in sum was too pragmatic to deal effectively with the chaotic situation in Soviet Russia. Since official British records are still not available to historians, the study cannot claim to be complete; nevertheless, it is clearly and effectively written and represents a very desirable contribution to the period under discussion.
        SR, 21:2:351-52; LJ, 98(1973):1282.

535.   Wheeler-Bennett, John W. **Brest-Litovsk: The Forgotten Peace, March 1918.** London: Macmillan, 1938; New York: St. Martin's Press, 1966; New York: W. W. Norton, 1971. 478p. $8.00.
This is the best known and still most valuable treatment of the first Soviet-German treaty, which helped Lenin sustain the Soviet seizure of power in Russia in 1917. This book stands as one of the classics for that particular period and should be in all library collections.
        JMH, 29:4:429.

536.   White, Stephen. **Britain and the Bolshevik Revolution: A Study in the Politics of Diplomacy, 1920-1924.** New York: Holmes & Meier, 1980. xiv, 317p. $32.00.
White argues persuasively that any ideological affinity between the Labour party and the Bolsheviks was secondary to more practical considerations. He has made exhaustive use of British public and private papers and available Soviet works and has produced a solid book.
        SR, 40:3:479-80; JMH, 53:4:724.

537. Wilson, Edward T. **Russia and Black Africa before World War II.** New York and London: Holmes & Meier, 1974. xvi, 397p.

The author's main theme is the continuity between tsarist and Soviet motivations for involvement in Africa. In both cases, "calculation of realpolitik had taken precedence over considerations of friendship or ideological affinity." With its wealth of hitherto unused sources, this volume provides valuable insight into the genesis of current Soviet involvement in Africa.

Choice, 12(1975):126.

538. Wolfe, Thomas W. **Soviet Power and Europe, 1945-1970.** Baltimore: The Johns Hopkins Press, 1970. 534p. $15.00. cl.; $3.95 pa. (A RAND Corporation Research Study.)

A main thesis of the book is that Soviet political objectives toward Europe with respect to neutralization of Germany, blocking the further buildup of NATO defenses, and preventing potential defections from the Soviet bloc have remained basically unchanged since Stalin's time. This unchanged image of Soviet policy is amply documented from primary sources through careful weighing of alternative interpretations and contrary evidence.

SR, 30:4:892-93; LJ, 96(1971):1267.

With Communist Countries

539. Ambroz, Oton. **Realignment of World Power: The Russo-Chinese Schism under the Impact of Mao Tse-Tung's Last Revolution.** 2 vols. New York: Robert Speller, 1972. Vol. 1: 388p., Vol. 2: 406p. $25.00 set.

This study discusses the effects of the Chinese cultural revolution on the two great Communist rivals, the Communist movement, and international relations. The author believes that the Sino-Soviet conflict presents the West with a major opportunity for new initiatives in foreign policy. He has made detailed use of Yugoslav, West German, and Chinese Nationalist accounts, in addition to the more familiar sources.

SR, 33:4:781-82; Choice, 10(1973):177.

540. An, Tai Sung. **The Sino-Soviet Territorial Dispute.** Philadelphia: Westminster Press, 1973. 254p. $8.95.

This study examines the background of the border problem. The author contends, "the Sino-Soviet conflict, which began as an ideological dispute in 1960, has degenerated into a nationalistic clash based on territorial issues." Since Moscow enjoys enormous nuclear superiority, An doubts that Peking will attempt any military adventures. An appendix containing English translations of Russo-Chinese treaties and protocols from 1689 through 1915 enhances this contribution.

SR, 33:4:781-82; JAS, 33(Nov. 1973):110.

541. Clubb, O. Edmund. **China and Russia: The "Great Game."** New York: Columbia University Press, 1971. 578p. 34 plates, 10 maps. $12.95.

The author has succeeded in producing a Toynbean survey of relations and contacts between the Chinese and Russians, from the Mongol conquests in the thirteenth century to the Sino-Soviet Cold War attitudes of 1970. He displays a talent for explaining in clear, concise prose what are, in fact, very complicated historical events. The book will be read with enjoyment by all people interested in the great game of Russian-Chinese relations.

CSP, 14:3:568-70; JAS, 31(May 1972):651; LJ, 97(1972):2636.

542. Floyd, David. **Mao against Khrushchev: A Short History of the Sino-Soviet Conflict.** New York and London: Praeger, 1964. 456p. $7.50.

This account narrates the Sino-Soviet split as it developed between 1956 and 1963, supported by an extensive chronology of documents and significant events. Well researched and readable, this is a valuable compendium for the general reader and for the student of Communist affairs.

SR, 23:3:597-98.

543. Ginsburgs, George, and Pinkele, Carl F. **The Sino-Soviet Territorial Dispute, 1949-1964.** New York: Praeger Publishers, 1978. viii, 145p. $17.50.

This excellent monograph provides a detailed and fascinating reconstruction of the Sino-Soviet territorial dispute in the 1962-64 period. After reviewing the evidence for possible conflict over border issues in the 1950s, the authors analyze the public exchanges sparked by Khrushchev's taunting criticism and the Chinese Communist party's threat to challenge the "unequal treaties" that provided the judicial basis of the Sino-Soviet border.

RR, 40:2:206-7; Choice, 16(1979):276.

544. Gittings, John. **Survey of the Sino-Soviet Dispute: A Commentary and Extracts from the Recent Polemics, 1963-1967.** London: Oxford University Press, issued under the auspices of the Royal Institute of International Affairs, 1968. 410p. $11.75.

The author has carefully culled the extensive Russian and Chinese materials for 1963-67, grouping explicit references under thirty categories. Because these documents as issued contained a hodgepodge of current and retrospective charges and countercharges, this reordering is particularly helpful for quick reference and will be of use to the undergraduate reader and paper-writer. The author prefaces each grouping, integrating where possible most recent Russian and Chinese materials.

SR, 29:4:703-4; Choice, 6(1969):140.

545. Griffith, William E. **Sino-Soviet Relations, 1964-1965.** Cambridge, MA: MIT Press, 1967. 425p. $7.50.

This study is a chronological continuation of the author's *The Sino-Soviet Rift,* treating the period from November 1963 through November 1965. It contains a detailed analytical assessment of several aspects of Sino-Soviet relations for that particular period.

AHR, 73:1:186; Choice, 4(1968):1427.

546. Griffith, William E. **The Sino-Soviet Rift.** Cambridge, MA: MIT Press, 1964. 512p. $7.95.

The author considers the Sino-Soviet rift as the single most significant ideological split since the Reformation in the sixteenth century. A chronological summary, analysis, and documentation of the developments in the dispute between February 1962 and November 1963 is contained in this treatment.

JP, 27:3:685; Choice, 2(1965):335.

547. Jones, Christopher D. **Soviet Influence in Eastern Europe: Political Autonomy and the Warsaw Pact.** New York: Praeger Publishers, 1981. xii, 323p. $29.95.

Examining the almost infinite and constantly shifting complexities of the Soviet Union's relations with each member of the Eastern Bloc, Jones focuses on the Soviet military and political policy in East Europe and the role of the Warsaw Pact. Three sections make up the text: the conflicts between the Soviet Union and the Communist parties of East Europe; Soviet military intervention in East Europe; and the Warsaw Pact countries' responses to the military doctrine, the structure and function of the official agencies, and the system of bilateral ties between the Soviet and East European military systems.

NP, 11:1:118-19.

548. Leong, Sow-Theng. **Sino-Soviet Diplomatic Relations, 1917-1926.** Honolulu: The University Press of Hawaii, 1976. 362p. $15.00.

The author argues that, from the beginning, Soviet diplomacy toward China was motivated by self-interest. The work relies extensively on primary source material, published and unpublished, from the Institute of Modern History in Taiwan, Japanese primary source material, and Russian works.

LJ, 102(1977):603; Choice, 14(1977):428.

549. Mehnert, Klaus. **Peking and Moscow.** Translated from German by Lelia Vennewitz. New York: Putnam's, 1963. 522p. $9.65.

Mehnert offers a comparison of the two countries and cultures and surveys their relationship in recent years. The author's extensive personal experience in both countries qualifies him to speak with authority on this problem.

550. Salisbury, Harrison E. **War between Russia and China.** New York: W. W. Norton, 1969. 224p. $4.95 pa.

This account of the centuries-old national hatreds between Russians and Chinese is useful, if exaggerated, but the suggestion that this deep-seated rivalry is inevitably escalating toward a military denouement underestimates the role that political leadership plays in deciding questions of war and peace. However, the book is to be welcomed for the main theme it stresses: that nuclear war between the Communist giants could be disastrous for the rest of the world as well.

SR, 30:1:159; BL, 66(Jan. 1970):585.

551. Shanor, Donald R. **The Soviet Triangle: Russia's Relations with China and the West in the 1980s.** New York: St. Martin's Press, 1980. 288p. $13.95.

This survey of Soviet foreign policy in the 1970s and prospects for the future treats Soviet relations with the People's Republic of China, the United States, and the European countries. Shanor focuses on two major elements of détente policies: arms control and trade. He enriches his analysis with summaries of interviews with influential and ordinary citizens, especially in the Soviet Union and Eastern Europe. This volume is recommended for both public and academic libraries.

BS, 40(1980):291.

552.   Thornton, Richard C. **The Comintern and the Chinese Communists, 1928-1931**. Seattle: University of Washington Press, 1969. 246p. $9.50.

This is an important and useful work, which presents considerable new material and successfully challenges previous interpretations on a number of points. Thornton is the first Western scholar to have been granted access to the six-volume stenographic report of the Sixth Congress of the Chinese Communist party, held in Moscow in the summer of 1928.

SR, 32:4:821-23; AHR, 75:5:1764; CH, 59(1970):170.

553.   Wich, Richard. **Sino-Soviet Crisis Politics: A Study of Political Change and Communication**. Cambridge, MA: Council on East Asian Studies, Harvard University, 1980. 313p. $15.00.

This study focuses on the political changes that took place between the Soviet invasion of Czechoslovakia and the opening a year later of Sino-Soviet negotiations over the bitterly disputed border between the Soviet Union and China. The seismic events that followed on the world scene, notably the Sino-American and Sino-Japanese rapprochements, underlined with the centrality of China to the major and decisive developments in the global balance of power.

AHR, 86:3:816; Choice, 18(1981):853.

554.   Zagoria, Donald S. **The Sino-Soviet Conflict, 1956-1961**. Princeton, NJ: Princeton University Press, 1962. 484p. $8.50.

The author has assembed an overwhelming number of facts and documents intended to convince the reader that specific traits in the development of Russian and Chinese Communism and differences in tactics are irrefutable indications that the conflict between the two countries is expanding and international Communism is disintegrating.

SR, 21:4:756-57.

HISTORY

General Reference Material, Sources, and Documents

555.   Adams, Arthur, et al. **An Atlas of Russian and East European History.**
       New York: Praeger, 1967. 204p. $6.00.
Through more than a hundred maps and a completely integrated text, the authors
trace both the growth of Russia and the kaleidoscopic history of Eastern Europe.
Subjects discussed are: geography, national groups, religious diversity, economy,
politics, and cultural development. This is an indispensable reference book for
students and teachers, for high school and college libraries.

556.   Chew, Allen F. **An Atlas of Russian History: Eleven Centuries of Changing
       Borders.** New Haven, CT, and London: Yale University Press, 1967. 113p.
       $3.95 pa.
This atlas is an essential supplement to the study of Russian history. It contains
thirty-four maps, each accompanied by concise, descriptive text.

557.   Crowther, Peter A., comp. **A Bibliography of Works in English and Early
       Russian History to 1800.** New York: Barnes & Noble, 1969. 236p. $9.50.
In this bibliography 2,164 entries are organized under twenty major divisions
(plus addenda through 1968). Each section is rationally subdivided and cross-
referenced. The index is thorough. The volume unquestionably belongs in every
library frequented by patrons interested in Russia.
       SR, 30:2:454-55; Choice, 7(1970):669.

558.   Dmytryshyn, Basil, ed. **Imperial Russia: A Source Book, 1700-1917.**
       New York: Holt, Rinehart & Winston, 1967; 2d ed. Hinsdale, IL: Dryden
       Press, 1974. 497p. $5.95 pa.
The work offers a collection of primary source selections, arranged chronologically,
dealing with the political, social, economic, and cultural life of Imperial Russia.
Many documents in the collection appear in English for the first time: official
decrees, proclamations, instructions, treaties, memoirs, and political programs.
The second edition includes documentary material dealing with Russia's foreign
relations.

559.   Dmytryshyn, Basil, comp. **Modernization of Russia under Peter I and
       Catherine II.** New York: John Wiley, 1974. 157p. $4.50 pa.

Due to the profound influence on the course of Russian history exerted by Peter I and Catherine II, the author attempts to explain these developments through the selection of relevent decrees, observations made by foreigners, and assessments by historians reflected in contemporary Soviet historiography. Many documents have here been made available in English for the first time.

560. Gilbert, Martin. **Soviet History Atlas.** London: Routledge & Kegan Paul, 1979. 69p. £6.75.
The first section of this book, up to the Russian revolution, contains ten maps, with the main section, "The Soviet Union," having fifty-nine maps. All the maps have been specially drawn, incorporating information from a broad range of atlases, maps, books, and articles.
SS, 31:2:460.

561. Harcave, Sidney, ed. **Readings in Russian History.** Vol. 1: **From Ancient Times to the Abolition of Serfdom.** Vol. 2: **The Modern Period.** New York: Crowell, 1962. 388p. and 330p., respectively. $3.75 pa. each.
This very useful collection contains fifty selections dealing with various subjects in Russian history. Each item is related to its historical background by a brief introduction. Many translations are available in English for the first time.

562. Hellie, Richard, comp. and trans. **Readings for Introduction to Russian Civilization: Muscovite Society.** Chicago: Syllabus Division, The College, The University of Chicago, 1967. 320p. $5.95.
The scope of this book covers Muscovite society as a whole, which Hellie follows group by group in nine chapters. He has drawn heavily on the Law Code (Ulozhenie) of 1649, and has also translated the Toropets Administrative Charter of 1590-91, and the petition on forbidding foreign merchants to trade, 1648-49. "The Enserfment of the Peasantry" and "Bondage in Muscovy" round out the selection.
SR, 29:2:302-3.

563. Pundeff, Marin, comp. and ed. **History in the U.S.S.R.: Selected Readings.** San Francisco: Chandler Publishing Co., published for the Hoover Institution, 1967. 313p. $6.50.
This collection of readings includes selections by Marx, Engels, Plekhanov, Lenin, Pokrovsky, Stalin, and Khrushchev, as well as official pronouncements and decrees, all of which have provided guidelines for the writing and teaching of history in the Soviet Union. All documents are provided with generally useful prefatory explanations for the beginning student.
SR, 28:4:656-57.

564. Riha, Thomas. **Readings in Russian Civilization.** Vol. 1: **900-1700**; Vol. 2: **1700-1917**; Vol. 3: **1917-1963**. Chicago: University of Chicago Press, 1964. $3.75 pa. each.
This selection includes religious, literary, philosophic, economic, ideological, and political aspects of Russian history.
JP, 27(Feb. 1968):245.

565. **The Russian Primary Chronicle: Laurentian Text (Povest' vremennykh let).** Translated and edited by Samuel H. Cross and Olgerd P. Sherbowitz-Wetzor. Cambridge, MA: Medieval Academy of America, 1953. 313p. $5.00. (Medieval Academy of America, no. 60.)

This is the English translation of a major source on the history of Kiev Rus'.

566. Shapiro, David, comp. **A Select Bibliography of Works in English on Russian History, 1801-1917.** Oxford: Basil Blackwell, 1962. 106p.

The bibliography lists 1,070 books and articles relevant to the study of Russian history. Only a few books are identified with references to critical reviews.

SR, 25:2:370-72.

567. Spector, Ivar, and Spector, Marion, eds. **Readings in Russian History and Culture.** Boston: Allyn & Bacon, 1965. 489p. $2.95 pa.

This volume comprises sixty-three readings, stressing historical and cultural aspects of Russian life. The editors also have provided appropriate up-to-date introductions to each selection. Suitable for undergraduates, this handy reader can also be used by high school students.

568. Vernadsky, George, and Fisher, Ralph T., Jr., et al., eds. and comps. **A Source Book for Russian History from Early Times to 1917. Vol. 1: Early Times to the Late Seventeenth Century. Vol. 2: Peter the Great to Nicholas I. Vol. 3: Alexander II to the February Revolution.** New Haven, CT: Yale University Press, 1972. Vol. 1: 306p.; Vol. 2: 307-584pp.; Vol. 3: 585-884pp. $12.50 each.

This three-volume work represents the most comprehensive source book in English encompassing various areas and fields of Russia's history. Documents and sources are accompanied by introductions and editorial explanations.

SR, 33:2:336-38; Choice, 10(1973):347; LJ, 38(1973):420.

569. Walsh, Warren B., comp. and ed. **Readings in Russian History: From Ancient Times to the Post-Stalin Era.** 4th ed., extensively rev. Vol. 1: **From Ancient Times to the Eighteenth Century.** 244p. Vol. 2: **From the Reign of Paul to Alexander III.** 245p. Vol. 3: **The Revolutionary Era and the Soviet Period.** 535p. Syracuse, NY: Syracuse University Press, 1963. $6.95 pa. each.

SR, 23:3:578-79.

570. Wieczynski, Joseph L., ed. **The Modern Encyclopedia of Russian and Soviet History (MERSH).** Gulf Breeze, FL: Academic International Press, 1976- . Vols. 1-7 in progress. $30.50 each.

This represents an ongoing project that is expected to reach more than fifty volumes before completion, at which time it will be the most comprehensive encyclopedic guide to Russian/Soviet history in the English language.

General Histories and Historiographies

571. Charques, Richard D. **A Short History of Russia**. New York: Dutton, 1956. 284p.
This is one of the best textbooks on Russian history for high school students.
SR, 27:3:352-53.

572. Dmytryshyn, Basil. **A History of Russia**. Englewood Cliffs, NJ: Prentice-Hall, 1977. xviii, 645p. Illustrated. $14.95.
This text is well organized, concise, and straightforward. It is divided into five parts: Kievan Rus', Divided Rus', Muscovy, Imperial Russia, and Soviet Russia. In addition to photographs and illustrations, there are a number of maps, tables, and charts.
SR, 37:2:290; AHR, 82:4:1290.

573. Ellison, Herbert J. **A History of Russia**. New York: Holt, Rinehart & Winston, 1964. 644p. $8.95.
Ellison endeavors to present an objective picture of the Russian historical past, to balance the failures and the achievements of prerevolutionary Russia. Especially sound is his analysis of the period 1906-14, which in fact exhibited "immense achievements in many areas of national life." The author also devotes much attention to the situation of the national minorities in the Russian Empire and in the Soviet Union.
SR, 24:2:323-24; JMH, 37:2:357.

574. Florinsky, Michael T. **Russia: A Short History**. 2d ed. London: Collier-Macmillan, 1969 (1964). 699p. $9.95.
Florinsky's well-known two-volume survey, *Russia: A History and an Interpretation* (1953), has subsequently been condensed into one volume, *Russia: A Short History* (1964), as a textbook for students of Russian history. Florinsky follows the Russian historical scheme on the question of Russia's origin, terminology, and periodization. Otherwise, his survey properly scrutinizes Russia's past. This second updated edition makes one of the better textbooks available.
JP, 27:1:242.

575. Harcave, Sidney. **Russia: A History**. Chicago: Lippincott, 1952. 668p.
This volume was published as one of the first American textbooks of Russian history adaptable to teaching in U.S. colleges. The author has provided a text that is easy to follow. He takes a primarily political approach to history, although other areas are not neglected. Sixteen maps and thirty-one illustrations, five chronological overviews, a useful bibliography, and a full index add to the value of this textbook.
SR, 14:1:126-28.

576. Hunczak, Taras, ed. **Russian Imperialism: From Ivan the Great to the Revolution**. New Brunswick, NJ: Rutgers University Press, 1974. 396p. $17.50.

Ten specialists have joined in an attempt to explain the historical and geopolitical aspects of Russian expansionism. The most interesting details presented are in the treatment of the geopolitical aspects of Russian expansionism. The original Russian state controlled an area of some fifteen thousand square miles in 1462, and it expanded at the rate of fifty square miles a day for four hundred years. The ethnic Russians established domination over a large number of nations, which actually outnumbered the dominant Russians.

SR, 34:3:584-85.

577. Kerner, Robert J. **The Urge to the Sea: The Course of Russian History. The Role of Rivers, Portages, Ostrogs, Monasteries and Furs.** New York: Russell & Russell, 1971, reprint of 1942 ed. by University of California Press. 212p. $14.00.

This represents the first American study attempting to explain Russia's territorial expansion from a geographic and geopolitical point of view. It is the first systematic treatment of the subject that has also drawn the attention of Russian historians, though they never elaborated on this aspect in historical continuity. The study remains among the standard works explaining factors of Russian imperialism.

578. Mazour, Anatole G. **Modern Russian Historiography.** Rev. ed. Westport, CT, and London: Greenwood Press, 1975 [1936, under the title *An Outline of Modern Russian Historiography*; 2d ed., 1958]. xiv, 224p. Illustrated. $6.50.

The latest edition, the third, includes some new materials on the chronicles and the earliest historians of Russia, but it deletes the previous editions' section on émigré historians, the Euro-Asian school, and scholarship (except that Siberian historiography is treated through the 1960s). The author designed this book "merely as a guide" to the important and complex subject of Russian historiography.

SR, 18:2:250-52.

579. Mazour, Anatole G. **The Writing of History in the Soviet Union.** Stanford, CA: Hoover Institution Press, 1971. 383p. $17.50. (Hoover Institution Publications, 87.)

Mazour offers as a supplement to his well-known *Modern Russian Historiography* (see entry 578) this survey of Soviet historical writing on some major themes in Russian history. The author provides a gripping description of the catastrophic impact of the Stalin cult on Soviet historiography.

SR, 31:3:684-86; LJ, 97(1972):1013; Choice, 9(1972):122.

580. Pipes, Richard. **Russia under the Old Regime.** New York: Charles Scribner's Sons; London: Weidenfeld and Nicolson, 1974. 361p. $17.50.

"The theme of this book is the political system of Russia. It traces the growth of the Russian state from its beginnings in the ninth century to the end of the nineteenth.... Unlike most historians who seek the roots of twentieth-century totalitarianism in Western ideas, I look for them in Russian institutions," states the author. A novel aspect of this work is the employment of analogies and comparisons in discussing the development of Muscovy-Russia.

SR, 34:4:812-14; LJ, 100(1975):580; Choice, 12(1975):738.

581.   Riasanovsky, Nicholas V. **A History of Russia**. 3d ed. New York: Oxford University Press, 1977. xx, 672p. Illustrated. $17.00.

This textbook is well organized along simple chronological lines and for the most part provides essential and reliable information on salient aspects of Russia's historical evolution. The account is lucid and tends to favor the more conservative interpretations. This third edition also treats post-1969 events such as the invasion of Czechoslovakia in 1968 and the talks leading up to SALT II.

582.   Vernadsky, George. **A History of Russia**. 6th rev. ed. New Haven, CT: Yale University Press, 1971 (1929). 531p. $3.95 pa.

According to the author, "in the present edition the course of events and the main trends of life in contemporary Russia have been related and analyzed. The bibliography has been expanded in order to list a number of important books published after 1960. The Appendix contains brief statistical data on the Soviet Union for 1966." Vernadsky represents the so-called Euro-Asiatic school of thought among Russian national historians.

583.   Vernadsky, George. **Russian Historiography: A History**. Edited by Sergei Pushkarev. Translated by Nickolas Lupinin. Belmont, MA: Nordland Publishing Company, 1978. x, 575p. $35.00.

At the time of his death, according to the editor, Vernadsky had completed this work except for a chapter on oriental studies and the history of the church, a chapter completed by Pushkarev. Though Vernadsky surveys the whole of Russia's history, emphasis in the work is on the late nineteenth and early twentieth centuries. This volume also contains four appendixes, an essay bibliography of Vernadsky's works, and bibliographies on the Russian Church and schism of the Old Believers.

NP, 9:1:161.

Pre-Petrinian Muscovy

584.   Fennell, John L. I. **Ivan the Great of Moscow**. New York: St. Martin's Press, 1961. 386p. $12.50.

This study is primarily concerned with the diplomacy and military ventures as well as the remarkable territorial expansion of Muscovy-Russia between 1462 and 1505. Because of the significance of that period in Russia's past, this detailed study deserves a place in a basic collection of Russia's history. The author has presented fresh views on the rule of Ivan III.

SR, 25:4:691-92.

585.   Grey, Ian. **Boris Godunov: The Tragic Tsar**. New York: Charles Scribner's Sons, 1973. $8.95.

In this volume Grey chronicles the narrative history of the life of Godunov, drawing heavily from the classic accounts by Karamzin, Soloviev, and Platonov and the more recent scholarship of Zimin and Vernadsky. For those who know little of this period of history, his work can serve as a useful introduction. The serious reader will be better served by S. F. Platonov's study of Godunov's reign, reissued in 1973 in English translation by Academic International Press.

SR, 33:2:344-5; Choice, 10(1974):1925.

586. Kliuchevskii, V. O. A. **A Course in Russian History: The Seventeenth Century.** Translated by Natalie Duddington. Introduction by Alfred J. Rieber. Chicago: Quadrangle Books, 1968. 400p. $8.95.

Based on the 1957 Soviet edition in Russian, this new version or translation flows smoothly and resounds the masterful style that made Kliuchevsky the most popular university teacher of history in Russia. In a solid, scholarly introduction, Rieber examines the work, life, and critics of Kliuchevsky the historian with a view to placing him in modern historiography. Both beginning and advanced students of Russian history will find the book valuable and highly readable, and because Kliuchevsky frequently differentiated between Russian and European experience, students of comparative historical methods will also be interested.

SR, 29:2:308-9; Choice, 5(1969):1625.

587. Payne, Robert, and Romanoff, Nikita. **Ivan the Terrible.** New York: Thomas Y. Crowell, 1975. x, 502p. $12.95.

This text is based on a wide range of contemporary narrative sources and is accompanied by well-chosen illustrations, maps, plans of the Kremlin, a glossary, and an index. The book concentrates on military campaigns, diplomatic negotiations, and the horrors of the *oprichnina.* And yet, in this book the Ivan that emerges is an Ivan that never existed.

SR, 35:4:730.

588. Pelenski, Jaroslaw. **Russia and the Kazan: Conquest and Imperial Ideology (1438-1560s).** The Hague: Mouton, 1974. 368p. 90 Dglds.

With the conquest of Kazan in 1552 the ethnic Russian state of Moscow became a multinational empire. The book's context is the unstable balance of power between the successor Khanates of the Golden Horde, Moscow, Lithuania-Poland, and peripheral powers from Kazan's independence in 1438-45 to 1552. The author shows that Kazan's submissiveness to Moscow was always episodic and generally unwilling.

RR, 34:1:92-93; CH, 44(1975):111.

589. Pravdin, Michael. **The Mongol Empire: Its Rise and Legacy.** Translated from the German by Eden and Cedar Paul. 2d ed. New York: The Free Press, 1967. 581p.

This is still the most accurate and authoritative account on the rise and fall of the world's largest empire. It describes the ascent of the Mongol people, who, through the military genius of one man, overwhelmed and subdued the nations of half the world. The book underlines the influence of Asia on Europe in general, and on Russia in particular.

590. Presniakov, A. E. **The Formation of the Great Russian State: A Study of Russian History in the Thirteenth to Fifteenth Centuries.** Translated by A. E. Moorhouse. Introduction by Alfred J. Rieber. Chicago: Quadrangle Books, 1970. 414p. $12.95.

The main value of the book lies in the new approach to explaining the rise of the Muscovite state and Russian autocracy. Presniakov describes the growth of the princely authority against an elaborate investigation of the social order of the period.

591. Presniakov, Alexander E. **The Tsardom of Muscovy**. Edited and translated by Robert F. Price. "Master and Man in Muscovy" by Charles J. Halperin. Gulf Breeze, FL: Academic International Press, 1978. xxii, 157p. $12.50.
This classic essay, first published in Petrograd in 1918, delineates in compressed fashion the major factors in the development of the Muscovite autocracy through the seventeenth century. On the whole, Presniakov focuses on the consolidation of central authority, which, in his view, had become a political necessity. This study should be required reading for all students of Russian history.
SR, 39:1:113-14.

592. Vernadsky, George. **The Tsardom of Moscow, 1547-1682**. 2 vols. New Haven, CT: Yale University Press, 1969. 873p. $20.00. (A History of Russia, vol. 5.)
The appearance of this work is the final step in Vernadsky's contribution to the ten-volume *History of Russia* started in 1943 jointly by him and Michael Karpovich. The epoch treated by Vernadsky is of crucial importance for Russian historical development: Ivan the Terrible's reign, the time of troubles, the evolution of serfdom, the Ukrainian wars and union of the Ukraine with Moscow, the church schism, the great territorial expansion—all within a span of 135 years. Vernadsky used Russian prerevolutionary and Soviet sources, as well as Ukrainian and Polish material.
SR, 29:4:691-93; AHR, 75:3:889.

593. Yanov, Alexander. **The Origins of Autocracy: Ivan the Terrible in Russian History**. Translated by Stephen Dunn. Foreword by Sidney Monas. Berkeley and Los Angeles: University of California Press, 1981. xvi, 339p. $19.95.
Yanov, Soviet émigré journalist and historian, has produced an extremely ambitious and uncommonly provocative book. It is a complex, multilayered endeavor: a reexamination of the reign of Ivan the Terrible; an attempt at a reinterpretation of Russian history; an extended and critical examination of the historiography on Ivan. In Yanov's view, autocracy originated in the reign of Ivan IV, specifically in the "revolution from above" embodied in the *oprichnina*.
SR, 42:1:104-6.

Imperial Russia

594. Avrich, Paul. **Russian Rebels, 1600-1800**. New York: Schocken Books, 1972. 309p. $10.00.
This study is an attempt to further explain and search for additional causes and explanations of the Bolshevik revolution reaching as far back as two centuries. Employing comparative and analytical insights, the author provides a deeper understanding of the nature of all major Russian rebellions during the seventeenth and eighteenth centuries. This study complements general textbooks.
LJ, 98(1973):540; Choice, 10(1973):836.

595. Byrnes, Robert F. **Pobedonostsev: His Life and Thought**. Bloomington: Indiana University Press, 1968. 495p. $15.00.
The author's description of Pobedonostsev's part in judicial reforms, his administration of the Holy Synod, and his work with primary education and censorship

provides a fascinating composite picture of the committed conservative in action. Pobedonostsev opposed introducing alien institutions where no natural base existed, and clung firmly to the unique need for autocracy in Russia.

SR, 28:3:486-87; AHR, 74:5:1665; Choice, 6(1969):892.

596. Charques, Richard D. **The Twilight of Imperial Russia.** Fair Lawn, NJ: Essential Books, 1959. 256p. $6.00.

This volume offers a vivid and penetrating analysis of the developments in Russia from 1861 to the opening of the revolution of 1917. The author's style is compact and even artistic. The content is interpretative rather than factual, and yet it is full of substance.

JMH, 31:3:380-81.

597. Curtiss, John Shelton. **The Russian Revolutions of 1917.** Princeton, NJ: Van Nostrand, 1957. 192p. (Anvil Originals, no. 16.)

As background to the tensions that produced the revolutions, the author sketches Russia's major unsolved problems from the emancipation of 1861 down to 1905, with special attention given the *Duma* period and Russia's role in World War I. High school students will profit from this narrative account.

SR, 16:3:392.

598. Curtiss, John Shelton. **Russia's Crimean War.** Durham, NC: Duke University Press, 1979. xi, 597p. $29.75.

Curtiss provides the first full treatment in English of the Russian side of the Crimean war. While the British public pushed the government into war, Napoleon drew the French along behind him; in Russia, however, "war feelings were strong in all classes," according to the author. This book provides a fresh new look at an important subject and a clear perception of its impact on Russia and the world.

RR, 39:1:240-41; AHR, 85:2:432; Choice, 16(1979):1356.

599. Daniels, Robert V. **Russia.** Englewood Cliffs, NJ: Prentice-Hall, 1965. 152p. $4.95.

This book presents a short summary of the main political features of the Soviet Union today, with an outline of Russian nineteenth-century history, an account of the revolutionary movement and the upheaval of 1917. The unifying theme is the view that the Soviet Union is largely a modern version of tsarist Russia, especially since Soviet totalitarianism is a direct outgrowth of the highly centralized tsarist autocracy. This text is suitable for high school instruction and as a supplementary reader in introductory history courses.

JMH, 38:4:423.

600. Florinsky, Michael T. **The End of the Russian Empire.** New York: Collier Books, 1961. 254p.

This is a documentary analysis of the forces behind the 1917 revolution and the formation of the Soviet state. It offers thought-provoking reading for the student of Russian history.

601.   Frankland, Noble. **Imperial Tragedy: Nicholas II, Last Days of the Tsars.**
       New York: Coward-McCann, 1961. 193p. $3.95.
The author repeats in popular fashion the story of the decline and fall of the last
of the Romanovs. The various parts of the account are skillfully assembled and the
book is engagingly written. It is light reading for secondary school students.
       SR, 21:1:161.

602.   Harcave, Sidney. **First Blood: The Russian Revolution of 1905.** New
       York: Macmillan, 1964. 316p. $5.75.
This excellent study exploits primary sources released by the Soviet government.
Concise summaries of the main currents of development toward revolution through
1904 precede a detailed examination of four phases of the revolution. The appendix contains translations of official documents, political programs of the opposition
parties, and the petition of Father Gapon, which he intended to submit to the
tsar on January 9.
       AHR, 70:4:1109-10; Choice, 2(1965):116.

603.   Harcave, Sidney. **Years of the Golden Cockerel: The Last Romanov Tsars,
       1814-1917.** New York: Macmillan, 1968. 515p. $12.50.
This study covers Romanov rule from Alexander I to the fall of Nicholas II. To the
average reader it is a fascinating and bewildering tale of political incapacity, over-
confidence, and self-deception. The last century of Russian autocracy represented
a trail that led logically to catastrophe. Great Russian nationalism often blinded
political behavior. The story is presented succinctly and soundly.
       AHR, 74:5:1663-65; BL, 65(Feb. 1969):634.

604.   Harrison, John A. **The Founding of the Russian Empire in Asia and Amer-
       ica.** Coral Gables, FL: University of Miami Press, 1971. 156p. $7.95.
The author summarizes the history of the Russian drive across northern Asia and
the northern Pacific from the ninth to the nineteenth century. He does so in three
parts: "The Land and the People," "The Gathering of Russia," and "The Moving
Frontier." Harrison succeeds in producing a coherent narrative that can be understood and followed with interest by college students.
       SR, 31:4:892; Choice, 9(1972):424.

605.   Healy, Ann Erickson. **The Russian Autocracy in Crisis, 1905-1907.**
       Hamden, CT: Archon Books, 1976. 328p. $15.00.
This study focuses on the hopes, achievements, and failures of the first Duma,
which was convened in St. Petersburg on May 10, 1906. Constitutional developments in Russia during the reign of Nicholas II have become a subject of special
interest. Healy's volume is among a number of recent monographs that deal with
the Russian experiment, and it is an interesting work.
       CSP, 19:2:226-27; AHR, 82:1:152; Choice, 13(1977):1484.

606.   Karpovich, Michael. **Imperial Russia (1801-1917).** Magnolia, MA: Peter
       Smith, 1932; 1964 printing. 114p. $2.50 pa.
This condensed discussion of Russian history of the nineteenth century, emphasizing reforms after 1855, is still a useful text for beginning students of Russian
history.

607. Kliuchevskii, Vasilii. **The Rise of the Romanovs.** Translated and edited by Liliana Archibald. London: Macmillan, 1970. 371p. $12.50

Kliuchevskii is considered the most capable *Geschichtsmaler,* who embodies in his excellent historical writing a summary of all the efforts of Russian historians, beginning with Tatishchev. He is representative of the methodological legal state school of thought, which considered the state to be the promoter of history. This work reflects Kliuchevskii's almost exclusive preoccupation with Russia's expansion to the south, west, and into Asia. He glorifies conquests and finds no sympathy for victims.

    SR, 32:2:374-75.

608. Kochan, Miriam. **The Last Days of Imperial Russia, 1910-1917.** New York: Macmillan, 1976. 224p. Illustrated. $12.95.

Kochan's book on the last days of imperial Russia is a handsomely illustrated volume intended for the general reader. Its primary aim is to convey some notion of the way people in various classes of society lived, combined with a description of the growing atmosphere of political apocalypse. The author has relied chiefly on memoirs, and has found a number of excellent old photographs, many of them unfamiliar, with which to illustrate her story.

    SR, 36:2:300.

609. Kohn, Hans. **Basic History of Modern Russia: Political, Cultural and Social Trends.** Princeton, NJ: Van Nostrand, 1957. 192p. (Anvil Originals, no. 24.)

This brief history of Russia in the nineteenth century is ideally suited for general readers and high school students.

    SR, 17:2:235.

610. Lensen, George Alexander, ed. **Russia's Eastward Expansion.** Englewood Cliffs, NJ: Prentice-Hall, 1964. 184p. $4.50.

The work consists of a collection of readings of Russian and Western authors on Russian expansion into Central Asia, Siberia, and the Far East since the Middle Ages. Six maps and a bibliography accompany this interesting reader.

611. Lincoln, W. Bruce. **Nicholas I: Emperor and Autocrat of All the Russias.** Bloomington and London: Indiana University Press, 1978. 424p. $15.95.

The goal of this study is to review the negative picture of Nicholas I presented in most accounts, not by way of "apology" but to "place [Nicholas] and his policies in a more balanced historical perspective." Lincoln concludes that Nicholas "sought to create the epitome of an eighteenth-century West European police state ... in the manner of an enlightened despot." Nicholas failed at his task, because it was impossible to govern this vast and diverse empire with programs designed for homogeneous states.

    SR, 38:1:109-10; Choice, 15(1978):1271.

612. Mazour, Anatole G. **The First Russian Revolution, 1825. The Decembrist Movement, Its Origins, Development and Significance.** Stanford, CA: Stanford University Press, 1965 (1937). 328p.

This detailed treatise remains the only significant study of the Decembrists in English. The only change in this edition is the inclusion of a bibliographic supplement, compiled in 1961.

SEER, 45:105:558-59.

613. Mazour, Anatole G. **Rise and Fall of the Romanovs**. Princeton, NJ: Van Nostrand, 1960. 192p. (Anvil Originals, no. 50.)

The author has provided a key to Russia's development from the accession to the throne of the first of the Romanovs in 1613 to the assassination of Russia's last tsar in 1917. The book illustrates how strongly the Romanovs influenced the course of modern European history by dictating Russia's foreign policy. A beginner will appreciate this study for its clarity and brevity.

SEER, 49:93:570.

614. Mosse, Werner E. **Alexander II and the Modernization of Russia**. Rev. ed. New York: Macmillan, 1958; Collier Books, 1962. 191p.

In this well-informed and perceptive account of the reign of Alexander II (1855-81) the author has successfully combined scholarship and popularization of the subject. The tsar reformer and tsar despot in one person, as presented in this volume, is among the most important figures in Russian history.

AHR, 65:1:180.

615. Oliva, L. Jay. **Russia in the Era of Peter the Great**. Englewood Cliffs, NJ: Prentice-Hall, 1969. 184p. $5.95.

This volume may herald a new trend in classroom-oriented writing on Russian history—away from the orthodox survey toward reinterpretations of more restricted periods and topics. Addressed to students and general readers, this concise study has something to offer the specialist, too. The author concentrates on the era rather than the man; he analyzes Petrine policies against the backdrop of early modern Europe. Also stimulating is his examination of the social forces that supported and opposed Peter's reforms.

SR, 29:3:505-6; BL, 66(Feb. 1970):649.

616. Pierce, Richard A. **Russian Central Asia 1867-1917: A Study in Colonial Rule**. Berkeley: University of California Press, 1960. 359p. $7.00.

It is widely believed in Europe and America that Russia is "untainted by the sin of colonialism," that she never had and does not have a subject empire. This study proves otherwise. It is a revealing account of Russian imperialism which has long been needed.

SEER, 49:93:547-48.

617. Presniakov, A. E. **Emperor Nicholas I of Russia: The Apogee of Autocracy, 1825-1855**. Edited and translated by Judith C. Zazek. With "Nicholas I and the Course of Russian History" by Nicholas Riasanovsky. Gulf Breeze, FL: Academic International Press, 1974. (Leningrad, 1925). 102p. $10.00. (The Russian Series, 23.)

Presniakov's essay on Nicholas I, written between 1923 and 1925, is "an interpretive essay which deals selectively with many features of the ruler's personality, purposes, programs, and policies," according to the translator. This is a valuable and stimulating piece of work. The book is further enriched by a brief essay by Riasanovsky.

618. Pushkarev, Sergei. **The Emergence of Modern Russia, 1801-1917.** Translated from Russian by Robert H. MacNeal and Tova Yedlin. New York: Holt, Rinehart & Winston, 1963. 512p. $8.75.

A Russian national historian discusses Russia's political structure, foreign relations, social and economic conditions, and cultural history.

619. Quested, R. K. I. **The Expansion of Russia in East Asia, 1857-1860.** Kuala Lumpur: University of Malaya Press, 1968. 339p. $9.75.

The seizure of the Far Eastern provinces, the subject of this study, represented the biggest mouthful of the Chinese empire that Russia was ever able to devour and digest. The period covered has not been comprehensively surveyed until now, even though the passing of this vast area to Russia was certainly one of the decisive events in the history of the Far East. Although the book encompasses a great deal of detail, the author has given a clear overall picture of the developments in policy-making at the diplomatic level without repeating slices of material found in published works in European languages.

SR, 29:2:311-12; AHR, 75:2:560; Choice, 6(1969):896.

620. Raeff, Marc. **The Decembrist Movement.** Englewood Cliffs, NJ: Prentice-Hall, 1966. 180p. $4.95.

The volume starts with an introduction by Raeff, followed by quotations from various sources, official accounts, testimonies, and constitutional projects drawn up by the Decembrists, and it ends with Pushkin's well-known poem, "Message to Siberia."

SR, 27:1:136.

621. Raeff, Marc. **Imperial Russia, 1682-1825: The Coming of Age of Modern Russia.** New York: Knopf, 1971. 176p. $2.95 pa. (Borzoi History of Russia, vol. 4.)

This is the first of six volumes which together will comprise a new general history of Russia. In this volume Raeff is offering a compendium of his work and thought. He has taken essays scattered in numerous publications and brought them into a single brief volume. It should provide useful supplementary reading for courses on the middle period of Russian history.

622. Raeff, Marc, ed. **Peter the Great: Reformer or Revolutionary?** Boston: Heath, 1966. 109p. $2.50.

This volume offers a selection of articles with an introduction that not only sets Peter's reforms in the pertinent Russian and European background, but also includes an interpretation of Peter I that is significant in its own right.

623. Ragsdale, Hugh. **Detente in the Napolenic Era: Bonaparte and the Russians.** Lawrence, KS: The Regents of Kansas, 1980. xii, 183p. $17.50.

This short book is really an essay based on considerable archival research. The point of the essay is to interpret Napoleon's foreign policy as a repeated effort to divide

Europe, and especially the Ottoman Empire, with Russia by peaceful or military means. The volume is clearly written and attractively presented.

RR, 40:2:186-87; AHR, 86:2:570; Choice, 18(1981):713.

624. Riasanovsky, Nicholas V. **Nicholas I and Official Nationality in Russia 1825-1855.** Berkeley: University of California Press, 1959. 296p. $6.50.

Riasanovsky has produced a general survey of the policies of Nicholas I, with special emphasis on the doctrine of official nationality, which, together with orthodoxy and autocracy, formed the famous threefold slogan of Count Uvarov. This book provides rewarding reading for the student who lacks knowledge of Russian.

SEER, 39:92:259-61.

625. Rogger, Hans. **Russia in the Age of Modernization and Revolution 1881-1917.** New York: Longman, 1983. 207p. $17.95.

A penetrating study of Russia under its last two tsars. The author examines how the Russians viewed tsardom as the central issue confronting their nation, and looks closely at the relationship between state and society and how that relationship affected politics, economics, and class relations in these critical years. Chapters examine the state apparatus and its personnel; the social classes from peasants to noblemen; political programs offered as solutions for poverty and the promise of progress; and Russia's dual role as imperial power and multinational state.

626. Schwarz, Solomon M. **The History of Menshevism.** Vol. 1: **The Russian Revolution of 1905; the Workers' Movement and the Formation of Bolshevism and Menshevism.** Chicago: University of Chicago Press, 1967. 361p. $8.95.

This book covers the crucial period during 1905 when social democracy emerged as a factor of consequence on the political scene, only to divide into the two parts that became Social-Democracy on the one hand and, on the other, the authoritarian labor movement that assumed the name of Communism. The author was a member of the Kerensky government.

AHR, 73:3:546; Choice, 4(1967):1166.

627. Seton-Watson, Hugh. **The Decline of Imperial Russia, 1855-1914.** New York: Praeger, 1962. 406p. $7.50.

This study aims at explaining the stages of the decline of Russian tsardom between the Crimean War and World War I. This book is an example of objectivity, balance, and clarity of presentation.

SR, 12:3:396-98.

628. Seton-Watson, Hugh. **The Russian Empire: 1801-1917.** Oxford: Clarendon Press, 1967. 813p. $10.00. (Oxford History of Modern Europe.)

This book is based on a wealth of information. Its foremost virtue is objectivity; the author tries to give everyone the credit he deserves. He is especially careful about telling the story of the non-Russian borderlands, from Finland and the Baltic areas to the usually neglected Caucasus and Central Asia.

AHR, 73:4:1201-2; Choice, 5(1968):398.

629. Stone, Norman. **The Eastern Front, 1914-1917.** New York: Charles
     Scribner's Sons, 1975. 348p. Maps. $15.00.
Stone has given much valuable information and analysis in this book, but is unable
to do full justice to this significant and neglected subject. Especially valuable are
Stone's clear and sensible discussions of the fundamental strategies that both sides
pursued. Despite its drawbacks, the study contains much fascinating material.
     SR, 36:2:301-2; LJ, 101(1976):1210; Choice, 13(1976):715.

630. Tarlé, E. V. **Napoleon's Invasion of Russia, 1812.** New York: Octagon
     Books, 1971 (1942). 422p. $13.00.
The author, one of the most controversial Russian historians of modern times, was
also responsible for the purges of those historians who refused to become tools of
Marxist dogma. He is a well-known authority on Napoleon's invasion of Russia and
the French Revolution who, in 1931, fell victim to the regime for his "errors"; he
had identified Soviet foreign policy with that of tsarist Russia. In 1937, however,
Tarlé was summoned back to Moscow from his place of banishment. In this volume,
in contrast to his previous statements, the author concluded that the war against
Napoleon was "solidly a national war." Tarlé initiated the glorification of Russia's
past, subordinating history to official Stalinist policy.

Revolution and Civil War

631. Avrich, Paul. **Kronstadt 1921.** Princeton, NJ: Princeton University Press,
     1970. 271p. $8.50. (Studies of the Russian Institute, Columbia
     University.)
Avrich describes the most tragic attempt to proclaim a republic of free soviets: the
rebellion of the Kronstadt sailors. The author concludes that the rebellion was
spontaneous in its inception, "anarcho-populist" in its program, and doomed, like
the Paris Commune, because of its lack of aggressiveness.
     SR, 30:1:150-1; AHR, 76:1:175.

632. Bradley, John. **Allied Intervention in Russia (1917-1920).** New York:
     Basic Books, 1968. 251p. $6.50.
Based chiefly on unpublished documents from British, French, and American
archives, the story starts with Allied efforts to get in touch with both the Bolsheviks and their Russian opposition, initially to restore the eastern front, possibly
with Japanese help. To strengthen their weak Red Army, the Bolsheviks formed
international Red units from war prisoners, which "ultimately consisted of some
twelve nationalities and amounted to 182,000 men."
     CSP, 16:1:109-11; LJ, 94(1969):543; Choice, 6(1969):123.

633. Brinkley, George A. **The Volunteer Army and Allied Intervention in South
     Russia, 1917-1921: A Study in the Politics and Diplomacy of the Russian
     Civil War.** Notre Dame, IN: University of Notre Dame Press, 1966. 446p.
     $8.95.
The book is a political and diplomatic history of the civil war in southern Russia,
focusing on the interrelations between the intervening powers and the Volunteer
Army. This remarkable work of historical scholarship also includes rich unpublished

materials from the archives of Columbia University and the Hoover Institution. Brinkley concludes that "Great Russian chauvinism" precluded a compromise between the Whites and the non-Russian nationalities striving for political independence.

SR, 28:4:648-49; Choice, 4(1967):562.

634.   Bunyan, James, and Fisher, H. H., eds. **The Bolshevik Revolution, 1917-1918.** Stanford, CA: Stanford University Press, 1961. 735p. $10.00.

This collection of documents, decrees, manifestos, press reports, and other materials tells how the Bolsheviks seized power in Russia and how they kept it during the first six months of their rule. Editorial notes, summarizing the events, accompany the documents in the collection.

635.   Chamberlin, William Henry. **The Russian Revolution 1917-1921.** Vol. 1: **From the Overthrow of the Czar to the Assumption of Power by the Bolsheviks, 1917-1918.** Vol. 2: **From the Civil War to the Consolidation of Power, 1918-1921.** New York: Grosset & Dunlap, 1965. 2 vols. $2.65 each.

This revised edition of the author's 1948 publication still maintains a leading place among studies examining the Soviet revolution. A chronological record of events between 1917 and 1921 is included.

636.   Daniels, Robert V. **Red October: The Bolshevik Revolution of 1917.** New York: Charles Scribner's Sons, 1967. 271p. $6.95.

Daniels has set out to separate myth from reality in the October revolution, and all who value truth will be indebted to him. In the last analysis, the Soviet regime was born as a result of chance developments and the fact that the Bolsheviks were less disorganized than their enemies. In every respect the book deserves a wider than college audience; it is also recommended for the general reader and especially for secondary school teachers.

SR, 29:3:518-19; Choice, 5(1968):112.

637.   Daniels, Robert V., ed. **The Russian Revolution.** Englewood Cliffs, NJ: Prentice-Hall, 1972. 184p. $5.95.

This is a book of selected extracts from older published accounts of the revolutionary year. The selections bring out the flavor of 1917, the folly, skill, desperation, and luck of its major participants, and the all-engulfing compass of the revolution for the Russian people.

CSP, 15:3:398-99; Choice, 10(1973):342.

638.   Ezergailis, Andrew. **The Latvian Impact on the Bolshevik Revolution.** Boulder, CO: *East European Quarterly,* 1983. 432p. $30.00. Distributed by Columbia University Press. (East European Monographs, no. 144.)

This study focuses on the character of the revolutionary tradition in Latvia, the specific character of the Latvian revolution of 1917, and the impact of the revolution in Latvia on the Bolshevik revolution in general.

639. Footman, David. **Civil War in Russia.** New York: Praeger, 1962. 328p. $8.00.

In this well-presented survey the story is told in a series of episodes or aspects of the war, each related to the role of one of the centers of the struggle. The author expresses his ideas clearly and writes with objectivity and insight, treating persons and events on their own merits. The book is well suited for the general and for the more specialized reader.

SR, 22:4:760-61.

640. Gill, Graeme J. **Peasants and Government in the Russian Revolution.** New York: Barnes & Noble, Harper & Row, 1979. xiv, 233p. $22.50.

Gill describes the attitudes and behavior of Russian peasants from March to October 1917 and details the programs and actions of successive governments toward the peasants during this period. Focus is on the hierarchical systems of land and food (supply) committees set up by the government, their overlapping competence and incompetence, and peasant participation in or rejection of them.

SR, 39:2:304-5; AHR, 85:3:687; Choice, 16(1980):1494.

641. Goldhurst, Richard. **The Midnight War: The American Intervention in Russia, 1918-1920.** New York: McGraw-Hill, 1978. xvi, 288p. + 16pp. photographs. Maps. $14.95.

The strength of this book, especially for aficionados of military history, is the great detail it provides on a number of individual military engagements. The tactics of American and other leaders of the intervention are subjected to microscopic investigation. The fate of the Czechs, hopelessly caught in the quagmire of advancing Bolshevik armies, the ineptitude of the Whites, and the confusion of the Allies serve as the main backdrop for the account.

SR, 39:4:486-87.

642. Keep, John L. **The Russian Revolution: A Study in Mass Mobilization.** New York: W. W. Norton, 1976. xvii, 614p. $19.50. (Revolutions in the Modern World Series.)

The author has amassed a rich store of facts, which confirm his claim that the peasants were at least as important as the workers in making the Russian revolution possible. They also confirm the impression obtained from other published sources that the workers, soldiers, and sailors provided the cadre without whom the revolution could not have triumphed. This detailed account shows that the Bolsheviks did not unleash the forces that contended for power in 1917. However, late in 1917 and in 1918, they succeeded in crushing the rest.

SR, 37:3:668-69; LJ, 102(1977):1377; Choice, 14(1977):1268.

643. Medvedev, Roy A. **The October Revolution.** Translated by George Saunders. New York: Columbia University Press, 1979. xix, 240p. $14.95.

A remarkable synthesis of recently advanced new considerations about the nature and development of the Bolshevik revolution has now come from within the Soviet Union itself, in the work of the renowned Marxist dissident Roy Medvedev. In this work the author looks for the sources of despotic degeneration in Soviet socialism.

RR, 39:3:497-98; Choice, 17(1980):277.

644.   Page, Stanley W., ed. **Russia in Revolution: Selected Readings in Russian Domestic History since 1855**. Princeton, NJ: Van Nostrand, 1965. 299p. $3.75 pa.

The editor includes several essays that illustrate the conditions which led to the revolution of 1917. Five major selections present the views of contemporaries, latter-day historians, and other writers. Some of the readings are translated here for the first time.

645.   Pipes, Richard. **The Formation of the Soviet Union: Communism and Nationalism, 1917-1923**. Cambridge, MA: Harvard University Press, 1954. 286p. Rev. ed. 1964. 365p. $7.95.

This study is among the outstanding contributions to our understanding of nationalism and its development as a political phenomenon in the non-Russian areas of the old tsarist empire. The book deals with the Soviet conquest of the Ukraine, Belorussia, and the Moslem territories. Lenin's exploitation of national sentiments of the non-Russian element receives a commendable scholarly treatment.
    JMH, 29:1:153-54.

646.   Rabinowitch, Alexander. **The Bolsheviks Come to Power: The Revolution of 1917 in Petrograd**. New York: W. W. Norton, 1976. xxxvi, 393p. Illustrated. $14.95.

The author's primary aim in this book is "to reconstruct as fully and accurately as possible, the development of the 'revolution from below'." In so doing, he comes to several conclusions, one of which is that in Petrograd in 1917 the Bolshevik party was successful precisely because it was flexible and responsive to the moods of the populace, in striking contrast to the traditional Leninist model.
    SR, 37:4:669-70; AHR, 82:3:701; Choice, 14(1977):114.

647.   Rabinowitch, Alexander. **Prelude to Revolution: The Petrograd Bolsheviks and the July 1917 Uprising**. Bloomington, IN: Indiana University Press, 1968. 229p. $8.50.

The author believes that a section of the Bolshevik party connected with the military organization and the Petersburg Bolshevik Committee was systematically preparing the disturbances that broke out on July 3, while at the same time the Central Committee of the party tried to create the impression that it urged soldiers and sailors to use the peaceful methods of political struggle to advance their power.
    SR, 31:4:896-97; JMH, 41:3:630.

648.   Reed, John. **Ten Days that Shook the World**. Foreword by V. I. Lenin. Introduction by Granville Hicks. [New York: Modern Library, 1935.] New York: Random House, Vintage Books, 1965. 371p. $1.45 pa.

The American journalist J. Reed, who later became a Communist, managed to get to Russia in time to witness the October revolution. In this book he gives a detailed day-by-day account of events as they took place during that fateful time. This is an illuminating historical document that has become part of the essential literature for that period. Reed's enthusiasm for the Bolsheviks does not diminish the value of this rare firsthand account.

649. Saul, Norman E. **Sailors in Revolt: The Russian Baltic Fleet in 1917.**
Lawrence, KS: The Regents Press of Kansas, 1978. xiv, 312p. + 8 pp.
plates. $17.50.

In attempting to determine why the sailors of the Baltic Fleet constituted one of
the most radical segments of the Russian population in 1917, Saul explores the
relationship between the war and the revolution, the nature of organizations and
leadership at various levels within the fleet, and the influence of party programs
on rank-and-file sailors, while noting the importance of factors peculiar to the
fleet. The author has used many original documents to support his presentation.

SR, 38:4:674-75; AHR, 84:1:215.

650. Snow, Russell E. **The Bolsheviks in Siberia, 1917-1918.** Madison, NJ:
Fairleigh Dickinson University Press, 1977. 269p. $13.50.

The author has broadened the geographic scope of the 1917 Russian revolution
with this study, and informed us about the Bolshevik activities in the vast region
of Siberia. He finds that Bolsheviks showed considerable strength there from the
very beginning of the revolution, and one of his important conclusions is that
the Bolshevik leadership was mostly locally generated, having little to do with
Lenin in Petrograd.

NP, 7:2:237.

651. Thompson, John W. **Revolutionary Russia, 1917.** New York: Charles
Scribner's Sons, 1981. xvi, 206p. Illustrated. Maps. Tables. $14.95.

This study does not pretend to originality of research; rather it is a balanced synthesis of old classic and a limited number of recent studies. Thompson argues that
the revolution might have been avoided had not the war disrupted a promising
course of evolutionary modernization. The February revolution was entirely
leaderless and spontaneous. Lenin is portrayed as single-minded, opportunistic,
but within a consistent theoretical framework. The book emphasizes the existence
and demands of the major social groups in society: soldiers, peasants, workers, and
national minorities. The book will serve well the general reader and the student.

SR, 41:4:709; Choice, 19(1982):979.

652. Williams, Albert Rhys. **Journey into Revolution: Petrograd, 1917-1918.**
Edited by Lucita Williams. Foreword by Josephine Herbst. Chicago:
Quadrangle Books, 1969. 346p. $8.95.

Williams was one of a small band of radical young journalists from the United
States who were drawn to Russia in the aftermath of the February revolution.
He was a correspondent for the New York *Evening Post* when he arrived in Petrograd in early June 1917. His first memoir, *Through the Russian Revolution,* glori-
fied the October revolution. At the time of his death he was reworking this
account, and *Journey into Revolution* is the product of this effort brought to
fruition by his widow.

SR, 29:1:93-94; BL, 66(Feb. 1970):647.

653. Wolfe, Bertram D. **An Ideology in Power: Reflections on the Russian Revolution.** Introduction by Leonard Schapiro. New York: Stein and Day, 1969. 406p. $10.00.

This volume is a collection of twenty-five essays originally published during the preceding twenty-eight years by the eminent scholar Bertram Wolfe. Central to Wolfe's view of history is the conviction that there are no general laws in accordance with which history proceeds. Rather history is the juxtaposition of specific and often unexpected, hence unpredictable, events. Wolfe gives an excellent analysis of the Soviet attempt to rewrite history.

      SR, 29:3:521-22; LJ, 95(1970):4370; Choice, 7(1970):142.

Soviet Union (RSFSR and USSR)

654. Black, Cyril E., ed. **Rewriting Russian History: Soviet Interpretation of Russia's Past.** New York: Praeger, 1956; Vintage Books, 1962. 413p. $7.50. (Praeger Publications in Russian History and World Communism, no. 39.)

In twelve essays the main trends of Soviet historical writing are discussed. In light of the meager literature in English on Russian historiography, this study is a welcome addition.

      SR, 17:2:234-35.

655. Carr, Edward Hallett. **A History of Russia.** Vol. 3: **Socialism in One Country, 1924-1926.** Parts 1 and 2. Baltimore: Penguin Books, 1970.

Volume 3, in two parts, completes Carr's monumental study of Soviet history up to 1926. His series *Socialism in One Country* has dealt exhaustively with the Soviet regime in the two-year period following Lenin's death: social and economic developments in volume 1; central and local politics in volume 2; and now foreign policy and the Communist International in the two parts of volume 3. This volume is, in fact, as much a history of the Communist movement and revolution around the world as it is a history of Soviet Russia.

656. Carrère d'Encausse, Hélène. **A History of the Soviet Union 1917-1953.** Vol. I: **Lenin: Revolution and Power.** Vol. II: **Stalin: Order Through Terror.** Translated by Valence Ionescu. New York: Longman, 1982. Vol. I: 279p.; Vol. II: 269p. $11.95 pa. each.

These two solid volumes, first published in 1979, are invaluable additions to any basic list of works on Soviet Russia in the period 1917-53 whatever the language. The volumes are so compactly written and arranged, and the discussion so informed, that they not only provide an excellent narrative of events but also develop the latest historiographical interpretations. For example, the discussion in the *Lenin* volume of the Bolshevik consolidation of power captures in two excellent paragraphs Lenin's contradictory attitudes toward the power he had seized and the practical realities of its exercise.

      HT, 33(Apr. 1983):41.

657. Dallin, Alexander. **German Rule in Russia 1941-1945: A Study of Occupation Policies.** 2d rev. ed. Boulder, CO: Westview Press, 1981. 707p. $36.00.

Widely acclaimed when first published in 1957, and considered the standard source on the German occupation of the Soviet Union, Dallin's study has now been enlarged by a new final chapter reflecting the author's second look at his own treatment of major issues and also sources and studies that have become available in the interim.

658. Dmytryshyn, Basil. **USSR: A Concise History**. 2d ed. New York: Charles Scribner's Sons, 1971. 585p. $12.50.

This book's distinctive feature is that the last third consists of forty-one appended documents, including in full such useful items as Lenin's "April Theses," the 1936 constitution, and Khrushchev's 1956 "secret speech." Thus it serves particularly well the teacher who wants students to work through and savor some key primary sources of Soviet history.

SR, 32:1:169-70.

659. Pundeff, Marin, ed. and comp. **History in the U.S.S.R.: Selected Readings**. San Francisco, CA: Chandler, 1967. 313p. $6.50. (Hoover Institution Publications.)

This selection of readings on Soviet historiography contains brief essays by Marx, Engels, Plekhanov, Lenin, Stalin, Pokrovsky, Khrushchev, A. M. Pankratova, and N. L. Rubinshtein, in addition to numerous other documents, decrees, and statements that offer an insight into Soviet historiography, interpretation, and changes.

SR, 28:4:565-57.

660. Shteppa, Konstantin F. **Russian Historians and the Soviet State**. New Brunswick, NJ: Rutgers University Press, 1962. 437p. $10.00.

This valuable study tells of Soviet historians and historiography whose services have been subordinated to the Communist ideology. The author's firsthand experiences, until 1941, lend more weight to the account. Soviet historiography underwent several revisions, which are discussed at length.

SR, 21:4:744-45.

661. Treadgold, Donald W. **Twentieth Century Russia**. 3d ed. Chicago: Rand McNally, 1972 (1959, 1964). 563p.

In this updated third edition, chapters 25 through 29 have either been rewritten or added, including the sections that cover Khrushchev's and Brezhnev's regimes. Although this is a history of the USSR, the title does not indicate so: "twentieth century Russia" ceased to exist officially in 1917. The book gives a chronological account up to the early 1970s. However, the author neglects the issue of the non-Russian nationalities and underestimates the size and tragedy of the purges, and the text appears to be written in the spirit of "coexistence."

SR, 21:3:542-44.

General Reference Material

662. Jones, David R., ed. **The Military-Naval Encyclopedia of Russia and the Soviet Union. Vol. 1: "A" (Gliders)-Administration, Military. Vol. 2: Administration, Military, Science of- Admiral Makarov (Ship).** Gulf Breeze, FL: Academic International Press, 1978. Vol. 1: viii, 247p. $29.50; Vol. 2: 1980. vi, 245p. Figures. Tables. $31.00.

This ambitious project should earn a solid place in the field of reference works on military history and Soviet/Russian studies. The volumes, the first of a series that is likely to run to forty to fifty volumes, live up to the editor's claims that "almost half of the contents ... concern items never recorded previously in other standard reference works" and that "if a topic might interest any general or specialist reader, or any student or teacher, it has been included."

SR, 39:3:505-6.

663. Norby, M. O. **Soviet-Aerospace Handbook.** Washington, DC: Government Printing Office, 1978. 223p.

This military manual provides information on the following: general administration, branches (air force, strategic missile forces, air defense, naval aviation, the space program, research and development), doctrine, manpower and finance, service conditions, biographies of twenty-one key figures, and Russian and Western bibliography. Illustrations include seventy pictures of aircraft and missiles and eighteen pages in color of uniforms, insignia, and medals.

664. Parrish, Michael, comp. **The Soviet Armed Forces: Books in English, 1950-1967.** Stanford, CA: Hoover Institution, 1970. 173p. $7.50. (Hoover Institution Bibliographical Series, 48.)

"This bibliography makes a systematic attempt to gather and organize publications on Soviet armed forces into appropriate categories which would allow students to find the material in the subject area of their interests." Listed are books, articles, documents, and special studies. The listing includes 2,146 entries without annotations, yet it is adequately organized by subjects and topics. The author index refers to entries.

Choice, 8(1971):204.

665. U.S. Department of the Army. **Soviet Military Power (Bibliography).** New York: Greenwood Press, 1969 (1959). 186p. $13.00.

First published in 1963 by the Army library, this is an extensive and updated bibliography on Soviet military affairs. The bibliography is arranged by specific subjects dealing with various aspects of the Soviet armed forces. An author index is provided.

History and General Studies

666. Armstrong, John A., ed. **Soviet Partisans in World War II.** Foreword by Philip E. Mosely. Madison, WI: University of Wisconsin Press, 1964. 792p. $12.50.

This work is an illuminating contribution which students of Soviet partisan warfare have long awaited. The volume is divided into two parts: the first consisting of essays about the various aspects of partisan warfare, the second containing five case studies. An appendix provides seventy-four Soviet partisan documents from German archives in translation, as well as a glossary of German and Russian military terms and abbreviations, a selected bibliography, and an index.

AHR, 70:2:461; CH, 49(Oct. 1965):236; Choice, 1(1965):586.

667. Bialer, Seweryn, ed. **Stalin and His Generals: Soviet Military Memoirs of World War II.** New York: Pegasus, 1969. 644p. $10.00.

The book's value lies in its revelation to the general student of Soviet affairs of the treasure house of nonmilitary information contained in the memoirs. Bialer's coverage considerably exceeds the period of Soviet participation in World War II; about one-fourth of the translated material deals with the military during the Great Purge, the Nazi-Soviet Pact period, and the Finnish war. The selections on the nature of military leadership in the USSR and the interaction of civilian and military leaders are especially revealing.

SR, 29:2:316-17; CH, 59(Oct. 1970):240.

668. Carell, Paul. **Scorched Earth: The Russian-German War, 1943-1944.** Translated from the German by Ewald Osers. Boston: Little, Brown, 1970. 556p. $12.50.

It is unusual to find a volume of military history so well written. This book, a sequel to the author's *Hitler Moves East,* continues its fascinating story of the Soviet-German campaigns of World War II. The author has combed through the official archives and has collected diaries and accounts of many German participants. He attributes decisive significance to the battle of Kursk in the summer of 1943. That battle, rather than Stalingrad, is held to have marked the turning point and the end of German prospects for victory.

SR, 30:3:669.

669. Chew, Allen F. **The White Death: The Epic of the Soviet-Finnish Winter War.** East Lansing: Michigan State University Press, 1971. 313p. $12.50.

This work is primarily a study of military tactics. Chew's sources are impressive: published documents, memoirs, and secondary works in English, Finnish, and Russian; archival materials in Washington and Helsinki; and personal interviews with a number of Finnish officers. The result is a more detailed study of the fighting than has hitherto been available in any Western language.

SR, 31:4:900; LJ, 97(1972):1320; Choice, 9(1972):422.

670.　Chuikov, Vasili I. **The Fall of Berlin.** Foreword by Alistair Horne. Translated by Ruth Kisch. New York: Holt, Rinehart & Winston, 1968. 261p. $5.95.

Marshal Chuikov's promise to be sincere did not enable him to avoid three biases. He is completely silent about the Warsaw uprising. His second bias is his ideological interpretation of what is not already established doctrine. Finally, he summarily dismisses everything the Germans have to say. Otherwise, the book is a treasure of information unavailable elsewhere.

　　　SR, 27:4:662-63.

671.　Clark, Alan. **Barbarossa: The Russian-German Conflict, 1941-45.** New York: Morrow, 1965. 522p. $10.00.

Essentially, *Barbarossa* is a military study of combat operations on a grand scale. As a narrative it is tremendously exciting. The author understands tactics and has a keen eye for the relevant and important. He chooses four critical battles: Moscow, 1941; Stalingrad, 1942; Kursk, 1943; and the Oder, 1945.

　　　JMH, 37:4:505-7; AHR, 71:2:549.

672.　Duffy, Christopher. **Borodino and the War of 1812.** New York: Charles Scribner's Sons, 1973. 208p. $10.00.

This is first and foremost a book for the military history enthusiast. It is a detailed descriptive account, based on a wide range of Russian and other sources, of the battle of Borodino, set within the framework of a rather brief sketch of the campaign as a whole. Duffy provides a competent account of the war as a whole and some valuable insights into the technical capabilities of the forces involved and how arms and troops were managed in combat.

　　　SR, 33:4:773-74; Choice, 10(1973):1615.

673.　Erickson, John. **The Road to Berlin.** Boulder, CO: Westview Press, 1983. 700p. $30.00.

This is an analysis of Soviet and German military operations from the temporary stalemate at Stalingrad to the total collapse of the German armed forces and political and administrative structures prior to the final destruction of the Berlin defense. It is a history of strategic and tactical moves and countermoves, of general staff work on the highest and also divisional levels, and of the total commitment of the two adversaries' military and intellectual resources. Erickson is considered the world's best expert on Soviet military history.

674.　Erickson, John. **The Road to Stalingrad: Stalin's War with Germany.** Vol. 1. New York: Harper & Row, 1975. x, 594p. + 8pp. photographs. $25.00.

Erickson, the noted British military historian and writer, is one of the most knowledgeable observers of Soviet military affairs, and his book is probably the best account to date of the first eighteen months of the Russo-German conflict of World War II. The work suffers from the inadequacies of official Soviet records that still remain unavailable to Western historians. A chapter on "Sources and References" presents a great deal of data and constitutes a most valuable source.

　　　SR, 35:2:337-38; Choice, 12(1976):1618.

675.   Erickson, John. **The Soviet High Command: A Military-Political History, 1918-1941.** New York: St. Martin's Press, 1962. 889p. $15.00.

This is a history of the origins and development of Soviet military leadership with an account of the relationship between the military and political rulers. Special attention is paid to the political administration of the armed forces and the commissars as well as the great purges within the army and the connection of military power and foreign policies.

AHR, 68:4:1065.

676.   Garder, Michel. **A History of the Soviet Army.** New York: Praeger, 1966. 226p. $7.50.

Colonel Garder is a first-class expert on Soviet military history whose account begins with Peter the Great, for Garder believes that the Soviet army is the product of two heritages, one based on the two hundred years of military experience accumulated before the revolution, the other on the experience of the Soviet regime itself. The bulk of the book is devoted to a narrative account of the military and politicomilitary history of the Soviet regime up to the fall of Khrushchev. The concluding section contains information on the personnel, structure, and doctrine of the Soviet army today.

SR, 27:1:138-39; LJ, 91(1966):5606.

677.   Garthoff, Raymond L., ed. **Soviet Military Policy: A Historical Analysis.** New York: Praeger, 1966. 285p. $6.50.

This book offers a comprehensive analysis of present-day Soviet, Chinese, and other Communist views and actions with respect to the relationship of war and revolution. Tracing the role of military power in Soviet society, ideology, and domestic and foreign policy, the author appraises the influence of the military in politics, technological developments, and the reorganization of class structure within the Soviet Union. This account is suitable for general and specialized readers.

SR, 27:1:138; JP, 29(1967):185.

678.   Hart, B. H. Liddell, ed. **The Red Army, 1918-1945; the Soviet Army, 1946 to the Present.** Gloucester, MA: Peter Smith, 1968. 480p. $6.75.

This reprint of a publication first issued in 1956 deals with the historical origins, evolution, and maturation of the Soviet army. The contributors treat the history of the Soviet army in a chronological fashion. The reader must be aware of the fact that this is not an updated source, especially on most recent developments concerning nuclear war capacity.

SR, 29:1:112-14.

679.   Higgins, Trumbull. **Hitler and Russia: The Third Reich in a Two-Front War, 1937-1943.** New York: Macmillan, 1966. 310p. $6.95.

In this book the noted military historian Higgins presents a view of the background and course of Hitler's war on the Soviet Union until the end of the Stalingrad campaign. Based on analysis of the memoir, documentary, and monographic literature and also on some recently available information from the Soviet Union, this book will serve both the scholarly community and the general public as an excellent introduction to this fascinating subject.

AHR, 72:3:965; Choice, 3(1967):1068.

680. Jones, David R., ed. **Soviet Armed Forces Review Annual**. Gulf Breeze, FL: Academic International Press, vols. 1-6, 1977-82. Vol. 6. $47.00.

SAFRA assembles and organizes all relevant public information on Soviet military affairs into one standard format on an annual basis. To these data are added analytical topical discussion, documentation, bibliography, and historical background. All entries are prepared by acknowledged experts. The major strength of the series rests with its valuable statistical overview of current Soviet military power accompanied by analyses that examine recent trends and events in the Soviet armed forces.

SR, 37:1:134-35.

681. Kolkowicz, Roman. **The Soviet Military and the Communist Party**. Princeton, NJ: Princeton University Press, 1967. 448p. $9.00.

In probing the relations between the military and the Communist party of the Soviet Union, Kolkowicz is not breaking new ground, but his book represents the most thorough, up-to-date, and sophisticated treatment of this subject. Approximately one-third of the book deals with the nature of institutional conflicts, including an examination of the structure, instruments, and methods employed by the CPSU to control the military establishment. Another third deals with specific issues of conflict that developed in the period 1953-63. Finally, the rise of the new technology and its present and possible future effects are discussed. The author finds that a mild form of pluralism has grown up in Soviet society and that the role and influence of the military are likely to rise in the future.

AHR, 73:3:864-65; Choice, 5(1968):670.

682. Lensen, George Alexander. **The Russo-Chinese War**. Tallahassee, FL: Diplomatic Press, 1967. 315p. $15.00.

Boxer attacks on the Russians and their properties in Manchuria provoked a Russian retaliation sufficient to bring Manchuria under Russian dominance for several years. A very small part of this development is singled out in this book for a detailed description. Lensen devotes his account mainly to military action between the Chinese and Russian soldiers and railwaymen in Manchuria. For the reader who is fascinated by factual description of military battles, this book will have value.

SR, 30:1:148; Choice, 5(1968):104.

683. O'Ballance, Edgar. **The Red Army: A Short History**. New York: Praeger, 1964. 237p. $7.50.

This book is more a popularization than a scholarly analysis, but it is no less worthy of attention. The author has a sound knowledge of Soviet military history, a shrewd eye for relevancies, and a sprightly style of presentation. The book will be pleasing to the general reader and also the specialist, who will know enough about the subject to appreciate the skill with which the narrative has been put together.

SR, 27:1:138-39; Choice, 1(1965):588.

684. Orgill, Douglas. **T-34 Russian Armor**. New York: Ballantine Books, 1971. 160p. $1.00 pa. (Ballantine's Illustrated History of World War II, Weapons Book, no. 21.)

This is an account of the conception, birth, development, and wartime role of the tank. The T-34 was a fast, medium tank with sloped and angled armor, an aspect to which the British and Germans had not then paid much attention, and almost forty thousand were produced, survivors being in action as late as 1967 in the Middle East.

SR, 31:3:680-81.

685.   Pipes, Richard, ed. **Soviet Strategy in Europe**. New York: Crane, Russak & Co., 1976. 316p. $14.50.

This collection of essays is concerned with Soviet strategy in Europe in the sense of a unified application of all means of state power in the service of foreign policy objectives. Four contributions address the political dimension of the problem. Two papers focus on the military dimension of the issues, and the final two papers probe the question of the degree of mutual economic dependence or the lack of it.

SS, 31:4:586; CS, 6(1977):459.

686.   Scott, Harriet Fast, and Scott, William F. **The Armed Forces of the USSR**. Boulder, CO: Westview Press, 1979. xvi, 439p. Illustrated. $24.00.

The authors' familiarity with the Soviet defense establishment and the evolution of Soviet military doctrine, as well as their attention to the institutional and ideological aspects of Soviet decision-making, contribute to an informative account. The study is divided into a historical prologue and three sections dealing with military doctrine and strategy, the contemporary structure of Soviet armed forces, and the integration of those forces into Soviet national life.

SR, 39:3:304-5; Choice, 16(1980):1643.

687.   Scott, Harriet Fast, and Scott, William F., eds. **The Soviet Art of War: Doctrine, Strategy, and Tactics**. Boulder, CO: Westview Press, 1982. 325p. $27.50.

No other country has invested as much intellectual capital and finances in the study of war as has the Soviet Union over the past six decades, and the doctrine, strategy, and tactics that have been developed by Soviet theoreticians are bound to guide any future Soviet military action. This book makes available to Western readers selections from the most significant and influential Soviet military writings from 1917 to the present.

CH:81(1982):335.

688.   Scott, William F. **Soviet Sources of Military Doctrine and Strategy**. New York: Crane, Russak & Co., 1975. viii, 72p. $2.75.

This is an invaluable reference book for anyone interested in Soviet military affairs. The bulk of the book is devoted to a critical examination of the most important Soviet works on military affairs that were published between 1960 and 1974. A list of English translations of Soviet military books is included.

SEER, 55:2:273-74.

689.   Seaton, Albert. **The Russo-German War, 1941-45**. New York: Praeger, 1971. 628p. $15.00.

This is a thorough study by a British colonel professionally familiar with both German and Soviet military establishments. The lay reader will often be more interested in the author's suggestive opinions regarding the reasons for successes and failures than in the abundant technical detail. Seaton finds that Hitler lost the war when, by political misjudgment, he embarked on a two-front war. The author has done a valuable job in sifting the mountains of confusing evidence on the military aspects of German-Soviet war.

SR, 31:2:431-32; AHR, 77:3:781.

690. Sokolovsky, V. D., ed. **Military Strategy: Soviet Doctrine and Concepts.** Introduction by Raymond L. Garthoff. New York: Praeger,. 1963. 416p. $6.50.

Fifteen leading Soviet military theoreticians offer an exposition of the general concepts of strategy, warfare, and mobilization. The book itself is a revealing historical document.

691. Walder, David. **The Short Victorious War: The Russo-Japanese Conflict, 1904-5.** New York: Harper & Row, 1974. 321p. $10.00.

According to the author, the last imperialist war is placed in its context, diplomatic and economic as well as military. Britain supported her new ally; the kaiser supported the tsar against the "Yellow Peril" but took advantage of the weakening of Russia, France's military ally. When Britain and Russia were on the brink of war, France, the ally of both, pulled them back. The United States was the first nation to realize the dangers of a militarily successful Japan. European and U.S. observers failed to appreciate the significance of this first glimpse of twentieth-century warfare.

JMH, 47:3:582; Choice, 11(1975):1822.

692. Zhukov, Georgii K. **The Memoirs of Marshal Zhukov.** New York: Delacorte Press, 1971. 703p. $15.00.

In this translation of Zhukov's memoirs, the author attempts to justify himself, blame others for failure, and answer a variety of critics and rivals. Although Zhukov praises Stalin's general leadership, force of personality, and steel nerves, he is far from the uncritical admirer that some Western writers portray.

SR, 30:1:154-55.

693. Yeremenko, A. I. **The Arduous Beginning.** Translated from the Russian *V Nachale Voiny* by Vic Schneierson. Moscow: Progress Publishers, 1966. 329p.

Marshal Yeremenko's memoirs of the beginning of the war, one of the first books by a senior Soviet commander about World War II, were first published in 1959. A revised edition appeared in 1964 and has now been translated into English. Both versions have given rise to controversy. Yeremenko is best known for his later command of the Stalingrad front.

SR, 27:1:139-41.

Air Force

694. Boyd, Alexander. **The Soviet Air Force since 1918.** Foreword by John Erickson. New York: Stein & Day, 1977. xx, 259p. + 12pp. photographs. $10.00.

Using a large number of Soviet and Western sources, Boyd has done a remarkable job of writing a detailed history of the Soviet air force, covering such fascinating subjects as the Russo-German cooperation in the 1920s; early Soviet theories about the deployment of air power; employment of imprisoned aircraft designers by the NKVD; the failures in the first two years of the Great Patriotic War; and, finally, victory and postwar rebirth.

SR, 37:1:138; AHR, 83:4:1063.

695. Higham, Robin, and Kipp, Jacob W., eds. **Soviet Aviation and Air Power: A Historical View.** Boulder, CO: Westview Press, 1977; London: Brassey's, 1978. xii, 328p. Illustrated. $25.00.

The eleven essays in this book investigate the evolution of Soviet air power from its feeble prerevolutionary origins through the perilous years of World War II to its present position of impressive strength, vitality, and leadership. Unlike most of the more technical works on the Soviet air forces, these essays do a good job of linking politics and leaders to both technical and organizational development.

SR, 38:3:496-97.

696. Wagner, Ray, ed. **The Soviet Air Force in World War II: The Official History, Originally Published by the Ministry of Defense of the USSR.** Translated by Leland Fetzer. Garden City, NY: Doubleday, 1973. 440p. $12.95.

"The original Russian text, as published in the Soviet Union, has been translated and edited by an American team. The history's scope is quite parochial; it confines itself to major Soviet air campaigns only, and does not go into aspects of the war in which their air force was not the largest participant." The main value of the work lies in making Soviet interpretations available to the English-speaking reader.

CR, 225(Aug. 1974):112.

Navy

697. Dismukes, Bradford, and McConnell, James M., eds. **Soviet Naval Diplomacy.** New York: Pergamon Press, 1979. xvii, 409p. $25.00.

A number of authors with the Center for Naval Analyses have contributed to this study of the Soviet navy's peacetime role. The unifying theme is that the Soviet ambition to communize the world has been constant, although the doctrine of the inevitable war with the capitalist West has been changed to one of "peaceful coexistence" to attain the ultimate goal.

RR, 39:2:257; PSQ, 95(Fall 1980):546.

698. Fairhall, David. **Russian Sea Power.** Boston: Gambit, 1971. 287p. $10.00.

This book provides more than adequate information and perspective for a layman interested in the problems posed by the dramatic expansion of Soviet sea power. Fairhall's major thesis is that the Soviet Union, with its centralized planning, is better equipped than any other nation to coordinate its efforts in support of its naval power. The author fully recognizes the immense political effect of the Soviet presence in seas that had never seen the Red flag.

> SR, 31:1:183-84.

699. Herrick, Robert Waring. **Soviet Naval Strategy: Fifty Years of Theory and Practice.** Annapolis, MD: U.S. Naval Institute, 1968. 198p. $9.00.

The author's principal, and most controversial, conclusion is that "current Soviet naval strategy is an essentially deterrent and defensive one." Anyone interested either in current world military affairs or in the Soviet field, as well as the smaller audience directly interested in Soviet military affairs, will find the book worth reading.

> SR, 28:4:649-50; Choice, 5(1969):1493.

700. MacGwire, Michael, ed. **Soviet Naval Developments: Capability and Contest.** New York: Praeger, 1973. 555p. $23.50.

This volume contains contributions by naval specialists and those in related fields who participated in a seminar on Russian naval policy. All participants were concerned with the significance of what seemed a break in the traditional pattern of Russian naval policy—a shift from the old task of coastal defense and support of the land forces to a posture of forward deployment that brought Soviet warships into the Mediterranean, the Caribbean, and the Indian Ocean.

> CASS, 9:1:124; LJ, 99(1974):664; CH, 67(Oct. 1974):177.

701. MacGwire, Michael; Booth, Ken; and McDonnell, John, eds. and comps. **Soviet Naval Policy: Objectives and Constraints.** Published for the Centre for Foreign Policy Studies, Department of Political Science, Dalhousie University, Halifax, Nova Scotia. New York: Praeger Publishers, 1975. xxvi, 663p. $32.50.

Twenty-seven British, Canadian, Australian, and American authors offer in this book informed analysis and debate on the Soviet naval policy. This volume is the second of a trilogy stemming from the conferences held in 1972, 1973, and 1974, providing a unique source of the latest developments concerning the Soviet navy.

> SR, 35:4:740-41.

702. MacGwire, Michael, and McDonnell, John, eds. **Soviet Naval Influence: Domestic and Foreign Dimensions.** Published for the Centre for Foreign Policy Studies, Department of Political Science, Dalhousie University, Halifax, Nova Scotia. New York and London: Praeger Publishers, 1977. xxxvi, 660p. $27.50.

The contributions of twenty-eight members of the third seminar at Dalhousie University are arranged under eight headings: aspects of Soviet foreign policy, the place of the navy in the policy processes, war fighting capability, projection capability, some analytical material, East-West naval interaction, the Soviet navy and the Third World influence building, and future prospects.

> SR, 37:1:138-40; CH, 75(Oct. 1978):124.

703. Moore, John E. **The Soviet Navy Today.** Introduction by John Erickson.
      New York: Stein & Day, 1976. 255p. Photographs. $15.95.
This book is divided by ship types, each section introduced by a short historical
narrative and each ship class replete with vital statistics, a silhouette, and one representative photograph. Using the historical development of the post-World War II
navy as his vehicle, Moore focuses on serious qualitative handicaps in the Soviet
navy, such as lack of experience in global naval operations, poor relations between
the navy and the political commissars, and other problems.
      SR, 36:2:319-20.

704. Murphy, Paul J., ed. **Naval Power in Soviet Policy.** Published under the
      auspices of the United States Air Force. Washington, DC: U.S. Govern-
      ment Printing Office, 1978. xiv, 341p. $5.25 pa. (Studies in Communist
      Affairs, vol. 2.)
Some of the sixteen contributors are former U.S. naval officers whose careers
included service directly concerned with the analysis of Soviet naval affairs. Four
essays focus on the origins of Soviet naval policy, eight articles are devoted to an
assessment of Soviet naval combat characteristics, and others concern naval arms
limitation efforts and Soviet naval deployment in the Mediterranean and the Indian
Ocean. This book is important for anyone interested in contemporary international
security affairs.
      SR, 39:2:316-17.

705. Ruge, Friedrich. **The Soviets as Naval Opponents, 1941-1945.** Annapolis,
      MD: Naval Institute Press, 1979. viii, 210p. $16.95.
Ruge served in the German High Seas Fleet in World War I and held various responsible posts in the *Kriegsmarine* during World War II, along with occupying high
positions in the Federal German navy. His book is not a memoir but a well-
considered narrative based on German war diaries, Soviet publications, and works
by Western scholars.
      RR, 39:2:257-59.

706. Watson, Bruce W. **Red Navy at Sea: Soviet Naval Operations on the High
      Seas, 1956-1980.** Boulder, CO: Westview Press, 1982. 245p. $27.00.
This is the only book to offer a detailed chronology of modern Soviet naval operations set within the framework of long-range Soviet foreign and domestic policy.
Watson argues that the physical configuration strategy and operations of the Soviet
navy are not merely pragmatic reactions to crises or shifts in world power trends;
rather they reflect a deliberate long-term pattern designed to attain equal-partner
status with other Soviet military forces.
      PSQ, 98(Summer 1983):355; Choice, 20(1982):648.

707. Wegener, Edward. **The Soviet Naval Offensive: An Examination of the
      Strategic Role of Soviet Naval Forces in the East-West Conflict.** Trans-
      lated from the German by Henning Wegener. Annapolis, MD: Naval Insti-
      tute Press, 1975 (1972, 1974). x, 135p. $11.00.
Wegener, a retired German naval officer who served both during World War II and
in NATO Command, has written an important book not only for strategists but

for all persons seriously concerned with Soviet foreign policy. He provides a plausible strategic doctrine for evaluation of Soviet and Western naval postures.
SR, 35:4:742.

708. Woodward, David. **The Russians at Sea: A History of the Russian Navy.** New York: Praeger, 1966. 254p. $6.95.
This book offers an able and informative account of Russian sea power from the time of Peter the Great. It deals at much greater length with the history of the Imperial Russian Navy than with the Soviet period. Woodward argues in this study that Russian and Soviet leaders alike looked to their navies to serve the strategic interests and prestige of an essentially landlocked power.
RR, 25:4:414-16; Choice, 3(1966):844.

Special Studies

709. Colton, Timothy J. **Commissars, Commanders, and Civilian Authority: The Structure of Soviet Military Politics.** Cambridge, MA, and London: Harvard University Press, 1979. xii, 365p. Tables. $25.00.
Colton challenges the specific conclusion that the CPSU leadership uses the military's *Glavpu* and its network of political officers to monitor and control the professional military men, as well as the general interpretation that the Soviet military leadership is locked in a zero-sum struggle for influence with the Soviet political leadership.
SR, 40:1:123-24; Choice, 16(1979):1228.

710. Deane, Michael J. **Political Control of the Soviet Armed Forces.** New York: Crane, Russak & Co., 1977. xi, 297p. $17.50.
Providing a historical overview of party-army relations from 1917 to Ustinov's promotion to defense minister in 1976, Deane concludes that civilian party leaders experience continuing problems in their efforts to control the MPA and the professional military. Unfortunately, the author relies too much on secondary sources for the pre-Khrushchev period.
SR, 37:1:134-35; AAPSS-A, 436(1978):165.

711. Gabriel, Richard A. **The New Red Legions.** Vol. 1: **An Attitudinal Portrait of the Soviet Soldier.** Vol. 2: **A Survey Data Source Book.** Westport, CT: Greenwood Press, 1980. Vol. 1: 312p. $22.50; Vol. 2: 280p. $40.00.
This is the first study of the Red army based on concrete empirical data. Gabriel conducted a comprehensive survey of recent émigrés from the Soviet Union, men who had served in the Soviet army. The study profiles Soviet soldiers of every rank and analyzes their leadership qualities, combat abilities, and relations with other ranks. Every aspect of daily army life is discussed. This is the most thoroughly researched work yet produced on the Soviet soldier.
Choice, 18(1981):1160.

712. Gallagher, Matthew P., and Spielmann, Karl F., Jr. **Soviet Decision-Making for Defense: A Critique of U.S. Perspectives on the Arms Race.** New York: Praeger, 1972. 102p. $12.50.

The authors conclude that defense policy is initiated at the top levels of the party hierarchy, that the military has a preferential but subordinate position in military policy formation, and that the scientists lack the institutional and political advantages to play the kind of role their American counterparts have enjoyed. These may be commonplace assertions, but the supporting argumentation is relatively fresh, and it cannot be repeated often enough that Soviet military policies are the product of truly political processes.

CSP, 16:1:116-18; Choice, 10(1973):1074.

713.   Garthoff, Raymond L. **Soviet Military Policy: A Historical Analysis.** New York: Praeger, 1966. 276p. $6.50.

The author tackles an elusive subject in his book on Soviet military policy, one that concerns an aspect of Soviet activity which intertwines with all the other activities by which the Soviet Union functions as a society. Garthoff succeeds in bringing all these relationships clearly into the field of vision of the reader while maintaining a sharp focus on the role of military power in Soviet policy. The book is packed with information.

SR, 27:1:136; JP, 29(1967):185.

714.   Goldhamer, Herbert. **The Soviet Soldier: Soviet Military Management at the Troop Level.** New York and London: Crane, Russak & Co. and Leo Cooper Ltd., 1975. xvi, 352p. $17.00.

The author of this book has put together a rather remarkable account of the life and times of the Soviet soldier and lower grade officer. He has made good use of the resources available, and shows that data exist upon which some critical judgments may be made. The book adds to the knowledge of the adversary and will serve students of the Soviet military.

SR, 36:1:131-32; Choice, 13(1976):428.

715.   Gouré, Leon, et al. **The Role of Nuclear Forces in Current Soviet Strategy.** Coral Gables, FL: Center for Advanced International Studies, University of Miami, 1974. 148p. $8.95.

The contributors to this significant volume argue that the West makes a dangerous mistake when accepting Soviet declarations at face value; that American behavior is based on wishful thinking; that illusions prevail over realities. Soviet declarations and actions are two different things, and to take public statements seriously is dangerously naive. The book deserves the attention of the American public because it conveys a realistic picture of the Soviet regime and its global strategies.

JP, 37(1975):870; Choice, 12(1975):142.

716.   Gouré, Leon. **War Survival in Soviet Strategy: USSR Civil Defense.** Foreword by Ambassador Foy D. Kohler. Coral Gables, FL: Center for Advanced International Studies, University of Miami, 1976. xxiv, 218p. $11.95 pa. (Monographs in International Affairs.)

The author addresses the subject from the standpoint of his—and the Miami Center's—broad concerns over Soviet political-military intentions and capabilities. The book includes an extensive review of the copious and detailed Soviet open literature on civil defense. The study makes a useful—if flawed—contribution to a subject that indeed deserves attention.

SR, 36:2:318-19.

717. Lomov, N. A., ed. **Scientific-Technical Progress and the Revolution in Military Affairs (A Soviet View).** Translated and published under the auspices of the U.S. Air Force.[Moscow: Voennoe Izdatel'stvo Ministerstva Oborony SSSR.] Washington, DC: Government Printing Office, 1973. 279p. $2.25 pa.

This book was written by a group of Soviet officers who were selected to contribute to the *Communist of the Armed Forces* and other journals. It describes the present stage in the development of Soviet military theory and practice as related to general scientific progress. How nuclear weapons have brought about a revolution in military thinking and the formulation of a new strategy is the underlying theme.

718. Milsom, John. **Russian Tanks, 1900-1970: The Complete Illustrated History of Soviet Armoured Theory and Design.** Harrisburg, PA: Stackpole Books, 1971. 192p. $11.95.

Milsom has compiled a complete illustrated history of Soviet armored theory and design. He traces the evolution and development of Soviet armor from its early confused and amateurish fumblings to present-day practical and professional efficiency. This work should be on the reference shelves and within easy reach of all military students, commentators, writers, and planners.

SR, 31:3:680-81.

719. Savkin, V. E. **The Basic Principles of Operational Art and Tactics (A Soviet View).** Translated and published under the auspices of the U.S. Air Force. [Moscow: Voennoe Izdatel'stvo Ministerstva Oborony SSSR.] Washington, DC: Government Printing Office, 1972. 284p. $3.20 pa.

The author reveals only partly the nature of the discussion and changes in the thinking of the Soviet military establishment. He examines more peripheral issues related to modern warfare and technology without providing details on Soviet armament and weaponry. He insists on the importance of maintaining strong ground forces supported by tanks and other conventional war equipment, and he concludes that achieving a nuclear balance with the United States makes Soviet conventional forces indispensable, considering geopolitical factors affecting the Soviet Union.

720. Smith, Myron J., Jr. **The Soviet Air and Strategic Rocket Forces, 1939-80: A Guide to Sources in English.** Foreword by Kenneth R.Whiting. Santa Barbara, CA, and London: ABC-Clio Press, 1981. xiv, 321p. Charts. $45.00. (War/Peace Bibliography Series, no. 10.)

This is a useful preliminary guide for research on Soviet aerospace forces, and it should constitute a welcome reference tool for libraries and specialists. The book contains seven main sections, each with a separate introduction and a note on cross reference. Each section is arranged alphabetically under the headings "books," "articles," and "documents, papers, and reports." The seven main sections are preceded by a chronology, and followed by four appendixes and the author index.

SR, 41:4:727-28; RQ, 21(Winter 1981):204.

721.   Spielmann, Karl F. **Analyzing Soviet Strategic Arms Decisions**. Boulder, CO: Westview Press, 1978. xvi, 184p. $16.00.

In this book, Spielmann considers "strategic factor" and plurastic (bureaucratic) decision-making models and then proposes an additional variant of both, which he calls a "national leadership decision-making" approach. The author presents an interesting "case study" of the deployment decision for the first Soviet ICBM system, the SS-6. The book should prove useful to those with particular interest in Soviet political-military affairs.

AAPSS-A, 445(1979):173.

RUSSIAN LANGUAGE

Dictionaries and Glossaries

722. Benson, Morton. **Dictionary of Russian Personal Names with A Guide to Stress and Morphology**. Philadelphia: University of Pennsylvania Press, 1964. 175p. $4.75. (University of Pennsylvania Studies in East European Languages and Literatures.)

This work, the most comprehensive of its kind, has been compiled with scrupulous care. The dictionary contains approximately twenty-three thousand surnames and a full list of Russian given names with their numerous diminutives. The introduction gives examples of the declension of surnames and of the stress movements in their declensions.

SEER, 45:104:220-21.

723. Borkowski, Piotr. **The Great Russian-English Dictionary of Idioms and Set Expressions: Over 8,600 Russian Entries**. London: Piotr Borkowski, 1973. xx, 384p. £5.00.

This book gives good English equivalents for the Russian entries, all of which are accented and labeled to indicate stylistic levels and usage. The work is arranged so that it is almost always easy to find the expression that one is looking for. In many cases, the Russian expressions are first translated by an English expression of the same stylistic level, which is then followed by a more literal and stylistically neutral translation, making it more comprehensive.

SR, 35:4:780-81.

724. Macura, Paul. **Russian-English Dictionary of Electrotechnology and Allied Sciences**. New York: Wiley Interscience Press, 1971. 707p. $32.50.

The dictionary contains about sixty thousand entries and is the largest of its kind. It will be most useful to anyone concerned with Russian electrotechnology.

SR, 31:4:949.

725. Müller, V. K. **Anglo-russkii slovar** (English-Russian Dictionary). Moscow: Izd. 'Sovetskaia entsiklopediia', 1971. 912p.; New York: E. P. Dutton & Co., 1976.

The dictionary covers about seventy thousand words and terms together with examples of their use.

726. Paternost, Joseph. **Russian-English Glossary of Linguistic Terms**. University Park: Department of Slavic Languages, Pennsylvania State University, 1965. 230p. $4.00 pa.

The photo-offset copy *Glossary* consists of 230 pages, each containing roughly fifty-two Russian items in the left column, and opposite each, in the right column, the English equivalent(s). This makes a total of around 11,960 Russian items. The *Glossary* is mainly intended to be of use to students at the level of either advanced grammar review or linguistic analysis of modern Russian. In addition, the *Glossary* will have a very substantial interest for Russian teachers and researchers and, in general, for anyone interested in the lexicon of Russian language study.

SEEJ, 10:1:93-95.

727. Vitek, Alexander J. **Russian-English Idiom Dictionary**. Edited by Harry H. Josselson. Detroit: Wayne State University Press, 1973. 328p. $19.95.

In this case, educated native speakers of Russian and English have worked together in an admirable combination of man and machine processing. Well over five thousand headword items are included in the dictionary. Headwords and English references are given in capital letters for easy identification.

SR, 33:4:838-39.

728. Wheeler, Marcus. **The Oxford Russian-English Dictionary**. Edited by B. O. Unbegaun with D. P. Costello and W. F. Ryan. Oxford: Clarendon Press, 1972. 918p. $18.00.

The Wheeler dictionary is superior to Smirnitsky's *Russko-angliiskii slovar'* in giving related forms. Both dictionaries, however, attempt to present the basic Russian vocabulary along with colloquial expressions, idioms, and technical words that might be encountered in the reading experience of an educated person. The Wheeler dictionary has some seventy thousand entries and Smirnitsky's about fifty thousand, though Smirnitsky is more generous with examples.

SR, 32:2:431-32.

729. Wilson, Elizabeth A. M. **The Modern Russian Dictionary for English Speakers**. Elmsford, NY: Pergamon Press, 1982. 715p.

The dictionary comprises over seventy-five thousand words and illustrative phrases. It is the first to be written primarily for the native speaker of English who wishes to speak and write Russian as it is used in the Soviet Union today. Words are shown in a broad spectrum of contexts, and shades of meaning are indicated.

730. Worth, Dean S.; Kozak, Andrew S.; and Johnson, Donald B. **Russian Derivational Dictionary**. New York: American Elsevier, 1970. 747p. $22.95.

This dictionary should prove an invaluable aid to the Russian linguist. It is likely to become as indispensable a work as the orthographic or the backwards dictionary. It is based on the 110,000-word corpus of the Ozhegov-Shapiro *Orfograficheskii slovar' russkogo izayka* (4th ed., Moscow, 1959) but is not as exhaustive as the Russian; it is, rather, a dictionary of Russian roots on vaguely etymological principles.

SEEJ, 18:4:455-56.

Textbooks and Grammars

731. Derwing, Bruce L., and Priestly, Tom M. **Reading Rules for Russian: A Systematic Approach to Russian Spelling and Pronunciation.** With notes on dialectal and stylistic variation. Columbus, OH: Slavica Publishers, 1980. vi, 247p. $10.95 pa.

In developing their rules, the authors provide a great deal of essential information about the phonological processes of Russian in a manner that is clear, concise, complete, and systematic enough for the student to grasp.
SR, 40:3:510.

732. Doherty, Joseph C., et al. **Russian: Book One.** Boston: D. C. Heath, 1968. 303p. **Russian: Book Two.** Boston: D. C. Heath, 1970. 382p.

Both volumes are intended to serve as a two-year introduction to the Russian language. The authors assume a five-period week. If less time is available, they suggest a three-year course. The two volumes together consist of an introduction and thirty-five lessons. Much of the text is devoted to drills, especially pattern drills. Each volume also contains appendixes giving declension and conjugation paradigms, lists of verbs dealt with in that volume, indexes, and a Russian-English and an English-Russian glossary.
SR, 29:2:355-56.

733. Gentilhomme, Y. **Russian for Scientists: A New Approach.** 4 vols. Translated by J. F. Henry. Preface by Jean Train. Paris: Dunod, 1970. Vol. 1: 163p.; Vol. 2: 165-345pp.; Vol. 3: 347-507pp.; Vol. 4: 659p.

The first volume begins with the alphabet and consists of ten chapters treating various parts of Russian grammar. In volume two we find articles to be read and translated. The third volume continues with articles to be translated, this time demonstrating the verb system as well as dative and instrumental cases. The fourth volume continues discussion of verbs, with still more articles for translation, followed by a table of units, a bibliography of recommended grammars, readers, and many dictionaries pertaining to specific fields of science, such as mathematics, nuclear physics, chemistry, and electricity. This work is one of the few serious treatments of Russian language study purely for a science student, and because of its completeness it should be highly recommended.
SR, 31:4:948.

734. Gould, S. H. **Russian for the Mathematician.** New York: Springer-Verlag, 1972. 211p. $8.80 pa.

This little book is intended to teach mathematicians and students of mathematics exactly enough Russian to be able to read mathematical Russian. For this limited objective the book is completely successful. The author himself is a mathematician and philologist who for many years directed the translation program of the American Mathematical Society.
SR, 32:2:432-33.

735. Harrison, William; Clarkson, Yelena; and Le Fleming, Stephen. **Colloquial Russian.** London: Routledge & Kegan Paul, 1973. 428p. $8.00.

This book is the latest in a series of language manuals devised primarily for the mature student working alone. A brief introduction deals with rules of Russian pronunciation, the alphabet, rules of spelling, and reading practice. The manual is divided into twenty-eight lessons, each consisting of four parts; reading text, vocabulary, grammar, and exercises. Highly motivated students should find this book most rewarding.

CSP, 15:4:623.

736. Levin, Jules F., and Kaikalis, Peter D., with Anatole A. Forostenko. **Reading Modern Russian**. Columbus, OH: Slavica Publishers, 1979. viii, 321p. $10.95 pa.

The stated aim of this book is to teach "the comprehension of Russian expository prose" to students with no prior knowledge of the language. The book is composed of thirty-one chapters, four appendixes, a vocabulary list, and a brief subject index. Each chapter begins with a vocabulary, followed by explanations of grammar and usage and lists of sample sentences in Russian.

SR, 39:4:722-23.

737. Nakhimovsky, Alexander, and Leed, Richard. **Advanced Russian**. Columbus, OH: Slavica Publishers, 1980. 380p. $11.95 pa.

This book represents a significant contribution to Russian textbook publishing. Being solidly based on original scholarly research, the volume goes considerably beyond previous textbooks in its treatment of certain grammatical problems that have thus far eluded satisfactory explanation. The text will be of great benefit to advanced language students.

SEEJ, 25:1:128-30.

738. Phillips, Roger W. **A Concise Russian Review Grammar with Exercises**. Madison, WI: University of Wisconsin Press, 1974. 108p. $2.95 pa.

This little handbook aims to provide "a trouble-shooting approach" to grammar review for students at the stage between the elementary and advanced levels. A positive feature of the book is that it gathers together much of the collective wisdom and commonsense judgments that Russian teachers have been disseminating in classrooms in one way or another.

SEEJ, 18:2:199-203.

739. Rudy, Peter; Youhn, Xenia L.; and Nebel, Henry M., Jr. **Russian: A Complete Elementary Course**. New York: W. W. Norton, 1970. 522p. $7.50.

This attractively printed volume is designed to integrate the functions of an elementary grammar, introductory conversation, and graded reader. The authors have aimed at combining both audiolingual and traditional methods and thus provide the basis for training in the fundamentals of aural comprehension. The book contains approximately fourteen hundred vocabulary items. Tape recordings are available from the publisher.

SR, 30:4:912-13.

740. Townsend, Charles E. **Continuing with Russian**. New York: McGraw-Hill, 1970. 426p. $9.95 pa.

This is the first grammar textbook with exercises written specifically for the American student at the intermediate-advanced level. It is also the first Russian textbook for this level of study to be firmly based on some of the more important linguistic research on Russian of the past half-century.

SEEJ, 16:1:113-16.

741. Walker, Gregory P. M. **Russian for Librarians.** London: Clive Bingley, 1973. 126p. $8.50. Distributed by Linnet Books, Hamden, CT.

This book fills a need in library literature as a concise, well-organized survey for English-speaking librarians and staff who work with Russian materials. Beginning with a review of Russian grammar, the author presents clear definitions, tables, and helpful exercises, using typical library words and phrases. Following this is a logical, although uneven, exposition on transliteration, cataloging, acquisitions, standard reference books, and identification of East European languages.

SR, 33:4:842-43.

RUSSIAN LITERATURE

General Reference Material

742. Moody, Fred, ed. **The Bibliographies of Twentieth Century Russian Literature.** Ann Arbor, MI: Ardis, 1977. 175p. $14.95.
Some of the bibliographies include introductory notes, some have indexes, some are in Cyrillic, some are transliterated; most are complete through 1971. They are all arranged differently: some by year of publication, others by broad categories of publications by and about these authors, and the rest by other arrangements.
SR, 38:3:546.

743. Weber, Harry B., ed. **The Modern Encyclopedia of Russian and Soviet Literatures (Including Non-Russian and Emigre Literatures).** Gulf Breeze, FL: Academic International Press, 1977-82. 6 vols.
MERSL is the most comprehensive reference source for the literary culture of the peoples of Russia and the Soviet Union. Volumes 1-6 (Ab-Ep) contain nearly 1,275 entries. Volumes 7 and 8 are planned for 1983; fifty volumes are planned, plus indexes and supplement.

744. Zenkovsky, Serge A., and Arbruster, David L., comps. **A Guide to the Bibliographies of Russian Literature.** Nashville, TN: Vanderbilt University Press, 1970. 62p. $4.50.
This is a concise compilation of all known existing bibliographies of Russian literature, in all languages, to 1970. There are two sections: "General Bibliography," subdivided by source, and "Literary Bibliography," subdivided by field. Entries are arranged according to the Library of Congress catalog.
WLB, 45(1971):883.

General Surveys and Histories

745. Brown, Deming. **Soviet Russian Literature since Stalin.** New York and London: Cambridge University Press, 1978. vi, 394p. $24.95.
This excellent survey of recent Soviet Russian literature is organized not chronologically as a history but by genres, topics, and individual authors. There are chapters on poets and prose, special concerns, and Solzhenitsyn and Siniavsky; one chapter is allotted to underground literature. Within these divisions, Brown provides biographical sketches and plot summaries.
SR, 37:4:716-17.

746. Čiževskij, Dmitrij. **History of Nineteenth-Century Russian Literature**. 2 vols. Translated by Richard Noel Porter. Edited by Serge A. Zenkovsky. Vol. 1: **The Romantic Period**. 236p.; Vol. 2: **The Age of Realism**. 218p. $5.95 each. Nashville, TN: Vanderbilt University Press, 1974 (1964, 1967).

These two books are the central portion of what will eventually be a four-volume history of Russian literature from the eleventh century to approximately 1920, the end of the Silver Age. It is an invaluable reference work by a distinguished scholar who has devoted his life to Russian literature.

RR, 34:2:226-27.

747. Drage, C. L. **Russian Literature in the Eighteenth Century: The Solemn Ode. The Epic. Other Poetic Genres. The Story. The Novel. Drama. An Introduction for University Courses**. London: Author's Publication, 1978. 281p. £4.00. Copies available from 94 Inverness Terrace, London W2, England.

The principal merit of this book is that it concerns itself undeviatingly with literature as a body of written texts; the author has obviously made a firsthand study of all the texts he discusses. No space is given to biographical, sociological, or political data.

SEER, 59:2:287-88.

748. Fennell, John, ed. **Nineteenth-Century Russian Literature: Studies of Ten Russian Writers**. Berkeley, CA: University of California Press, 1973. 356p. $15.00.

This volume consists of eight studies of Russian writers—seven prose writers and three poets: Turgenev, Dostoevsky, Tolstoy, Pushkin, Gogol, Chekhov, and others. Each essay contains a select bibliography and some also offer biographical and critical literature.

SR, 34:1:191-93; Choice, 10(1973):1394.

749. Freeborn, Richard; Donchin, Georgette; and Anning, N. J. **Russian Literary Attitudes from Pushkin to Solzhenitsyn**. Edited by Richard Freeborn. London: Macmillan; New York: Barnes & Noble, Harper & Row, 1976. viii, 158. $22.50.

This is a collection of essays on the total literary careers of six authors (chronologically presented): Pushkin, Dostoevsky, Tolstoy, Gorky, Pasternak, and Solzhenitsyn.

SR, 36:2:345-46; Choice, 14(1977):209.

750. Gifford, Henry. **The Novel in Russia: From Pushkin to Pasternak**. London: Hutchinson University Library; New York: Hillary House, 1964. 208p. $3.00 pa.

This book gives a comprehensive, enlightened view of the subject. Some excellent parallels with English literature help considerably. For example, Turgenev is compared with Thackeray, Saltykov-Shchedrin with George Eliot, and the beginning of Sholokhov's *The Quiet Don* is likened to Thomas Hardy.

SR, 29:3:555-57; Choice, 2(1965):393.

751. Hosking, Geoffrey. **Beyond Socialist Realism: Soviet Fiction since Ivan Denisovich.** New York: Holmes & Meier, 1980. x, 260p. $27.50.
This volume attempts to reevaluate what the author calls the "socialist realist tradition," and he discovers in recent Soviet literature evidence not only of departures from that tradition but also of its persistence, even in certain dissident and émigré writers. The author has surveyed and analyzed a representative sample of contemporary Russian writing.
RR, 39:4:520-22.

752. Markov, Vladimir. **Russian Futurism: A History.** Berkeley: University of California Press, 1968. 467p. $12.00.
This is the first history of Russian futurism either in Russian or in any Western language. A wealth of bibliographic material is supplied, and over thirty pages of reproductions are included: photographs and portraits of prominent futurists and pages, drawings, and book covers from some of the most characteristic futurist publications. Thus, all major poets and many others are presented as men and artists in this book.
SEEJ, 14:1:67-69; Choice, 6(1969):44.

753. Mihailovich, Vasa D., comp. and ed. **Modern Slavic Literatures.** Vol. 1: **Russian Literature.** New York: Frederick Ungar, 1972. 424p. $15.00. (A Library of Literary Criticism.)
Mihailovich has examined a wide range of materials concerning each author (sixty-nine in all of the twentieth century), and selected from these materials excerpts that are stimulating. Many of these selections are translated from Russian for the first time, and the translations read well.
SR, 32:3:665; Choice, 10(1973):600.

754. Segel, Harold B. **Twentieth-Century Russian Drama: From Gorky to the Present.** New York: Columbia University Press, 1979. xviii, 502p. Photographs. $27.50.
This is a richly illustrated history of Russian drama since Chekhov. It is indeed a pioneering work that succeeds in an ambitious task.
SR, 40:1:145-47; LJ, 104(1979):2573; Choice, 17(1980):80.

755. Slonim, Marc. **Soviet Russian Literature: Writers and Problems, 1917-1967.** Rev. ed. New York: Oxford University Press, 1967. 373p. $2.25 pa.
Slonim's book is not something entirely new; originally it formed part of the second volume (*Modern Russian Literature: From Chekhov to the Present, 1953*) of his two-volume history of Russian literature. Revised, corrected, and enlarged, it was then published under its present title in 1964. Since then it has been once more revised and brought up to date—that is, its account of Soviet literature was extended from 1963 to 1967. Slonim's book is meant for the general reader, and it certainly provides such a reader with a good overall, vividly written survey of Soviet literature during the fifty years of its existence.
SR, 27:2:352-53.

756.　Stacy, R. H. **Russian Literary Criticism: A Short History**. Syracuse, NY: Syracuse University Press, 1974. 268p. $8.00 pa.

The book is well-informed and well-balanced—a pioneer study of Russian literary criticism from Lomonosov to the 1970s. It will serve the English-speaking student well. There is no bibliography, but all the important relevant literature available in English is listed at the end of each chapter.

　　　　RR, 34:3:345-46; Choice, 12(1975):690.

757.　Struve, Gleb. **Russian Literature under Lenin and Stalin, 1917-1953**. Norman, OK: University of Oklahoma Press, 1971. 454p. $9.95.

The author masterfully structures and controls a mass of unwieldy materials. The footnotes make fascinating reading all by themselves. Incisive periodization is supported by a lucid grasp of what the regime has done to the literary life of the country.

　　　　SR, 31:1:197-98.

758.　Waliszewski, Kazimierz. **A History of Russian Literature**. Port Washington, NY: Kennikat, 1969 (1927). 451p. $15.00.

The first edition of this popular history of Russian literature was published in 1900. Though written in journalistic form, the book provides adequate information on the various subjects and offers pertinent criticism, explanations, and analyses that are not always found in other histories. This work makes good reading for the general reader who is not interested in academic complexities.

Anthologies

759.　Carlisle, Olga Andreyev, and Styron, Rose, eds. and trans. **Modern Russian Poetry**. New York: Viking Press, 1972. 210p. $6.95.

The collection reads quite easily. The survey is accompanied by an index with a chronological chart of Russian history, 1613-1968. Each poet is introduced by a short chatty essay, often incorporating family recollections and accounts of meetings between the editors and the poets.

　　　　SR, 32:4:855-57.

760.　Erlich, Victor, ed. **Twentieth-Century Russian Literary Criticism**. New Haven, CT: Yale University Press, 1975. ix, 317p. $15.00.

Erlich attempts to provide the nonspecialist with a selection of the best Russian literary criticism of this century. Seventeen essays provide information on the symbolists, formalists and near-formalists, early Soviet Marxists, émigré critics, and the recent scene. The editor also gives a brief sketch of the highlights of Russian twentieth-century criticism. The anthology is an especially useful introduction for the general reader.

　　　　CSP, 19:3:390-91; Choice, 13(1976):78.

761.　Field, Andrew, comp. **The Complection of Russian Literature: A Cento**. New York: Atheneum; Toronto: McClelland & Stewart, 1971. 324p. $8.95.

This is an interesting and well-chosen anthology of Russian literary criticism, slightly over half of it by Russian creative writers themselves, with a little literary gossip, psychological speculation, and paranoid slander thrown in for spice.

　　　　SEEJ, 16:3:356-57.

762.   Ginsburg, Mirra, ed. and trans. **The Ultimate Threshhold: A Collection of the Finest in Soviet Science Fiction.** New York: Holt, Rinehart & Winston, 1970. 244p. $5.95.

The author has emerged as one of the finest translators of contemporary Soviet Russian literature. *The Ultimate Threshhold* is the first English translation of Soviet science fiction, which is increasingly becoming popular with Soviet writers and young Soviet readers eager to escape from the monotony of "Socialist realism."

763.   Kuzminsky, Konstantin K., and Kovalev, Gregory L. **The Blue Lagoon: Anthology of Modern Russian Poetry.** Vol. 1. Newtonville, MA: Oriental Research Partners, 1980. 606p. $28.00.

This first of a projected series of five volumes includes forty poets, sixty articles, and ninety-seven photographs. The anthology draws upon almost exclusively unpublished archival materials from Moscow and Leningrad. Forthcoming volumes, all with rare illustrations smuggled out of the USSR, will be published soon.

764.   Olgin, Moissaye J. **A Guide to Russian Literature (1820-1917).** New York: Russell & Russell, 1971 (1920). 323p. $14.00.

The author has selected from the literary production of the nineteenth and twentieth centuries only those literary pieces which are of certain value because of their artistic qualities or which represent some aspect of Russian life. Olgin also surveys the growth of a national literature, the "modernists," and "the recent tide" (1900-1917).

765.   Pachmuss, Temira, ed. and trans. **Women Writers in Russian Modernism: An Anthology.** Chicago and London: University of Illinois Press, 1978. xvi, 340p. $17.50.

This anthology fascinates and intrigues the reader by its novelty—it introduces new facts, faces, and unfamiliar personalities demanding further investigation. The book can be recommended to readers seeking to gain greater familiarity with the variety of literary experiences comprising the Silver Age. Pachmuss provides basic data about each author.

SR, 39:1:162; Choice, 16(1979):398.

766.   Pomorska, Krystyna, ed. **Fifty Years of Russian Prose: From Pasternak to Solzhenitsyn.** 2 vols. Cambridge, MA: MIT Press, 1971. Vol. 1: 278p.; Vol. 2: 354p. $10.00 each.

The first volume consists mainly of works by Pasternak, Tsvetaeva, Zamyatin, Babel, and Pilnyak. Volume two, emphasizing works written in the fifties and sixties, includes stories by Yashin, Nagibin, Zhdanov, Solzhenitsyn, and other contemporaries. This well-designed anthology will be of interest to the selective reader.

CSP, 15:3:425-26; Choice, 9(1972):653.

767.   Proffer, Carl, and Proffer, Ellendea, eds. **The Ardis Anthology of Recent Russian Literature.** Ann Arbor, MI: Ardis, 1975. xvi, 420p. Illustrated. $5.00 pa.

The emphasis of this volume is on poetry. A fourth of the book is devoted to translations of poems, with twenty-nine poets represented.

SR, 36:1:157-60.

768.   Proffer, Carl R., ed. **From Karamzin to Bunin: An Anthology of Russian Short Stories.** With a critical commentary and eleven translations by Carl R. Proffer. Bloomington, IN: Indiana University Press, 1969. 468p. $12.50.

Not claiming to be a "history" of the Russian short story, the collection is representative and offers the reader the near "best." Proffer's critical examination of the stories includes "information on style, structure, characterization, and theme." This book is intended for the general reader.

CSP, 12:4:487-88.

769.   Yarmolinsky, Avrahm, ed. and intro. **Two Centuries of Russian Verse: An Anthology from Lomonosov to Voznesensky.** New York: Random House, 1966. 322p. $6.95.

This collection contains over 350 of the finest Russian poems written between the early 1800s and the present day. Eighty-two poets are represented in this anthology, ranging from Pushkin and Lomonosov to the young Soviet poets who are now voicing protests against the Soviet totalitarian system.

Choice, 3(1966):778.

PHILOSOPHY AND POLITICAL THEORY

General Surveys and Bibliographies

770. Berlin, Isaiah. **Russian Thinkers.** Edited by Henry Hardy and Aileen Kelly. Introduction by Aileen Kelly. New York: The Viking Press, 1978. xxiv, 312p. $14.95.

Under Sir Isaiah's pen, Russia's intelligentsia and literary élite come to life—the reader can recognize men of emotion and commitment, with all their human weaknesses and spiritual glory. He shows how these emotions, lives, friendships, and dislikes were diffracted in the ideas of these men and in the ideas of succeeding generations. This collection of essays on Russia's intellectual past offers many a lesson for the thoughtful reader in the Western world.

SR, 38:1:106-7; Choice, 15(1978):1335.

771. Edie, James M., et al., eds. **Russian Philosophy.** With the collaboration of George L. Kline. Chicago: Quadrangle Books, 1965. Vol. 1: **The Beginnings of Russian Philosophy: The Slavophiles; the Westernizers.** 434p. $7.50. Vol. 2: **The Nihilists; the Populists; Crisis of Religion and Culture.** 311p. $6.50. Vol. 3: **Pre-Revolutionary Philosophy and Theology; Philosophers in Exile; Marxists and Communists.** 521p. $8.50.

These three volumes are comprehensive and break new ground by making available in careful, readable translations many works that were hitherto untranslated and often difficult to obtain even in Russian. Thus they provide a good source book, useful for general reading by those interested in Russian culture. The three volumes contain selections from twenty-seven thinkers.

Choice, 2(1966):779.

772. Laszlo, Ervin, comp. and ed. **Philosophy in the Soviet Union: A Survey of the Mid-Sixties.** Dordrecht, The Netherlands: D. Reidel; New York: Praeger, 1968. 208p. $10.00.

The purpose of this book is to acquaint the reader with the various aspects of Soviet philosophy and its recent accomplishments, and to provide evidence that this thought is of philosophical as well as social importance. The book contains thirteen articles, of which ten are systematic studies and three are concerned with the relation of Soviet and Western thought.

SR, 29:1:709-10.

773. Treadgold, Donald W. **The West In Russia and China: Religious and Secular Thought in Modern Times.** New York and Cambridge: Cambridge University Press, 1973. Vol. I: **Russia, 1472-1917.** 324p. Vol. 2: **China, 1582-1949.** 251p. $11.95.

This book seeks to understand one of the central phenomena of our time: the establishment of Communist ideologies in Russia and China. Its most interesting feature is the weight and attention Treadgold gives to religious encounters in the deeper past, and the common typology he finds in successive phases of the West's intellectual invasion of both Russia and China.
  SR, 33:2:342-43; CH, 43(March 1974):127.

774. Ulam, Adam B. **Ideologies and Illusions: Revolutionary Thought from Herzen to Solzhenitsyn.** Cambridge, MA, and London: Harvard University Press, 1976. x, 335p. $15.00.

In this book, Ulam touches on the birth of Russian radicalism, utopia and socialism, the roots of Marxism, the personalities of the founders of Russian Social Democracy, Lenin and the Bolsheviks, Stalin and Stalinism, and Titoism before lingering over Soviet foreign policy. Ulam traces the influence of a number of what he regards as significant ideas shaping Russian history.
  CSP, 20:1:122-24; JP, 39(1977):849.

775. Utechin, S. V. **Russian Political Thought: A Concise History.** London: Dent, 1964. 320p. $6.00.

The author has attempted to write a concise history of Russian political thought in the form of a survey intended "for students of politics" and assuming "no more than a very elementary knowledge" of Russian history. Utechin has much that is cogent and stimulating to say about some of the thinkers he discusses.
  SEER, 44:102:220-22; PSQ, 80(1965):512.

776. Walicki, Andrzej. **A History of Russian Thought from the Enlightenment to Marxism.** Translated by Hilda Andrews-Rusiecka. Stanford, CA: Stanford University Press, 1979 (1973). xx, 456p. $25.00.

This book's interpretive narrative combines chronological progression with concentration on specific topics in different periods. The author is at his best in the fundamental analysis of thought, whether the specific subject of investigation is Chaadaev's total world view, the manifold Hegelian influences in Russia, or the different kinds of positivism.
  SR, 40:1:102.

Non-Marxist Movements

777. Avrich, Paul. **The Russian Anarchists.** Princeton, NJ: Princeton University Press, 1967. 303p. $7.50. (Studies of the Russian Institute, Columbia University.)

This compact book is the first full-scale history in a Western language of the anarchist movement in Russia. It is an admirably balanced and informative account of one of the more quixotic revolutionary movements in twentieth-century Russia. The author succeeds in describing their views and their pathetic fate with seriousness, detachment, and understanding.
  SR, 27:1:137; Choice, 4(1968):143.

778. Brower, Daniel R. **Training the Nihilists: Education and Radicalism in Tsarist Russia.** Ithaca, NY, and London: Cornell University Press, 1975. 248p. $17.50.

This book provides a historical interpretation of the sociology of the radical intellectuals in mid-nineteenth-century Russia. The author argues that in Russian higher education, a "recruitment" system developed that fed a steady, if small, stream of committed revolutionaries into the life of the country, and that the radical intelligentsia was drawn from much the same social strata as university students in general.

SR, 35:1:129-30; AAPSS-A, 424(1976):139.

779. Brown, Edward J. **Stankevich and His Moscow Circle, 1830-1840.** Stanford, CA: Stanford University Press, 1966. 149p. $5.00.

Brown is interested in discovering both the "true" N. V. Stankevich as a historical person and "the intellectual concerns and motives" of the man who created the idealized image of the saintly and contemplative Stankevich. The author has separated fact from fiction in regard to Stankevich, having consulted the available literature during his trips to the Soviet Union.

RR, 26:1:76-78.

780. Chaadaev, Peter Iakovlevich. **Philosophical Letter and Apology of a Madman.** Translated and with an introduction by Mary-Barbara Zeldin. Knoxville: University of Tennessee Press, 1970. 203p. $7.50.

With a taste for high style and a flair for color and imagery, Zeldin has produced one of the most successful and literate English translations of the works of an important Russian thinker.

SR, 30:3:664-65; Choice, 8(1971):683.

781. Christoff, Peter K. **An Introduction to Nineteenth-Century Russian Slavophilism: A Study in Ideas.** Vol. 2: **I. V. Kreevskij.** The Hague, The Netherlands: Mouton, 1972. 406p. 68 Dgds. (Slavistic Printings and Reprintings, no. 23/2.)

The author presents the Slavophile doctrine as a major, uniquely Russian contribution to the theory of knowledge. Kireevsky is viewed as the theoretician of the movement. He sees the Slavophiles as authentic philosophers of Orthodoxy, and this leads him to minimize their debt to German Idealism.

SR, 33:1:134-35.

782. Galai, Shmuel. **The Liberation Movement in Russia, 1900-1905.** New York: Cambridge University Press, 1973. 325p. $22.50.

This monograph represents a comprehensive history of Russian liberalism from the late 1870s to 1905. It is distinguished by impressive attention to detail, and it fully exhausts the published sources available to a Western historian.

SR, 33:1:137; AHR, 79:3:822.

783. Gleason, Abbott. **European and Muscovite: Ivan Kireevsky and the Origins of Slavophilism.** Cambridge, MA: Harvard University Press, 1972. 376p. $13.50. (Russian Research Center Studies, 68.)

Gleason limits his inquiry to those figures who entered Kireevsky's life. A biographical strategy suits the subject admirably: like many Romantic thinkers, Kireevsky was fascinated by the genesis of ideas and demanded that intelligence respond to the totality of experience. Kireevsky's final transformation from European to Muscovite is interpreted along psychological lines.

SR, 32:1:167-68.

784. Gleason, Abbott. **Young Russia: The Genesis of Russian Radicalism in the 1860s.** New York: The Viking Press, 1980. xvi, 437p. $16.95.
Gleason focuses on what is Russia's most crucial decade before 1917. His analysis probes below the surface to see how certain individuals came to their particular ideas. What is their contribution to the radical aim of liberating the people from the state, and how do they relate to that people and the state? This is a lively, readable book.

JMH, 53:1:155.

785. Hardy, Deborah. **Petr Tkachev, the Critic as Jacobin.** Seattle and London: University of Washington Press, 1977. xiv, 339p. $12.50.
This volume provides a detailed account of Petr Tkachev' social background, copious writings, and revolutionary activities at home and abroad, which were typical of prominent Russian rebels in the 1860s and 1870s. Tkachev emerges as a lonely and secretive man, better at wielding the pen than at organizing resistance to authorities. This book tells us all about the man and his impact during his lifetime.

SR, 37:2:296; Choice, 14(1978):1698.

786. Lukashevich, Stephen. **Ivan Aksakov, 1821-1886: A Study in Russian Thought and Politics.** Cambridge, MA: Harvard University Press, 1965. 191p. $5.50. (Harvard Historical Monographs, 57.)
This important monograph presents systematically a leading Slavophile's ideas on a wide range of topics, as those ideas developed from the 1860s to the 1880s. The book is a significant contribution to an understanding of Russian attitudes toward the West that continue to manifest themselves in a variety of ways.

AHR, 72:1:242; Choice, 3(1966):706.

787. MacMaster, Robert E. **Danilevsky: A Russian Totalitarian Philosopher.** Cambridge, MA: Harvard University Press, 1967. 368p. $7.95.
According to MacMaster, Danilevsky belonged to a group of nineteenth- and twentieth-century thinkers who advocated the use of violence, war, or revolution to attain religious or metaphysical ends. Danilevsky, like other radicals, sought a new form of modernity to take the place of the "dehumanized" and European one then being forced upon Russian society.

SR, 28:3:487-80; PSQ, 83(March 1968):107.

788. Malia, Martin. **Alexander Herzen and the Birth of Russian Socialism, 1812-1855.** Cambridge, MA: Harvard University Press, 1961; New York: Grosset & Dunlap, 1965. 486p. $10.00.
This study of Herzen, his philosophy, and his role in the formation of Russian political and philosophical thought is not only a singularly outstanding English-language work, but the only extensive study in any language. Herzen, the "father

of Russian socialism," is also seen as a liberal, revolutionary democrat and promoter of national self-determination. This noble intellectual was one of the first Russians who opposed Russia's oppression of Poles and Ukrainians.

SR, 21:3:540-42.

789. McConnell, Allen. **A Russian Philosopher: Alexander Radishchev, 1749-1802.** The Hague, The Netherlands: Nijhoff, 1964. 228p. 24.25 Dglds.

This is an interesting study, giving a balanced account of Radishchev's life, thought, and enduring influence, and it should be of interest to many readers besides specialists. McConnell does an excellent job of putting Radishchev into context; he effectively explains the most important influences on his hero. His family background, his religious faith, and the several stages of his education are cogently set forth. So is the development of his ideology.

SR, 24:4:724-25; AHR, 70:4:1204.

790. McNally, Raymond T. **Chaadayev and His Friends: An Intellectual History of Peter Chaadayev and His Russian Contemporaries.** Tallahassee, FL: Diplomatic Press, 1971. 315p. $15.00.

McNally offers in this volume a revised portrait of Chaadayev. His main contention is that Chaadayev's later thinking was significantly shaped by his efforts to substantiate the thesis about Russia's backwardness proclaimed in his first letter, and that this switch from attack to defense was a result of relentless probing by the Slavophiles.

SR, 32:4:809-10.

791. Pereira, N. G. O. **The Thought and Teachings of N. G. Černyševskij.** Paris and The Hague, The Netherlands: Mouton, 1975. xii, 144p. DM.20. (Slavistic Printings and Reprintings, 308.)

This work offers an intelligent review of Černyševskij's interaction with his cultural milieu. After a short introduction to his life and historical situation, the author provides a summary of Russian radical premises.

SR, 39:4:678-79; Choice, 12(1975):1297.

792. Perrie, Maureen. **The Agrarian Policy of the Russian Socialist-Revolutionary Party: From Its Origins through the Revolution of 1905-1907.** New York and London: Cambridge University Press, 1976. xii, 216p. $15.95.

In this work, the emphasis is primarily on political behavior of the Social Revolutionists and on their programmatic statements, as shaped by the challenge of Marxism and Chernov's inspiring political contacts with the peasants in the 1890s. Perrie focuses on an analysis of the social composition of the Socialist-Revolutionary party and the peasant movement in 1905-7.

SR, 37:2:294-95; Choice, 14(1977):928.

793. Pipes, Richard. **Struve: Liberal on the Right, 1905-1944.** Cambridge, MA: Harvard University Press, 1980. xix, 526p. $32.50.

Peter B. Struve (1870-1944) emerges as a genius, a man with an extraordinary range of intellectual interests and accomplishments, an outstanding scholar, and a superb journalist. Pipes discusses extensively Struve's economic theory.

RR, 40:2:158-62; JMH, 53:1:159.

794.   Pomper, Philip. **Peter Lavrov and the Russian Revolutionary Movement.**
        Chicago: University of Chicago Press, 1972. 250p. $7.95.
Drawing skillfully on Amsterdam, Hoover, Columbia, and, to a lesser extent, Soviet
archives, Pomper richly documents his novel interpretation of Lavrov's personality.
The author has presented a fine analysis of the interplay of personality, ideas, and
external circumstance.
        SR, 32:4:812-13; Choice, 10(1973):170.

795.   Pomper, Philip. **Sergei Nechaev.** New Brunswick, NJ: Rutgers University
        Press, 1979. x, 273p.
This is a skillfully written, well-produced, and thought-provoking book that makes
for spellbinding reading. The key to understanding Nechaev's career, Pomper
hypothesizes, was his single-minded pursuit of "both martyrdom and revenge."
        RR, 39:1:78-79; Choice, 16(1980):1495.

796.   Thaden, Edward C. **Conservative Nationalism in Nineteenth-Century
        Russia.** Seattle: University of Washington Press, 1964. 271p. $9.50.
In this study Thaden discusses, at least briefly, almost all important representatives
of conservative Russian nationalism, and quite a few of these names appear for the
first time on the pages on an English-language book. This is an objective and
interesting survey of Russian conservative national thought.
        RR, 25:2:190-92; Choice, 2(1965):118.

797.   Ulam, Adam B. **In the Name of the People: Prophets and Conspirators
        in Prerevolutionary Russia.** New York: The Viking Press, 1977. xiv, 418p.
        Illustrated. $15.00.
The period under discussion is rather brief—from the emancipation of the serfs in
1861 until the collapse of the People's Will organization in about 1883 after the
repression that followed the assassination of Alexander II. The main thread of the
narrative runs from publicity and propaganda to terrorism, from Herzen to the
People's Will. The author's chief preoccupation is with the character and causes
of the change.
        SR, 37:1:126-27; APSR, 72(1978):1136.

798.   Venturi, Franco. **Roots of Revolution: A History of the Populist and
        Socialist Movements in Nineteenth Century Russia.** Introduction by Sir
        Isaiah Berlin. Translated from the Italian by Francis Haskell. New York:
        Grosset & Dunlap, 1960. 850p. $3.45 pa.
Venturi's study of the Russian Populist movement is still the most comprehensive
and perhaps most authoritative account in any language. An impartial judgment,
mature handling of this most complex aspect of Russian history, and consultation
of primary sources combined with exhaustive research, make this work indispensable learning material for the student of Russian history. Recommended for both
the student and the instructor, obligatory for the specialist, yet too advanced for
the general reader.
        SR, 20:4:710-11.

799.   Walicki, Andrzej. **The Slavophile Controversy: History of a Conservative Utopia in Nineteenth Century Russian Thought**. Translated by Hilda Andrews-Rusiecka. Oxford: Clarendon Press, 1975. viii, 609p. $43.95.

The Polish historian Walicki defines the Slavophile utopian model in terms of its consistencies as well as its vagaries; he explains not only intellectually, but sociologically and psychologically, the genesis of this model and its attraction for many nineteenth-century Russians. He confirms that the Slavophiles were in large measure reactionary noblemen worried about how capitalism would affect their traditional positions.

   CSP, 19:1:94-95; Choice, 13(1976):678.

800.   Yanov, Alexander. **The Russian New Right: Right-Wing Ideologies in the Contemporary USSR**. Berkeley, CA: Institute of International Studies, University of California, 1978. xvi, 185p. $3.95 pa.

Yanov chronicles the mid-1960s rise of a new Russian nationalist movement that shows potential for repeating the paradox of nineteenth-century Russian nationalism. The author is at his best when describing events and personalities he was professionally and personally close to in the USSR. Policy-makers and planners will especially profit from Yanov's labors.

   RR, 39:1:91-94.

Marxism in Russia and in the USSR

801.   DeGeorge, Richard T. **Patterns of Soviet Thought: The Origins and Development of Dialectical and Historical Materialism**. Ann Arbor: University of Michigan Press, 1966. 293p. $6.95.

This book does a commendable job of summarizing and giving a detailed critique of the basic works of Marxist-Leninist philosophy from its German origins to its latest developments in the Soviet Union. DeGeorge points out that one must avoid the danger of systematizing the writings of Marx, Engels, and Lenin; nevertheless, he manages to present the content of their works in a clear and organized way. Besides the intrinsic interest, DeGeorge presents a persuasive case for studying Soviet philosophy—not as the axioms from which Soviet behavior may be deduced, but as a world view whose presuppositions and general conceptual mode cannot but influence the way in which Soviet citizens frame problems and solve them. The greatest merit of DeGeorge's book is the good common sense that comes forward at every point in it.

   LJ, 20(1967):1017; SR, 26:4:695-96.

802.   DeGeorge, Richard T. **Soviet Ethics and Morality**. Ann Arbor, MI: University of Michigan Press, 1969. 184p. $2.95 pa.

The author clearly delineates the predicament of the contemporary Soviet philosopher, who is faced with real moral problems but is able to deal with them only within the confines of a very dogmatic system and under the watchful eye of a none-too-sophisticated political establishment. He shows how the collectivist notion of man underlies all Soviet ethical discussion.

   SR, 29:2:334.

803.   Grier, Philip T. **Marxist Ethical Theory in the Soviet Union.** Dordrecht, The Netherlands, and Boston: D. Reidel Publishing Company, 1978. xviii, 276p. DM. 65.00.

One of the central problems of Marxism has been whether Marxism can have an ethics. Grier presents the views of those leading Soviet philosophers who interpret Marx's writings as implying a definite ethical standpoint. Any student of Marxism will find valuable information and perceptive interpretations in this book.

SR, 39:1:136-37.

804.   Lane, David. **The Roots of Russian Communism: A Social and Historical Study of Russian Social-Democracy 1898-1907.** Assen, The Netherlands: Van Corcum, 1969. 240p. New, rev. ed.: University Park: Pennsylvania State University Press, 1975. 240p. $4.95 pa. (Publications of Social History issued by the Internationaal Instituut voor Sociale Geschiedenis, Amsterdam, no. 6.)

This study is strictly a sociological and statistical analysis of participants up to 1907. The author shows great resourcefulness in making use of the available data, employing an impeccable methodology in constructing samples, defining concepts, computing margins of error, and cross-checking his sources where possible. The result is probably the best picture we are likely to get of the distribution according to social class, education, occupation, age, and nationality. One is not surprised to find a heavy concentration of gentry, workers of peasant background, Great Russians, and persons of a younger mean age among the Bolsheviks, and of minority nationalities and city dwellers of all grades among the Mensheviks.

RR, 29:2:215-17; SR, 26:4:695-96.

805.   Senn, Alfred Erich. **The Russian Revolution in Switzerland, 1914-1917.** Madison, WI: University of Wisconsin Press, 1971. 250p. $12.50.

The principal theme of the work is the "nationalist-internationalist" schism in the ranks of the Russian exiles—a theme whose importance to events in Russia in 1917 and 1918 cannot be doubted. In his approach to the great range of problems with which he deals, the author examines the Polish political exiles and their relations with the Germans, Lenin's relations with various secondary non-Russian figures of the Second International and with the German government, and similar circumstances.

SR, 31:1:164-65.

806.   Tompkins, Stuart Ramsay. **The Triumph of Bolshevism: Revolution or Reaction?** Norman, OK: University of Oklahoma Press, 1967. 331p. $5.95.

Tompkins, the author of *The Russian Mind* (1953) and *The Russian Intelligentsia* (1957), presents his concluding work, *The Triumph of Bolshevism,* which brings the story up to the revolution itself. This is an intellectual history of Russian Marxism: its origins, its application, its ascendancy. The author is primarily concerned with the motivations of the Russian Social Democrats and the ideological vagaries they pursued in emigration. He is relatively uninterested in the broader Russian panorama of the time, in the illegal underground, or in the actual events of 1905 and 1917. Tompkins allows himself to be more interpretive than many of his younger predecessors.

SR, 27:4:653-54; AHR, 73:2:543.

807. Tucker, Robert C., ed. **The Lenin Anthology**. New York: W. W. Norton, 1975. xiv, 764p. $18.95.

Tucker has prefaced this collection with an essay on Lenin's emergence as the revolutionary leader who single-mindedly combined Marxist thought with Russian revolutionary tradition. The Lenin that emerges from this volume is the familiar charismatic messiah of the Russian revolution.

SR, 35:2:335-36.

808. Ulam, Adam B. **The Bolsheviks: The Intellectual and Political History of the Triumph of Communism in Russia**. New York: Macmillan; London: Collier-Macmillan, 1965. 598p. $9.95.

Vigorously written, this study covers the ground with exemplary thoroughness from the nineteenth century to Lenin's death in 1924, roughly half the total space being allotted to the post-revolutionary epoch. Ulam bases his narrative on extensive research but carries his learning lightly; his judgments are fair and will command wide assent. If the interpretation is on the whole a familiar one, this is largely due to the state of the sources. All students of modern Russia will be grateful to Ulam for a highly stimulating account of the origins of Soviet Communism. Regrettably, there is no bibliography and no index.

SR, 25:1:155-56; AHR, 72:1:245.

809. Wildman, Allan K. **The Making of a Workers' Revolution: Russian Social Democracy, 1891-1903**. Chicago: University of Chicago Press, 1967. 271p. $7.95. (The Hoover Institution, Inter-University Project on the History of the Menshevik Movement.)

Wildman focuses on the ambivalent relations between the rank-and-file factory workers and their intellectual mentors. According to the author, there was continuous contact between the two groups, and their destinies were inextricably intertwined. The Marxist intellectuals stirred new hope among the factory hands and gave coherent expression to their dreams and aspirations.

RR, 27:3:354-55; Choice, 5(1968):400.

Intellectual and Cultural Histories

810. Billington, James H. **The Icon and the Axe: An Interpretive History of Russian Culture**. New York: Knopf, 1966. 786p. $15.00.

This is an extremely interesting and well-written book. The author has aimed at presenting an overall interpretation of Great Russian culture—the culture of the Russian North—and he has traced the two symbols of his title into the period of the Communists. Unfortunately, like most American writers, he persists in applying the word "Russian" to the culture of Kiev, which is far more characteristic of Ukraine throughout its history than it is of Moscow and the Great Russians.

AHR, 72:5:1476; Choice, 4(1967):743.

811. Herzen, Alexander. **My Past and Thoughts: The Memoirs of Alexander Herzen**. 4 vols. Introduction by Isaiah Berlin. Translated by Constance Garnett. New York: Knopf, 1968. 1908p. $30.00.

The memoirs cover the years 1817-70 and contain, in addition to autobiographical materials, Herzen's activities, thoughts, and writings in Russia and, after 1847, abroad. This publication is a potentially rich mine of information not only about the events in Russia but also about philosophical, social, and political movements of the time in Western Europe. Herzen was the publisher of *Kolokol,* and he left a marked imprint on Russian intellectual and social history.

HR, 22(Summer 1969):334.

812. Lampert, E. **Sons against Fathers: Studies in Russian Radicalism and Revolution.** Oxford: Clarendon Press, 1965. 405p.

This is a lively, provocative book; both learned and entertaining, it shows a fine density of appropriately chosen dramatic detail worked into a sturdy but sufficiently playful and fluent style. It resembles Franco Venturi's *Roots of Revolution* in its point of view, as well as its subject matter, though it is not so long, not so complete and exhaustive. It is about Chernyshevsky, Dobroliubov, and Pisarev, and in particular about the conflict between generations. The chapters on Dobroliubov and Pisarev, especially the latter, are more interesting and more convincing than that on Chernyshevsky.

SR, 24:4:725-26; AHR, 71:4:1020.

813. Miliukov, Paul. **The Origins of Ideology.** Translated from *Ocherki po istorii russkoi kul'tury* (Paris, 1930-37), vol. 3, by Joseph L. Wieczynski. Gulf Breeze, FL: Academic International Press, 1974. $12.50. (The Russian Series, 19-1.)

This work has long figured as an essential element in the education of serious students of Russia. Fuhrmann's introduction, "The Two Worlds of Paul Miliukov," will convey to the student some useful information on Miliukov's life and work. The translator has furnished a set of notes; however, the editor has omitted Miliukov's introduction and notes from this translation.

JMH, 47:3:324.

814. Pomper, Philip. **The Russian Revolutionary Intelligentsia.** New York: Thomas Y. Crowell, 1970. 216p. $3.25 pa.

The subject of this study is, in fact, the road to the revolutionary fate of the intelligentsia. Nearly half of the book is devoted to the radical intelligentsia in the reign of Alexander II. Much of the value of the study lies in its method. Men create, discover, and use ideologies "in a given historical context"; ideologies "reflect the diversity of human temperament and personality."

SR, 30:4:881-82.

815. Raeff, Marc. **Origins of the Russian Intelligentsia: The Eighteenth-Century Nobility.** New York: Harcourt, Brace & World, 1966. 248p. $2.45 pa.

In this brilliant study Raeff analyzes the forces that shaped the behavior and attitudes of the eighteenth-century Russian nobility, especially of its educated component, who served as "fathers" to the first generation of the Russian intelligentsia. Drawing on a wealth of material, the author illuminates the function of family and service in the lives of the nobility, the impact of the nobleman's education on his behavior and outlook, and the way in which Western ideas and culture were assimilated by the Russian elite.

SR, 27:2:317-18.

816.   Raeff, Marc, ed. **Russian Intellectual History: An Anthology.** With an introduction by Isaiah Berlin. New York: Harcourt, Brace & World, 1966. 404p. $4.50 pa.

The purpose of this anthology is to acquaint the English-speaking reader with the writings and ideas that have helped to shape the history of Russia. Most of the documents included are of the eighteenth- and nineteenth-century intelligentsia and never published in English. Among these are writings of F. Prokopovich, M. V. Lomonosov, M. M. Shcherbatov, N. I. Novikov, N. M. Karamzin, I. P. Panin, P. Ia. Chaadaev, I. A. Kireevski, A. S. Khomiakov, K. S. Aksakov, K. D. Kavelin, L. N. Tolstoy, A. A. Blok, and M. O. Gershenzon. This volume will be most useful to students of Russian intellectual history and should serve as a handy reference for quotations as well.

Choice, 3(1967):1168.

PSYCHOLOGY AND PSYCHIATRY

817. Krippner, Stanley. **Human Possibilities: Mind Exploration in the USSR and Eastern Europe**. Garden City, NY: Anchor Press & Doubleday, 1980. xi, 348p. $14.95.

This is an extensive study of the status, development, and application of psychology in the Soviet Union as personally observed by Dr. Krippner during his trip to the USSR in 1971. Subjects and material include parapsychology, hypnosis, suggestopedia, problems of the unconscious, and holographics.

LJ, 106(1981):62.

818. Lur'e, A. R. **The Selected Writings of A. R. Luria**. Edited and with an introduction by Michael Cole. White Plains, NY: M. E. Sharpe, 1978. xxii, 351p. $22.50.

Cole has assembled several articles by the eminent Soviet psychologist A. R. Lur'e (1902-77). The papers focus on child development, language acquisition, mental imagery, mental ability, and neuropsychology.

SR, 39:4:697.

819. Payne, T. R. S. **L. Rubinstejn and the Philosophical Foundations of Soviet Psychology**. Dordrecht, The Netherlands: Reidel Publishing, 1969. 184p. $14.25. Distributed by Humanities Press, New York.

The reader who thinks it unfair to call Marxist-Leninist psychology a mystification should read Payne's book. "As the unifying principle in psychology Rubinstejn sees the so-called Marxist-Leninist theory of determinism. As a general theory, applicable to all parts of the material world, it is formulated as follows: the outer cause works through, and is refracted by, the inner conditions of the object on which it acts. In the light of this principle psychic events are the result of the interaction of the individual with the outer world."

SR, 33:4:786-87.

820. Rahmani, Levy. **Soviet Psychology: Philosophical, Theoretical, and Experimental Issues**. New York: International Universities Press, 1973. 440p. $17.50.

The author provides an elaborate survey of Soviet psychological research together with a critique of the theoretical foundation of the Soviet doctrinaire approach toward the methodology of research. He explains the Soviet concept of psychology and its function in various applications within the context of dialectical materialism. The study is aimed at professionals and informed readers.

Choice, 10(1974):1789.

821.   Rollins, Nancy. **Child Psychiatry in the Soviet Union: Preliminary Observations**. Cambridge, MA: Harvard University Press, 1972. 293p. $12.95.

This is the first book in English dealing with the theory, practice, and organization of child psychiatry in the Soviet Union. This study is not only of interest and value in the area of professional therapy, it also provides numerous insights into Russian cultural attitudes that have an effect on character and personality development. It should therefore attract the attention of an audience considerably beyond the scope of medicine.

SR, 33:4:787; Choice, 10(1973):1084.

RELIGION

822. Alexeev, Wassilij, and Stavrou, Theofanis G. **The Great Revival: The Russian Church under German Occupation.** Minneapolis: Burgess Publishing Co., 1976. xvi, 229p. Illustrated. $21.95.

The work details by geographic region the experiences of Russian Orthodox hierarchs and parishes. Alexeev presents accounts of church services in a number of localities, indicating the sweep of the religious movement that affected most of the German-occupied region and played its part in convincing Stalin to come to terms with the church at home.

SR, 36:3:501-3.

823. Bennigsen, Alexandre, and Lamercier-Quelquejoy, Chantal. **Islam in the Soviet Union.** Introduction by Geoffrey E. Wheeler. New York: Praeger, published in association with the Central Asian Research Centre, London, 1967. 272p. $7.00.

This book unfolds a broad survey of political change among the formerly Muslim people of Russia for the purpose of determining what survives from the Islamic past and how much weight may be assigned such remnants today. Two chapters, out of sixteen, deal directly with the practices of Islam.

SR, 28:1:143-45; APSR, 62(1968):1002.

824. Bourdeaux, Michael. **Patriarch and Prophets: Persecution of the Russian Orthodox Church Today.** New York: Praeger, 1970. 359p. $10.00.

Prefaced by an introduction on church-state relations in the USSR, the volume presents documentation of the persecution of the Orthodox church. The documents deal with such aspects as the persecution of the clergy, the suppression of monasteries and seminaries, destruction of parish life, and reactions of the believers. The account will be read with intense interest by laymen and specialists.

SR, 30:1:164-65.

825. Bourdeaux, Michael. **Religious Ferment in Russia: Protestant Opposition to Soviet Religious Policy.** New York: St. Martin's Press, 1968. 255p. $8.95.

This book deals with the so-called Initiators' Movement, which began around 1962 among the Baptist communities in opposition to the government's attempts to gain control over the internal affairs of religious organizations. It is a unique and profound study, bringing to the fore the problems of the Christian conscience in

Russia. The author tells of the organized opposition of a small group of people who dared to protest governmental pressure upon their personal lives and their organizations.

SR, 30:2:403-5; Choice, 6(1969):228.

826. Conquest, Robert, ed. **Religion in the U.S.S.R.** New York: Praeger, 1968. 135p. $5.00.

The purpose of this volume is to demonstrate the irreconcilable hostility of Communist ideology to any manifestation of religion. The author has listed many acts of the Soviet government regarding religion without any attempt to interpret or discuss their meaning.

SR, 30:2:403-4.

827. Dunn, Dennis J. **The Catholic Church and the Soviet Government, 1939-1949.** Boulder, CO: *East European Quarterly,* 1977. viii, 267p. $17.00. Distributed by Columbia University Press, New York. (East European Monographs, 30.)

This work attempts to shed light on the crucial period 1939-49 by examining a heretofore seldom explored aspect: Soviet-Catholic relations. It reveals Soviet and papal motivation in the elaboration of war and postwar policy; Soviet rationale in the formulation of domestic religious policy after the war in Lithuania, West Ukraine, and Carpatho-Ukraine; as well as attitudes in the evolution of governmental policies in those regions.

NP, 7:2:239-40; LJ, 103(1978):458; Choice, 15(1978):286.

828. Dunn, Dennis J., ed. **Religion and Modernization in the Soviet Union.** Boulder, CO: Westview Press, 1977. x, 414p. Illustrated. $21.75.

This symposium on the governmental administration and politics of religion in the USSR consists of three major topics: underlying forces and values; policies and practices in the control of religion, including the use of antireligious satire; and the status of various religions.

SR, 39:2:326; Choice, 15(1978):894.

829. Fletcher, William C., comp. **Christianity in the Soviet Union: An Annotated Bibliography and List of Articles; Works in English.** Los Angeles: Research Institute on Communist Strategy and Propaganda, University of Southern California, 1963. 95p.

This booklet lists 588 entries, including a list of translations of articles from the Soviet press.

830. Fletcher, William C. **Religion and Soviet Foreign Policy, 1945-1970.** London: Oxford University Press, published for the Royal Institute of International Affairs, 1973. 179p. $11.25.

The church is seen in the role of forming a favorable picture of the Soviet Union through the participation of its members in international peace conferences and ecumenical movements. The author explores the role of Soviet churchmen in the World Peace Council, the Christian Peace Conferences, the World Council of Churches, and relations with the Vatican.

SR, 33:1:147; AAPSS-A, 410(Nov. 1973):198.

831. Fletcher, William C. **The Russian Orthodox Church Underground, 1917-1970.** New York: Oxford University Press, 1971. 314p. $12.75.
Fletcher draws several conclusions from his study of underground Orthodoxy: it is a response to Soviet persecution; persecution of Orthodoxy does not succeed, for it does not eradicate religion but drives it underground; this underground opposition serves as insurance that organized religious institutions may continue to exist. This study corrects and dismisses the view popularized by Harrison Salisbury and others that the "Church indulges in no undercover activities."
SR, 34:1:151; Choice, 9(1972):226.

832. Kolarz, Walter. **Religion in the Soviet Union.** New York: St. Martin's Press, 1961. 518p. $12.50.
Unlike most of the works on religion in Russia, this one deals not only with the Orthodox church but also with all the other religious denominations in the USSR. In this regard it is the most complete study of the religious spectrum in the Soviet Union and a valuable source of information.
SR, 22:3:588-89.

833. Marshall, Richard H., et al., eds. **Aspects of Religion in the Soviet Union, 1917-1967.** Chicago: University of Chicago Press, 1971. 489p. $19.75.
The major portion of the book consists of essays by seventeen contributors covering virtually every major aspect of the subject and every major group in the USSR (Orthodox, Moslems, Jews, Baptists, Catholics) as well as national churches (Georgian, Armenian) and even minor groups such as the Mennonites and the animistic Siberian tribes. The volume also has an appendix containing the text of all the major laws pertaining to religion in the USSR.
SR, 31:1:175; JMH, 44:2:302.

834. Simon, Gerhard. **Church, State and Opposition in the U.S.S.R.** Translated by Kathleen Matchett in collaboration with the Centre for the Study of Religion and Communism. Berkeley: University of California Press, 1974. 248p. $12.00.
This translation of a study by an outstanding expert on religion in Russia is of equal value to general readers and specialists. The author deals with the Russian church on the eve of revolution; church relations, and religious persecution today; Pastor Richard Wurmband's mission and its impact on the Western churches and documents translated from the Russian originals complete this survey on church-state relations.

835. Spinka, Matthew. **The Church in Soviet Russia.** New York: Oxford University Press, 1956. 162p.
The author reports on the relations of the Russian Orthodox church and the Soviet state. This small volume answers many questions frequently asked on this topic.
JMH, 29:2:302.

836. Zatko, James J. **Descent into Darkness: The Destruction of the Roman Catholic Church in Russia, 1917-1923.** Notre Dame, IN: University of Notre Dame Press, 1965. 232p. $6.95.
This is an authoritative study on the systematic destruction of the Catholic church in the Soviet Union, an event that has been scarcely publicized.
AHR, 71:2:628.

837.   Zernov, Nicolas. **The Russian Religious Renaissance of the Twentieth Century.** New York: Harper & Row, 1964. 410p. $7.00.

Central to the author's arguments is the view that Russia achieved its national and cultural identity through the Orthodox church. A large portion of this volume is devoted to discussion of the nature and role of the intelligentsia, described by the author as a group that tried to destroy religious unity by the "preaching of socialism based on materialism and atheism." An appendix lists the leading figures of the religious movement and their major writings.

SR, 24:1:159-60.

SCIENCE AND RESEARCH

838. Fischer, George, ed. **Science and Ideology in Soviet Society**. New York: Atherton Press, 1967. 176p. $6.95.
Four contributors to this study reinforce a basic truth the West should have recognized long ago: Soviet ideology is a very fuzzy and elusive thing: simply pointing to it does not explain why Soviet leaders have taken changing stands in various sciences, including no stand at all. The authors discuss sociology, philosophy, cybernetics, and economics.
SR, 28:4:665-66.

839. Graham, Loren R. **The Soviet Academy of Sciences and the Communist Party, 1927-1932**. Princeton, NJ: Princeton University Press, 1967. 225p. $6.50. (Studies of the Russian Institute, Columbia University.)
The author tells the story of "the renovation of the Academy of Sciences" during the crucial period of the First Five-Year Plan with special attention to the details of the purging of the Academy with its concomitant terror. The events are related to a broader context—economic planning in the Soviet Union and the relations of governments to science and scientists outside the Soviet Union. Graham also emphasizes the relationship of the Communist rulers to the Academy and how they successfully dominate the institution and its members.
RR, 27:4:476-77; Choice, 5(1968):252.

840. Graham, Loren R. **Science and Philosophy in the Soviet Union**. New York: Knopf, 1972. 624p. $15.00.
Graham offers a discipline-by-discipline account of the interaction of science and Marxist philosophy in the work of the leading Soviet scientists, the controversies in which they have been involved, and the contributions they have made to contemporary world science.
AHR, 78:1:131.

841. Heiliger, William S., comp. **Bibliography of the Soviet Sciences, 1965-1975**. 2 vols. Troy, NY: Whitson, 1978. v, 996p. $65.00 set.
The more than 9,300 entries, which have been culled from the *Ezhegodnik izdanii* of the Soviet Academy of Sciences, are given in English translation and are grouped by year within each institute or journal. A name and subject index is appended.
ARBA, 10(1979):193.

842. Hutchings, Raymond. **Soviet Science, Technology, Design: Interaction and Convergence.** London: Oxford University Press, 1976. xiv, 320p. + 8 pp. plates. Tables. $27.50.

In his pioneering study, Hutchings analyzes these three categories as applied to the scientific-industrial complex in the Soviet Union. The basic thesis of the book is that although Soviet science, technology, and design depend heavily on borrowing from the West, they are not without distinct national characteristics which, in their own way, illuminate some of the vital components of the Soviet political system, social arrangements, and cultural values.

      SR, 36:2:321-22.

843. James, Peter N. **Soviet Conquest from Space.** New Rochelle, NY: Arlington House, 1974. 256p. $8.95.

The author reveals the little publicized implementation of militarism in the Soviet space program. According to James, space research in the Soviet Union is determined, controlled, and utilized exclusively by the Soviet armed forces. The program as such is part of an overall Soviet strategic planning that is subordinated to Soviet global policy and ideological aims as outlined by the CPSU program.

844. Korol, Alexander. **Soviet Research and Development: Its Organization, Personnel and Funds.** Cambridge, MA: MIT Press, 1965. 375p. $11.00.

This is a pioneering work in an area that is commanding increasing attention on both sides of the ideological frontier, and as such it should not be missed by a wider audience. The author's central aim is to examine the magnitude and distribution of national resources allocated to scientific research and development in the Soviet Union.

      RR, 25:2:198-99; Choice, 2(1966):852.

845. Lewis, Robert. **Science and Industrialization in the USSR.** London: Macmillan, in association with the Centre for Russian and East European Studies, University of Birmingham, 1979. xiv, 211p. Tables. $30.00 (Studies in Soviet History and Society Series.)

This is a fairly detailed study of the historical evolution of the structure and subordination of Soviet research and development establishments. There are also chapters on research planning, science at the factory, and industrial research and innovation. The aircraft industry is singled out for more detailed analysis. Appendixes cover expenditures, costs, and manpower.

      SEER, 59:1:122-23.

846. Medvedev, Zhores A. **Nuclear Disaster in the Urals.** Translated by George Saunders. New York: W. W. Norton, 1979. vii, 214p. $12.95.

Medvedev, a Russian biologist exiled in 1973 and now in London, has written on a nuclear disaster in the Ural mountains that occurred in the winter of 1957-58. The book has the merit of drawing attention to an event that appears to be both real and important. Since that time, the Soviet Union has published many details of peaceful uses of nuclear explosives, for example in extinguishing a resistant gas-well fire.

      RR, 40:1:69-70.

847. Medvedev, Zhores A. **Soviet Science**. New York and Toronto: W. W. Norton and George J. McLeon Ltd., 1978. xii, 262p. + 12pp. photographs. $15.95.

This is an interpretive, historical account of the changing conditions in Soviet science since the Bolshevik revolution. The book is well written and appeals to a wide audience. Medvedev focuses on individual scientists affected by the needs and demands of a political system more concerned with its own security than with the advancement of knowledge.

LJ, 104(1979):551; Choice, 15(1978):1237.

848. Vladimirov, Leonid. **The Russian Space Bluff: The Inside Story of the Soviet Drive to the Moon**. Translated by David Floyd. Foreword by Anatoli Fedoseyev. New York: Dial Press, 1973. 190p. $10.95.

The author makes it clear that the chief cause of the Soviet lag in the space exploration efforts was the gross interference of the Communist politicians with that nation's scientists and engineers. Only the talents and the incredible ingenuity of experts allowed the late Sergei Korolev to achieve whatever was achieved before 1969—despite the rulers' ignorant caprices. And the reason the false impression in the West lingered so long was the colossal Western gullibility.

SR, 38:4:692-93; LJ, 99(1974):620.

849. Vucinich, Alexander. **Science in Russian Culture, 1861-1917**. Stanford, CA: Stanford University Press, 1970. 575p. $18.50.

The author is concerned not only with science and scholarship proper but also with relevant institutional structure and government policies, Russian education as a whole, and indeed the entire intellectual and cultural history of the period. It is a rich and rewarding account of numerous Russian scientists, scholars, and their work.

SR, 31:1:159-60; Choice, 8(1971):856.

850. Zaleski, E., et al. **Science Policy in the USSR**. Paris: Organization for Economic Co-operation and Development, 1969. 615p. $15.00.

The topics of this collection of five essays range from organizational problems and the financing of research within the general framework of Soviet economic planning to the employment of scientists and engineers, from a brief history and description of the USSR Academy of Sciences to research in higher education and industrial research and applied technology.

SR, 29:1:139-40; JP, 32(1970):1027.

SOCIOLOGY

General Studies and Bibliographies

851. Alliluyeva, Svetlana. **Twenty Letters to a Friend**. Translated by Priscilla Johnson McMillan. New York: Harper & Row, 1967. 256p. $5.95.
This is a dramatic story told by the daughter of the late dictator Josef Stalin about herself and her family's life in the Soviet Union during the Stalin regime. The *Letters* shed light on the Soviet society, its contexture, and its struggle for power and influence.
LJ, 92(1967):4275; Choice, 4(1968):1431.

852. Hindus, Maurice. **The Kremlin's Human Dilemma: Russia after Half a Century of Revolution**. Garden City, NY: Doubleday, 1967. 395p. $5.95.
This is an informative and stimulating book by an author who has intimate knowledge of the country and its peoples. Hindus presents a remarkable panorama of Soviet life—the city, the village, the economy, and the social classes; the plight of dissident intellectuals, the national minorities, and religious believers; and the ways in which a dogmatic ideology creates impossible dilemmas for those whose aspirations are in conflict with the system.
SR, 31:2:426-28; APSR, 62(1968):286.

853. Inkeles, Alex. **Social Change in Soviet Russia**. Cambridge, MA: Harvard University Press, 1968. 477p. $12.50. (Russian Research Center Studies, 57.)
In this collection of essays the author offers his views with regard to the nature of social structure in the Soviet Union. The topics range from "Social Stratification in the Soviet Union" and "Developments in Soviet Mass Communications" to "The Totalitarian Mystique: Some Impressions of the Dynamics of Totalitarian Society."
SR, 29:1:136-37; LJ, 94(1969):92; Choice, 6(1969):584.

854. Inkeles, Alex, and Bauer, Raymond A. **The Soviet Citizen: Daily Life in a Totalitarian Society**. New York: Atheneum, 1968 (1959). 533p.
This book resulted from examination of three thousand questionnaires filled out by refugees from the Soviet Union in connection with the Harvard Project on the Soviet Social System. A wide spectrum of daily life is investigated. The work constitutes a historical record of major importance pertaining to the nature of the totalitarian Soviet state.
BRD, May 1960.

855.   Matthews, Mervyn. **Class and Society in Soviet Russia.** New York: Walker & Co., 1972. 366p. $12.50.

Although the author mainly focuses on social and economic inequality, the study also includes a useful discussion of recent Soviet demographic trends, a summary of rural-to-urban migration studies, and an attempt to estimate the magnitude of Soviet youth unemployment.

SR, 33:2:377-78; LJ, 98(1973):1182.

856.   Mehnert, Klaus. **Soviet Man and His World.** Translated from the German by Maurice Rosenbaum. New York: Praeger, 1962. 310p.

The author evaluates the impact of three primary influences on the present-day Russian: his heritage of traditional Russian characteristics, the forces of industrialization, and the pressures of Communist social engineering.

SR, 22:1:158-59.

857.   Meissner, Boris, ed. **Social Change in the Soviet Union: Russia's Toward Industrial Society.** Notre Dame, IN: University of Notre Dame Press, 1972. 427p. $9.95.

The main theme of this collection of articles is the interaction between historical antecedents and industrialization and its impact on Soviet social and political structure. Among the highlights of the volume is an excellent and well-documented discussion of the restratification of Soviet society, which culminated in a new, well-ordered hierarchical society.

CSP, 17:2:337-38.

858.   Nogee, Joseph L., ed. **Man, State, and Society in the Soviet Union.** New York: Praeger, 1972. 599p. $15.00.

About thirty authors, including Marx, Engels, and Lenin, have contributed to this collection of essays, which attempts to assess the present-day Soviet system and society from various vantages such as ideology, politics, economy, judicial process, personal life, social groups, and national minorities. The variety of viewpoints offers rich insights into a complex matter.

Choice, 19(1973):674.

859.   Shipler, David K. **Russia: Broken Idols, Solemn Dreams.** New York: New York Times Books, 1983. 404p. $17.95.

Shipler was the *New York Times'* bureau chief in Moscow from 1975 to 1979. He presents an unsparing view of the Soviet Union as a hopelessly closed, ideologically and spiritually desiccated society. The intelligentsia, he observes, is gripped by a powerful contempt for workers and peasants. Well-educated Russians reflect their society's general lack of concern for the abused and injured, whose very existence, because it clashes with Soviet ideology, is categorically denied. Shipler attributes "a state of moral weightlessness" in the Soviet Union to the absence of any system of belief that is thorough and enveloping enough to satisfy the Russian's ingrained need for some truth, some abiding faith to guide their lives.

860. Simirenko, Alex, ed. and intro. **Social Thought in the Soviet Union.** Chicago: Quadrangle Books, 1969. 439p. $14.95.
Twelve contributors to this collection of essays analyze social science ideology, philosophy, psychiatry, structural linguistics, political science law, historiography, economics, character education, psychology, psychiatry, ethnography, and sociology.
    SR, 29:1:137-38; AHR, 75:3:892.

861. Thaden, Edward C. **Russia since 1801: The Making of a New Society.** New York: John Wiley & Sons, 1971. 682p. $10.95.
Most of the study concentrates on domestic issues, such as agriculture, industry, education, science, music, literature, social classes, and bureaucracy. The author has given the most diligent attention to the nationality problem—before, during, and since the Revolution—in a clear and impartial fashion.
    SR, 31:1:154-55.

862. Vucinich, Alexander. **Social Thought in Tsarist Russia: The Quest for a General Science of Society, 1861-1917.** Chicago and London: University of Chicago Press, 1976. xi, 294p. $15.50.
This volume presents a comprehensive picture of the impact of scientific thought and the development of a rationalistic tradition in Russia. Interesting surveys of several schools of thought are presented here. The author has done well to make some of Russia's thinkers accessible to nonspecialists.
    SR, 36:1:117-18; AHR, 81:4:1174.

863. Weinberg, Elizabeth Ann. **The Development of Sociology in the Soviet Union.** London: Routledge & Kegan Paul, 1974. 173p. $14.00.
The achievements of sociology in the Soviet Union since 1956 constitute the central theme of this book. Weinberg has gathered interesting and highly relevant information on the historical roots of Soviet sociology and on the present-day efforts of Soviet scholars to bring historical materialism and sociology into a symbiotic relationship and to effect a full separation of ideological and scientific approaches to social reality.
    RR, 34:2:218; Choice, 12(1975):299.

Medical Care and Social Welfare

864. Field, Mark G. **Soviet Socialized Medicine: An Introduction.** New York: Free Press; London: Collier-Macmillan, 1967. 231p. $6.95.
Its wide scope and abundance of quoted sources make this publication valuable to anyone interested in the origins and development of the Soviet medical system. Its range of topics includes history, organization, health personnel, salaries, and clinical facilities. Through this medical portal one can see the whole of Soviet life, since the author very skillfully fits the medical system into the total Soviet structure.
    SR, 26:4:691.

865. Madison, Bernice Q. **Social Welfare in the Soviet Union**. Stanford, CA: Stanford University Press, 1968. 298p. $8.50.

This study reviews Soviet achievements and shortcomings, particularly in the areas of family and child welfare services. In the first part of the book the author deals briefly with social welfare policy formation between 1917 and 1966; in the second part she turns to current practices, an analysis that is tempered and enhanced by her own expertise and two extended stays in the Soviet Union. Her book is thus unique in this underexplored field.

SR, 28:3:519-20; Choice, 6(1969):284.

866. McAuley, Alistair. **Economic Welfare in the Soviet Union: Poverty, Living Standards, and Inequality**. Madison, WI, and Herts, England: University of Wisconsin Press and George Allen & Unwin, 1979. xx, 389p. $25.00.

This book makes an important contribution to knowledge of an area of Soviet life about which Soviet sources are notably reticent and published data obscure. The author evaluates data related to trends in total money incomes and earnings from wages and the prevalence of poverty in the USSR as a whole. The evidence shows that the Soviet welfare state has a long way to go before it can match even its own internal criteria, to say nothing of levels of living achieved in the West.

867. Osborn, Robert J. **Soviet Social Policies: Welfare, Equality, and Community**. Homewood, IL: Dorsey Press, 1970. 294p. $3.95pa.

Osborn examines three broad areas of post-Stalin Soviet social policies: (1) social security and claims to assistance and benefits in a system where concepts of welfare and wages are determined centrally, (2) the motivations provided for the individual to select appropriate levels of education and remain committed to his work, and (3) the organization and shaping of the urban environment, where meaningful social interaction is promoted in communities that would be conducive to social, occupational, and ethnic integration.

CSP, 14:3:547-48; Choice, 8(1971):740.

868. Ryan, Michael. **The Organization of Soviet Medical Care**. Oxford: Basil Blackwell, 1978. 168p. £10.00.

This book describes advances in Soviet medical care as well as its weaknesses. We learn that this care is not a single monolithic system; that in many ways medicine is business (with "second-economy" features); that the gap in expenditures between republics widened during the 1960s; and that total expenditures have not risen relative to national wealth.

RR, 39:3:380-81; AAPSS-A, 442(March 1979):176.

Social Problems and Social Change

869. Churchward, L. G. **The Soviet Intelligentsia: An Essay on the Social Structure and Roles of Soviet Intellectuals during the 1960s**. London: Routledge & Kegan Paul, 1973. 204p. $10.00.

Many of the disputes concerning the functions and attributes of Soviet intellectuals hinge on the definition of the intellectual. In this study Churchward offers his interpretation: "I regard the intelligentsia as consisting of persons with a tertiary education, tertiary students, and persons lacking formal tertiary qualification but

who are professionally employed in jobs which normally require a tertiary qualification." Thus he classifies them as careerist professionals, humanist intelligentsia,
open opposition, and the lost intelligentsia—in order of alienation from the system.
SR, 34:1:160-61; JP, 36(1974):259.

870. Connor, Walter D. **Deviance in Soviet Society: Crime, Delinquency, and
Alcoholism**. New York: Columbia University Press, 1972. 327p. $12.50.
The author analyzes the content of discussions in professional journals and the
press in the Soviet Union and describes the formal mechanisms that have been set
up to control deviance of different kinds, thus exposing a very serious social problem to the Western audience.
SR, 32:3:625-26; PSQ, 88(June 1973):331.

871. Juviler, Pater H. **Revolutionary Law and Order: Politics and Social Change
in the USSR**. New York and London: The Free Press and Collier-
Macmillan, 1976. xiv, 274p. $13.95.
In this wide-ranging review of Russian and Soviet responses to the phenomenon of
crime from 1864 to the present day, Juviler seeks to identify the basic patterns of
and trends in criminal policy, with emphasis on the post-Stalin era. The author
has explored a highly pertinent facet of Soviet life.
LJ, 101(1976):2496; Choice, 14(1977):596.

872. Matthews, Mervyn. **Privilege in the Soviet Union: A Study of Elite Life-
Styles under Communism**. London: George Allen & Unwin, 1978. 197p.
$17.25.
The author addresses the touchy question of Soviet privilege, its extent, and its
recipients. He defines the Soviet elite and describes its material privileges, its legal
underpinnings and the historical evolution of privilege, and its recipients. Finally,
Matthews assesses mobility into the Soviet elite and compares it to the elites of
Eastern Europe and the United States. This book is a lively and painstaking docu-
mentation of a dusky corner of Soviet society presented in an admirable form.
SR, 39:3:509-10; ARBA, 10(1979):355.

873. Yanowitch, Murray. **Social and Economic Inequality in the Soviet Union:
Six Studies**. White Plains, NY: M. E. Sharpe, 1977. xvii, 197p. Tables.
$15.00.
This volume brings together findings that illuminate many facets of social inequity
in the USSR. After first reviewing changes in Soviet conceptions of the social
structure, he examines income differentials, inequality of access to education,
patterns of social mobility, authority relations in the workplace, and aspects of
sexual inequality. This study should be of interest to a wide spectrum of readers.
SR, 38:2:317.

874. Yanowitch, Murray, and Fisher, Wesley A., eds. **Social Stratification and
Mobility in the USSR**. White Plains, NY: International Arts and Sciences
Press, 1973. 402p. $20.00.
Represented here are some of the best Soviet writings of the last decade, reflecting
on the increasing horizontal and vertical complexity of Soviet society, a con-
sequence of ongoing occupational differentiations that can no longer be contained

within the descriptive formula of "two classes, one stratum" (collective farmer, worker; intelligentsia).

RR, 34:3:337-38.

Women, Family, Youth

875. Blekher, Feiga. **The Soviet Woman in the Family and in Society: A Socio-logical Study**. New York: John Wiley, 1979. ix, 234p. $37.95.

The author simultaneously presents a historical survey, while describing marriage and family problems, women's work, and the way women experience everyday life. No fewer than thirty-seven topics are discussed and a great deal of material is brought together and organized in an orderly fashion around the topics discussed. The author recognizes that "women's problems" reflect many aspects of life.

RR, 40:3:348-49; LJ, 105(1980):994.

876. Brown, Donald R., ed. **The Role and Status of Women in the Soviet Union**. New York: Teachers College Press, 1968. 139p. $6.25.

This volume grew out of a "Symposium on Russian Women" held at Bryn Mawr College. The editor presents three useful papers, short commentaries, introduction, and conclusion on the Soviet woman in her various roles, her changing image, and the changing Soviet family.

SR, 29:3:548-49; LJ, 94(1969):772.

877. Dodge, Norton T. **Women in the Soviet Economy: Their Role in Economic, Scientific, and Technical Development**. Baltimore, MD: Johns Hopkins University Press, 1966. 311p. $10.00.

This work is essentially a demographic study of the female population of the Soviet Union with respect to age, geographic distrubution, education, social stratification, and employment. The data assembled in this study indicate that the Soviet Union over the past five decades has made headway toward guaranteeing equality of the sexes.

SR, 28:4:664-65; AER, 57(March 1967):319.

878. Geiger, Kent H. **The Family in Soviet Russia**. Cambridge, MA: Harvard University Press, 1968. 381p. $11.25.

The study is centered around three themes: the views of Marx and Engels on the family; the interpretation of these views by Soviet leaders, writers, and educators; and the differences in "life styles" of families at various social levels in the Soviet Union. The author exhibits great insights, and his book is highly recommended to both the expert and the layman.

CSP, 11:1:129-30; Choice, 5(1969):1624.

879. Liegle, Ludwig. **The Family's Role in Soviet Education**. Translated from the German by Susan Hecker. Foreword by Ure Bronfenbrenner. New York: Springer Publishing Co., 1975. xiv, 186p. $9.95.

The author focuses primarily on Soviet family life, the work careers of Soviet females, and the intertwined relationship between the family and the state as competing educational institutions. He observes wide gaps between espoused Marxist ideology and the everyday realities of family, female work, and the educational system. He concludes that Soviet society has failed to transfer the family's and the female's traditional household and educational activities to society at large. Household work continues to fall to the mother or wife, not the father or husband.

SR, 35:4:749-51; LJ, 100(1975):2141; Choice, 12(1965):1374.

880. McAuley, Alastair. **Women's Work and Wages in the USSR**. London: George Allen & Unwin, 1981. xi, 228p. $37.50.

The author has sifted and sorted the considerable body of Soviet material to produce a detailed study of the changing position of women in the Soviet economy since World War II, to present persuasive evidence that Soviet women at present earn between 60 and 70 percent of the average male wage, and to offer a careful assessment of the factors responsible for this differential.

SS, 34:2:307-9.

881. O'Dell, Felicity Ann. **Socialization through Children's Literature: The Soviet Example**. New York and London: Cambridge University Press, 1978. x, 278p. Tables. $32.50.

The author's attempt to assess the success of character education in the Soviet school is the most important aspect of her book. This well-researched study reaffirms the assumption that only an education in which there is no disparity between the textbook and real life, and in which there is a measure of tolerance for dissenting views, is able to bring out the best in young individuals.

SR, 39:1:139; Choice, 16(1979):431.

882. Taubman, William. **The View from Lenin Hills: Soviet Youth in Ferment**. New York: Coward-McCann, 1967. 249p. $5.50.

This is an entertaining and illuminating book, instructive for the general public. Taubman's subject is student life at Moscow University in the year 1965-66. He conveys worthwhile information about many things, including the admission process, the system of courses and examinations, student recreation, the atmosphere and daily routine in the dormitory, and discussions among students of various types and between students and party spokesmen. Throughout, the people he met are described with color and clarity.

SR, 28:4:667-68; LJ, 92(1967):4277.

Special Studies

883. Bailes, Kendall E. **Technology and Society under Lenin and Stalin: Origins of the Soviet Technical Intelligentsia, 1917-1941**. Princeton, NJ: Princeton University Press, 1978. xiii, 469p. $32.00.

Bailes is concerned with the selection of young people for technological jobs, the problems they face at work, their collective relations with the regime, and a number of related matters. This is a most worthwhile and readable book.

SEER, 58:2:307-8; Choice, 16(1979):132.

884. Brine, Jenny; Perrie, Maureen; and Sutton, Andrew, eds. **Home, School and Leisure in the Soviet Union**. London: George Allen & Unwin, 1980. xiv, 279p. $28.50.

With its main theme the study of daily life in Soviet society, the three main sections of this book are devoted to topics that are of intrinsic value in people's everyday lives: housing, the family, and the role of women; education and child care; and recreation. Most of the authors sympathize with the Soviet system, but their essays reflect a balanced approach.

Choice, 18(1981):856.

885. Chalidze, Valery. **Criminal Russia: Essays on Crime in the Soviet Union.** Translated from the Russian by P. S. Falla. New York: Random House, 1977. xiv, 241p. $10.00.

Chalidze is a prominent human rights activist. Deprived of his Soviet citizenship, he now lives in New York. The book opens with a brief essay on the Russian criminal tradition. Toleration of crime, glorification of brigands, disrespect for property, and widespread violence and cruelty in the pre-Soviet era are noted. According to the author, the Soviet criminal tradition absorbed many features of this earlier period. Various forms of violence and lawlessness are discussed in detail.

SR, 37:3:511; JP, 40(1978):845.

886. Cox, Terence M. **Rural Sociology in the Soviet Union: Its History and Basic Concepts.** New York: Holmes & Meier, 1979. vi, 106p. $17.00.

According to the author, rural society in the Soviet Union is rich empirical ground for testing the concepts of Marxist sociology. A basic tenet of Soviet and Marxist sociology is that property relations define class structure and nourish its antagonism. In the Soviet Union, only rural society contains the two property relationships allowed by Soviet law: collective and state ownership. Differences in rural and urban settlements, age, ethnicity, sex, and education have also emerged to complement the relations based on property.

SR, 37:1:143; Choice, 16(1979):1373.

887. Sacks, Michael Paul. **Work and Equality in the Soviet Union: The Division of Labor by Age, Gender, and Nationality.** New York: Praeger Publishers, 1982. 208p. $18.95.

A comprehensive examination of the occupational structure of the individual Soviet republics from 1939-1970, this book analyzes the relationship between industrialization and labor force changes, and between industrialization and age groups within each republic. Sacks examines differences between occupations of men and women of all ages, and tests theories relating the consequences of economic development to changes in the labor force. In addition, the author discusses the extent of equality in the republics and analyzes the extent to which recently developing regions, industries, and professions have experienced change in women's participation in the labor force.

SRNB, 10(Feb. 1983):7.

3

USSR — NON-RUSSIAN REPUBLICS, JEWS, OTHER PEOPLES

GENERAL STUDIES

888.   Allworth, Edward, ed. **Soviet Nationality Problems.** New York: Columbia
University Press, 1971. 296p. $9.95.
This collective work focuses on theoretical issues; it covers in nine chapters such
topics of Soviet nationality problems as "Theory," "Imperial Policies," "Commu-
nist Views," "Implications for the Soviet State," "Legal Reflection of National
Differences," "The Islamic Legacy," and "Ethnicity and Cultural Differences."
An extensive bibliography, data from the 1970 USSR census, and an index augment
the basic chapters.
SR, 31:3:700-1; Choice, 9(1972):271.

889.   Azrael, Jeremy R., ed. **Soviet Nationality Policies and Practices.** New York
and London: Praeger Publishers, 1978. xii, 393p. $25.00.
The essays in this volume "share a common concern with the character, functioning
and development of the USSR as a multi-national polity and society." Contributors
concentrate mainly on three issues: elites, planning, and identity. This is one of the
pioneering solid contributions to the understanding of Soviet nationality policy and
the role of non-Russian peoples of the USSR.
SR, 39:1:140-41; Choice, 16(1979):118.

890.   Bailey, Barnadine. **The Captive Nations: Our First Line of Defense.**
Chicago: Chas. Hallberg, 1969. 191p.
In 1969, twenty-seven formerly independent nations, with a population of
1,161,373,000—one-third of the world—were living under Communist domination.
Of the fifteen so-called republics of the USSR, only one is Russian. The others
have their own languages and cultures and yearn for independence, but are subjected to a ruthless campaign of Russification. This book deserves a wide
distribution.

891.   Carrère d'Encausse, Hélène. **Decline of an Empire: The Soviet Socialist
Republics in Revolt.** Translated by Martin Sokolinsky and Henry A.
LaFarge. New York: Newsweek Books, 1979. 304p. $10.95.
A particular merit of the work is its emphasis on historical context. The first chap-
ter is a detailed consideration of the historical roots of Soviet nationality problems.
The author is careful to give proper consideration to the theoretical views and aims
of the Bolsheviks of all nationalities in the period up to and immediately after the

revolution. Her lengthy discussion of birth rates, migration, language adherence, and labor supply is accurate and highly readable.
NP, 9:2:242-43; LJ, 105(1980):619.

892. Clem, Ralph S., ed. **The Soviet West: Interplay between Nationality and Social Organization.** Foreword by Edward Allworth. New York: Praeger Publishers, 1975. xvi, 161p. $15.00.
The Soviet West, which includes Estonia, Latvia, Lithuania, Belorussia, Ukraine, and Moldavia, is an area with traditional ties to Europe and with a record of national dissent. This collection of articles focuses on the interaction between the efforts of national groups to preserve their identities and the pressures for integration from the Party, the press, the schools, and the economy.
SR, 35:1:145.

893. Conquest, Robert. **The Nation Killers: The Soviet Deportation of Nationalities.** Rev. ed. New York: Macmillan, 1970 (1960, under the title: *The Soviet Deportation of Nationalities*). 222p. $6.95.
Conquest's book deals specifically with the relatively unknown Soviet deportations of entire peoples. Stalin transplanted to Siberia some 1.6 million people simply because they were Chechens, Ingushi, Karachai, Balkars, Kalmyks, Volga Germans, Crimean Tatars, and Meskhetians; and thus he depopulated 62,021 square miles of territory. This book describes how in the Soviet society the Orwellian "unperson" was supplanted by the new category of "unnation." Revealing as this book is, it tells the reader little about any amends that have been made thus far to the former deportees. More particularly, it has virtually nothing to offer on the implications of such forced mass transplantations. The book tells much about important but heretofore obscure events and so it deserves attention.
JBS, 3:2:140-41.

894. Conquest, Robert, ed. **Soviet Nationalities Policy in Practice.** New York: Praeger, 1967. 160p. $5.25.
This is a well-documented survey of Soviet nationalities policy in theory and practice, from Lenin's 1903 Party program to the present. The volume embraces five chapters, heavily studded with references based almost entirely on Soviet sources. There is an editor's preface, an introduction, two appendixes, and a very extensive bibliography. The nationality problem in the USSR has indeed proved to be the Gordian knot of the Kremlin.
JP, 30(1968):865; Choice, 4(1968):1442.

895. Goldhagen, Erich, ed. **Ethnic Minorities in the Soviet Union.** New York: Praeger, for the Institute of East European Jewish Studies of the Philip W. Lown School of Near Eastern and Judaic Studies, Brandeis University, 1968. 351p. $8.75.
The eleven essays in this volume were originally presented at a symposim held at Brandeis University in the fall of 1965. Three of them, almost half of the book, deal broadly with the nationality problem in the Soviet Union in general. Each of the remaining eight essays deals with a specific ethnic group or national minority region. All of the essays are scholarly and informative, but they lack a common

focus of attention. Also, the volume is highly unbalanced in its coverage; twice as many pages are devoted to the Jews as to the Ukrainians, and some important groups, for instance the Georgians, are simply left out.

CSP, 12:4:496-98; CH, 56(Apr. 1969):233.

896. Grimsted, Patricia K. **Archives and Manuscript Repositories in the USSR, Estonia, Latvia, Lithuania, and Belorussia.** Princeton, NJ: Princeton University Press, 1980. 782p. $40.00.

A landmark survey of institutions in Soviet Estonia, Latvia, Lithuania, and Belorussia with archival and manuscript materials is offered in this work. It has appendixes on archival organization and access requirements, geographic names, maps, and a glossary of archival terms.

897. Hodnett, Grey. **Leadership in the Soviet National Republics: A Quantitative Study of Recruitment Policy.** Oakville, Ontario: Mosaic Press, 1978. xx, 410p. Tables. $20.00.

This "strictly quantitative" study examines recruitment policies and practices for the top Communist party and governmental positions in the Soviet non-Russian republics between 1955 and 1972. The fifty republic positions that are analyzed range from key republic Party positions to the Central Committee department heads, members of the council of ministers, the chairman of the Presidium of the Supreme Soviet, the president of the Academy of Sciences, and the chairman of the Union of Writers. Data collected on these positions resulted in 1,182 biographies.

NP, 8:2:241-42; APSR, 74(1980):245.

898. Horak, Stephan M., ed. **Guide to the Study of the Soviet Nationalities: Non-Russian Peoples of the USSR.** Littleton, CO: Libraries Unlimited, 1982. 265p. $35.00.

The *Guide* brings together much of the Western literature on all major Soviet nationalities, and arrangement is not only by nationality but also by subject area. The utility of the bibliography is enhanced by the fact that the great majority of the entries are annotated. Each of the ten major sections is introduced by a specialist on the nationalities with a brief survey on the historical and current status of the ethnic groups, and a list of Western library and archival holdings on the nationality.

SR, 42:4:310-11; CRL, 44(Jan. 1983):52.

899. Kamenetsky, Ihor, ed. **Nationalism and Human Rights: Processes of Modernization in the USSR.** Littleton, CO: Libraries Unlimited for the Association for the Study of the Nationalities (USSR and East Europe), 1977. 246p. $18.50. (ASN Series in Issues Studies [USSR and East Europe], no. 1.)

This volume offers a sampling of some of the better works now being done in the West on Soviet nationality policy by historians, sociologists, and political scientists. The volume's fourteen articles are arranged under three broad headings: "the historical-theoretical background, the broader all-Union issues related to nationalities and human rights, and an evaluation of trends."

CRSN, 6:1:117-20.

900.   Katz, Zev; Roberts, Rosemarie; and Harned, Frederic, eds. **Handbook of Major Soviet Nationalities.** New York: Free Press, 1975. 481p. $25.00.
This handbook offers a general survey of major Soviet nationalities divided into five groups: Slavs, Baltics, Transcaucasians, Central Asians, and others such as Jews, Tatars, and Moldavians. In each case, the information includes history, economy, demography, culture, and a select bibliography. All of these topics are discussed for each nationalitiy in relationship to the Russians, who in 1970 constituted 53 percent of the population of the USSR.
  SR, 35:4:751-52; LJ, 101(1976):967; Choice, 13(1976):348.

901.   Koropeckyj, I. S., and Schroeder, Gertrude E., eds. **Economics of Soviet Regions.** New York: Praeger, 1981. xi, 461p. Figures. Map. Tables.
The volume provides a short overview of the study of Soviet regions, followed by a section that discusses some specific problems of regional development such as regional labor supply, growth and productivity, living standards, and fixed capital. The main part of the book is devoted to a region-by-region analysis. One chapter deals with the European USSR, while three other chapters focus on the Ukraine, Moldavia, Belorussia, and the Baltic republics. Other chapters deal with the Caucasian and Central Asian republics.
  SS, 35:2:264-65.

902.   Luckyj, George S., ed. **Discordant Voices: The Non-Russian Soviet Literatures, 1953-1973.** Oakville, Ontario: Mosaic Press, 1975. viii, 149p. $9.95.
Six essays in this study are devoted to the literature of Armenia, Belorussia, Latvia, Tatar, and Ukraine. Valuable lists for further study in Western languages and the vernacular languages are also included.
  SR, 37:3:539-40.

903.   Nekrich, Aleksandr M. **The Punished Peoples: Deportation and Fate of Soviet Minorities at the End of the Second World War.** New York: W. W. Norton, 1978. xii, 238p. $10.95.
The Punished Peoples was prepared in the USSR before Nekrich emigrated to the United States in 1976. He makes excellent use of very restricted access to the sources. Human aspects come through forcibly without detriment to the scholarly level of the book. This is not simply a case study—it offers new insights on wartime collaboration, Soviet nationality policies in the past and today, and the fate of peoples under a totalitarian Communist regime.
  AHR, 84:2:509.

904.   Pennar, Jaan; Bakalo, Ivan I.; and Bereday, George Z. F. **Modernization and Diversity in Soviet Education with Special Reference to Nationality Groups.** New York: Praeger, 1971. 395p. $20.00. (Praeger Special Studies in International Economics and Development.)
This work includes a vast array of statistics from tsarist to post-Khrushchev times. Without polemicizing, the authors present some evidence to suggest that under

Stalin, and even after, Soviet personnel have been moved from non-Russian to Russian areas, and vice versa, more to promote Russification than for the sake of economic efficiency.

NP, 3:1:47-48; APSR, 66(1972):665.

905. Rockett, Rocky L. **Ethnic Nationalities in the Soviet Union: Sociological Perspectives on a Historical Problem**. New York: Praeger Publishers, 1981. xiii, 171p. $20.95.

Using the case of Soviet nationalities as a test, Rockett surveys six representative groups—Russians, Ukrainians, Estonians, Jews, Armenians, and Uzbeks—and examines in detail their historical beginnings as a people, their relation with the Russian empire, their experiences during the revolutions of 1917, and the impact of past and current Soviet nationalities policy. He concludes that the prognosis as to the assimilation is complex. Differences persist in relative economic development, urbanization, and other measures of sociological development.

906. Szporluk, Roman, ed. **The Influence of East Europe and the Soviet West on the USSR**. New York: Praeger Publishers, 1976. x, 260p. Tables. Figures. $17.50.

The papers presented in this volume, resulting from a symposium of the same title, prove beyond any doubt that in many borderland areas and satellite countries things are done and problems are solved differently from what is done in the Soviet Union itself. Information about the Soviet West is brought out in several essays.

SR, 35:4:754-55.

907. Tillett, Lowell. **The Great Friendship: Soviet Historians on the Non-Russian Nationalities**. Chapel Hill: University of North Carolina Press, 1969. 468p. $12.50.

American East European historiography, while making progress in Russian and Soviet areas during the last two decades, almost completely neglected at the same time the non-Russian aspect of the USSR. Tillett's work represents, therefore, a remarkable breakthrough. Part 1 describes the making of the myth of friendship among Soviet nationalities, and Part 2, arranged topically, analyzes the substance of the myth. Laboring diligently through hundreds of Soviet works, articles, and official documents, the author exposes the Soviet claims that Leninist nationality policy had created something entirely new in history—a multinational society without national conflicts—and that the party's nationality policy created the friendship among the peoples. A 34-page bibliography, an index, a glossary of historical terms, and a map of nationalities enhance the reference value of this pioneering contribution.

AHA, 76:5:1576-77; AAPSS-A, 392(1970):224.

BALTIC REPUBLICS

General Reference Works

908. Balys, Jonas, ed. **Lithuania and Lithuanians: A Selected Bibliography.**
New York: Published for the Lithuanian Research Institute by Praeger
Publishers, 1961. 190p.

The volume has 1,182 entries divided into areas on reference, history, geography,
etc. The author, a specialist with the Library of Congress, has periodically updated
his research with articles in Baltic journals and periodicals.

909. **Encyclopedia Lituanica.** Edited by Simas Suziedlis, et al. 6 vols. Boston:
Juozas Kapocius, 1970-78.

This encyclopedia in English is a major reference guide that provides a "comprehensive and easily accessible source of information for those who wish to learn
about Lithuania and its people." The set contains a valuable collection of maps,
charts, and photographs.

910. Jēgers, Benjamiņš. **Bibliography of Latvian Publications Published outside
Latvia, 1940-1960.** 2 vols. Stockholm: Daugava, 1968-72.

The citations, listed alphabetically, are not annotated. Volume 1, with 2,677
entries, deals with monographs and pamphlets, and volume 2 lists catalogues, maps,
music, serials, and other items, numbering 1,523 entries.

911. Kantautas, Adam, and Kantautas, Filomena, comps. **A Lithuanian Bibliography: A Checklist of Books and Periodicals Held by the Major Libraries
of Canada and the United States.** Edmonton: University of Alberta Press,
1975. 725p.

Supplement to a Lithuanian Bibliography. Edited by A. Ulpis et al.
Edmonton: University of Alberta Press, 1980. 728p. + 16pp. illustrations.

This valuable reference tool has 10,168 entries—and in excess of 4,000 in its
updated supplement—that describe and locate an extensive list of books, journals,
and other types of printed literature in 43 Canadian, 458 American, and 11 European institutions. The listing is divided into various topical areas.

912. Page, Stanley W. **The Formation of the Baltic States: A Study of Great Power Politics upon the Emergence of Lithuania, Latvia, and Estonia.** Cambridge: Harvard University Press, 1959; reprint, New York: Howard Fertig, 1970. 193p.

This book surveys the struggle of Estonia, Latvia, and Lithuania for independence between 1918 and 1920. Their fight was a complex affair that involved many different ideological forces. The book details the intricate military and diplomatic struggle that took place between the Baltic nationals, Germans, Bolsheviks, and Western powers to acquire control of this region in the midst of the Russian civil war.

913. Parming, Marju Rink, and Parming, Tönu. **A Bibliography of English-Language Sources on Estonia: Periodicals, Bibliographies, Pamphlets, and Books.** New York: Estonian Learned Society in America, 1974. 72p. $5.50.

This basic reference tool of 662 entries is divided into various sections on periodicals, reference works, general works, description and travel, language and literature, culture, law, history, etc., with cross references.

JBS, 6:1:81-82.

914. Rank, Aino. **A Bibliography of Works Published by Estonian Historians in Exile, 1945-1969.** Stockholm: Institutum Literarum Estonicum, 1969. 56p.

This bibliography covers books, periodical articles, and reviews written on history, archaeology, history of art, music, religion, and law. This publication is the second in a series—the first being *Works by Estonian Ethnologists in Exile* (1966)—and the third bibliography was issued in 1971 under the title *A Bibliography of Works Published by Estonian Philologists.* 117p.

History, Politics, Government

915. Allworth, Edward, ed. **Nationality Group Survival in Multi-Ethnic States: Shifting Support Patterns in the Soviet Baltic Region.** Published in cooperation with the Program on Soviet Nationality Problems, Columbia University. New York and London: Praeger Publishers, 1977. xvi, 302p. Tables. $21.00.

Focusing on Lithuania, Latvia, and Estonia, this collection of essays is concerned with determining what factors are important for the survival of nationality groups, especially in a multinational and authoritarian society. The individual studies explore, among other subjects, the roots of nationality differences, the significance of culture and religion, social distance between the groups, and the special problem of Baltic Jews.

SR, 37:4:692.

916. Bilmanis, Alfred. **A History of Latvia.** Princeton, NJ: Princeton University Press, 1951. 441p.

This survey, the first in English, traces Latvian history from its beginning to the time of Soviet annexation in 1940. It explains the birth of national consciousness and quite thoroughly covers the period of Latvian independence, 1920-1940.

SR, 11:3:237-39.

917.   Budreckis, Algirdas Martin. **The Lituanian National Revolt of 1941.** Boston: Juozas Kapocius, 1968; distributed by Lithuanian Encyclopedia Press. 147p. $4.00.

The story of Lithuania's revolt of June 23, 1941, against the Soviet regime is not often told. The revolt, involving an estimated one hundred thousand armed Lithuanian rebels, took place at the outbreak of the German-Soviet war and was reported by the neutral press of Sweden. Budreckis expounds the clearly defined thesis that the Lithuanian revolt was a genuine patriotic uprising and that its sponsor, the Lithuanian Activist Front, cooperated with the Germans only for the purpose of reestablishing Lithuania's statehood, which the Soviets had destroyed in 1940. For this end the rebels were willing to make concessions to the Germans so far as Lithuanian national interests permitted them, but the Germans rejected the offered cooperation and suppressed the provisional government that the LAF had established.

SR, 28:4:653-54.

918.   Ezergailis, Andrew. **The 1917 Revolution in Latvia.** Boulder, CO: *East European Quarterly*, 1974; distributed by the Columbia University Press, New York. 281p. $12.50. (East European Monographs, no. 8.)

This work has as its central focus the revolutionary development of Latvia and the Latvian Social Democratic movement. The author explains why both before and during 1817 Latvia was more receptive to radical ideas than Russia proper and thus, in part, why the Bolsheviks were able early in the year to triumph in various worker, peasant, and military organizations.

CSP, 17:4:677-78; Choice, 12(1975):442.

919.   Gerutis, Albertas, ed. **Lithuania: 700 Years.** Translated by Algirdas Budrekis. 2d rev. ed. New York: Manylands Books, 1969. 458p. $12.00.

This is a popular history of Lithuania and its people, covering the period from the beginning of statehood to the present. The story is aimed at the general reader, in particular to make Lithuanian-Americans aware of their national historical heritage.

Choice, 6(1970):1819.

920.   Gimbutas, Marija. **The Balts.** New York: Praeger, 1968 (1963). 286p. $6.95. (Ancient Peoples and Places, vol. 33.)

This volume provides nonspecialized readers with all the information they are likely to need on the archeology of the Baltic tribes before the appearance of large-scale states in that area, before the beginning of the feudal period. The book offers detailed and very interesting illustrations and its general information will encourage readers to dig further into a field that is sadly neglected in the West.

SR, 24:1:131-32.

921.   Jurgela, Constantine R. **History of the Lithuanian Nation.** New York: published for the Lithuanian Cultural Institute, Historical Research Division, by John Felsberg, 1947. 544p.

A detailed history of Lithuania from 1200 to 1918. The first major section is divided into four segments that deal with Lithuania from 1200 to 1795. The second section covers the period 1795-1918. There are a collection of maps, photographs, and a bibliography.

922. Kaslas, Bronis J. **The Baltic Nations: The Quest for Regional Integration and Political Liberty.** Pitton, PA: Euramerica Press, 1976. 319p. $12.00.
This study traces the evolution of Poland's, then Estonia's, Latvia's, and Lithuania's, efforts to form a viable Baltic entente. The author feels their efforts were successful in several diplomatic, economic, and administrative areas, though the three nations failed to stop Soviet aggression.

923. Kaslas, Bronis, J., ed. **The USSR-German Aggression against Lithuania.** New York: Robert Speller, 1973. 543p. $15.00.
The documentary materials contained in this work concern Lithuania's relations with Germany and the Soviet Union. The collection consists of treaties, diplomatic correspondence, excerpts from speeches, and statements by former government members. The author's comments attempt to clarify and interpret some of the documents.
JBS, 4:3:283.

924. Kavass, Igor I., and Sprudzs, Adolf, eds. **Baltic States: A Study of Their Origin and National Development, Their Seizure and Incorporation into the U.S.S.R.** Third Interim Report of the Select Committee on Communist Aggression, U.S. Congress, House. 83d Congress, 2d Session, 1954; reprint, Buffalo, NY: William S. Hein & Co., 1972.
This congressional investigation of the Soviet absorption of Estonia, Latvia, and Lithuania in June-August 1940 is based on historical research, committee hearings, and other sources. The bulk of the study centers on events in 1939-40, with emphasis on cultural, political, economic, and social development.

925. Manning, Clarence A. **The Forgotten Republics.** New York: Philosophical Library, 1952. 264p.
This is a balanced account of the singular fate of the three Baltic nations, Estonia, Latvia, and Lithuania, from the dawn of their history to their annexation by the Soviet Union in 1940.
SR, 12:4:572-73.

926. Nodel, Emanuel. **Estonia: Nation on the Anvil.** New York: Bookman Associates, 1964. 207p. $5.00.
This account tells of the struggle of the Estonian nation against Germanization and Russification from 1721 to 1940. The author traces the attitude of the Baltic German nobility toward the emancipation of the Estonian people and records its negative and positive aspects on the growth of Estonian national consciousness.
SR, 24:3:542-43.

927. Parming, Tönu, and Jarvesoo, Elmar, eds. **A Case Study of a Soviet Republic: The Estonian SSR.** Boulder, CO: Westview Press, published in cooperation with the Estonian Learned Society in America, 1978. 432p. $22.00.
This pioneering work covers the period since 1940 and provides an excellent glimpse into all aspects of Estonian society in the USSR's most prosperous, Westernized republic. Parming predicts a further decrease in the percentage of

ethnic Estonians in the republic and Rein Taagepera offers valuable insights into Estonian attitudes toward Soviet rule. This is an indispensable book for students of Baltic affairs and of the Soviet nationality policy.
SR, 39:1:143-44; AHR, 84:1:218.

928.   Rauch, Georg von. **The Baltic States: The Years of Independence: Estonia, Latvia, Lithuania, 1917-1940.** Translated by Gerald Onn. Berkeley: University of California Press, 1974 (1970). 265p. $10.95.
Originally published in German (1970), its text in English is slightly enlarged. Von Rauch has the distinction of being the first Baltic German historian who follows the line of modern historians about the conception of Baltic history which covers the entire Baltic area, including Estonia, Latvia, and Lithuania. The author surveys in particular the period between 1918 and 1940, and reports on educational, cultural, economic, and ethnic policies of each Baltic state as well as their political and diplomatic concerns.
RR, 34:1:99-100; Choice, 11(1974):1534.

929.   Remeikis, Thomas. **Opposition to Soviet Rule in Lithuania 1945-1980.** Chicago: Institute of Lithuanian Studies Press, 1980. 280p. + 24pp. plates.
This volume is an impressive contribution to the study of relations between the nationalities of the USSR since the end of World War II. About one-fourth of it consists of a careful account of the changing character of Lithuanian behavior, and the remaining three-fourths contains documents amassed by Remeikis and translated from Lithuanian.
BS, 41(April 1981): 34.

930.   Rodgers, Hugh I. **Search for Security: A Study in Baltic Diplomacy, 1920-1934.** Hamden, CT: Shoe String Press, 1975. xi, 181p. $15.00.
Rodgers' account of frantic Latvian diplomacy, in the period between World War I and the rise of Hitler, presents a special case study for a small nation caught between two great powers. Although there was really no escape for the Latvian frog trapped in the German-Russian-Polish snake pit, it was only natural for Latvian statesmen to act the role of mini-Talleyrands. Their survival-oriented ploys are detailed in this book.
SR, 41:2:336-37.

931.   Rutkis, Janis, ed. **Latvia: Country and People.** Stockholm: Latvian National Foundation, 1967. 683p. $17.00.
Thirty-one exiled Latvians from six countries have joined "to make facts about Latvia and the Latvians readily available to interest foreign students." They have achieved this primary objective. Contributors discuss geology, climate, flora and fauna, geographic description of regions and towns, the social and economic system, history of the Latvians, and the political system since 1918.
SEEJ, 14:2:257-59.

932.   Sabaliunas, Leonas. **Lithuania in Crisis: Nationalism to Communism, 1939-1940.** Bloomington, IN: Indiana University Press, 1972. 293p. $11.50.

The author argues that before the international crises that foredoomed Lithuania's independence there were internal ones—economic, social, political—that were reaching a peak at about the same time as the external one. To a large measure, he attributes the easy collapse of democratic Lithuania to emulation of West European political patterns and the disregard with which democracy was held in the world.

SR, 31:3:711-12; Choice, 9(1972):1192.

933.   Senn, Alfred Erich. **The Emergence of Modern Lithuania**. New York: Columbia University Press, 1959; reprint, Westport, CT: Greenwood Press, 1975. 272p. $6.00.

Lithuania's efforts to achieve independence involved complex diplomatic and military struggles. This history details, chronologically, efforts by Lithuanian nationalists during the Russian civil war, particularly against Soviet Russia, to obtain nationhood.

AHR, 65:2:425-26.

934.   Senn, Alfred Erich. **The Great Powers, Lithuania, and the Vilna Question, 1920-1928**. Leiden: E. J. Brill, 1967. 242p.

This study investigates the international problems that surrounded Lithuania's claim to its historical capital, Vilnius (Vilna), and the impact on Lithuanian politics of its failure to acquire the district. Senn surveys the complex diplomatic, economic, ethnic, and nationalistic issues that were part of the dispute, providing a glimpse of the tremendous problems that plagued that segment of Europe after World War I.

AHR, 72:4:1383.

935.   Tarulis, Albert N. **Soviet Policy toward the Baltic States, 1918-1940**. Notre Dame, IN: University of Notre Dame Press, 1959. 276p. $8.95.

The volume offers a basic study of relations between the USSR and the Baltic states during their twenty-two years of independence. Coverage is heaviest for the 1918-20 and 1938-40 periods.

SR, 25:3:100-1.

936.   Thaden, Edward C., ed. **Russification in the Baltic Provinces and Finland, 1855-1914**. Lawrenceville, NJ: Princeton University Press, 1981. 497p. Maps. Figures. $44.00.

This volume serves as a solid and comprehensive introduction to the nationalist movements in the Baltic provinces and Finland against the background of Russification. Five contributors discuss in depth the process of acculturation of minorities into the Great Russian empire, institutional integration, and efforts to impose the Russian language, culture, and Orthodox religion on subject peoples so that they would become Russians.

NP, 12:1:137-38; AHR, 87:1:222.

937.   Tomingas, William. **The Soviet Colonization of Estonia**. New York: Kultuur Publishing House, 1973. 312p.

Tomingas reviews in detail the events that led to the loss of independence of Estonia in June 1940. He provides a background of the emergence and history of

Estonia until 1940 and, in a chapter "Life in Estonia under the First Soviet Occupation 1940-1941," describes the situation under the Soviet occupiers.

938. Vardys, V. Stanley. **The Catholic Church, Dissent and Nationality in Soviet Lithuania.** Boulder, CO: *East European Quarterly,* 1978, distributed by Columbia University Press. xiii, 336p. $18.00. (East European Monographs, 43.)

Lithuania's Catholic struggle remains very closely intertwined with national dissent and constitutes a considerable part of the general Soviet civil rights movement. Thus, while focusing attention on the goals, scope, and social dynamics of Lithuanian Catholic dissent, the author examines it in the perspective of Lithuania's modern development.

NP, 7:2:238-39; AHR, 84:4:1109; Choice, 16(1979):284.

939. Vardys, V. Stanley, ed. **Lithuania under the Soviets: Portrait of a Nation, 1940-65.** New York: Praeger, 1965. 299p. $7.00.

The contributors seem unanimous in the belief that the Lithuanian nation fared better in an independent state than it does now under Soviet rule. The authors offer frank accounts of the years of Lithuania's independence, omitting none of the major aspects of that period, but entertain no doubts that the happiest course would be for Lithuania to be politically independent.

SR, 24:3:543-44; AHR, 71:4:1390.

940. Ziedonis, Arvidis, et al., eds. **Problems of Mininations: Baltic Perspectives.** San Jose, CA: Association for the Advancement of Baltic Studies, 1973. 214p.

While all mininations face the same basic difficulties—inability to defend themselves militarily and to achieve "industrial versatility"—the primary concern of the subjected peoples of the Baltic states has been the preservation of their ethnic substance in view of the persistent pressure of Russification. This pressure is especially strong in Latvia and Estonia, where the postwar influx of Russians dramatically undermined the numerical preponderance of the titular nationality.

CSP, 26:4:648-49; JBS, 5:1:53-54.

Languages and Literatures

941. Belzēja, et al. **English-Latvian Dictionary.** The chapter on "American Slang, New Words, Proverbs, and Sayings" compiled and edited by V. Silmalis. Waverly, Iowa: Latvjugrāmata, National Latvian Publishers, 1971. 1133p.

The most comprehensive dictionary available comprising over fifty-five thousand words, idiomatic phrases, colloquial expressions and terms, including technical, medical, and other scientific words.

942. Budina, Lazdina T. **Teach Yourself Latvian.** London: English Universities Press, 1966. 335p.

This book is a Latvian course for the English-speaking student. It consists of thirty-two lessons, each of which has a reading passage, vocabulary, grammar, and exercises. The grammatical rules are clearly expressed and skillfully graduated, and examples for practical application are given.

SEER, 45:104:264-65.

943. Dambriunas, Leonardas, et al. **Introduction to Modern Lithuanian.** Brooklyn, NY: Franciscan Fathers Press, 1966. 471p. $7.00.

This is a full introductory grammar of Lithuanian in English. It has a long introductory chapter on pronunciation, spelling, accentuation, etc., followed by forty lessons in which Lithuanian grammar is systematically presented. The keys and tapes are also available.

944. Ekmanis, Rolfs. **Latvian Literature under the Soviets 1940-1975.** Belmont, MA: Nordland Publishing Co., 1978. 533p. $27.50.

Ekmanis is concerned with "the policy of the Communist Party of the Soviet as, in its shifting formulations, it has affected Soviet Latvian literature and culture." He is particularly successful in his selection and presentation of various samples of mutilated art as they correspond to shifting Party policies.

NP, 8:2:250-51.

945. Oinas, Felix J. **Basic Course in Estonian.** Bloomington, IN: Indiana University Press, 1975. 398p.

This Estonian-English text emphasizes conversation, with an Estonian-English glossary and an index.

946. Oras, Ants. **Estonian Literary Reader.** Bloomington, IN: Indiana University Press, 1963. 386p.

This collection begins with a short history of Estonian literature, though its strength is its careful selection of works by Estonian poets and writers. It has an excellent glossary.

947. Piesarskas, B., and Svecevicius, B. **Lietuviu-Anglu Kalbu Zodynas** (Lithuanian-English Dictionary). Vilnius: Mokslas Publishers, 1979. 911p.

The dictionary contains some fifty thousand words.

948. Rubulis, Aleksis. **Baltic Literature: Survey of Finnish, Estonian, Latvian, and Lithuanian Literatures.** Notre Dame, IN: University of Notre Dame Press, 1970. 215p. $8.50.

This book on Baltic literature briefly but adequately discusses the principal literary movements and their major representatives. Each Baltic nation and trend is represented by examples of prose and poetry of first-rate quality. This study is the first and only one of its kind in English.

SR, 30:2:451-52.

949. Saagpakk, Paul F. **Eesti-Inglise Sõnaraamat** (Estonian-English Dictionary). New Haven, CT, and London: Yale University Press, 1982. 1180p.

This dictionary provides philologists and students of language with a means of learning Estonian thoroughly. To this end the author has included a concise grammatical survey which explains the essentials of Estonian pronunciation, spelling, and inflection.

NP, 12:1:148-49.

950. Schmalstieg, William R., and Klimas, Antanas. **Lithuanian-English Glossary of Linguistic Terminology.** University Park, PA: Department of Slavic Languages, Pennsylvania State University, 1971. 115p. $4.00.

This glossary was prepared for students and scholars in the fields of Baltic and Lithuanian linguistics. The terms were taken from Lithuanian books and periodicals within the past fifty years and also from textbooks, dictionaries, and word lists. It contains 3,915 entries with English definitions and appears to be extremely accurate and complete.

SEEJ, 16:3:385.

951. Straumanis, Alfreds, ed. **Confrontation with Tyranny: Six Baltic Plays with Introductory Essays.** Prospect Heights, IL: Waveland Press, 1977. 363p. $15.00.

This is a collection of two Estonian, two Latvian, and two Lithuanian plays. Three were written by authors in the Soviet Baltic republics, while the others were composed by exiles. Each play has been translated, with commentary. The selection of the plays ranges from political to abstract, from realistic to symbolic.

JBS, 11:3:267-68.

BELORUSSIA

History, Politics, Government

952. Lubachko, Ivan S. **Belorussia under Soviet Rule, 1917-1957**. Lexington, KY: University Press of Kentucky, 1972. 219p. $10.00.
The Belorussians were relatively late in developing a national consciousness in the modern sense. Their awakening coincided roughly with the advent of Bolshevism in Russia. During the early 1920s, Lenin succeeded in gaining the support of Belorussian nationalists. This détente came to a bloody end with the help of Stalin's purges in the 1930s, which literally decimated the Belorussian nation. No fewer than one million Belorussians perished.
CRSN, 1:2:196-97; Choice, 9(1972):1343.

953. Vakar, Nicholas P. **Belorussia: The Making of a Nation--a Case Study**. Cambridge, MA: Harvard University Press, 1956. 296p. (Russian Research Center Studies, no. 21.)

   Bibliographic Guide to Belorussia. Cambridge, MA: Harvard University Press, 1956. 63p.
This rare study deals with a little-known nation of Eastern Europe. Belorussian nationalism revived only at the beginning of the twentieth century. The country's recent history is a fascinating and often horrifying case study in the interplay of nationalism and communism.
JMH, 29:2:172-73.

Language and Literature

954. Adamovich, Anthony. **Opposition to Sovietization in Belorussian Literature (1917-1957)**. New York: The Institute for the Study of the USSR, Scarecrow Press, 1958. 204p.
Adamovich analyzes one of the most complex periods in the development of Belorussian literature. He bases his study largely on personal knowledge and experience of the literature and of the epoch considered. He includes biographical data, references, translations of poems, and a list of works of over forty writers.

955. Bykov, Vasily. **The Ordeal (A Novel)**. Translated by Gordon Clough. New York: Dutton, 1972. 170p. $5.95.
The Ordeal was first published in the Soviet Union in 1970. The main character is the soldier Sotnikov, whose wartime experience of fighting Germans as a member

of a Soviet partisan unit and later as a prisoner of war in a German camp is the theme of the novel. What makes this work unique is its realistic description of wartime events, hitherto excluded from officially sanctioned Soviet literature.

956. Mayo, Peter J. **A Grammar of Byelorussian.** Sheffield, England: Anglo-Byelorussian Society in association with the Department of Russian and Slavonic Studies, University of Sheffield, England, 1976. 66p. £1.50.

The first part of the *Grammar* acquaints the reader with the alphabet, stress, pronunciation, and spelling; the remainder deals with the morphology of Belorussian.

957. McMillin, Arnold B. **A History of Byelorussian Literature: From Its Origins to the Present Day.** Giessen, Germany: Wilhelm Schmitz Verlag, 1977. 447p. DM 60.00.

This work is a general survey of Belorussian literature from the twelfth century to 1975. In spite of its numerous shortcomings, the book has merit, since it is a summary of serious studies.

CSP, 20:2:275-76.

958. McMillin, Arnold B. **The Vocabulary of the Byelorussian Literary Language in the Nineteenth Century.** London: Anglo-Byelorussian Society, 1973. 336p. £2.00.

This study focuses on a neglected aspect of the origins and development of a "new" literary language based mainly on the literary works of the Byelorussian writer Dunin-Marcinkievich. The author studied in detail the vocabulary and presents a statistical analysis of 3,378 words.

CSP, 16:4:684.

959. Pashkievich, Valentina. **Fundamental Byelorussian.** Books I and II. Toronto: Byelorussian-Canadian Coordinating Committee, 1974-78. Book I: 312p.; Book II: 422p.

This is a textbook for the study of Belorussian. It covers the fundamentals of grammar, offers a short but complete course on phonetics and morphology, indicates stresses, presents written and oral drill exercises, and contains an extensive Belorussian-English dictionary. Book II contains an appendix with grammatical tables summarizing the declensions of nouns, adjectives, and pronouns, conjugations of verbs, and tables of numerals. The dictionary lists over twenty thousand words.

960. Rich, Vera, trans. **Like Water, Like Fire: An Anthology of Byelorussian Poetry from 1828 to the Present Day.** London: George Allen & Unwin, 1971. 347p. £4.50. (UNESCO Collection of Representative Works, European Series.)

This is the first anthology of Belorussian poetry to appear in English. Vera Rich has been translating Belorussian poetry for about twenty years, and she is known for her own books of original poetry in English. The volume can be enjoyable for general readers. The book contains 221 poems by 41 authors. Contemporary Soviet Belorussian poetry is represented most extensively.

SR, 32:4:863-64.

UKRAINE

General Reference Works

961. Lawrynenko, Jurij. **Ukrainian Communism and Soviet Russian Policy toward the Ukraine: An Annotated Bibliography, 1917-1953.** Foreword by John S. Reshetar. New York: Praeger, 1953. 454p.
The most comprehensive bibliography in Ukrainian, Russian and western languages on the development of Communism in the Ukraine. Arranged chronologically under various subjects, including Soviet Russian policy in the Ukraine.
SR, 14:3:414.

962. Magocsi, Paul Robert. **Galicia: A Historical Survey and Bibliographic Guide.** Downsview, Ontario: University of Toronto Press in association with the Canadian Institute of Ukrainian Studies and the Harvard Ukrainian Research Institute, 1983. 300p. $19.50.
The volume surveys the history of Ukrainian Galicia from the earliest times to the present. It includes over one thousand notes and three thousand references about archeological, political, social, economic, literary, linguistic, and cultural developments in Galicia. A separate chapter is devoted to Galicia's minorities—Poles, Jews, Germans, and Karaites.

963. **Ukraine: A Concise Encyclopedia.** 2 vols. Prepared by Shevchenko Scientific Society. Edited by Volodymyr Kubijovič. Foreword by Ernest J. Simmons. Toronto: University of Toronto Press, published for the Ukrainian National Association, 1963 and 1971. Vol. 1: 1185p.; Vol. 2: 1394p. $70.00 ea.
Nearly a hundred Ukrainian scholars have been involved in providing this comprehensive library of information about Ukraine in English. The value of the work is enhanced by the extensive bibliographies, which include Soviet works, by the numerous illustrations and maps in color, and by the up-to-date charts and graphs.
SR, 31:2:456-57.

964. Weres, Roman. **Ukraine: Selected References in the English Language.** 2d ed. Chicago: Ukrainian Research and Information Institute, 1974. 312p.
This volume contains 1,958 entries, listing works, both monographic and serial, related to the history, economy, and culture of the Ukrainian people. Annotations indicate the nature and scope of books and articles listed.

History, Historiography, Politics, Government

965. Adams, Arthur E. **Bolsheviks in the Ukraine: The Second Campaign, 1918-1919.** Port Washington, NY: Kennikat Press, 1973. 440p. $20.00.
Much of the book describes the Bolsheviks' unsuccessful attempt to administer and defend the Ukraine against the Whites. Once in power, the Ukrainian Communist party "remained insensitive to Ukrainian needs and stubbornly reluctant to adapt itself to Ukrainian realities."
JMH, 37:1:112-13.

966. Armstrong, John A. **Ukrainian Nationalism, 1939-1945.** Rev. ed. New York: Columbia University Press, 1963; reprint, Littleton, CO: Ukrainian Academic Press, 1980. 361p. $30.00.
This is a dramatic account of nationalists struggling to establish Ukrainian independence during World War II, while powerful forces fought for control of Eastern Europe. The revised and expanded edition includes such postwar developments as: the armed struggle of the UPA (Ukrainian Partisan Army) against the Soviet regime in the years 1945-50, the Soviet policy following the UPA's defeat, and further activities of the Ukrainian emigration.
SR, 23:4:771; JMH, 28:4:404-6.

967. Bilinsky, Yaroslav. **The Second Soviet Republic: The Ukraine after World War II.** New Brunswick, NJ: Rutgers University Press, 1964. 539p. $12.50.
The author of this study analyzes the political, socioeconomic, and cultural development of the Ukraine for the past twenty years and ponders its effect on the attitudes of Ukrainians toward the problem of separation. Some of the chapters describe the rapid industrial strides of the Soviet Ukraine and the rise of Ukrainians to positions of power. But the author's documented analysis also points to discriminatory policies in behalf of Russification, such as the absence of courses in Ukrainian literature and history in the republic's primary and secondary schools.
AHR, 70:4:1112-13; SR, 26:3:493-95.

968. Borys, Jurij. **The Sovietization of Ukraine: The Communist Doctrine and Practice of National Self-Determination.** Rev. ed. Edmonton and Toronto: Canadian Institute of Ukrainian Studies, 1980. 488p. $37.50 Distributed by the University of Toronto Press.
This is the second revised edition of the author's work originally published under the title *The Russian Communist Party and the Sovietization of Ukraine.* Its value lies in its emphasis on sociological and economic elements.
NP, 12:1:139-41.

969. Braichevskyj, Mykhailo I. **Annexation or Reunification? Critical Notes on One Conception.** Edited and translated by George P. Kulchycky. Munich: Ukrainisches Institut für Bildungspolitik, 1974. 139p.
This essay written by a Soviet historian in 1966 was refused publication in Soviet Ukraine. It subsequently received wide circulation in *samvydav.* Two other essays by Kulchycky and Ohloblyn are part of this volume. It is a landmark work in Ukrainian historiography.

970.   Dmytryshyn, Basil. **Moscow and the Ukraine, 1918-1953: A Study of Russian Bolshevik Nationality Policy.** New York: Bookman Associates, 1956. 310p.

The motives of the Russian Bolsheviks in their occupation of Ukraine and the reasons behind them are the topic of this volume. The author finds two main causes: the Russian revolutionary intellectuals of the nineteenth century ignored the national problem, and they considered the amalgamation of small nations contrary to their aims. Lenin's promises to the minority nationalities were temporary expedients.

SR, 17:1:123-24.

971.   Doroshenko, Dmytro. **A Survey of Ukrainian Historiography,** and Ohloblyn, Olexander, **Ukrainian Historiography, 1917-1956.** *Annals of the Ukrainian Academy of Arts and Sciences in the U.S.* Vols. V-VI (1957). New York: The Ukrainian Academy of Arts and Sciences in the U.S., 1957. 456p.

This study represents the most comprehensive and objective account of the development of Ukrainian historiography from its beginning in the eleventh century up to 1956. Three essays updating this study have since been published.

972.   Doroshenko, Dmytro. **A Survey of Ukrainian History.** Edited and updated by Oleh W. Gerus. Winnipeg: Humeniuk Publication Foundation, 1975. xiii, 873p. $25.00.

Dmytro Doroshenko (1882-1951) authored approximately six hundred historical studies. The present work appeared first in 1932 in Ukrainian; the first English edition was published in 1939, and the present edition is based on the Ukrainian text as well as the earlier English edition. The editor has added six new chapters, new maps, bibliography, and pictorial materials, as well as a brief biographical sketch of Doroshenko. The study begins with prehistory and covers all periods of Ukrainian history.

CSP, 19:2:248-49.

973.   Farmer, Kenneth C. **Ukrainian Nationalism in the Post-Stalin Era: Myths, Symbols and Ideology in Soviet Nationalities Policy.** The Hague, The Netherlands: Martinus Nijhoff, 1980. 241p. $36.50.

This is a combined chronological and analytical study of the Ukrainian national movement from 1956 to 1972, with emphasis on the Ukrainian dissent movement of the 1960s and 1970s. The theme of this study is the manipulation of symbols in the popular culture by proponents of "proletarian internationalism" and by proponents of greater national political and cultural autonomy in Ukraine and other republics.

NP, 10:1:83-84; SR, 40:4:660-61.

974.   Fedyshyn, Oleh S. **Germany's Drive to the East and the Ukrainian Revolution, 1917-1918.** New Brunswick, NJ: Rutgers University Press, 1971. 401p. $15.00.

The author attempts to evaluate the interplay of the German *Ostpolitik* and the Ukrainian endeavors for national self-determination during the eventful years of

the Ukrainian revolution in 1917-18. The study is unique in that it examines the German war aims and the German occupation policy in particular reference to the Ukraine and the events occurring at that time.
SR, 31:1:166-67; AHR, 77:1:182.

975.   Gajecky, George, ed. **The Cossack Administration of the Hetmanate.** 2 vols. Cambridge, MA: Harvard Ukrainian Research Institute, 1978. xvi, 775p. Maps. (Harvard Ukrainian Research Institute, Sources and Documents Series.)
This book consists of a comprehensive description of the structure of the Ukrainian Cossack state of the seventeenth century. It includes a list of all officers at both regimental and company levels, and an index of the names of more than three thousand Cossack officers.

976.   Goldelman, Solomon J. **Jewish National Autonomy in Ukraine, 1917-1921.** Chicago: Ukrainian Research and Information Service, 1968. 140p.
This is a study of the legal status of Jews in Ukraine during 1917-21 by a Ukrainian-Jewish émigré, who is a former member of the Ukrainian diplomatic corps.

977.   Hrushevsky, Michael. **A History of the Ukraine.** Edited by O. J. Frederiksen. Preface by George Vernadsky. Hamden, CT: Archon Books, 1970 (1941). 629p. $15.00.
This book represents the reprinting of the first and thus far the only translation of Hrushevsky's condensed *History of Ukraine*. The story is presented in popular style for the general reader and student who is interested in a general survey of Ukrainian history. The English-speaking reader does not yet have access to Hrushevsky's prolific writings: his *Istoriia Ukrainy-Rusy*, in ten volumes, his almost two thousand other works, articles and documents which he edited, almost all written in Ukrainian. This survey, dating from about 1900, presents the history of Ukraine from the so-called populist point of view, which is by now largely obsolete. An inadequate translation makes for heavy reading.

978.   Hunczak, Taras, ed. **The Ukraine, 1917-1921: A Study in Revolution.** Assisted by John T. Von der Heide. Introduction by Richard Pipes. Cambridge, MA: Harvard University Press, 1977. viii, 424p. $15.00.
This is a collection of essays by fourteen specialists in modern Ukrainian history. The book includes articles on Communist tactics in the takeover of Ukraine; the Orthodox church in Ukraine; and political parties in Ukraine before the Communist takeover.
CSP, 21:1:131-33; Choice, 15(1978):289.

979.   Kamenetsky, Ihor. **Hitler's Occupation of the Ukraine, 1941-1944.** Milwaukee, WI: Marquette University Press, 1956. 101p. (Marquette Slavic Studies, no. 2.)
In a survey of Nazi planning for the occupation of the Ukraine, Hitler was determined to turn the country into a German colony in which the Ukrainian population would be reduced to serfdom.
SR, 16:3:411-12.

980. Kolasky, John. **Education in Soviet Ukraine: A Study in Discrimination and Russification.** Toronto: Peter Martin, 1968. 238p. $3.50pa.

Kolasky, a veteran Canadian Marxist formerly highly sympathetic to the USSR, accumulated very strong evidence of the existence of an opposition to Soviet policy among Ukrainian intellectuals during his two years' study in Kiev, Ukraine. The bulk of his work consists of statistics on the relative education of nationalities.
SR, 28:4:503-4.

981. Kostiuk, Hyrhory. **Stalinist Rule in the Ukraine: A Study of the Decade of Mass Terror, 1929-1939.** New York: Praeger, 1960. 162p.

This is a dispassionate description of Stalin's terror in the Ukraine. The book contains valuable information on the purges and the history of Ukraine under Soviet rule.
SR, 20:3:532-33.

982. Magocsi, Paul Robert. **The Shaping of a National Identity: Subcarpathian Rus', 1848-1948.** Cambridge, MA: Harvard University Press, 1978. xvi, 640p. Maps. $27.50.

The theme of this book is that Subcarpathian Rusyns failed to develop into an independent nationality because their intelligentsia suffered from a sense of inferiority vis-à-vis other closely related nationalities.
NP, 7:2:221-22; Choice, 15(1979):1713.

983. Majstrenko, Ivan. **Borotbism: A Chapter in the History of Ukrainian Communism.** Translated by G. Luckyj. New York: Research Program of the USSR, 1954. 325p.

The Borotbists, a Ukrainian social revolutionary faction, joined the Bolsheviks and became the foremost advocate of national communism in Ukraine in the early 1920s.

984. Manning, Clarence A. **Hetman of Ukraine: Ivan Mazeppa.** New York: Bookman Associates, 1957. 234p.

Hetman Mazeppa, in alliance with King Charles XII of Sweden, led the unsuccessful war against Russia in 1709. The account elucidates the Russo-Ukrainian relation and conflict.

985. Manning, Clarence A. **The Story of the Ukraine.** New York: Philosophical Library, 1947. 326p.

The author provides primarily an account of the relations of the Ukraine to Russia. The story is lucidly composed and suitable for the general reader.
SR, 6:18-19:183-84.

986. Manning, Clarence A. **Ukraine under the Soviets.** New York: Bookman Associates, 1953. 223p.

This is a brief historical account of the significant political, economic, and cultural changes in Ukraine since 1917. Manning discusses the effects of the NEP in Ukraine, the literary and scholarly developments of the "Ukrainization" period, the intensive re-Russification, and events during and after World War II, with emphasis on the resistance of the Ukrainian population.

987. Margolin, Arnold. **Ukraine and the Policy of the Entente**. Translated by V. P. Sokoloff. Los Angeles: L. A. Margolina, 1977. 261p.

Following the Bolshevik coup, Margolin, former minister in the Central Rada, lent his support to the Ukrainian movement as a jurist and diplomat. He thus views many aspects of the Ukrainian problem from firsthand experience. These recollections were first published in 1921.

RR, 38:3:369-70.

988. Mazlakh, Serhii, and Shakhrai, Vasyl. **On the Current Situation in the Ukraine**. Edited and translated by Peter J. Potichnyj. Introduction by Michael M. Luther. Ann Arbor: University of Michigan Press, 1970. 220p. $8.95.

This is a translation of a book-length pamphlet originally published in early 1919. The authors, prominent Ukrainian Communists, were convinced that the drift of the Ukrainian revolution was toward national statehood, and advocated a fully independent Ukrainian Soviet republic. The book exposes the contradiction between Bolshevik slogans of national self-determination and actual Bolshevik practices in Ukraine.

SR, 31:1:172-75; Choice, 8(1971):133.

989. Nahayewsky, Isidore. **History of Ukraine**. Philadelphia: America Publishing House, 1962. 295p. $5.00.

This work offers a concise popular historical account of the Ukrainian people from the dawn of their existence to the present, with special emphasis on religious life.

SR, 22:3:559-60.

990. O'Brien, C. Bickford. **Muscovy and the Ukraine from the Periaslav Agreement to the Truce of Andrusovo, 1654-1667**. Berkeley: University of California Press, 1963. 138p. $3.00.

O'Brien examines the activities of individual hetmans after the death of Hetman Khmelnytsky, emphasizing the anti-Muscovite attitude of the Ukrainian population, especially the clergy. The study centers on the very complex "Period of Ruin" in Ukrainian and East European history and on two agreements that became focal points in Russo-Ukrainian relations.

SR, 23:4:744-46.

991. Palij, Michael. **The Anarchism of Nestor Makhno, 1918-1921: An Aspect of the Ukrainian Revolution**. Seattle and London: University of Washington Press, 1976. xiv, 248p. Photographs. $14.50. (Institute for Comparative and Foreign Area Studies, Publications on Russia and Eastern Europe, no. 7.)

The author draws the political, ideological, and military profile of Makhno and describes his impact on the revolution by analyzing his attitudes and relations to the Bolsheviks, to various Ukrainian governments, and to the White Guards under the command of Denikin and Wrangel. The book is composed in a highly readable form.

NP, 6:1:75-79; AHR, 83:2:491; Choice, 14(1978):1554.

992.   Pidhainy, Oleh S. **The Formation of the Ukrainian Republic: The Ukrainian Republic in the Great East-European Revolution.** Vol. 1. Toronto: New Review Books, 1966. 685p. $10.75.
This massive and well-documented study describes how Ukrainian statehood was brought about in 1917-18. The author concludes that Ukraine had "consolidated its sovereignty, had completed its period of formation and entered as an equal into the world community of states."
CSP, 11:2:290-92.

993.   Reshetar, John S., Jr. **The Ukrainian Revolution, 1917-1920: A Study in Nationalism.** Princeton, NJ: Princeton University Press, 1952. 363p.
This volume is an important part of East European literature on a crucial period. The author has traced the movement of nationalism from its origins in the mid-seventeenth century to the ultimate collapse of the Ukrainian national state in 1920.
SR, 12:1:145-47.

994.   **Russian Oppression in Ukraine: Reports and Documents.** London: Ukrainian Publishers, Ltd., 1972. 576p. $8.00.
This voluminous book contains seventeen essays on various aspects of Soviet policy in Ukraine, in addition to several reports and eyewitness accounts. Photographs documenting the Soviet terror and famine of 1932-33 complement the text.

995.   Sawczuk, Konstantyn. **The Ukraine in the United Nations: A Study in Soviet Foreign Policy, 1944-1950.** Boulder, CO: *East European Quarterly,* 1975. 158p. $10.00. Distributed by Columbia University Press, New York. (East European Monographs, 9.)
This is a study of how Ukraine came to be a founding member of the United Nations in 1945; its political role and activities in the early years, especially the impact of the U.N. delegate Dmytro Manuilsky; and the complicated question of the juridicial status of the Ukrainian SSR in the international community.

996.   Shandruk, Pavlo. **Arms of Valor.** Translated by Roman Olesnicki. Introduction by Roman Smal-Stocki. New York: Robert Speller and Sons, 1959. 320p.
These are the memoirs of Pavlo Shandruk, lieutenant general of the general staff, Ukrainian National Army. The memoirs cover three important periods in his life: the era of Ukrainian independence after World War I, his experience under the Polish occupation; and his experiences during World War II.
SR, 20:4:611-12.

997.   Stachiw, Matthew. **Ukraine and Russia: An Outline History of Political and Military Relations (December, 1917-April, 1918).** Translated from the Ukrainian by Walter Dushnyck. Preface by Clarence A. Manning. New York: Schevchenko Scientific Society, 1967. 215p.
The work consists of a factual and accurate outline history of the first invasion and war of Soviet Russia against Ukraine.
SR, 34:3:623-24.

998.   Stachiw, Matthew, and Sztendera, Jaroslaw. **Western Ukraine at the Turning Point of Europe's History, 1918-1923.** 2 vols. Edited by Joan L. Stachiw. Scranton, PA: Ukrainian Scientific-Historical Library, 1969. (Shevchenko Scientific Society Ukrainian Studies, English Section, vol. 5.) This is the only study in English that uses original sources to show the conflicting interests over Western Ukraine, namely among the Poles, Russians, Austrians, Jews, and Ukrainians, during the last crucial years of World War I and at the peace conference in Paris. By briefly sketching the history of Western Ukraine, the work lays a good foundation for understanding the differences that brought these groups to the battlefield where, eventually, the fate of an independent West Ukraine was decided.
CASS, 7:2:272-73.

999.   Stachiw, Matthew; Stercho, Peter G. (vol. I only); and Chirovsky, Nicholas L. F. **Ukraine and the European Turmoil, 1917-1919.** 2 vols. New York: Shevchenko Scientific Society, 1973.
The authors present a history of the Ukrainian National Republic (UNR) from 1917 to March 1919 and offer much information that is new in English. The account is somewhat biased and polemical in its presentation.
SR, 34:3:623-24.

1000.   Stercho, Peter G. **Diplomacy of Double Morality: Europe's Crossroads in Carpatho-Ukraine, 1919-1939.** New York: Carpathian Research Center, 1971. 496p. $15.00.
This book will for some time serve as an authoritative source work on Carpatho-Ukraine for the critical period covered. Methodically arranged, the work is suitably divided into nine chapters dealing with various aspects of the history of that land. Virtually every page is heavily footnoted with source and documentary proof for the author's observations and historical narrative. Explanatory maps are conveniently provided, and supporting tables of statistical data enable the reader to appreciate more precisely the more pointed observations made by the author.
SR, 33:1:163-64.

1001.   Subtelny, Orest. **The Mazepists: Ukrainian Separatism in the Early Eighteenth Century.** Boulder, CO: *East European Quarterly,* 1981. vii, 280p. $20.00. Distributed by Columbia University Press, New York. (East European Monographs, no. 87.)
The bulk of this study deals with the colossal diplomatic efforts of Mazepa's successor in exile, Hetman Pylyp Orlyk, to forge a broad anti-Russian coalition involving Sweden, Turkey, Poland, Austria, and Germany, which might reconstitute an autonomous Cossack state in Ukraine. Orlyk's ultimate failure is attributed to his fickle allies and to his own despondent mood in exile.
SR, 41:3:564-65; HRNB, 10(July 1982):211.

1002.   Sullivant, Robert S. **Soviet Politics and the Ukraine, 1917-1957.** New York and London: Columbia University Press, 1962. 438p. $8.50.
The study concerns Soviet Russian policies in Ukraine, which are described as aimed at the reassertion of Russia's authority over the continuously dissenting

Ukrainian "nationalist" forces. The book's considerable value lies in its character as a broad survey of events that are little known in the Western world.

SR, 23:1:146-47.

1003. Sydorenko, Alexander. **The Kievan Academy in the Seventeenth Century.** Ottawa, Canada: University of Ottawa Press, 1977. xvi, 194p. + 34pp. plates. (University of Ottawa Ukrainian Studies.)

The Kievan Academy became a major intellectual and educational center in East Europe and was patterned after Western academic institutions of the time. The author describes the political and cultural setting in seventeenth-century Ukraine and emphasizes the precarious Polish-Russian-Ukrainian relationships and the struggle of the Ukrainian Orthodox church with Polish Catholic influences.

NP, 7:1:106-7; SR, 38:3:486.

1004. Tys-Krokhmaliuk, Yurjy. **UPA Warfare in Ukraine.** Preface by Ivan Wowchuk. Translated from the Ukrainian by Walter Dushnyck. New York: Society of Veterans of Ukrainian Insurgent Army of the U.S. and Canada, 1972. 449p.

In the introduction the author offers general information about Ukraine prior to and during World War II. Then he proceeds with the history of the formation and activities of the Ukrainian Partisan Army (UPA) fighting both invaders, Nazi Germany and Soviet Russia. The UPA continued the fighting until 1950. This story of the struggle of the Ukrainian underground is hardly known in the West.

1005. Vernadsky, George. **Bohdan Khmelnytsky, Hetman of Ukraine.** New Haven: Yale University Press, 1941. 150p.

This is a biography of the most prominent figure of the Ukrainian Cossacks whose leader led the fight against the Poles. Khmelnytsky founded the Cossack state in the middle of the seventeenth century.

BRD, Jan. 1942.

1006. Yaremko, Michael. **Galicia-Halychyna: From Separation to Unity.** Introduction by Clarence A. Manning. Toronto, New York, Paris: Shevchenko Scientific Society, 1967. 292p. $7.00.

This is a popular account of the history of Galicia from earliest times to the present. Yaremko discusses Galicia's past in four parts: the princely period, 907-1340; Galicia under Polish occupation, 1349-1772; Galicia under the Habsburgs, 1772-1918; and Galicia from 1914 to 1945.

AHR, 74:1:221.

Economics

1007. Kononenko, Konstantyn. **Ukraine and Russia: A History of Economic Relations between Ukraine and Russia, 1654-1917.** Milwaukee, WI: Marquette University Press, 1958. 257p. (Marquette Slavic Studies, no. 4.)

The Ukraine's natural resources made her vulnerable to economic exploitation and the victim of Russian colonialism. The Soviet regime continues to follow the tsarist example of investing in less than taking from the Soviet Ukraine.

1008.   Koropeckyj, I. S. **Location Problems in Soviet Industry before World War II: The Case of the Ukraine.** Chapel Hill: University of North Carolina Press, 1972. 219p. $11.95.

The problem analyzed is whether the USSR was correct in stressing the development of heavy industry "behind the Urals" during the 1928-40 period. Under Stalin heavy industry expanded in the Ukraine, but not as rapidly as elsewhere; in particular, the Ural-Kuznetsk Combine created a second iron and steel base for the USSR. This study contributes to the understanding of Soviet investment policies.

SR, 31:4:909-10.

1009.   Koropeckyj, I. S., ed. **The Ukraine within the USSR: An Economic Balance Sheet.** New York: Praeger Publishers, 1977. xxi, 316p. $26.95.

Two important conclusions flow from this collection of essays: Ukraine is a region of relative decline, and there is a definite drain of resources and revenues from the Ukrainian SSR. The contributors are unanimous in estimating the costs incurred by Ukraine's economy and population and on the role of Ukraine's economy within the USSR.

1010.   Melnyk, Zinowij Lew. **Soviet Capital Formation: Ukraine, 1928/29-1932.** Munich: Ukrainian Free University Press, 1965. 182p.

This study of Soviet internal finances is well supplied with tables and well documented. The author concludes that Ukraine was being exploited by the rest of the USSR in its capital formation drive when almost 30 percent of total revenue collected by the central government of Ukraine during the period examined was withdrawn and spent elsewhere in the Soviet Union.

SEER, 45:105:568-71.

Dissent Movement

1011.   Browne, Michael, ed. **Ferment in the Ukraine: Documents by V. Chornovil, I. Kandyba, L. Lukyanenko, V. Moroz and Others.** Foreword by Max Hayward. New York: Praeger Publishers, 1971. 267p. $15.00.

The volume contains documents of protest. Of special interest are the documents related to the secret trial of seven Ukrainian defendents who demanded the exercise of Ukrainian rights as provided for in the Soviet constitution. The trial took place in a KGB prison and not in a courtroom.

SR, 31:4:910-12.

1012.   Chornovil, Vyacheslav, comp. **The Chornovil Papers.** Introduction by Frederick C. Barghoorn. New York: McGraw-Hill, 1969. 246p. $6.95.

The Chornovil Papers is an annotated translation of Chornovil's lengthy petitions, enumerating in detail the violations of the constitution and of criminal law and procedure committed in the course of the arrests, investigation, and trials by the very guardians of Soviet legality.

SR, 29:2:343-44; Choice, 7(1970):550.

1013.   Dzyuba, Ivan. **Internationalism or Russification? A Study in the Soviet Nationalities Problem.** Preface by Peter Archer. Edited by M. Davies. London: Weidenfeld & Nicolson, 1968. 240p. 42s.

The author's main thesis is that Lenin's nationality policy called for a free and unrestricted Ukrainian culture as a part of the international proletarian culture. He accuses the present Soviet regime of violating Lenin's principles. He charges that the turmoil and upheaval in Ukraine is a direct result of the Russification of the non-Russian peoples, and that the present Soviet Russian policies in Ukraine are the same as the previous tsarist policies.

SR, 28:3:503-4; Choice, 6(1969):574.

1014. Khodorovich, Tatyana, ed. **The Case of Leonid Plyushch**. Boulder, CO: Westview Press, 1976. xvii, 152p. $10.75.

Plyushch, a Ukrainian cyberneticist and member of the Ukrainian Academy of Sciences, who confessed to being a "convinced Marxist," endured thirty months of psychiatric torture in the Dnipropetrivsk psychiatric prison for asking embarrassing questions about Stalinist terror and a nationalities policy that was cast in the "tsarist pattern." This volume contains a collection of his letters and petitions and articles concerning his case.

CSP, 19:3:381.

1015. Liber, George, and Mostovych, Anna, comps. **Nonconformity and Dissent in the Ukrainian SSR, 1955-1975: An Annotated Bibliography**. Cambridge, MA: Harvard Ukrainian Research Institute, 1978. xxxix, 245p. $8.50. (Harvard Ukrainian Research Institute, Sources and Documents Series, no. 3.)

This bibliography includes 1,242 items and stresses national, religious, and civil rights movements in Ukraine, covering the uncensored material published between 1955 and 1975 in numerous *samvydav* publications. The material is arranged by names and subjects with a complete bibliographic description and brief annotation.

NP, 7:2:242-43; ARBA, 10(1979):270.

1016. Moroz, Valentyn. **Boomerang: The Works of Valentyn Moroz**. Edited by Yaroslav Bihun. With an introduction by Paul L. Gersper. Baltimore: Smoloskyp Publishers, 1974. 272p. $3.25 pa.

Boomerang is a book that tells of the life and works of Moroz, a fighter for universal freedom and a martyr of the Soviet totalitarian system. In 1965 he was sentenced to four years at hard labor. While in prison he wrote several treatises, all dealing with his prison experiences, Russification of Ukraine, and man's eternal quest for freedom and justice.

1017. Moroz, Valentyn. **Report from the Beria Reserve: The Protest Writings of Valentyn Moroz**. Edited and translated by John Kolasky. Chicago: Cataract Press, 1974. 162p. $2.95 pa.

While Moroz served four years at hard labor in the Yavas concentration camp in Mordovia he wrote this first significant essay. His writings are almost exclusively concerned with the oppression and persecution of the Ukrainian people. In addition to the title piece, the translation includes "Moses and Dathan," "A Chronicle of Resistance," "In the Midst of the Snows," "The First Day," and "Instead of a Final Statement."

1018.   Plyushch, Leonid. **History's Carnival: A Dissident's Autobiography.**
        Edited, translated, and with an introduction by Marco Carynnyk. New
        York and London: Harcourt Brace Jovanovich, 1979. xvii, 429p. $14.95.
This is a moral and philosophical autobiography of one of the best-known dissidents, now living in Paris, who spent two years in the notorious Dnipropetrivsk
psychoprison for his political views. The book also contains little-known information about the Democratic movement in the USSR, especially in Ukraine.
Plyushch's encounter with the KGB offers new insights into the practices of this
organization.
        NP, 10:2:237-43.

1019.   Prychodko, Nicholas. **Stormy Road to Freedom.** With a foreword by
        Igor Gouzenko. New York: Vantage Press, 1968. 356p. $5.95.
The book by a Ukrainian political refugee, now a Canadian citizen, presents in the
form of a novel the drama-packed story of a Ukrainian family under the Stalin
regime. The author unveils a vast panorama of life: how ordinary men and women
in Ukraine lived, loved, and laughed throughout years of terror, Siberian slave
labor camps, tortures by the Soviet secret police, the German-Soviet war, and
finally exit to freedom, emigration to Canada.

1020.   Stetsko, Slava, ed. **Revolutionary Voices: Ukrainian Political Prisoners
        Condemn Russian Colonialism.** Foreword by Ivan M. Lombardo. Munich:
        Press Bureau of ABN; 2d ed., 1971. 269p.
This is a comprehensive record of the writings, appeals, and petitions of a number
of Ukrainian political prisoners, most of whom are in a Soviet prison, a concentration camp, or a psychoprison. Many of these appeals first appeared in Ukrainian
samvydav publications and eventually were smuggled out of Ukraine to the West.

1021.   **The Ukrainian Herald, Issue no. 6: Dissent in Ukraine.** Translated and
        edited by Lesya Jones and Bohdan Yasen. Toronto: Smoloskyp Pub-
        lishers, 1977. 215p.

        **The Ukrainian Herald, Issue no. 7-8 (Spring 1974). An Underground
        Journal from Soviet Ukraine: Ethnocide of Ukrainians in the U.S.S.R.**
        Compiled by Maksym Sahaydak. Introduction by Robert Conquest.
        Translated and edited by Olena Saciiuk and Bohdan Yasen. Baltimore,
        MD: Smoloskyp Publishers, 1976. 209p. $6.95.
Issue no. 6 contains commentaries and appeals by individual Ukrainians who
represent the movement for human and national rights in Ukraine. The first part
of Issue 7-8 offers statistical analysis of the imposed denationalization of Ukraine
through linguistic Russification. The second part consists of discussion of the purge
in Ukraine during the early 1930s and of the repression of Ukrainian national
culture.

1022.   Verba, Lesya, and Yasen, Bohdan, with Osyp Zinkewych, eds. **The Human
        Rights Movement in Ukraine: Documents of the Ukrainian Helsinki
        Group, 1976-1980.** Introduction by Nina Strokata. Baltimore, MD,
        Washington, DC, and Toronto: Smoloskyp Publishers, 1980. xvi, 258p.
        Photographs.
The volume is a product of the activities of the Ukrainian monitors of the Helsinki
Final Act, signed in 1975, from 1976 to the fall of 1980 on behalf of human rights

in Ukraine. It is a chronicle of the recent cycle of dissent and repression. The volume is completed with fifty-two illustrations, biographical sketches of the thirty-seven Ukrainian Helsinki monitors, and a name index.

Language and Literature

1023. Andrusyshen, C. H., and Krett, J. N., assisted by Helen Virginia Andrusyshen. **A Complete Ukrainian-English Dictionary.** Saskatoon: University of Saskatchewan, 1955. 1165p.
This dictionary contains about ninety-five thousand words with their derivatives and equivalents in English. In addition, it contains about thirty-five thousand idiomatic, popular, and proverbial phrases, neologisms, and dialectical expressions of regional literature.

1024. Barantsev, K. T. **Anhlo-ukrains'kyi frazeolohichnyi slovnyk** (English-Ukrainian Phrase-Dictionary). Kiev: Vyd. 'Radians'ka Shkola,' 1969. 1052p.
The dictionary covers more than thirty thousand English set phrases, idioms, proverbs, and sayings, which are arranged in alphabetical order. Each expression is followed by a corresponding Ukrainian equivalent, and many expressions are illustrated from books by English, American, and Canadian writers, both classic and modern, or different magazines and newspapers. The dictionary is useful for students, teachers, or those engaged in translation from English into Ukrainian.

1025. Čyževs'kyj, Dmytro. **A History of Ukrainian Literature (from the Eleventh to the End of the Nineteenth Century).** Translated by Dolly Ferguson, Doreen Gorsline, and Ulana Petyk. Edited and with a foreword by George S. N. Luckyj. Littleton, CO: Ukrainian Academic Press, 1975. xii, 681p. $25.00.
This work represents a milestone in Ukrainian literary criticism because it presents in an original way a comprehensive description of the literary periods with their principal trends and an analysis of the works of their representatives. It is a comprehensive history of Ukrainian literature.
SR, 36:2:355-57.

1026. Duravetz, G. N. **Ukrainian: Conversational and Grammatical.** Level I and Level II. Toronto: Ukrainian Teachers' Committee, Level I, 1973. 312p.; Level II, 1976. 435p.
These textbooks were developed to meet curriculum requirements set by the Ontario Ministry of Education for oral and written language instruction. Level I contains twenty-two lessons and introduces twelve hundred words. Level II provides advanced lessons and a seventy-five-page bilingual dictionary.

1027. Humesky, Assya A. **Modern Ukrainian.** Edmonton and Toronto: The Canadian Institute of Ukrainian Studies, 1980. 438p. $8.00 pa.
This text covers the basics of Ukrainian phonology and morphology as well as some elements of sentence structure and intonation. Twenty lessons include dialogues and narrative passages, grammar notes, explanatory notes, and exercises. The text is accompanied by tapes and can be used for independent study by both beginning and advanced students. Twelve cassette tapes are available.

1028.   Luchkovich, Michael, ed. **Their Land: An Anthology of Ukrainian Short Stories**. Preface by Clarence A. Manning. Introduction by Luke Luciw. Biographical Sketches by Bohdan Krawciw. Jersey City, NJ: Svoboda Press, 1964. 325p.

This collection of translations of Ukrainian short fiction from the nineteenth and twentieth centuries contains mostly stories that had been printed in the Ukrainian weekly *Svoboda*. Included are twenty-six stories by twenty-one authors.

1029.   Luckyj, George S. N. **Between Gogol and Ševčenko: Polarity in the Literary Ukraine: 1798-1847**. Munich: Wilhelm Fink Verlag, 1971. 210p. DM38.

This book concentrates on the crucial period in the first half of the nineteenth century when Ukrainian writers were struggling to decide whether to make their special contribution to Russian or whether to develop a complete Ukrainian literature in the Ukrainian language. As the title implies, Gogol made the first choice and Shevchenko the second.

        SR, 34:1:189.

1030.   Luckyj, George S. N. **Literary Politics in the Soviet Ukraine, 1917-1934**. New York: Columbia University Press, 1956. 323p.

The study documents the efforts of Ukrainian authors and playwrights to promote Ukrainian nationalism in the face of Soviet domination. Luckyj discusses, in particular, the literary figures of the 1920s and early 1930s who experienced brutal Soviet efforts to suppress their works.

1031.   Luckyj, George S. N., ed. **Modern Ukrainian Short Stories**. Parallel text edition. Littleton, CO: Ukrainian Academic Press, 1973. 228p. $8.50.

The fifteen stories in this volume, written between 1897 and 1968, are the work of eleven authors and reflect the similarities between literary developments in various periods. These stories all reflect new trends that began in Ukrainian literature around 1900.

        CSP, 17:2-3:559-61.

1032.   Podvez'ko, M. L., comp. **Ukrainian-English Dictionary. English-Ukrainian Dictionary**. 2d rev. ed. Kiev: Radians'ka Shkola; distributed by Saphrograph, New York, 1963. 1018p.

Published in Soviet Ukraine, this is the most comprehensive and current dictionary of Ukrainian. Each part contains sixty thousand words and gives, in addition to definitions, examples in sentences for words which have several meanings or are difficult to translate.

1033.   Slavutych, Yar. **Conversational Ukrainian**. Preface by Orest Starchuk. Edmonton and Winnipeg: Gateway Publishers, 1959. 368p.

This is a textbook for schools and self-study, with emphasis as well on the geography, history, and culture of Ukraine and information about Ukrainians in the United States and Canada.

1034. Struk, Danylo Husar. **Ukrainian for Undergraduates.** Oakville, Ontario: Mosaic Press, for the Canadian Institute of Ukrainian Studies, 1978. xxv, 350p.

The book is divided into twenty-three chapters and an introduction to phonetics. Each lesson in the book contains a rather extensive vocabulary list with English equivalents. Good explanations of grammatical rules and usage are given.

CSP, 22:3:445-46.

1035. **Ukrainian dumy: Original Texts.** Translated by George Tarnawsky and Patricia Kilina. Introduction by Natalie K. Moyle. Toronto: Canadian Institute of Ukrainian Studies, 1979. 219p. $5.95.

Thirty-three Ukrainian *dumy*, or epics, are here translated into English. Since *dumy* have verses of different lengths, the translators tried to reflect this in English, while omitting peculiar rhyming observed in the originals. In the introduction these epics are compared to the *Niebelungenlied* and the *Chanson de Roland*.

CSP, 22:3:443-44.

CAUCASIAN REPUBLICS AND PEOPLES

1036.   Agathangelos' **History of the Armenians**. Translated and edited by R. W. Thomson. Albany: State University of New York Press, 1976. xcviii, 527p. $50.00.

Agathangelos' *History* purports to be an eyewitness account of the conversion to Christianity of Greater Armenia, although its surviving Armenian recension was probably compiled some 150 years after the fact (about A. D. 460). The translation is accompanied by a useful introduction and an index of biblical quotations and allusions. The text used is that of the Tiflis 1914 Lukasean edition.

SR, 38:4:699-700; Choice, 13(1977):1567.

1037.   Allen, W[illiam] E. D. **A History of the Georgian People: From the Beginning Down to the Russian Conquest in the Nineteenth Century**. London: Kegan Paul, Trench, Trubner & Co., 1932; reprint, London: Routledge & Kegan Paul; New York: Barnes & Noble, 1971; New York: Gordon Press, 1978. 429p. $75.00.

This book, brilliantly written and apolitical, presents Georgia's history within an area-wide cultural and historical perspective. Final sections show Georgia's medieval social and political structure, art, literature, trade, and material welfare. There are numerous illustrations.

SEER, 12:34:220-26.

1038.   Baddeley, John F. **The Russian Conquest of the Caucasus**. London and New York: Longmans, Green & Co., 1908; reprint, New York: Russell & Russell, 1969. 518p.

Baddeley writes vividly, without bias, and with precise detail. The mountain tribes held their own for two generations against a great despotic empire. The book is especially recommended to soldiers and to those interested in the present renascence of Islam.

1039.   Bardakjian, Kevork B., and Thomson, Robert W. **Textbook of Modern Western Armenian**. Delmar, NY: Caravan Books, 1977. 319p.

Each lesson teaches assorted pieces of grammar. Tapes and cassettes are available. Pending a fully revised edition, this is the best introductory text.

1040.   Bedrossian, Matthias. **New Dictionary: Armenian-English**. Venice, Italy: St. Lazarus Armenian Academy, 1875-79; reprint, Beirut, Lebanon: Librairie du Liban; distributed by International Book Centre, Troy, MI, 1974. 786p.

This dictionary contains literary, scientific, and colloquial Armenian vocabulary—over thirty thousand main entries, plus their compounds—and a choice of English equivalents. Idiomatic expressions are included, and unpredictable genitive forms are indicated.

1041.   Gidney, James B. **A Mandate for Armenia**. Kent, OH: Kent State University Press, 1969. 270p. $7.50.
The book tells the story of Armenia since the end of World War I, with particular reference to America's interest in the settlement of the Armenian question. This is an informative and objective presentation of events from 1917 to 1923. The author concludes that Armenia can exist only in union with the Soviet Union or with Turkey; prospects for an independent Armenia are almost nil. This lucidly written, tragic story of a much-suffering nation is recommended for the general reader.

1042.   Gvarjaladze (Gvardzhaladze), Tamar (S.), and Gvarjaladze, Isidore (S.), comps. **English-Georgian and Georgian-English Dictionary**. English-Georgian Dictionary, 4th ed.; Georgian-English Dictionary, 3d ed. Tbilisi: Ganatleba, 1974. 549p.
This work—unlike the **Georgian-English Dictionary** by E. Cherkesi, Oxford, 1950—is based upon the spoken and written Georgian of the current (Soviet) period, with its many new terms. Prefatory matter is in Georgian.

1043.   Householder, Fred W., and Mansoor, Lofti. **Basic Course in Azerbaidzhani**. Bloomington: Indiana University Press, 1965. 275p. (Uralic and Altaic Series, vol. 45.)
This course is designed to introduce the student to spoken Azerbaijani. It is divided into twenty-five lessons and includes a glossary.

1044.   Hovanessian, Diana Der, and Margossian, Marzbed, eds. and trans. **Anthology of Armenian Poetry**. New York: Columbia University Press, 1978. xxii, 357p. $20.00.
This fine collection includes all periods and types of poetry, from folk and early Christian to Soviet and diaspora. Brief biographical notes are included. The smooth translations, in modern American poetic idiom, have immediacy but at some sacrifice of stylistic identity.

1045.   Hovannisian, Richard G. **Armenia on the Road to Independence, 1918**. Berkeley: University of California Press, 1967. 364p. $8.50.
This study is a detailed account of the eighteen months from the Russian March revolution of 1917 to the conclusion of the Mudros Armistice between Turkey and the Allied powers in November 1918: the period of the creation and collapse of the ephemeral Transcaucasian Federative Republic and of the proclamation of the independence of its three component republics, Georgia, Azerbaijan, and Armenia, in May 1918.
SR, 27:2:320-21; Choice, 5(1968):408.

1046.   Hovannisian, Richard G. **The Republic of Armenia**. Vol. 1: **The First Year, 1918-1919**. Berkeley: University of California Press, 1971. 547p. $15.00. Vol. 2: **From Versailles to London, 1919-1920**. Berkeley: University of California Press, 1982. 603p. $35.00.

The first winter (1918-19) in the Armenian republic was a demographic disaster second only to the massacres of 1915-16. The author states that about two hundred thousand people, almost 20 percent of the republic's population, died of hunger or disease by mid-1919. The disaster would have been greater had it not been for the help of American Near East Relief.

SR, 31:3:731-32; NP, 12:1:147-48.

1047. Kazemzadeh, Firuz. **The Struggle for Transcaucasia (1917-1921).** Introduction by Michael Karpovich. New York: Philosophical Library; London: George Ronald, 1951. 356p.

The book's value lies in its description of the very complicated interplay of national, social, ideological, and strategic factors. Transcaucasian disunity, the importance to Russia of Baku, and the attitude of Turkey helped doom Transcaucasian independence.

LJ, 77(1952):594.

1048. Lang, David Marshall. **Armenia: Cradle of Civilization.** Rev. ed. London: George Allen & Unwin, 1978 (1970). 320p. + 8pp. plates. Illustrated. $29.00.

Focusing primarily on prehistorical, classical, and early Christian Armenia, this work provides the general reader with pertinent information and an easy narrative, accompanied by an abundance of photographs.

SR, 38:4:700.

1049. Lang, David Marshall. **The Georgians.** New York: Praeger Publishers, 1966. 244p. $7.50. (Ancient Peoples and Places, no. 51.)

Although Lang is not primarily an archeologist, he has conformed to the general emphasis of the series to which this volume belongs by concentrating on the earlier period and giving an extensive and conscientious account of the prehistoric and pre-Christian era. The author has given a great deal of information in this volume.

SR, 27:1:133-35; Choice, 4(1967):733.

1050. Lang, David Marshall. **The Last Years of the Georgian Monarchy, 1658-1832.** New York: Columbia University Press, 1957. 333p. $5.50.

This is the history of one of the oldest states conquered by Russia and subjected to Russification and a gradual destruction of native culture and tradition.

LJ, 82(1957):547.

1051. Lang, David Marshall. **A Modern History of Soviet Georgia.** New York: Grove Press, 1962; Praeger Publishers, 1963. 298p. $6.50.

Georgia's national independence of 1917-20 was put to an end by Soviet Russian troops. This study surveys the Soviet period of the Georgian republic and as such throws light on the problems of nationalities in the Soviet Union.

1052. Matossian, Mary K. **The Impact of Soviet Policies in Armenia.** Leiden, The Netherlands: E. J. Brill, 1962. 239p.

This work is the first study of the impact of the Soviet system on the political, social, economic, religious, and cultural life in Soviet Armenia. The Communists' eventual, difficult triumph over traditional institutions was due to merciless means, but also to astute identification of Soviet policies with traditional values.

1053. Mepisashvili, Rusudan, and Tsintsadze, Vakhtang. **The Arts of Ancient Georgia**. New York: Thames & Hudson, 1977 and 1979. 309p. $29.95.
The authors present a visual and verbal display of the artistic, principally architectural, achievements of the Georgians. This work chronicles not only the arts of the most ancient past, but the full range of the more prolific medieval and even the early modern periods. Rich in fine photographs, plans, and explanatory text, the book is a handsome contribution to the study of Caucasian art.
RR, 39:3:274; Choice, 16(1979):1162.

1054. Nalbandian, Louise Z. **The Armenian Revolutionary Movement: The Development of Armenian Political Parties through the Nineteenth Century**. Berkeley: University of California Press, 1963. 247p. $6.00.
This book describes the armed struggle of Armenian rebels against the Ottoman Turks, from the first major uprising in 1863 to the massacres of 1896.

1055. Rustaveli, Shota. **The Lord of the Pantherskin: A Georgian Romance of Chivalry**. Translated with an introduction and notes by R. H. Stevenson. Afterword by A. G. Baramidze. Albany: State University of New York Press, 1977. xxix, 240p. $17.00.
This is the translation of Rustaveli's great medieval romance. In the introduction Stevenson discusses the poem in an international context.
WLT, 53(Winter 1979):179.

1056. Suny, Ronald Grigor. **The Baku Commune, 1917-1918: Class and Nationality in the Russian Revolution**. Princeton, NJ: Princeton University Press, 1972. 412p. $15.00. (Studies of the Russian Institute, Columbia University.)
This study of the Baku Commune is set against the long train of events, from the turn of the twentieth century onward, that culminated in the proclamation of Soviet rule in Baku. The author is especially effective in recreating the dizzying array of political-administrative bodies that operated in Baku after the February-March revolution, and has illuminated the interracial enmity that characterized Transcaucasian life.
SR, 31:3:673-75; AHR, 79:2:549.

1057. Toumanoff, Cyril. **Studies in Christian Caucasian History**. Washington, DC: Georgetown University Press, 1965. 601p.
The legendary ancient cities of Colchis, Iberia, and Armenia have been yielding up their treasures. Toumanoff's essays extend roughly from 500 B.C. to A.D. 1000. He treats the social background, states and dynasties, and Armeno-Georgian marchlands.

1058. Walker, Christopher J. **Armenia: The Survival of a Nation**. London: Croom Helm; New York: St. Martin's Press, 1980. 446p. $30.00.
This historical survey of Armenia and the Armenians, starting with ancient and medieval times, covers Armenia under the Russian and Ottoman Empire

occupations, along with the attempts to establish a republic after each empire collapsed. It ends with the history of the Armenian SSR within the USSR. This book is recommended for students and lay readers.

AHR, 86:3:627; Choice, 18(1981):579.

CENTRAL ASIAN REPUBLICS AND PEOPLES

History and General Studies

1059.   Allworth, Edward, comp. **Soviet Asia: Bibliographies.** New York: Praeger Publishers, 1975. 687p. $35.00.
This massive bibliography with the subtitle "A Compilation of Social Science and Humanities Sources on the Iranian, Mongolian, and Turkic Nationalities" contains approximately fifty-two hundred entries published between 1850 and 1970. It comprises general works and works related to specific national groups. This volume is a basic source for libraries.
CRL, 37(July 1976):356.

1060.   Allworth, Edward, ed. **Central Asia: A Century of Russian Rule.** New York: Columbia University Press, 1967. 552p. $12.95.
Several specialists set out to tell "what has happened to the land and its people and why, during the last hundred years, Russian-style civilization has been superimposed upon the traditional Central Asian culture." There are chapters on people, languages, and migrations; geography, industrialization, and agriculture; nationalism and social and political reform movements; intellectual and literary developments; musical tradition and innovation; and architecture, art, and town planning.
SR, 26:3:486-87; PSQ, 83(1968):444.

1061.   Allworth, Edward, ed. **The Nationality Question in Soviet Central Asia.** New York: Praeger Publishers, 1973. 221p. $16.50.
Fifteen contributors discuss various aspects of Soviet nationality policy in Central Asia, stressing such subjects as literature, ethnic intermarriage, assimilation trends, national identity, and ethnic consciousness. A selected list of recent books in English about Central Asia and short biographical sketches of the contributors complete the study. Appended are a number of valuable maps and tables.
APSR, 70(March 1976):234.

1062.   Bacon, Elizabeth E. **Central Asians under Russian Rule: A Study in Culture Change.** Ithaca, NY: Cornell University Press, 1966, 1980. xxxix, 273p. $6.50.
The 1980 edition contains a fascinating new introduction by Michael M. J. Fischer and lovely photographs. Much of the book deals with the pastoral nomads and

settled oasis people by periods: prior to Russian conquest in the mid-nineteenth century, under tsarist rule, and after 1917. The book is recommended as "one of the best places to start" the study of cultural change in Central Asia, since field research for Western anthropologists is still impossible.

AHR, 72:5:1449; LJ, 92(1967):253; Choice, 4(1967):190.

1063.   Bennigsen, Alexandre A., and Wimbush, S. Enders. **Muslim National Communism in the Soviet Union: A Revolutionary Strategy for the Colonial World.** Chicago: The University of Chicago Press, 1979. 267p. $20.00.

This book begins with an account of the experiences and aims that by 1917 had led various Muslim leaders in the Russian empire to look to the Bolshevik party as a means of national liberation of their people. However, as the book recounts, these dreams were frustrated as early as 1928, and most of the leading national Communists were physically purged soon after that.

NP, 9:1:139-40; JP, 42(1980):580.

1064.   Demko, George J. **The Russian Colonization of Kazakhstan, 1896-1916.** Bloomington: Indiana University Publications; The Hague, The Netherlands: Mouton, 1969. 271p. $9.50. (Uralic and Altaic Series, vol. 99.)

In 208 pages of text, of which nearly half consist of maps and statistical tables, the author reviews the chief aspects of Russian settlement in Kazakhstan and attempts incidentally to derive from it—for the comparative history of migrations—theoretical lessons. A brief historical and geographical overview is the aim of the first part, which traces the chief stages of Russian penetration. There follows in the second part the depiction of the peasant immigration, for which the author strives to draw up in the third part—the fullest and most detailed—an agricultural, economic, and human balance sheet. A brief conclusion is followed by statistical tables, notes, and a rather uneven bibliography.

SR, 30:2:430-31.

1065.   Donnelly, Alton S. **The Russian Conquest of Bashkiria: A Case Study in Imperialism.** New Haven, CT: Yale University Press, 1968. 114p. $6.50. (Yale Russian and East European Studies, 7.)

The author finds five major causes for Russian movement toward the southeast and into Bashkiria: the necessity for terminating harmful raids by the nomads, the desire to increase government income through tribute, Peter's interest in metallurgy, his intention to trade with the East, and official and unofficial migration of Russians into the area.

AHR, 74:4:1043.

1066.   Massell, Gregory J. **The Surrogate Proletariat: Moslem Women and Revolutionary Strategies in Soviet Central Asia, 1919-1929.** Princeton, NJ: Princeton University Press, 1974. 448p. $18.50.

Massell has written a masterful historical and analytical account of Soviet efforts during the 1920s to develop a productive strategy for social change in Central Asia. Basically this is a study of the modernization of a traditional society. That

Muslim women came to be viewed as a surrogate proletariat in Soviet eyes becomes abundantly clear as Massell delves into the process by which the regime sought to modernize Central Asia.

SR, 34:2:398-99; Choice, 11(1974):1531.

1067. Masson, V. M., and Sarianidi, V. I. **Central Asia: Turkmenia before the Achaemenids.** Translated and edited by Ruth Tringham. New York: Praeger Publishers, 1972. 219p. $12.50.

Two Soviet archeologists have provided an up-to-date account of man's efforts and successes in exploiting the deserts and mountain valleys from the first Pleistocene trace to the middle of the first millennium B.C. This is a well-illustrated account.

SR, 32:1:156; Choice, 8(1973):1644.

1068. McCagg, William O., Jr., and Silver, Brian D., eds. **Soviet Asian Ethnic Frontiers.** New York: Pergamon Press, 1979. xx, 280p. $22.50.

This collection of essays focuses on the nationalities that straddle the volatile Soviet frontiers with Afghanistan, China, Iran, and Turkey. Several of the contributions add new information and insights on the area and its peoples. The book is equipped with six helpful maps.

RR, 39:4:511.

1069. Nove, Alec and Newth, J. A. **The Soviet Middle East: A Communist Model for Development.** New York: Praeger Publishers, 1967. 160p. $6.50.

The authors have explored the economic development of Transcaucasia and Soviet Central Asia. The picture that emerges from their study is clear: starting from abysmally low levels, the Soviet Middle East has made very rapid economic, especially industrial, and social progress.

SR, 26:3:503-5; Choice, 4(1967):1052.

1070. Rakowska-Harmstone, Teresa. **Russia and Nationalism in Central Asia: The Case of Tadzhikistan.** Baltimore, MD: The Johns Hopkins Press, 1970. 325p. $10.95.

This is a case study of the Soviet nationalities policy as applied to the Muslim peoples of Soviet Central Asia. The author examines the various aspects of the Soviet experiment: the formation of the Tadzhik SSR; the ethnic structure of the republic; the nature and extent of Soviet control; and the reactions of the indigenous elite to Russian, socialist, economic, and cultural regimentation. The book provides great insight into Soviet policy and methods and into native reaction to them up to 1956.

SR, 30:1:156; APSR, 65(1971):1254.

1071. Rywkin, Michael. **Moscow's Muslim Challenge: Soviet Central Asia.** Armonk, NY: M. E. Sharpe, 1982. 200p. Maps. $25.00.

This volume presents in a succinct, lucid, and yet comprehensive manner the historical and cultural background of Central Asian Muslims and the effect of contemporary economic, social demographic, and international forces in reshaping

the political destiny of these people. This text is highly recommended for the specialist and the public audience alike.
NP, 12:1:138-39.

1072.   Sauvaget, Jean. **Introduction to the History of the Muslim East: A Bibliographical Guide.** Edited by Claude Cahen and based on the second edition. Berkeley: University of California Press, 1965. 252p.
Sauvaget was one of the most famous French Arabists and the author of many works in Arabic and Islamic studies. The present volume is an annotated guide to the literature on the history of the Muslim East.
AHR, 71:5:1392.

1073.   Shnitnikov, Boris N. **Kazakh-English Dictionary.** Preface by Nicholas Poppe. London; The Hague, The Netherlands; Paris: Mouton & Co., 1966. 301p. (Indiana University Publications. Uralic and Altaic Series, vol. 28.)
This Kazakh-English dictionary is the most complete ever compiled and the first to be compiled outside the USSR.

1074.   Wheeler, Geoffrey. **The Modern History of Soviet Central Asia.** New York: Praeger Publishers, 1964. 272p. $7.00.
The author has surveyed briefly the impressive cultural traditions as well as the distinctive international role of the region during its long history. The Soviet government inherited this typically colonial problem and has, like the imperial government before it, pursued goals in Central Asia that were essentially its own rather than those of the largely non-Russian local population.
RR, 25:4:430-31; LJ, 90(1965):1903; Choice, 2(1965):114.

Languages and Literatures

1075.   Bennigsen, Alexandre, and Lemercier-Quelquejoy, Chantal. **The Evolution of the Muslim Nationalities of the USSR and Their Linguistic Problems.** London: Central Asian Research Center, 1961. 57p.
This is a survey of the history and linguistic development of Russia's Muslims before and since the October revolution.

1076.   Menges, Karl. **The Turkic Peoples and Languages: An Introduction to Turkic Studies.** Wiesbaden, Germany: Otto Harrassowitz, 1968. 248p. Charts. Maps.
The study is primarily an analysis of the phonology and grammar of the Turkic languages, with introductory chapters on the evolution of Turkic studies and the distribution and historical migrations of the Turkic peoples.

1077.   Wurm, Stefan A. **Turkic Peoples of the USSR: Their Historical Background, Their Languages and the Development of Soviet Linguistic Policy.** London: Central Asian Research Center, 1954. 51p.
This slim publication contains a brief and authoritative summary of the subject.

JEWS

General Reference Works

1078. Braham, Randolph L. **Jews in the Communist World: A Bibliography, 1945-1960.** New York: Twayne Publishers, 1961. 64p.
This bibliography of English publications on Jews in Communist Eastern Europe includes a section on Jews in the USSR. It differentiates between critical and apologetic publications and arranges them accordingly. Most listings are of a journalistic nature.

1079. **Encyclopedia Judaica.** 16 vols. Edited by Cecil Roth and Geoffrey Wigoder. Jerusalem: Keter, 1972. Index.
This includes a lengthy entry on the history of the Jews in Russia and the USSR, as well as a wealth of updated information on various aspects of Jewish life and Jewish personalities in Russia and the Soviet Union.

1080. Fluk, Louise R., comp. **Jews in the Soviet Union: An Annotated Bibliography.** New York: The American Jewish Committee; Institute of Human Relations, 1975. 44p.
This bibliography consists of a selection of the most significant and accessible writings, both scholarly and popular, on Soviet Jewry published in English between January 1, 1967, and September 1974. It includes 314 entries—books, pamphlets, and articles.

1081. **The Jewish Encyclopedia.** 12 vols. Cyrus Adler et al., eds. New York: Funk and Wagnalls, 1901-1906.
This first modern Jewish encyclopedia includes entries pertaining to the history of some Jewish communities in tsarist Russia.

1082. Pinkus, Binyamin, comp. **Soviet Jewry, 1917-1973: A Bibliography of Jewish History.** Jerusalem: The Zalman Shazar Center for the Furtherance of the Study of Jewish History, The Historical Society of Israel, 1974. 79p.
This bibliography attempts to list the most important books and articles in Hebrew, English, and French dealing with the various aspects of Jewish existence in the USSR published since World War II. It is arranged by subjects such as History,

Jewish Settlement, Political and Social Literature, Anti-Semitism, Zionism, Religion, Culture and Education, and Belles-Lettres.

1083. Pinkus, Binyamin, ed., and Dombrovska, D., comps. **Soviet and East European Jewry as Reflected in Western Periodicals: An Annotated Bibliography for 1970.** Jerusalem: Centre for Research and Documentation of East European Jewry; Society for Research on Jewish Communities, 1972. 67p.

This annotated bibliography covers about 120 journals, and the 1970 bibliography is the first in a series. Subsequent bibliographies were published in *Behinot.*

History, Politics, Government

1084. Baron, Salo W. **The Russian Jew under Tsars and Soviets.** New York: Macmillan, 1964. 427p. $7.50.

Traditionally, Muscovy-Russia was against Jewish settlement until, ironically, the partitions of Poland confronted Catherine II with nearly a million Jewish subjects in the western provinces of her empire. The manner in which this growing Jewish hinterland was dealt with oscillated between attempted vocational and cultural "amalgamation" and cynical and brutal quarantine. Yet for those Jews who welcomed the Bolshevist revolution as the emancipator, the years following 1917 proved a total disillusionment.

JMH, 37:2:230-31; CH, 48(1965):235.

1085. Brym, Robert J. **The Jewish Intelligentsia and Russian Marxism: A Sociological Study of Intellectual Radicalism and Ideological Divergence.** New York: Schocken Books, 1978. viii, 157p. Figures. $16.95.

The central question this book addresses is: Why were members of the Russian Jewish intelligentsia in the late nineteenth and early twentieth centuries drawn to one or another of four distinct but related radical organizations—the Poalei Zion, the Bund, the Menshevik party, and the Bolshevik party? The choices made depended on a variety of situational factors, and also on the particular sociocultural characteristics of the population among whom each worked.

SR, 38:4:671-72; Choice, 15(1978):1269.

1086. Cang, Joel. **The Silent Millions: A History of the Jews in the Soviet Union.** London: Rapp & Whitting, 1969. 246p.

A popular reader may learn a great deal from this book. Detailed information is presented on the rich Jewish cultural life both in tsarist and postrevolutionary Russia, before Stalin liquidated it. The reader gains an insight into the great contribution of the Jews to the establishment of the Soviet state.

LJ, 95(1970):2671; Choice, 7(1970):918.

1087. Dawidowicz, Lucy S., ed. **The Golden Tradition: Jewish Life and Thought in Eastern Europe.** New York: Holt, Rinehart & Winston, 1967. 502p. $8.95.

In a concise, highly informative essay, Dawidowicz traces the origins of the various Jewish reactions to the sudden encounter with a Gentile world that was hitherto so distant except as an ever-looming threat. To some of Eastern Europe's Jews the partial emancipation (after the French Revolution) appeared as a propitious time for complete assimilation. In fact, the former goal may help explain the attraction of so many East European Jews to a variety of reformist and revolutionary political causes. But there were also those who saw in political emancipation an opportunity to remain Jews by choice rather than coercion. The nineteenth century witnessed the birth of a specifically Jewish socialism (the Bund), of a sophisticated neo-orthodoxy in religion, and of modern Jewish nationalism (Zionism). World War II resulted in the all but complete disappearance of the Bund. The religious orthodoxy, perhaps surprisingly, is holding its ground, while Zionism emerged triumphant with the establishment of the state of Israel.

SR, 26:3:518.

1088.   Dubnov, Semen M. **History of the Jews in Russia and Poland: From the Earliest Times until the Present Day.** 3 vols. Philadelphia: The Jewish Publication Society, 1916-20.
This work is by now a classic of Jewish historiography. It presents a comprehensive account of the history of the Jews in Russia up to World War I, and is permeated by the author's historical approach to the possibility and acceptability of Jewish national existence in the Diaspora.

1089.   Frankel, Jonathan. **Prophecy and Politics: Socialism, Nationalism and the Russian Jews, 1867-1917.** Cambridge: Cambridge University Press, 1980. 650p. $49.50.
This book discusses the Jewish socialist movements in Russia before 1917 and emphasizes the importance of the 1881 pogroms as a turning point in the history of modern Jewish politics. The author also traces the development of these movements and their ideologies among the émigrés in the United States and Palestine. Particular emphasis is placed on leading ideologists and how they reconciled their socialist internationalist convictions with Jewish interest and nationalism.

LJ, 106(1981):1418.

1090.   Gilboa, Yehoshua A. **The Black Years of Soviet Jewry, 1939-1953.** Boston: Little, Brown and the Graduate Center for Contemporary Jewish Studies, Brandeis University, 1971. 418p. $15.00.
Gilboa affirms that the Soviet governmental antagonism to Jewish culture beginning in the thirties—temporarily interrupted by the war—reached its climax in the 1950s. Only with the death of Stalin in 1953 was even greater tragedy averted. His book, scrupulously documented and temperate in tone, has the qualities that make it a work of abiding reference. It is also extremely readable. So far as present evidence allows, here is a remarkable contribution to our knowledge of the campaign against "worthless cosmopolitans," the Crimean affair of 1952, the Prague trial at the end of that year, and the "doctor plot" early in 1953. Gilboa brings Stalin's Jewish policy into perspective with Soviet developments in general—as indeed he does throughout this most valuable work.

SR, 31:2:447-48; Choice, 8(1972):185.

1091.   Gitelman, Zvi Y. **Jewish Nationality and Soviet Politics: The Jewish Sections of the CPSU, 1917-1930.** Princeton, NJ: Princeton University Press, 1972. 573p. $20.00.

The author, in a heavily researched and lengthy work, seeks to examine Jewish national existence in the first generation of Soviet power. He concerns himself particularly with the Jewish experience "as a history of the modernization and secularization of an ethnic and religious minority resulting from attempts to integrate this minority into a modernizing state." The bulk of the volume deals with the *Evsektsiia's* major tasks to destroy the old order, the Bolshevization of the Jews, and the reconstruction of Jewish national life. He presents well the difficulties of the Jewish Bolsheviks with their dilemmas—to assimilate or to help build a pluralistic culture within the Communist framework.

SR, 33:3:549-50; Choice, 10(1973):517.

1092.   Goldberg, Ben Zion. **The Jewish Problem in the Soviet Union: Analysis and Solution.** New York: Crown Publishers, 1961. 374p. $4.95 pa.

This work has two main themes. The first is Stalin's destruction of Jewish culture, accompanied by the execution of the leading Yiddish writers. The second is milder but equally persistent—present-day persecution of Soviet Jewry as a whole. The author shows the extraordinarily unfair position in which the Jews find themselves.

LJ, 86(1961):2332.

1093.   Goldman, Guido G. **Zionism under Soviet Rule, 1917-1928.** New York: Herzl Press, 1960. 136p.

This is a pioneering study of Soviet attitudes and policies toward Zionism and Zionists during the first decade of Communist rule in Russia. The author concludes that moderate Soviet policies toward Zionism in the 1920s stemmed from specific foreign policy and domestic considerations.

1094.   Greenberg, Louis. **The Jews in Russia: The Struggle for Emancipation.** With a new foreword by Alfred Levin. 2 vols. in 1. New Haven, CT, and London: Yale University Press, 1965. $10.00.

The first half of this book, which originally appeared in 1944, deals with the background of the Jewish question in Russia, leading up to the assassination of Alexander II. The second volume, which appeared in 1951, five years after the death of Greenberg, was edited by Mark Wischnitzer, and it deals with the years up to 1917.

LJ, 91(1966):2837.

1095.   Kochan, Lionel, ed. **The Jews in Soviet Russia since 1917.** London: Oxford University Press, published for the Institute of Jewish Affairs, London, 1970. 357p. $7.95.

The Jews in the Soviet Union made an extremely important contribution to the various revolutionary parties and subsequently participated in large numbers in the early Soviet government and party apparatus on all levels. However, they soon were affected by the introduction of a quota system of sorts for Jews in Soviet state, industrial, and educational institutions. Aspects of these various changes, as well as the role of Jews in Soviet society and their plight, are treated in this collection of essays.

CSP, 15:4:571-71; AHR, 76:2:529.

1096. Levitats, Isaac. **The Jewish Community in Russia, 1772-1844.** New York: Octagon, 1970. 300p.

This study deals primarily with the relationship between the Jewish community ("Kahal") and the Russian State, from the reign of Catherine II to that of Nicholas I. Despite limiting governmental legislation, the Jewish community succeeded in maintaining control of the religious, educational, judicial, and socioeconomic aspects of Jewish life during the period discussed.

Choice, 8(1971):462.

1097. Mendelsohn, Ezra. **Class Struggle in the Pale: The Formative Years of the Jewish Workers' Movement in Tsarist Russia.** Cambridge: Cambridge University Press, 1970. 180p. $8.50.

By use of the rich and unused literature in Yiddish, the history of the Jewish labor movement suddenly comes alive and takes on sharp new contours in this informative book. Mendelsohn deals with the legal status, demography, and social-occupational stratification of Jews in tsarist Russia and provides a wealth of concrete details on techniques and associational forms of the Jewish movement.

SR, 31:1:163-64; AHR, 76:4:1194.

1098. Shaffer, Harry G. **The Soviet Treatment of Jews.** New York: Praeger Publishers, 1974. 232p. $13.50.

In this objective analysis Shaffer deals with such topics as the identity of anti-Semitism and anti-Zionism, the treatment of Judaism as a religion, discrimination in education and employment facilities, and the right to emigrate.

SR, 34:3:614-15.

1099. Smolar, Boris. **Soviet Jewry Today and Tomorrow.** New York: Macmillan, 1971. 228p. $5.95.

Born in Russia and well acquainted with the earlier phases of the Soviet period, Smolar is able to connect the current problems of Russian Jewry with both pre- and postrevolutionary experience. The author expresses fears that Jewish identity may disappear in the Soviet Union.

SR, 32:1:176; BS, 31(March 1972):562.

1100. Teller, Judd L. **The Kremlin, the Jews and the Middle East.** New York and London: Yoseloff, 1957. 202p.

A seasoned analyst of overseas Jewish affairs, Teller demonstrates that Communistic policy, far from reversing tsarist intolerance, was a calculated enlargement of its dimensions for unconscious totalitarian purposes.

1101. Tobias, Henry J. **The Jewish Bund in Russia: From its Origins to 1905.** Stanford, CA: Stanford University Press, 1972. 409p. $16.50.

It was the Bund which, in 1898, organized the first conference of the Social-Democratic Workers Party of Russia, one faction of which, led by Lenin, dissolved the Bund some twenty years later, and left it to Stalin to murder many of its members. Tobias describes step by step the policy of Lenin's Bolsheviks to force the Bund out of the Social-Democratic Workers Party, which in 1905 represented thirty thousand members.

SEER, 53:130:128-29; Choice, 9(1972):1346.

1102.	West, Binyamin. **Struggles of a Generation: The Jews under Soviet Rule.** Tel Aviv: Massadah, 1959. 216p.

Some chapters of this book offer a very general treatment of significant issues in the history of Soviet Jews, such as World War II and the situation of Jews in the territories annexed by the USSR in 1939-40. Others contain personal accounts of Soviet attitudes toward Zionism and Hebrew, and personal testimonies on the vicissitudes of World War II.

Education and Religion

1103.	Greenbaum, Alfred Abraham. **Jewish Scholarship and Scholarly Institutions in Soviet Russia, 1918-1953.** Jerusalem: Centre for Documentation and Research of East European Jewry, The Hebrew University, 1978. 224p.

The author contends that Jewish "bourgeois" and Soviet-sponsored scholarship still coexisted until the late 1920s. Growing limitations and pressures in the sphere of Soviet nationalities policies after 1928 resulted in the disappearance of the former; and World War II and Stalin's liquidation of Jewish scholarship and institutions in the USSR brought Jewish culture to an end.

1104.	Halevy, Zvi. **Jewish Schools under Czarism and Communism: A Struggle for Cultural Identity.** With a foreword by George Z. F. Bereday. New York: Springer Publishing, 1976. 298p. $14.50.

There were virtually no non-Russian-language Jewish secular schools in Russia prior to 1917. The author attempts to explain the creation of the Yiddish school system in the 1920s, the reason for its subsequent elimination, and the way this was accomplished. The schools declined because of governmental policy.

SR, 38:2:322-23; Choice, 14(1977):580.

1105.	Rothenberg, Joshua. **The Jewish Religion in the Soviet Union.** New York: KTAV Publishing House and the Philip W. Lown Center for Contemporary Jewish Studies, Brandeis University, 1971. 242p. $10.00.

This is an immensely important book, a milestone in the study of Jews in the Soviet Union. It confines itself strictly to the religious aspects of its subject, without succumbing to the temptation to confuse the issue with cultural and national repressions suffered by Jews in the USSR.

SR, 31:3:700; Choice, 9(1972):829.

1106.	Schulman, Elias. **A History of Jewish Education in the Soviet Union.** New York: KTAV Publishing House and the Institute for East European Jewish Studies, Brandeis University, 1971. 184p.

In this study, Schulman makes it clear that Jewish educational officials in the Soviet Union had to emphasize that their work on behalf of the Yiddish language had no connection with Yiddish-speaking activities outside the USSR. They feared the accusation of nationalism.

Dissent Movement and Anti-Semitism

1107.   **Antisemitism in the Soviet Union: Its Roots and Consequences.** 2 vols. Jerusalem: Centre for Documentation and Research of East European Jewry, The Hebrew University. Vol. 1: 1979. 332p.; Vol. 2. 1980. 295p.
The contributions in these two volumes indicate that contemporary Soviet anti-Semitism has its roots in pre-1917 Russia and is used by the regime today for various purposes. A list of anti-Semitic and anti-Israeli publications in the USSR in the 1960s and 1970s supplements this compendium.

1108.   Eliav, Arie L. **Between Hammer and Sickle.** Updated edition. New York: New American Library, 1969. 237p.
Eliav, who served for three years as first secretary of the Israeli embassy in Moscow, is a keen observer who has traveled widely throughout the Soviet Union and met with a great variety of Jews in all walks of public life. The work highlights the extraordinary contradiction in Soviet policy: on the one hand, the authorities attempt to obliterate any sense of Jewish self-identity; on the other hand, the government insists on maintaining Jewish nationality identity in the required internal passport.
        SR, 29:1:706-7.

1109.   Glazer, Nathan, et al. **Soviet   Jewry: 1969.** New York: Academic Committee on Soviet Jewry, 1969. 95p.
This is a collection of essays stemming from a symposium on Soviet Jewry. The contributions deal with such topics as "Jewish National Consciousness in the Soviet Union," "Soviet Policy and Anti-Semitism," "The Jews and Soviet Foreign Policy," and commentaries.

1110.   Grossman, Leonid. **Confession of a Jew.** Translated with an introduction and notes by Ranne Moab. New York: Arno Press, a *New York Times* Company, 1975. viii, 189p. $12.00.
Dostoyevsky devoted half of the March 1877 issue of his *Diary of a Writer* to the "Jewish Question," that is, the question of his own anti-Semitism, of which he was accused by a reader, Avraam Kovner. As a consequence, a correspondence developed between Kovner and Dostoyevsky. In this study Grossman examines Kovner's life and writings, which appeared first in Russian in Leningrad in 1924. This is the first English translation.
        SR, 35:4:753-54.

1111.   Korey, William. **The Soviet Cage: Antisemitism in Russia.** New York: Viking Press, 1973. 369p. $12.50.
At the heart of this book is the author's account of the 1970 Leningrad trial for the attempted hijacking of a Soviet plane, and the subsequent, related trials in

Kishinev and Riga. These marked the zenith of the official Soviet attempt to crush the renaissance of Jewish national feeling in the USSR.
SR, 34:3:614-15.

1112.   Kuznetsov, Edward. **Prison Diaries**. Translated by Howard Spier, with an introduction by Leonard Schapiro. New York: Stein & Day, 1975. 254p. $8.95.
This translation consists of prison stories and memoirs from the labor camps. It is part of a growing list of dissent literature emanating from the Soviet Union.

1113.   Lawrence, Gunther. **Three Million More?** New York: Doubleday, 1970. 214p.
This very general account of the status and situation of Soviet Jews in the 1960s was written by a person who was actively involved in Jewish public activities on behalf of Soviet Jewry. The most interesting parts of the book are the descriptions of the author's visit to the USSR, and of early U.S. government attempts to influence Soviet policies in regard to Jewish emigration from the Soviet Union.

1114.   Rass, Rebecca. **From Moscow to Jerusalem: The Dramatic Story of the Jewish Liberation Movement and Its Impact on Israel.** New York: Shengold, 1976. 256p. $8.95.
Rass has chosen an attractive and informative style of presentation. She presents events in chronological order, which enables her to discuss the political background as well as the obstacles awaiting the would-be emigrant. The distinct, abrupt sentences draw the reader into a world in which one can live only armed with idealism.
SJA, 7:2:75-79.

1115.   Rubin, Ronald I., ed. **The Unredeemed: Anti-Semitism in the Soviet Union.** Foreword by Abraham J. Heschel. Chicago: Quadrangle Books, 1968. 317p. $10.00.
This is a collection of essays, documents, and eyewitness accounts, all bearing on the precarious position of Jews in the Soviet Union.
SR, 28:4:666-67.

1116.   Rusinek, Ala. **Like a Song, Like a Dream: A Soviet Girl's Quest for Freedom.** With an afterword by Ezra Rusinek. New York: Scribner's, 1973. 267p.
This highly fascinating and vividly written personal account comes from a young Moscow Jewess. She describes the events and feelings that accompanied her growing national identity in the early 1970s, and her struggle to leave the USSR for Israel. Of particular interest is the description of contacts between groups of young Soviet Jews from Moscow and Riga.

1117.   Schroeter, Leonard. **The Last Exodus.** New York: Universe Books, 1974. 432p. $10.95.
The author has used an impressive collection of Soviet underground *samizdat* publications in this book, which provides the first extensive account of the awakening and activities of the Jewish national movement in the Soviet Union. In a sense this work is a collection of case studies of persons and small groups who triggered a mass movement.
SR, 34:2:402.

1118.　Stern, August, ed. **The USSR vs. Dr. Mikhail Stern.** Translated from the
Russian by Marco Carynnyk. New York: Urizen Books, 1977. 267p.
$9.95.

This is an account of the investigation and trial of Dr. Mikhail Stern, based on tape
recordings smuggled out of the USSR. Soviet police interrogated more than two
thousand of Stern's patients in rural Ukraine, intimating that the Jewish doctor
was ritually murdering Gentile children and poisoning patients. Despite this official
anti-Semitism, many of the Ukrainian peasants demonstrated considerable heroism
by defying the prosecution and rejecting falsified pretrial testimony being passed
in their names.

　　　　BL, 74(Jan. 1978):720; Choice, 14(1978):1710.

1119.　Svirsky, Grigory. **Hostages: The Personal Testimony of a Soviet Jew.**
Translated from the Russian by Gordon Clough. New York: Alfred A.
Knopf; London: Bodley Head, 1976. 305p. £4.95.

Svirsky has made a reputation as a novelist but cannot reconcile himself to the
pernicious influence of anti-Semitism. The bitterness of rejection is shared by many
Soviet Jews and flavors every chapter of *Hostages.*

1120.　Taylor, Telford, et al. **Courts of Terror: Soviet Criminal Justice and
Jewish Emigration.** New York: Alfred Knopf, 1976. xi, 187p. $6.95.

The authors have concentrated on a limited aspect of the wide range of Soviet
Jewry's problems—the use of judicial procedure as a means of repression against
the Jewish emigration movement.

　　　　SJA, 7:2:75-76.

1121.　Wiesel, Elie. **The Jews of Silence: A Personal Report on Soviet Jewry.**
Philadelphia: The Jewish Publication Society of America, 1967. 143p.

The author tells, more vividly than anyone else has yet been able to, the strange
and contradictory nature of the Jewish problem. No one reading this book will
be able to deny that the state of Russian Jewry remains a legitimate cause for concern in the outside world.

Language and Literature

1122.　Friedberg, Maurice. **The Jew in the Post-Stalin Soviet Literature.** Washington, DC: B'nai B'rith International Council, 1970. 59p.

In this lengthy essay, covering the years 1954-67, the author attempts to study
the public image of the Jew through a historical, sociological, and political examination of Soviet literature. His thorough knowledge of the Soviet literary scene, as
well as of Soviet Jewry, makes this task possible.

1123.　Howe, Irving, and Greenberg, Eliezer, eds. **Ashes out of Hope: Fiction by
Soviet Yiddish Writers.** New York: Schocken Books, 1977. 218p. $10.95.

Ashes out of Hope, the fifth volume of Yiddish literature in translation on which
the editors have collaborated, contains five stories by three Soviet Yiddish writers,
David Bergelson, Moshe Kulbak, and Der Nister, all of whom, along with so many
of their confreres, died in prison or were executed under Stalin.

　　　　SR, 39:4:720; TLS, (May 1978):561.

1124.   Howe, Irving, and Greenberg, Eliezer, eds. **A Treasury of Yiddish Poetry.**
        New York: Schocken Books, 1976. 378p. $5.95 pa.
This English anthology of modern Yiddish poetry includes a section on Yiddish
poets in the Soviet Union. Seven poets are represented here, together with a brief
introduction on Yiddish poetry in the USSR.

1125.   Kuznetsov, Anatoli A. **Babi Yar: A Document in the Form of a Novel.**
        London: Jonathan Cape, 1970. 478p.
Kuznetsov's documentary novel on the years of Nazi occupation in his native Kiev
was first published in a censored form in the Soviet youth journal *Yunost'* in the
mid-1960s. After his defection in 1969, it was republished in the West in its original
form. The parts of the book related to Jews and anti-Semitism in the USSR, and
the opportunity it presents for studying the techniques of Soviet censorship, make
this a highly unusual literary and historical document.
        LJ, 96(1971):1289.

1126.   Lvov-Rogachevsky, V. **A History of Russian Jewish Literature.** Edited
        and translated by Arthur Levin. Essay by B. Gorev. Ann Arbor, MI: Ardis,
        1979. 213p. $14.00.
This is a stimulating potpourri of useful information on the Jews in Russia. The
volume consists of an essay on the treatment of Jews in Russian literature, written
by B. Gorev in 1917, followed by an extended essay on Jewish writers in the
Russian language, published by Lvov-Rogachevsky in 1922.
        SR, 39:4:719.

1127.   Markish, Esther. **The Long Return.** New York: Ballantine, 1978. 307p.
Originally written in French, this memoir by the widow of Perets Markish provides
a highly interesting insight into the world of Soviet-Jewish intellectuals in Stalin's
days. Markish, perhaps the leading Soviet-Yiddish poet, was at one time part of the
Soviet cultural elite. When Stalin decided to destroy whatever remained of Yiddish
culture in the USSR after World War II, Markish was one of his most illustrious
victims.

1128.   Shmeruk, Kh. **Jewish Literature in the Soviet Union during and following
        the Holocaust Period.** With a bibliography of Yiddish publications by A.
        Ben Yosef. Jerusalem: Yad Vashem Studies Reprint, vol. 4, 1960. 72p.
The author, a foremost authority on Soviet-Yiddish literature, discusses the vicissitudes of Yiddish publishing in the USSR from the late 1930s to 1948. He suggests
the following chronological breakdown into subperiods, based on Soviet policies
and Jewish reactions regarding both the scope and contents of Yiddish publications: 1939-41; 1941-45; 1946-48.

MOLDAVIANS

1129.   Bruchis, Michael. **One Step Back, Two Steps Forward: On the Language Policy of the Soviet Communist Party of the Soviet Union in the National Republics** (Moldavian: A Look Back, A Survey, and Perspectives, 1924-1980). Boulder, CO: *East European Quarterly,* 1982. 371p. $25.00. Distributed by Columbia University Press. (East European Monographs, no. 109.)
Bruchis examines the evolution of the Romanian language in Soviet Moldavia or former Romanian Bessarabia. This is an encompassing presentation of what happened to the Romanian language in Soviet Moldavia and the incredible schemes and struggle behind the language.
NP, 11:2:302-3; SR, 42:3:509-10.

1130.   Clark, Charles Upson. **Bessarabia.** New York: Dodd, Mead, 1927. 333p.
This is a fundamental work on the history of Bessarabia by an American student of Romanian and international affairs.

1131.   Dima, Nicholas. **Bessarabia and Bukovina: The Soviet-Romanian Territorial Dispute.** Boulder, CO: *East European Quarterly,* 1983. 256p. $20.00. Distributed by Columbia University Press. (East European Monographs, no. 110.)
A thorough study of historical and contemporary problems which includes important data on the national minority problems of interwar Romania. Dima also presents the historical evolution of this territorial conflict and illuminates the political, socioeconomic, and ethnodemographical changes that have taken place in the area between 1944 and 1980.
NP, 12:1:145-47.

1132.   Jewsberry, George F. **The Russian Annexation of Bessarabia, 1774-1828: A Study of Imperial Expansion.** Boulder, CO: *East European Quarterly,* 1976. 199p. $18.00. Distributed by Columbia University Press.
The author concentrates on the administrative challenges to the Russian government in a newly conquered non-Russian land. Only with the participation of the Bessarabian boyars did Russia succeed in governing the territory, a tactic employed by Moscow in many other areas before and after Bessarabian autonomy was abrogated in 1828.
AHR, 82:1:393.

1133. Duin, Edgar C. **Lutheranism under the Tsars and the Soviets.** 2 vols. Ann Arbor, MI: Xerox University Microfilms, for Lutheran Theological Seminary, 1975. 926p.
Duin presents a thorough history of Lutheranism in Russia from the Middle Ages to the 1970s under the Soviets. Though most of the book deals with the Baltic Germans, there are also sections related to the German Russians.

1134. Fisher, Alan. **The Crimean Tatars.** Stanford: Hoover Institution Press, Stanford University, 1978. xiv, 264p. Photographs. $14.95. (Studies of Nationalities in the USSR, vol. 1.)
This is the first work in which a historian has approached the history of the Tatar nation as a whole, from the foundation of the Khanate in the fifteenth century to the present. The author treats the three main periods of Tatar history: the glorious era of the Crimean Khanate; Crimea as a province of the tsarist empire (1783-1917); and the Crimean Soviet Republic, the genocide of 1943, and the struggle for survival.
    NP, 7:1:102-4; Choice, 15(1978):1270.

1135. Fisher, Alan W. **The Russian Annexation of the Crimea, 1772-1783.** Cambridge: Cambridge University Press, 1970. 180p.
Fisher details the events leading to annexation, with special attention to the precarious independence of the Crimean state in the decade prior to 1783. This thorough study is based on archival sources mainly.
    SR, 30:2:392.

1136. Giesinger, Adam. **From Catherine to Khrushchev: The Story of Russia's Germans.** Battleford, Saskatchewan: Marian Press, 1974. 443p. Maps.
The Russian Germans are an interesting case study in the history of provincial Russia since most of them migrated to the Volga, the Black Sea region, Volhynia, and other parts of the Russian empire. They lived in scattered settlements, were mainly farmers, and rarely received more than a basic elementary education. Disruption of families, forced labor, loss of property, and the experience of total terror characterized the history of the Germans after 1917.
    SR, 35:4:733.

1137. Heitman, Sidney. **The Soviet Germans in the USSR Today.** Cologne: Bundesinstitut für ostwissenschaftliche Studien, 1980. 135p.

The author has presented a study of the ethnic Germans, descendants of colonists invited to Russia by Catherine the Great and Alexander I. He focuses on the interaction between the efforts of the Soviet Germans to preserve their identity and the pressures for integration from the Party, the press, the schools, and the economy.

NP, 10:1:88.

PEOPLES OF SIBERIA AND THE VOLGA BASIN

1138. Hajdu, Peter. **The Samoyed Peoples and Languages.** Translated by Marianne Esztergar and Attila P. Csanyi. Bloomington: Indiana University Press; The Hague: Mouton, 1963. 114p. (Uralic and Altaic Series, no. 14.)
Hajdu has provided a summary of Samoyedic culture, history, folklore, and language. He stresses the importance of patriarchy, clan organization, and blood revenge for Samoyeds, in part reflected in their epics.

1139. Jakobson, Roman; Huttl-Worth, Gerta; and Beebe, John Fred. **Paleosiberian Peoples and Languages: A Bibliographical Guide.** New Haven, CT: Human Relations Area Files, 1957. 222p.
This is a superb compendium of resources, both published and archival, for several major Siberian native groups: Gilyak, Chukcheee, Yukagir, and "Yeniseians." It includes an appendix with useful ethnographic, demographic, and linguistic information.

1140. Kennan, George. **Siberia and the Exile System.** New York and London: Praeger Publishers, 1970; London: Osgood, McIlvaine & Co., 1891. 575p. Maps. Photographs.
This is a classic documentation of tsarist Siberian exiles and prisons by a distinguished traveler whose goals are to provide a "vivid impression of the scenery, the people, and the customs of Siberia," as well as to analyze government attitudes and practices. Focus is on the lives, ideals, and fates of Russian revolutionaries, but insights into the relatively independent lives of Siberian natives are also given.

1141. Kolarz, Walter. **The Peoples of the Soviet Far East.** New York: Praeger Publishers, 1954. 194p. Illustrations. Maps.
The author analyzes the political, economic, and cultural framework of Soviet rule in the Far East, discussing "aboriginal," Yakut, Mongolic, and Tuvinian peoples. Early tense Soviet relations with Koreans, Chinese, and Japanese are also explored. Kolarz disputes the Soviet claim to have provided material progress and cultural enlightenment in the Far East.
SR, 14:3:415.

1142. Levin, M. A., and Potapov, L. P., eds. **The Peoples of Siberia.** English translation edited by Steven Dunn. Originally printed in Russian. Chicago and London: University of Chicago Press, 1964. 948p. Moscow: Akademiia nauk, 1956.

This work covers southern and northern cultures, and Slavic relations with them. It includes essays on archeology, physical anthropology, settlers, and Soviet development. Basic information on traditional economies and history is provided, while social and religious practices are only briefly outlined.

1143.   Michael, Henry N., ed. **Studies in Siberian Ethnogenesis.** Toronto: University of Toronto Press for Arctic Institute of North America, 1962. 313p. Maps. Charts. Photographs. (Anthropology of the North Series, no. 2.)
This compendium was written by Soviet authors and deals with the origins of various Siberian cultures, and with the transition from kinship to territorial relationships.

1144.   Michael, Henry, ed. **Studies in Siberian Shamanism.** Translated by Stephen and Ethel Dunn. Toronto: University of Toronto Press for Arctic Institute of North America, 1964. 229p. Illustrations. (Anthropology of the North Series, no. 4.)
The editor has organized a group of Soviet articles that are crucial for an understanding of Siberian religions. They are written by ethnographers with extensive field experience and sensitivity to native traditions.

1145.   Riazanovsky, Valentin A. **Customary Law of the Nomadic Tribes of Siberia.** Bloomington: Indiana University Press; The Hague, The Netherlands: Mouton, 1965. 151p. (Uralic and Altaic Studies, no. 48.)
This reprint of a work originally published in Tientsin in 1938 surveys the jural practices among Turkic, Mongolic, Tungusic, and Ugric peoples and provides crosscultural comparisons. There are discussions of ancient codes and various cultural influences, as well as of native government.

1146.   Rubel, Paula G. **The Kalmyk Mongols: A Study in Continuity and Change.** Bloomington: Indiana University Press, 1967. 282p.
This is a field investigation among American Kalmyk groups conducted in 1960-61. The author resided with a Kalmyk family and learned their language. The book offers some historical background, the past of the Kalmyk nation.

1147.   Treadgold, Donald. **The Great Siberian Migration: Government and Peasant in Resettlement from Emancipation to the First World War.** Princeton, NJ: Princeton University Press, 1957. 278p. Maps. Charts. Photographs.
The author asks crucial questions regarding the nature of Siberian settlement in the late tsarist period. He compares American and Siberian frontier experiences, and his discussion of population pressures in Russia sets the stage for understanding both migration policies and realities.
        SR, 17:4:538; BRD, Aug. 1958.

4  EASTERN EUROPEAN COUNTRIES

GENERAL WORKS

Reference Works

1148. Horecky, Paul L., and Kraus, David H., eds. **East Central and Southeast Europe: A Handbook of Library and Archival Resources in North America.** Santa Barbara, CA: ABC-Clio Press, 1976. xii, 466p. $35.75. (Joint Committee on Eastern European Publication Series, no. 3.)
A total of forty-three different institutions are included in this book, from the Library of Congress and major university libraries to such little-known collections as the Noli Library of Albanian and Eastern Orthodox Culture in South Boston.
SR, 37:1:146-48.

1149. Horecky, Paul L., ed. **East Central Europe: A Guide to Basic Publications.** Chicago: University of Chicago Press, 1970. 956p. $50.00.

   Southeastern Europe: A Guide to Basic Publications. Chicago: University of Chicago Press, 1970. 755p. $31.00.
The first, *East Central Europe,* covers Czechoslovakia, East Germany, Hungary, Poland, and the Sorbians (Lusatians) and Polabians (the latter are treated to eleven pages listing fifty-two items!). About sixty specialists contributed approximately thirty-five hundred entries in European languages. The second, *Southeastern Europe,* covers Albania, Bulgaria, Greece, Rumania, and Yugoslavia. More than fifty experts submitted sections containing about three thousand entries. A considerable number of the contributors are natives of the regions about which they write but which they no longer inhabit.
SR, 30:2:457-58.

1150. Kraus, David H., et al. **National Science Information Systems: A Guide to Science Information Systems in Bulgaria, Czechoslovakia, Hungary, Poland, Rumania, and Yugoslavia.** Cambridge, MA: MIT Press, 1972. 325p. $12.50.
This study of the organizational aspect of national information systems first provides an overview of the common characteristics of the six national systems and then a detailed account of each country's national information system.

1151. Nowak, Chester Michael, comp. **Czechoslovak-Polish Relations, 1918-1939: A Selected and Annotated Bibliography.** Stanford, CA: Hoover Institution Press, 1976. xii, 219p. $10.00. (Hoover Institution Bibliographical Series, 55.)

This work contains 869 citations to bibliographies and published primary and secondary sources. Literature published up to 1972 is included; all items are annotated. Use of the book is facilitated by cross-references and an author index.

Geography

1152.   Hoffman, G. W., ed. **Eastern Europe: Essays in Geographical Problems.** London: Methuen, 1971. 502p. £5.00.
This volume is a collection of papers presented at a conference on east-central and southeastern European geography. The work reflects the role of ideology in shaping or changing the cultural landscape and man's participation in it.

1153.   Mellor, Roy E. H. **Eastern Europe: A Geography of the Comecon Countries.** New York: Columbia University Press, 1975. x, 358p. Tables. Illustrations. $17.50.
The three main parts of this book deal with the physical environment and political geography; the demographic and economic framework of the region; and Comecon and the national economies.
SR, 35:2:367-68; GJ, 141(1975):464.

1154.   Osborne, R. H. **East-Central Europe: An Introductory Geography.** New York: Praeger Publishers, 1967. 384p. $7.50.
This compendium of geographic information on Eastern Europe provides a factual and descriptive survey and is a very valuable reference work. The author provides information on land, climate, soils, agriculture, industry, population, transportation, and trade, in addition to introductory chapters on "The Peoples" and "The Geographical Background," and historical background sketches on each country, from Albania to Romania.
SR, 27:3:497-98; Choice, 4(1967):1038.

1155.   Turnock, David. **Eastern Europe: Studies in Industrial Geography.** Boulder, CO, and Folkstone, England: Westview Press and William Dawson & Sons, 1978. xii, 273p. $19.50.
This work treats all eight Communist states of Eastern Europe, excluding the USSR, and is useful to a wide range of readers. The material is organized in a framework that is traditional in studies of economic geography. There are thirty-seven maps.
GJ, 145(1979):311; Choice, 15(1978):1428.

History and General Studies

1156.   Bannan, Alfred J., and Edelenyi, Achilles. **Documentary History of Eastern Europe.** New York: Twayne Publishers, 1970. 392p. $7.50.
The purpose of this book is to provide a collection of source materials on Eastern Europe (excluding the USSR) from the first Slavic invasion before A.D. 1000 to the Czech crisis of 1968. The sources include selections from chronicles, law codes, constitutions, treaties, letters, travel accounts, and historical events, episodes and periods.
SR, 31:3:702; Choice, 8(1971):278.

1157. Borsody, Stephen. **The Triumph of Tyranny: The Nazi and Soviet Conquest of Central Europe.** New York: Macmillan, 1960. 285p. $4.50.
This highly stimulating book combines political history with a political program. It displays in detail the fascinating and tragic picture of internecine political infighting among the smaller powers of East and Central Europe since they achieved independence as a result of World War I.
SR, 20:2:313-15.

1158. Brown, J. F. **The New Eastern Europe: The Khrushchev Era and After.** New York: Praeger Publishers, 1966. 306p. $2.25 pa.
Brown examines in detail the decade that followed the events of 1956 in Eastern Europe by individual countries, describing political, economic, cultural, and diplomatic events.
SR, 26:2:326-28; JP, 29(1967):224.

1159. Dvornik, Francis. **The Slavs in European History and Civilization.** New Brunswick, NJ: Rutgers University Press, 1962. 688p. $15.00.
This work treats the political, constitutional, social, and cultural history of the region between the Baltic, Adriatic, and Black seas. It is a continuation of the author's *The Slavs, Their Early History and Civilization* (1956) and, to some extent, of his *The Making of Central and Eastern Europe* (1949).
SR, 22:3:547-48.

1160. Fischer-Galati, Stephen, ed. **Eastern Europe in the Sixties.** New York and London: Praeger Publishers, 1963. 239p. $6.00.
This is a collaborative attempt of historians, economists, and political scientists to explain and analyze conditions in Eastern Europe. Through a variety of topics the work provides a good picture of this area in the early 1960s.
SR, 24:1:139-40.

1161. Fischer-Galati, Stephen, ed. **Eastern Europe in the 1980s.** Boulder, CO: Westview Press, 1981. xvii, 292p. $26.25.
The volume offers a good analysis of past developments in Eastern Europe and of the direction of change, and thus of the seeds of future changes. Ten contributors treat the major trends, agriculture and rural development, industrialization, patterns of trade, the political order, relations to world Communism, relations with non-Communist countries, education, and cultural development.
NP, 10:2:265.

1162. Fisher-Galati, Stephen, ed. **Twentieth Century Europe: A Documentary History.** Philadelphia: Lippincott, 1967. 416p. $3.95 pa.
This collection of significant documents, speeches, treaties, and other like material reflects the historical process that led to the current division of Eastern and Western Europe.

1163. Halecki, Oscar. **Borderlands of Western Civilization: A History of East Central Europe.** New York: Ronald Press, 1952. 503p. $6.00.
The author focuses on the significant events in the life of the various national identities of this area along with the policies of churches and empires, and the

repercussions between Eastern and Western Europe occasioned by the periodic shift in the balance of power in either or both divisions.

SR, 12:1:147-49.

1164.   Jelavich, Charles, and Jelavich, Barbara. **The Establishment of the Balkan National States, 1804-1920.** Edited by Peter F. Sugar and Donald W. Treadgold. Seattle and London: University of Washington Press, 1977. xvi, 358p. Maps. $18.95. (A History of Central Europe, vol. 8.)

The general theme of this volume is the emancipation of the Balkan nations from Ottoman rule and the involvement of the Great Powers in the process. Each nation receives its own treatment, but there are also chapters that surmount the narrow boundaries of one nation, such as a survey of Balkan cultural development and an account of the Balkan nationalities in the Habsburg empire.

CSP, 20:3:443-44; LJ, 103(1978):35; Choice, 15(1978):457.

1165.   Kann, Robert A. **A History of the Habsburg Empire, 1526-1918.** Berkeley: University of California Press, 1974. xiv, 646p. Maps. $25.00.

The author surveys in a clear style the development of both the Austro-German and Hungarian parts of the monarchy from the Turkish and religious wars of the sixteenth and first half of the seventeenth centuries through World War I.

SR, 35:1:157-58; Choice, 12(1975):279.

1166.   Kohn, Hans. **Pan-Slavism: Its History and Ideology.** Notre Dame, IN: University of Notre Dame Press, 1953. 356p.; 2d rev. ed., New York: Vintage Books, 1960. 468p.

Pan-Slavic ideology, originated among the Slavs, became an instrument of Russian foreign policy. This comprehensive survey is highly provocative and informative. It is recommended for all types of readers.

SR, 12:3:419-21.

1167.   Lendvai, Paul. **Eagles in Cobwebs: Nationalism and Communism in the Balkans.** Garden City, NY: Doubleday, 1969. 396p. $6.95.

The oldest and most endemic political problem of the Balkans is the irrepressible force of nationalism. "The twin assault of a Communist takeover and Soviet domination has not solved the national problem. On the contrary, it has intensified national animosities," according to the author. He shows almost conclusively that the rise of nationalism has led to a dramatic decline of Soviet influence not only in this region but also in neighboring countries.

Choice, 6(1970):1645.

1168.   Macartney, C. A. and Palmer, A. W. **Independent Eastern Europe: A History.** London: Macmillan. New York: St. Martin's Press, 1962; reprint, 1966. 499p. $12.00.

This is mainly a history of Eastern European states between the two World Wars, a period during which the nations in that area formed sovereign and national states on the ruins of large supranational empires: Turkey and the Austro-Hungarian monarchy.

SR, 23:1:147-49.

1169. Orton, Lawrence D. **The Prague Slav Congress of 1848**. Boulder, CO: *East European Quarterly,* 1978. vii, 185p. $13.50. Distributed by Columbia University Press, New York. (East European Monographs, 46.)
Orton emphasizes that when the Danubian Slavs organized a congress in Prague in the spring of 1848, they aimed to develop a common platform and policy to protect and enhance their national well-being, calling their meeting expressly a "Slav," not a "Pan-Slav," congress, thereby distancing themselves from the Russian-dominated Pan-Slav orientation.
NP, 8:2:132; AHR, 84:4:1092.

1170. Polonsky, Anthony. **The Little Dictators: The History of Eastern Europe since 1918**. London and Boston: Routledge & Kegan Paul, 1975. xii, 212p. Maps. Statistical appendix. $16.50.
This volume introduces the reader to the many political, economic, social, demographic, ideological, and international problems that rocked the East European countries. It then outlines the extent to which some of these problems persist today or have been replaced by new ones.
SR, 35:4:757.

1171. Ristelhueber, René. **A History of the Balkan Peoples**. Edited and translated by Sharman David Spector. New York: Twayne Publishers, 1971. 470p. $7.50.
This French study manages to include a whole series of subtleties, and no serious reader can put it down without having acquired a knowledge of the ethnic clashes, religious complications, and power politics of the area over the centuries.
AHR, 80:5:1361; LJ, 97(1972):873.

1172. Rothschild, Joseph. **East Central Europe between the Two World Wars**. Seattle: University of Washington Press, 1974. 420p. $14.95. (A History of East Central Europe, vol. 9.)
This is a history of the interwar period of all countries between the Baltic Sea and Greece. The author chose a mixture of handbook and interpretive monograph to provide a historical survey of each of the ten countries he covers.
LJ, 100(1975):760.

1173. Seton-Watson, Hugh. **East European Revolution**. 3d ed. New York: Praeger Publishers, 1955. 435p. $6.50. (Praeger Publications in Russian History and World Communism.)
This is a most readable survey of Eastern Europe, covering the years 1941-49. It concentrates on Poland, Czechoslovakia, Hungary, Romania, Bulgaria, Albania, Yugoslavia, and Greece, describing the gradual Communization of these countries. It contains a bulk of factual information.
SR, 11:2:150-54.

1174. Seton-Watson, Hugh. **Eastern Europe between the Wars, 1918-1941**. Cambridge: Cambridge University Press, 1945. 442p.; 3d ed.: Hamden, CT: Shoe String Press, 1963. $10.00.
This survey of East Europe during the interwar period is a precursor to the author's *East European Revolution* and is regarded as an excellent textbook, which also serves the general reader well.

1175.   Seton-Watson, Hugh, and Seton-Watson, Christopher. **The Making of a New Europe: R. W. Seton-Watson and the Last Years of Austria-Hungary.** Seattle, WA: University of Washington Press, 1981. xii, 458p. Illustrations. $50.00.

This book should be read by anyone interested in the first two decades of twentieth-century Europe. There are basically four parts to the book: a brief informative prologue, written by R. W. Seton-Watson in the 1940s; a study of the period from 1905 to 1914, when the elder Seton-Watson became a keen observer of the Habsburg empire; the war and the plans for the breakup of the empire; and the peace settlements and creation of the new states. This valuable study underscores the dramatic periods in modern European history and Seton-Watson's role.

   SR, 41:2:360-62; AHR, 86:4:1118.

1176.   Seton-Watson, Robert William. **The Rise of Nationality in the Balkans.** London: Constable, 1917; reprint, New York: Howard Fertig, 1967. 308p. $8.50.

This account, the most authoritative work in English on the historical evolution of the Balkan nations, begins with the period of Turkish hegemony and continues through the national struggles for independence in the nineteenth century, the Berlin settlement, and the Balkan wars.

1177.   Singleton, Frederick B. **Background to Eastern Europe.** Oxford and New York: Pergamon Press, 1965. 226p.

This is a general introduction to the history, economy, and political conditions of the East European countries. It offers the reader a wide range of information related to the peoples and countries of Eastern Europe.

1178.   Stavrianos, Leften S. **The Balkans, 1815-1914.** New York: Holt, Rinehart & Winston, 1963. 135p. $2.75 pa.

In this study emphasis is on the national awakening of the southern Slavs. This condensed history of the Balkans is ideally suited for high school use.

1179.   Stavrianos, Leften S. **The Balkans since 1453.** New York: Holt, Rinehart & Winston, 1958. 970p. $14.50.

This work is more than a textbook; it makes available in summary form monographic material otherwise inaccessible to the reader. The author has provided rich bibliographic material that can be used for further study.

   SEER, 39:92:253-54.

1180.   Sugar, Peter F., and Lederer, Ivo J., eds. **Nationalism in Eastern Europe.** Seattle, WA: University of Washington Press, 1969. 465p. $15.00. (Far Eastern and Russian Institute Publications on Russia and Eastern Europe, no. 1.)

Each one of the East European countries is treated separately in this compendium concentrating on the history of nationalism in the nineteenth and twentieth centuries. The essays cover Albania, Bulgaria, Czechoslovakia, Greece, Hungary, Romania, and Yugoslavia.

   SR, 29:1:119-21; LJ, 95(1970):1850; Choice, 7(1970):1428.

1181.   Wolff, Robert Lee. **The Balkans in Our Time**. Cambridge, MA: Harvard
         University Press, 1974 (1956, 1967). 647p. $15.00.
During World War II the author served in the Balkan division of the Office of
Strategic Services and undertook three trips to various parts of the Balkans. This
account is based on his own observation and background knowledge and tells
mainly about Yugoslavia, Romania, and Bulgaria. The book is recommended to
the student and lay reader for general information related to events in the Balkans
since the beginning of World War II and up to the 1960s.
         SEER, 39:92:281-82.

Government and Politics

1182.   Benes, Vaclav; Gyorgy, Andrew; and Stambuk, George. **Eastern European
         Government and Politics**. New York: Harper & Row, 1966. 247p.
The authors treat contemporary governments and politics of Czechoslovakia,
East Germany, Hungary, Poland, Romania, and Yugoslavia. They explain the
development and structure of individual Communist parties and the problem of
leadership and relations with the Soviet Union since World War II.
         Choice, 4(1967):908.

1183.   Brzezinski, Zbigniew. **The Soviet Bloc: Unity and Conflict—Ideology
         and Power in the Relations among the USSR, Poland, Yugoslavia, China
         and Other Communist States**. With an introduction by Robert R. Bowie.
         Cambridge, MA: Harvard University Press, 1960. 470p.; rev. and enl.
         ed., New York: Praeger Publishers, 1967. 565p. $2.95 pa.
The author analyzes the intricate relations within the Soviet bloc. The central
theme is the role of ideology and power in the Communist orbit.
         Choice, 4(1967):1048.

1184.   Kamenetsky, Ihor. **Secret Nazi Plans for Eastern Europe: A Study of
         Lebensraum Policies**. New York: Bookman Associates, 1961. 236p. $5.00.
The expansionist plans of National Socialism are the theme of this study. The book
analyzes the geographic patterns of German colonization in Eastern Europe and the
differential treatment of subject nationalities in the eastern regions, particularly
in relation to the Baltic, Belorussian, and Ukrainian groups.
         AHR, 67:3:785-86.

1185.   Roberts, Henry L. **Eastern Europe: Politics, Revolution, and Diplomacy**.
         New York: Knopf, 1970. 352p. $6.95.
This book is a compilation of essays written by Roberts during various phases
of his career; it reflects the wide range of his interests and provides the reader with
analyses of the various problems affecting Eastern Europe.
         SR, 30:3:678.

1186.   Seton-Watson, Hugh. **The "Sick Heart" of Modern Europe: The Problem
         of the Danubian Lands**. Seattle and London: University of Washington
         Press, 1975. xii, 76p. $4.95.
The Danubian lands have been the sick heart of twentieth-century Europe.
According to the author, World War I grew out of the "clash of conflicting national-
isms in Central Europe," World War II grew out of "the national and social conflicts

in the Danube lands," and the current situation in Eastern Europe is one of "national humiliation" for eighty million Europeans.

> SR, 35:3:548.

1187. Skilling, H. Gordon. **The Government of Communist East Europe**. New York: Crowell, 1966. 256p. $2.50 pa.

This book presents a first-class description of the Communist governments of Eastern Europe. The study is well written and carefully organized and can be used as a handy reference.

> SR, 26:2:326-28; Choice, 3(1967):1081.

1188. Staar, Richard F. **The Communist Regimes in Eastern Europe**. 2d rev. ed. Stanford, CA: Hoover Institution Press, 1971 (1967). 304p. $3.95 pa.

This little reference book introduces the reader to the basic political, social, and economic factors influencing the development and course of eight East European satellites. Staar deals country by country with the current situations in these countries. He explains how the Communist party came to control and how Party decisions are implemented in each country. The general reader will benefit from this handy book.

> LJ, 93(1968):1990.

Communism, Communist Parties

1189. Bromke, Adam and Uren, Philip E., eds. **The Communist States and the West**. New York: Praeger Publishers, 1967. 256p. $6.50.

Twelve essays describe and evaluate changes in the Communist world in terms of East-West relations. Covered are such questions as power versus ideology, alliance structures, and international equilibrium.

> APSR, 62(1968):311.

1190. Burks, R. V. **The Dynamics of Communism in Eastern Europe**. Princeton, NJ: Princeton University Press; London: Oxford University Press, 1961. 244p. $5.00.

This volume contains an analytical history of Communist parties in East European countries. The author explains the different forms of Communist activities prior to seizure of power.

1191. Fischer-Galati, Stephen, ed. **The Communist Parties of Eastern Europe**. New York: Columbia University Press, 1979. viii, 393p. $20.00.

This is a collection of eight case studies. The articles take the stories of the East European Communist parties up to 1976-77. The following countries are covered: Poland, Albania, Bulgaria, Romania, Czechoslovakia, and Yugoslavia.

> SR, 39:4:699-700; LJ, 105(1980):212; Choice, 17(1980):282.

1192. Lendvai, Paul. **The Bureaucracy of Truth: How Communist Governments Manage the News**. Boulder, CO, and London: Westview Press and Burnett Books, 1981. 285p. $24.75.

Lendvai, a journalist in Hungary until his departure in 1957, has written this book from the perspective of a practicing journalist in the lively style of newspaper journalism. The book brings together a substantial number of interesting anecdotes and impressions and culls from Western newspaper coverage a corpus of examples. The impressions and supporting newspaper stories about these systems provide the reader with the most interesting material in the book.

    SR, 42:2:307-8; JC, 32(May 1982):148.

1193. McCauley, Martin. **Communist Power in Europe 1944-1949.** New York: Barnes & Noble, Harper & Row, 1977. xxvi, 424p. $21.50.

This collection of thirteen essays deals with the mechanics of Communist Party takeovers in Soviet-occupied East Europe; with Communist parties that failed to come to power despite substantial support; and with the Baltic states; and it includes general surveys of Eastern Europe during and after the war. The book has a coherent theme.

    SR, 39:2:329-30; Choice, 15(1978):128.

1194. Rakowska-Harmstone, Teresa, and Gyorgy, Andrew, eds. **Communism in Eastern Europe.** Bloomington, IN, and London: Indiana University Press, 1979. x, 338p. $17.50.

This symposium of twelve essays stresses the importance of two conflicting forces shaping political life in postwar Eastern Europe: the diverse historical, political, economic, and cultural traditions of East European people; and the determination of the Soviet Union to integrate them and subject them to Moscow's control.

    NP, 9:1:158-59; Choice, 16(1979):1366.

1195. Skilling, H. Gordon. **Communism National and International: Eastern Europe after Stalin.** Toronto: University of Toronto Press, 1964. 168p. $4.95.

Skilling presents a refreshing discussion of Communism and its encounter with local nationalism in the examples of East European countries. The book stimulates interest in further reading.

    SR, 24:2:337-38; Choice, 2(1965):118.

Foreign Relations

1196. Byrnes, Robert F., ed. **The United States and Eastern Europe.** Englewood Cliffs, NJ: Prentice-Hall, 1967. 179p. $4.95.

The contributions by specialists who participated in the Thirty-first American Assembly (1967) reflect on the land and peoples in history, politics and political change, economic modernization, social forces and cultural change, Eastern Europe in the Communist world, Europe, East and West, and American opportunities and dilemmas.

    SR, 28:1:157-58; Choice, 5(1968):261.

1197. Calder, Kenneth J. **Britain and the Origins of the New Europe, 1914-1918.** Cambridge: Cambridge University Press, 1976. x, 268p. $19.95. (International Studies Series.)

This study deals with east-central Europe as it was reconstructed after the dissolution of the Habsburg monarchy and the demise of the Romanov empire. The book is most useful where it illustrates the operation of the bureaucracy in its exploitation of the subject nationalities, that is, in fighting the war.

  SR, 36:2:327-28; AHR, 81:4:1114.

1198. Campbell, John C. **American Policy toward Communist Eastern Europe: The Choices Ahead.** Minneapolis, MN: University of Minnesota Press, 1965. 136p. $4.50.

Campbell brings into the picture the question of Germany and its paramount importance to developments in Eastern Europe. He also attaches great importance to the revival of nationalism. He presents various alternatives that may be pursued at the diplomatic, cultural, economic, and military levels.

  SR, 25:3:547-49; JP, 28(1966):451.

1199. Kovrig, Bennett. **The Myth of Liberation: East-Central Europe in U.S. Diplomacy and Politics since 1941.** Baltimore, MD: Johns Hopkins University Press, 1973. 360p. $11.50.

The worth of this book is not in puncturing a myth but in analyzing its place in the continuing evolution of U.S. policy on east-central Europe over a quarter-century. The book deals fully with the Hungarian revolt, less so with the Prague Spring.

  SR, 33:1:158-59.

1200. Lundestad, Geir. **The American Non-Policy towards Eastern Europe 1943-1947: Universalism in an Area Not of Essential Interest to the United States.** Oslo: Universitetsforlaget, 1978. 654p. Distributed by Columbia University Press. $18.00 pa.

Lundestad limits his analysis to U.S. policy in Eastern Europe and most of his material comes from the U.S. National Archives. The work offers a sober exposition of the views and actions of official Washington.

  SR, 38:4:696-97; Choice, 15(1978):1264.

1201. Mamatey, Victor S. **The United States and East Central Europe, 1914-1918: A Study in Wilsonian Diplomacy and Propaganda.** Princeton, NJ: Princeton University Press, 1957. 431p. $10.00.

This study explores various facets of Wilsonian diplomacy in the latter part of World War I. It discusses the aims and aspirations of ethnic groups in the Danubian area, the Czech and Slovaks, the Southern slavs, and the Romanians.

  JMH, 30:3:263-64.

1202. Radu, Michael, ed. **Eastern Europe and the Third World: East vs South.** Foreword by William T. R. Fox. New York: Praeger Publishers, 1981. xviii, 358p. Tables. $24.95.

The importance of the Third World in the foreign policies of the Soviet bloc states has grown considerably for both politicomilitary and economic reasons. The essays in this volume describe the new relations that have evolved between the East European states and the Third World. They present an informed picture of the current status of Eastern Europe and the Third World.

  SR, 41:4:735-36; HRNB, 10(Jan. 1982):50.

1203. Remington, Robin Alison, ed. **The International Relations of Eastern Europe.** Detroit: Gale Research Co., 1979. xvi, 273p. $22.00.
The first part of this annotated bibliography covers titles related to Communist Eastern Europe as a whole, and the second part identifies and describes sources and books related to Albania, Bulgaria, Czechoslovakia, the GDR, Hungary, Poland, Romania, and Yugoslavia.
   NP, 8:1:133; ARBA, 11(1980):240.

1204. Remington, Robin Alison. **The Warsaw Pact: Case Studies in Communist Conflict Resolution.** Cambridge, MA: MIT Press, 1971. 268p. $10.00. (Studies in Communism, Revisionism, and Resolution.)
The book is a study in coalition politics and focuses mainly on three specific examples of conflict (Romania, Czechoslovakia, and East Germany). Fifteen documents round out the text. One is impressed with the analysis of the December 1970 crisis in Poland.
   SR, 31:3:703-4; Choice, 9(1972):123.

1205. Wandycz, Piotr S. **France and Her Eastern Allies, 1919-1925: French-Czechoslovak-Polish Relations from the Paris Peace Conference to Locarno.** Minneapolis: University of Minnesota Press, 1962. 454p. $8.50.
The author examines a three-way diplomatic relationship that both reflected and contributed to the ambiguous and uncertain international scene in the years immediately following the Versailles settlement. The implications of Locarno had little to encourage a brighter future for this part of Europe.
   SEEJ, 7:2:234; SR, 22:1:150-52.

Economics

1206. Gianaris, Nicholas V. **The Economies of the Balkan Countries: Albania, Bulgaria, Greece, Romania, Turkey, and Yugoslavia.** New York: Praeger Publishers, 1983. 204p. $23.95.
This book reveals the main characteristics of Balkan economies and outlines developmental trends leading to closer cooperation. The emphasis is given to more vital recent phases of the economic and social life of the Balkan peoples. Subjects covered include land and natural resources, human resources and population, inflation and productivity, taxation, and capital to output studies. Also covered are agriculture and heavy and service industries.

1207. Höhmann, Hans-Hermann, et al., eds. **The New Economic Systems of Eastern Europe.** Berkeley and Los Angeles: University of California Press, 1975. xxiv, 585p. $22.50.
This is a very useful and handy reference, for it covers the broad features of contemporary industrial and agricultural systems in all East European nations, including Albania and Yugoslavia, and it contains much information, particularly on laws, decrees, and regulations, that is not readily available elsewhere.
   SR, 35:3:546-48; Choice, 13(1976):409.

1208.   Kaser, Michael. **Comecon: Integration Problems of the Planned Econo-mies.** London and New York: Oxford University Press, 1965. 215p. $5.60.
The author examines the many aspects of Comecon in terms of cooperation and diversity of interests among the individual member countries.

1209.   Kaser, Michael, and Zielinski, Janusz G. **Planning in East Europe: Indus-trial Management by the State; a Background Book.** London: The Bodley Head, 1970. 184p. $4.95.
This is a background book, according to its own subtitle, and it offers, unencum-bered with footnotes, a succinct and precise description of the East European systems before and after the reforms of the mid-1960s, from central planning to worker consultation, via tiers of authority, finances, price-setting, and success criteria for management. Anyone working in this general area should be acquainted with this study.
        SR, 31:1:238; Choice, 8(1971):876.

1210.   Mieczkowski, Bogdan, ed. **East European Transport: Regions and Modes.** The Hague, The Netherlands; Boston; and London: Martinus Nijhoff, 1980. xiv, 353p. Figures. Maps. Tables. Distributed by Kluwer Boston, Hingham, MA.
Since the economies of Eastern Europe are very interesting these days, and trans-port is an important aspect of their problems, this is a very useful book. Inter-action between Western and Eastern Europe has become substantial.

1211.   Mieczkowski, Bogdan. **Personal and Social Consumption in Eastern Europe: Poland, Czechoslovakia, Hungary, and East Germany.** New York: Praeger Publishers, 1975. xxiv, 342p. Tables. $21.50.
This study consists of three parts. The first part is a discussion of the theory and the political economy of consumption in Marxist thought and in socialist East Europe. Part 2 consists of studies of consumption in each of the four countries. Comparisons among these and conclusions make up part 3. The serious student will find much here that is illuminating.
        SR, 35:3:549; Choice, 12(1975):1345.

1212.   Mieczkowski, Bogdan. **Transportation in Eastern Europe: Empirical Findings.** Boulder, CO: *East European Quarterly,* 1978. xvi, 221p. Tables. Figures. Distributed by Columbia University Press, New York. $14.50. (East European Monographs, 38.)
This volume provides a comprehensive view of transport in East European countries covering the period between 1945 and 1975. Among the modes of transport covered are railroad, road, water, pipelines, and air. It is both a systematic evalua-tion of the transport system in Eastern Europe as a whole and a detailed study of transport in each country.
        NP, 7:2:230-31; Choice, 16(1979):124.

1213.   Schnitzer, Martin. **U.S. Business Involvement in Eastern Europe: Case Studies of Hungary, Poland, and Romania.** New York: Praeger Publishers, 1980. ix, 156p. Tables. $19.95.

Focusing on the three states with which U.S. cooperation and trade expanded most during détente, Schnitzer provides a useful primer for several kinds of readers interested in business with Communist Europe. The reader will find numerous details about specific statutes, taxes, and other matters affecting the conduct of business in Eastern Europe or with East European capital. The volume can be of use to American companies contemplating cooperative arrangements with Eastern Europe.

SR, 41:4:736-37.

Society, Sociology

1214. Carlton, Richard K., ed. **Forced Labor in the "People's Democracies."** New York: Praeger Publishers, published for the Mid-European Studies Center of the Free Europe Committee, 1955. 248p.

This collective work covers the legal framework of forced labor in the "socialist countries," the administration and the operation of the forced labor system. The impact of de-Stalinization on this aspect of socialist structures is also discussed.

1215. Faber, Bernard Lewis, ed. **The Social Structure of Eastern Europe: Transition and Process in Czechoslovakia, Hungary, Poland, Romania, and Yugoslavia.** New York: Praeger Publishers, 1976. xvi, 419p. $25.00.

This solid and useful volume on the sociology of Eastern Europe relies heavily on contributions from East European sociologists. It also includes contributions on the family, urban life, and factory organization.

SR, 36:3:514-15; Choice, 13(1976):1366.

1216. Grant, Nigel. **Society, Schools and Progress in Eastern Europe.** Oxford: Pergamon Press, 1969. 363p. $7.00 pa.

This book surveys the social, political, and historical background of Eastern Europe; the Marxist theory of education and Soviet educational practice; common characteristics, aims, structure, and overall development of the national systems of education in Poland, East Germany, Czechoslovakia, Hungary, Romania, Yugoslavia, Bulgaria, and Albania from their prewar antecedents to the mid-1960s.

SR, 31:1:210.

1217. Gutkind, E. A., ed. **Urban Development in East-Central Europe: Poland, Czechoslovakia, and Hungary.** Edited by Gabriele Gutkind. New York: Free Press; London: Collier-Macmillan, 1972. 339p. $25.00. (International History of City Development, vol. 7.)

Gutkind, E. A., ed. **Urban Development in Eastern Europe: Bulgaria, Romania, and the U.S.S.R.** Edited by Gabriele Gutkind. New York: Free Press; London: Collier-Macmillan, 1972. 457p. $19.95. (International History of City Development, vol. 8.)

These two volumes represent a collective work of leading Polish, Czechoslovak, Hungarian, Bulgarian, Romanian, and Soviet authorities on the subject. The books seek to describe and analyze the origins and development of towns. At the end of each volume is a long list of bibliographic sources which examine the field of town evolution from many angles.

SR, 33:3:562-63.

1218. Mieczkowski, Bogdan. **Social Services for Women in Eastern Europe.** Charleston, IL: The Association for the Study of the Nationalities (USSR and East Europe), 1982. 130p. $8.50 pa. (ASN Series in Issues Studies [USSR and East Europe], no. 3.)

The author describes Marxist theoretical views on women and relates these attitudes to the present. He notes that in many cases the reality conflicts with long-term goals of the socialist states. For example, the new freedom accorded to women to keep them in the labor market caused women to wish to limit the size of their families, which in turn will reduce the overall labor force in years to come. Statistical data support the author's findings.

NP, 11:1:106-7.

1219. Scott, Hilda. **Does Socialism Liberate Women?: Experiences from Eastern Europe.** Boston: Beacon Press, 1974. 240p. $7.95.

The book is a rather thorough documentation of the author's negative answer to the question in the title. It describes the situation in present-day Czechoslovakia; provides an interesting discussion of socialist ideas about women from Marx and Engels onward; and deals with the status of women as it has developed in Eastern Europe, particularly in Czechoslovakia, since World War II, and the relationship between socialism and women's liberation.

SR, 34:3:619-20.

National Minorities and Dissent

1220. Dawidowicz, Lucy S. **The War against the Jews, 1933-1945.** New York: Holt, Rinehart & Winston, 1975. xviii, 460p. $15.00.

In addition to discussing Nazi extermination of Jews, the author analyzes prevailing forms of anti-Semitism in East European countries. Her stirring account should be read by all interested in the recent history of Central and Eastern Europe.

SR, 34:4:821-23; JSS, 38(Winter 1976):82.

1221. Horak, Stephan M., et al. **Eastern European National Minorities, 1919-1980: A Handbook.** Littleton, CO: Libraries Unlimited, 1985. circa 375p. $42.50.

Ten specialists discuss all aspects of national minorities in the following East European countries: Albania, Bulgaria, Czechoslovakia, Hungary, Poland, Romania, and Yugoslavia. Introductory surveys of each country for the period 1919-80 precede annotated international bibliographic selections. The handbook includes an extensive general introduction, an index, and 980 entries in its bibliographic sections.

1222. King, Robert R. **Minorities under Communism: Nationalities as a Source of Tension among Balkan Communist States.** Cambridge, MA: Harvard University Press, 1973. 326p. $14.00.

The subtitle of this book is more descriptive of its contents than is the main title. King is interested in ascertaining how the relations between a *Staatsvolk* and the

ethnic minorities in any particular Communist state become a source of international tension between and among several Communist states. The thesis of this
study is that Communism has not solved the nationality problem in Eastern
Europe.
SR, 33:4:805-6; Choice, 11(1974):161.

1223.   Klein, George, and Reban, Milan J., eds. **The Politics of Ethnicity in
Eastern Europe.** Boulder, CO: *East European Quarterly*, 1981. vi, 273p.
Tables. $20.00. Distributed by Columbia University Press, New York.
(East European Monographs, no. 93; ASN Series in Issues Studies [USSR
and East Europe], no. 2.)
This collection of essays assesses nationalism and its ramifications for ethnic minori-
ties in contemporary Eastern Europe. The short introductory essay and the editors
emphasize the remarkable resilience and continuing relevance of nationalism in
nominally internationalist Marxist-Leninist state systems.
SR, 42:1:128-29; Choice, 19(1982):962.

1224.   Lendvai, Paul. **Anti-Semitism without Jews: Communist Eastern Europe.**
Garden City, NY: Doubleday, 1971. 393p. $7.95.
Lendvai examines the present conditions and status of Jews in Poland, Czechoslovakia, Hungary, and Romania. Despite the enormous numerical decrease of Jews
since World War II (to about 0.2 percent of the population), many of the problems
remain, including anti-Semitism in various forms.
TLS, (Sept. 15, 1972):1068.

1225.   Mastny, Vojtech, ed. **East European Dissent.** Vol. 1: **1953-1964**; Vol. 2:
1965-1970. New York: Facts on File, 1972. 292p. $8.95 set pa.
The two volumes contain a collection of documents revealing the existence of
dissent and covering the years 1953 through 1970. The editor has included all
forms of opposition, including armed uprising. The material, chronologically
arranged, is taken from *Facts on File.* The collection will enable the reader to
examine firsthand information, which he can then put in proper perspective by
reading monographs discussing these events.

1226.   Mendelsohn, Ezra. **The Jews of East Central Europe between the World
Wars.** Bloomington, IN: Indiana University Press, 1983. 320p. $27.50.
This is an illuminating and ambitious study of the demographic, cultural, and
socioeconomic conditions of East Central European Jewry between the wars.
The book focuses on the internal life of Jewish communities in the region as well
as on the relationships between Jews and Gentiles in a highly nationalistic environment.

1227.   Pearson, Raymond. **National Minorities in Eastern Europe 1848-1945.**
London: Macmillan Press, 1983. x, 249p.
The author of this attempt at an overview of national minorities in Eastern Europe
sees the problem of the minorities as a reaction to the tendency of most historians
to concentrate exclusively on the particular state nation and very often to ignore
large groups of minorities.

1228.   Sugar, Peter F., ed. **Ethnic Diversity and Conflict in Eastern Europe.** Santa
         Barbara, CA: ABC-Clio Press, 1980. xii, 400p. Tables. $20.75.
Ten contributors describe the influence of ethnicity on the development of Eastern
Europe, strongly underscoring the importance of Eastern Europe in the sociological
investigation of ethnicity. This volume documents the role of language and the
influence of government, religion, and economic factors on class structures, ethnic
minorities, and nationality.
         Choice, 18(1981):1016.

1229.   Tökes, Rudolf L., ed. **Opposition in Eastern Europe.** Baltimore, MD, and
         London: Johns Hopkins University Press, 1979. xiv, 306p. $22.50.
The aim of this volume is to present the chronological development of regime
opposition in Czechoslovakia, Poland, the German Democratic Republic, and
Hungary since 1968, while locating this development within a political sociology
of the working class, the intelligentsia, and the peasantry.
         SEER, 59:1:136-38; Choice, 17(1980):284.

1230.   Trunk, Isaiah. **Judenrat: The Jewish Councils in Eastern Europe under
         Nazi Occupation.** Introduction by Jacob Robinson. New York: Mac-
         millan, 1972. 664p. $14.95.
The study centers on the questions of why and how the Councils (Judenrat)
worked and whether Jewish-Nazi cooperation was decisive in the destruction of
European Jewry. To arrive at an answer, the author spent five years of study and
research in various Jewish archives in the United States, Israel, and Germany, in
addition to making a personal collection of notes and summaries of documents
assembled in Poland during the years 1946-50.
         Choice, 10(1973):347.

1231.   Vago, Bela, and Mosse, George L., eds. **Jews and Non-Jews in Eastern
         Europe, 1918-1945.** New York, Toronto, and Jerusalem: J. Wiley and
         Sons; Israel Universities Press, 1974. 334p.
This book is a valuable first attempt to introduce to an English-speaking audience
the whole gamut of Jewish problems in Eastern Europe between the wars.
         Choice, 12(1975):736.

ALBANIA

1232. Griffith, William E. **Albania and the Sino-Soviet Rift**. Cambridge, MA: MIT Press, 1963. 423p. $7.95.
In addition to a short history of Albania, the author gives a careful analysis of the primary causes of the rift between Moscow and Tirana. The author has aimed his study at the general reader.
SR, 23:1:158-59.

1233. Logoreci, Anton. **The Albanians: Europe's Forgotten Survivors**. Boulder, CO: Westview Press, 1978. 230p. + 8pp. plates. $16.00.
This account consists of an overview of Albanian history from the fourteenth-century Ottoman invasions to the end of World War II and a survey of Albanian history prior to the establishment of the present regime. A major portion of the book is devoted to a discussion and analysis of political, diplomatic, economic, social, and cultural developments from 1945 to the early 1970s. This book will be enjoyed by the nonspecialist reader.
CSP, 23:1:107.

1234. Mann, Stuart E. **An English-Albanian Dictionary**. Cambridge: Cambridge University Press, 1957. 434p.
The dictionary attempts to express the essential vocabulary of the English literary language in modern literary Albanian. No attempt has been made to represent such scientific or technical terms as are without general literary currency.

1235. Pano, Nicholas C. **The People's Republic of Albania**. Baltimore, MD: Johns Hopkins University Press, 1968. 185p. $6.50.
This volume is part of the "Integration and Community Building in Eastern Europe" series. It serves well as an introduction to Albanian modern history and politics, especially to the interested layman.
SR, 29:1:127-28.

1236. Prifty, Peter R. **Socialist Albania since 1944: Domestic and Foreign Developments**. Cambridge, MA: The MIT Press, 1978. 311p. $25.00. (Studies in Communism, Revisionism, and Revolution, 23.)
Prifty bases his information mostly on Albanian sources and offers the most up-to-date reference work on the development in that country. The author also provides information on Albanians in Yugoslavia.
Choice, 15(1979):1577.

1237. Skendi, Stavro, ed. **Albania**. New York: Published for the Mid-European Studies Center of the Free Europe Committee, Inc., by Praeger Publishers, 1956. 389p. $7.50.

This handbook is designed for the general reader and for reference use, and will benefit the librarian as well with its broad scope and voluminous factual detail. The work includes biographical data on twenty-seven leading Communists, a brief chronology for 1944-55, and a list of treaties.

1238. Skendi, Stavro. **The Albanian National Awakening, 1878-1912**. Princeton, NJ: Princeton University Press, 1967. 498p. $13.75.

Skendi reconstructs the complex process of Albanian national identity and cohesion, whereby Albanians overcame the factors of fragmentation and achieved a sense of national needs and interests and, by 1912, independence. This valuable study is based on far-reaching research in archives, the contemporary press, and secondary sources.

SR, 26:4:680-82; AHR, 73:2:537.

1239. Thomas, John I. **Education for Communism: School and State in the People's Republic of Albania**. Stanford, CA: Hoover Institution Press, 1969. 131p. $6.50.

This is a concise technical report on education in Albania since 1944, based on Albanian sources. The study is supplied with tables that provide the necessary statistics. In content, the author has found the obvious: education in Albania under the Communists has been thoroughly politicized.

EEQ, 4:2:110-11.

BULGARIA

Bibliography

1240.　Pundeff, Marin V., ed. **Bulgaria: A Bibliographic Guide**. Washington, DC: Slavic and Central European Division, Reference Department, Library of Congress, 1965; reprinted by Arno Press, 1968. 98p. $5.50.
This bibliography consists of a discussion of sources, grouped into various categories, and an alphabetical listing of all the sources discussed in the previous section. All entries contain pertinent bibliographic data.
　　　SR, 28:3:531-33; LJ, 94(1969):2906.

History, Politics, Government

1241.　Anastasoff, Christ. **The Bulgarians: From Their Arrival in the Balkans to Modern Times. Thirteen Centuries of History**. Hickesville, NY: Exposition Press, 1977. 380p. $20.00.
This is a popular history of the Bulgarians from ancient times to 1944, with special emphasis on the Bulgarian renaissance of the eighteenth century and the emergence of modern Bulgaria and the fate of its people. Several maps and photographs enhance the usefulness of this book, which is aimed at the general reader and student.

1242.　Brown, J. F. **Bulgaria under Communist Rule**. New York: Praeger Publishers, 1970. 338p. $11.00.
Brown presents a comprehensive account of Communism in Bulgaria in the past two decades. The once volatile Bulgarians have remained politically docile during the last generation. Bulgaria has neither deviated from the political standards set by the Soviet Union nor produced visible internal combustions of any consequence. The impact of Stalin's death on the Bulgarian Communist hierarchy is well analyzed in this study.
　　　SR, 31:4:933-34; CH, 60(1971):303.

1243.　Chary, Frederick B. **The Bulgarian Jews and the Final Solution, 1940-1944**. Pittsburgh, PA: University of Pittsburgh Press, 1972. 246p. $9.95.
This heavily documented study revolves around the principal question, "Who saved the Bulgarian Jews?" Despite the author's ability to collect a mass of information,

his conclusions are unclear; he refuses to give credit where credit is due—for example, to the Bulgarian Orthodox church and to the countless sincere Bulgarians from top to bottom of the social structure.

HRNB, 1(March 1973):106; Choice, 10(1973):1058.

1244.   Crampton, Richard J. **Bulgaria, 1878-1918**. Boulder, CO: *East European Quarterly,* 1983. 592p. $35.00. Distributed by Columbia University Press, New York. (East European Monographs, no. 138.)

This study, which fills a noticeable gap in Western historiography, examines the first forty years in Bulgaria after it emerged from five centuries of Ottoman rule, and how it went about finding political stability, promoting internal economic development, and establishing a foreign policy.

1245.   Dellin, L. A. D., ed. **Bulgaria**. New York: Praeger Publishers, published for the Mid-European Studies Center of the Free Europe Committee, 1957. 457p. $8.50.

This volume contains a collection of 1,243 items of general reference, including land and people, language and literature, history, politics, government, and law.

SEER, 44:103:529-30.

1246.   Georgeoff, Peter John. **The Social Education of Bulgarian Youth**. Minneapolis, MN: University of Minnesota Press, 1968. 329p. $10.00.

The author gives a detailed picture of all existing Bulgarian educational institutions, which are modeled mainly on Soviet patterns. He also deals with social education, defined as the introduction of youth into the traditions, values, mores, ethics, and ideology that characterize Communist society.

SR, 28:4:668; Choice, 5(1969):1472.

1247.   MacDermott, Mercia. **A History of Bulgaria, 1393-1885**. New York: Praeger Publishers, 1962. 354p. $8.75.

This is a general history of Bulgaria. The information on the liberation movement is both new and relevant.

AHR, 68:2:528-29.

1248.   Miller, Marshall Lee. **Bulgaria during the Second World War**. Stanford, CA: Stanford University Press, 1975. xiv, 290p. $10.95.

The author investigates the political history of Bulgaria during its involvement in World War II, skillfully interweaving threads of domestic and foreign politics. He reveals that Nazi Germany exercised little control over the policies of its satellite, and the relatively human treatment of the Bulgarian Jews provides a good illustration of this point. He pays relatively little attention to the purely military history.

SR, 35:3:565-66; AAPSS-A, 424(March 1976):142.

1249.   Oren, Nissan. **Bulgarian Communism: The Road to Power, 1934-1944**. New York: Columbia University Press, 1971. 288p. $12.50. (East Central European Studies of Columbia University and the Research Institute on Communist Affairs.)

In presenting the Bulgarian Communist party's history within the context of more general political developments in Bulgaria, the author illuminates certain themes important to Bulgarian history as a whole. Considerable attention is given to quarrels over personalities and tactics.

SR, 32:4:848-49; LJ, 97(1972):1433; Choice, 9(1972):270.

1250. Oren, Nissan. **Revolution Administered: Agrarianism and Communism in Bulgaria.** Baltimore, MD: Johns Hopkins University Press, 1973. 204p. $8.50. (Integration and Community Building in Eastern Europe, no. 8.)

This book offers the most readable short political survey of contemporary Bulgaria, from the end of World War I to the present. The account is a powerful and convincing summary of the tragic fate of modern Bulgaria. The main emphasis is on the conflict between the peasant majority and the Communist minority.

SR, 33:3:602-3; Choice, 10(1973):1444.

1251. Rothschild, Joseph. **The Communist Party of Bulgaria: Origins and Development 1883-1936.** New York: Columbia University Press, 1959. 354p. $7.50.

This noteworthy book displays a high standard of scholarship in a lucidly written account of the historical development of Socialism-Communism in the Balkans.

SR, 20:1:144-46.

Language and Literature

1252. Chakalov, G.; Liakov, I.; and Stankov, Z. **Bulgarsko-angliiski rechnik** (Bulgarian-English Dictionary). Sofia: Derzh, Izd. "Nauka i izkustvo," 1961. 982p.

The dictionary contains over fifty thousand words and is recommended for students, specialists, translators, and teachers of foreign languages.

1253. Kirilov, Nikolai, and Kirk, Frank, eds. **Introduction to Modern Bulgarian Literature: An Anthology of Short Stories.** New York: Twayne Publishers, 1969. 480p.

There are thirty-six selections from twenty-eight authors, all but five of whom were living at the time of compilation. On the whole, the collection is quite entertaining, though the verbosity of Bulgarian writers is in evidence.

LJ, 95(1970):1502; Choice, 7(1970):847.

1254. Lord, Albert B., and Bynum, David E. **A Bulgarian Literary Reader.** The Hague, The Netherlands: Mouton, 1968. 200p. 25 Dglds.

The introductory essay provides a capsule background of Bulgarian literature up to the time where the selections begin. Each selection is preceded by a brief biographical sketch in English. The glossary is excellent. It provides not only meanings but all the grammatical information a student needs. The selections themselves are representative in both time and variety.

1255. Moser, Charles A. **A History of Bulgarian Literature, 865-1944.** The Hague, The Netherlands: Mouton, 1972. 286p. 35 Dglds. (Slavistic Printings and Reprintings, 112.)

It was not until after 1878 that Bulgarian literature began to mature and branch out. Bulgarian literature from 1878 to 1896 was still geared to serve social ends. The last two chapters of the book, dealing with the period 1896-1944, are fascinating as well as unique contributions to the history of Bulgarian letters.

SR, 29:1:761-62.

CZECHOSLOVAKIA

Reference Works

1256. Busek, Vratislav, and Spulber, Nicholas, eds. **Czechoslovakia.** New York: Praeger Publishers, published for the Mid-European Studies Center of the Free Europe Committee, 1957. 520p.
This handbook concentrates on four major topics: geography and demography, the Party and the government, the society, and the economy. An appendix contains biographical sketches of leaders of the postwar regime, a brief chronology, and a list of treaties and agreements from 1943 to 1956.
JMH, 31:1:68-69; LJ, 82(1957):5112.

1257. Hejzlar, Zdenek, and Kusin, Vladimir V. **Czechoslovakia 1968-1969: Chronology, Bibliography, Annotation.** New York and London: Garland Publishing, 1975. 316p. $28.00.
The authors have performed an important service by putting order into this unwieldy body of source material. This volume serves as a handy reference.
SR, 35:1:156-57; ARBA, 7(1976):164.

1258. Parrish, Michael, ed. **The 1968 Czechoslovak Crisis: A Bibliography, 1968-1970.** Santa Barbara, CA: ABC-Clio Press, 1971. 41p. $6.00 pa.
This is a bibliography of books, pamphlets, monographs, special studies, documents, and journal articles from worldwide sources covering Soviet military intervention in Czechoslovakia.
Choice, 8(1972):1570.

1259. Sturm, Rudolf. **Czechoslovakia: A Bibliographic Guide.** Washington, DC: Library of Congress, 1967; reprinted by Arno Press, 1968. 157p. $6.00.
The bibliography is divided into two parts: the first is a discussion of sources, grouped into various categories, and the second is an alphabetical listing of all the sources discussed in the previous section. The individual entries contain all the pertinent bibliographic data.
SR, 28:3:531-33.

1260. Zeman, Jarold K. **The Hussite Movement and the Reformation in Bohemia, Moravia and Slovakia (1350-1650): A Bibliographical Study Guide (with Particular Reference to Resources in North America).** Ann Arbor, MI: Published under the auspices of the Center for Reformation Research, Michigan Slavic Publications, 1977. xxxvi, 389p. $14.00. (Reformation in Central Europe, no. 1.)

The data were collected between 1972 and 1977. There are 3,853 entries in four-teen languages, arranged with several thousand cross-references in four major parts: "Historical Development (1350-1650)," "Biographical Studies," "Topical Studies," and "Study Aids." This guide is also a useful reference aid for librarians.
SEER, 58:3:337-38.

History

1261. Brock, Peter. **The Slovak National Awakening: An Essay in the Intellec-tual History of East Central Europe**. Toronto and Buffalo, NY: Univer-sity of Toronto Press, 1976. x, 104p. $12.50.
This small book covers the essential facts of the evolution of Slovak linguistic and political consciousness from the latter decades of the eighteenth century to the revolution of 1848. This work is the most complete account of the subject available in English.
SR, 36:2:336-37; AHR, 82:4:1022.

1262. Eidlin, Fred H. **The Logic of "Normalization": The Soviet Intervention in Czechoslovakia of 21 August 1968 and the Czechoslovak Response**. Boulder, CO: *East European Quarterly,* 1980. 278p. $20.00. Distributed by Columbia University Press, New York. (East European Monographs, no. 74.)
The nearly unanimous response of Czechoslovakia's population, rulers, and institu-tions to the 1968 Soviet invasion was to reject the intervention. The study explains how the outlines of a stalemated political situation emerged as both the occupation and the Czechoslovak response to it became consolidated.
CH, 80(1981):178.

1263. Kaminsky, Howard. **A History of the Hussite Revolution**. Berkeley: University of California Press, 1967. 580p. $15.00.
This is a fascinating ideological and sociological analysis of Hussite history seen as a movement of reformation and revolution. The author sees the two as intimately tied together. He sets the Hussite revolt in the larger context of "world-historical terms" in its relationship both to late medieval history and to the old order.
SR, 29:3:502-3; AHR, 73:3:796.

1264. Kirschbaum, J. K., ed. **Slovakia in the 19th and 20th Centuries**. Toronto: Slovak World Congress, 1973. 368p.
The articles in this collection were written from the position that the Slovaks are a "distinct central European nation" and thus have rights to self-determination and equality of rights.
CSP, 16:4:682.

1265. Lettrich, Jozef. **History of Modern Slovakia**. New York: Praeger Pub-lishers, 1955. 239p. $5.00.
The book provides a brief sketch of Slovak history before 1918 and principal trends in Slovak politics and events during the first Czechoslovak republic. The greater part of the study is devoted to events since 1938, when, as a result of the Munich verdict, Czechoslovakia disintegrated and Slovakia was set up as a German

protectorate. The author favors the so-called Czechoslovak idea as a solution to the Czech-Slovak relationship.

JMH, 28:1:103.

1266.   Littell, Robert, ed. **The Czech Black Book.** New York: Praeger Publishers, 1969. 303p. $6.95.

What happened in Czechoslovakia from August 21 through August 27, 1968, is dramatically described in this document, prepared by members of the Institute of History of the Czechoslovak Academy of Sciences. It is a compilation of eye-witness testimony, broadcasts from the free Czechoslovak radio stations, newspaper articles, statements from participants in official government and party proceedings, and notes from high-level clandestine meetings.

JP, 32(1970):1015.

1267.   Luža, Radomir. **The Transfer of the Sudeten Germans: A Study of Czech-German Relations, 1933-1962.** New York: New York University Press, 1964. 365p. $7.50.

The subtitle of this book gives a somewhat more accurate picture of its content than does the title. The bulk of the volume deals not with the actual transfer of the Germans from Czechoslovakia in 1945 but with the background of this momentous event in East European history. A thorough examination of the economic and social foundations of the Czech-German problem provides the necessary foundation for understanding and appraising the difficult decision made by the Czechoslovak government in exile, and endorsed by the allied governments, to transfer more than three million Germans from Czechoslovakia.

SR, 25:4:701-2; AHR, 70:3:757.

1268.   Mamatey, Victor S., and Luža, Radomir, eds. **A History of the Czecho-slovak Republic, 1918-1948.** Princeton, NJ: Princeton University Press, 1973. 534p. $9.75.

This book is a product of many hands, with fourteen authors contributing seventeen chapters grouped in three themes: "The Czechoslovak Republic 1918-1938," "Occupation, War, and Liberation 1938-1945," and "Czechoslovakia between East and West 1945-1948." The volume contains several maps, pictures, and photographs.

EEQ, 8:3:389-91; Choice, 11(1974):815.

1269.   Masaryk, Tomas. **The Making of a State: Memories and Observations, 1914-1918.** Edited and introduced by Henry Wickham Stee. New York: Howard Fertig, 1969 (1927). 461p. $15.00.

Masaryk, who created a new state by the force of his own will, narrates events that brought about the freedom of Czechoslovakia. He describes how he organized abroad the fight and support of the Czech people and of Western statesmen, including Woodrow Wilson. His comments and observations reveal his thoughtful mind and character.

1270.   Mastny, Vojtech. **The Czechs under Nazi Rule: The Failure of National Resistance, 1939-1942.** New York: Columbia University Press, 1971. 274p. $10.00.

Mastny describes the fall of Czechoslovakia. His central thesis is simply stated: the Czechs failed to challenge the Nazi authorities with an effective resistance. By 1942 the resistance movement was destroyed, never to play a significant role until the end of the war.

SR, 34:3:628-30.

1271.   Odložilik, Otakar. **The Hussite King: Bohemia in European Affairs; 1440-1471.** New Brunswick, NJ: Rutgers University Press, 1965. 337p. $10.00.

The author concentrates on the skein of religious, political, and military involvements—on the king's attempt to mediate between Catholics and Utraquists within the kingdom and to maintain his throne against the papacy and his secular rivals.

SR, 25:3:532-33; Choice, 2(1966):814.

1272.   Pech, Stanley Z. **The Czech Revolution of 1849.** Chapel Hill, NC: University of North Carolina Press, 1969. 386p. $10.00.

The author makes it clear that the revolution in Bohemia bore little resemblance to those in Moravia, Silesia, and Slovakia. He also discusses the national, liberal, and social aspects of the revolution. The study is based on documents the author collected in several archives in Prague, a large number of contemporary newspapers, and other published contemporary sources.

SR, 31:1:218-19; LJ, 95(1970):67; Choice, 7(1970):448.

1273.   Perman, Dagmar Horna. **The Shaping of the Czechoslovak State: Diplomatic History of the Boundaries of Czechoslovakia, 1914-1920.** Leiden, The Netherlands: Brill, 1962. 339p. (Studies in East European History, no. 7.)

The dissolution of the Habsburg Empire and the consequent rise of the successor states were accompanied by many frontier problems. This book examines the manner in which the Paris Peace Conference reached the decision fixing newly created Czechoslovakia's boundaries in the winter of 1918-19.

AHR, 69:3:844.

1274.   Ripka, Hubert. **Munich: Before and After; a Fully Documented Czechoslovak Account of the Crises of September 1938 and March 1939.** Translated by Ida Sindelková and Comdr. Edgar P. Young. New York: Howard Fertig, 1969 (1939). 523p. $14.00.

This account of events leading to, and related to, the Munich agreement was written by a prominent Czech journalist who joined Beneš's government-in-exile in London. This account complements George F. Kennan's study *From Prague after Munich. Diplomatic Papers, 1938-1940* (1968).

1275.   Skilling, Gordon. **Czechoslovakia's Interrupted Revolution.** Princeton, NJ: Princeton University Press, 1976. xvi, 924p. $45.00.

The author's extensive research, persuasive interpretation, and detailed biographical footnotes combine to make this the best volume available on the history of the Dubček era. The study's detailed treatment of 1968 presents a vast amount of information and conveys the complexities and contradictions of the reform movement.

SR, 37:1:152-53; Choice, 13(1977):1488.

1276. Szporluk, Roman. **The Political Thought of Thomas G. Masaryk.** Boulder, CO: *East European Quarterly,* 1981. viii, 244p. $20.00. Distributed by Columbia University Press, New York. (East European Monographs, no. 85.)

The author shows that by 1900 Masaryk believed that "a self-governing state was the most desirable goal for any nation." He observes that Masaryk's Republik, to the extent that it reflected his ideas, was indeed flawed; it nevertheless embodied his humanism and was a haven for the oppressed of many other nations and states. Masaryk's commitment to his nation and his state was unwavering.

    SR, 42:1:140-41.

1277. Vyšný, Paul. **Neo-Slavism and the Czechs 1898-1914.** Cambridge: Cambridge University Press, 1977. xiv, 287p. $21.95. (Soviet and East European Studies.)

This interesting, well-written volume offers a valuable treatment of Neo-Slavism, a short-lived but significant movement that sought to promote Slavic cooperation, particularly between Czechs and Russians. Its creator and main driving force was the Czech politician Karel Kramař. This thoughtful analysis illuminates a crucial area of politics and diplomacy in prewar Eastern Europe.

    NP, 7:1:109-10; SR, 34:4:701-2.

1278. Wallace, William V. **Czechoslovakia.** London and Tonbridge, England: Ernest Benn, 1977; Boulder, CO: Westview Press, 1976. xvi, 374p. Illustrations. Maps. $24.00.

This is a history of the Czechs and Slovaks from 1849 until the present time. It is informative on economic history of the nineteenth century and has many interesting things to say on the resulting social developments. It gives the Slovaks their proper place in the story before and during the creation of their common state with the Czechs. This book is a comprehensive guide for the general reader.

    SEER, 56:1:133-34; LJ, 102(1977):920; Choice, 14(1977):739.

1279. Zacek, Joseph Frederick. **Palacký: The Historian as Scholar and Nationalist.** The Hague, The Netherlands: Mouton, 1970. 137p. 28 Dglds. (Studies in European History, no. 5.)

This is a biography of František Palacký's accomplishments as a historian and as the chief leader of the Czech national movement. The author has done this by making a critical "synthesis of the published material" and combining it with the result of his own "researches into the pertinent primary sources."

    SR, 33:2:379; Choice, 8(1971):1078.

Government and Politics

1280. Ello, Paul, comp. **Czechoslovakia's Blueprint for "Freedom": "Unity, Socialism and Humanity," Dubček's Statements—the Original and Official Documents Leading to the Conflict of August, 1968.** Washington, DC: Acropolis Books, 1969. 304p. $4.95.

The publication of some of Alexander Dubček's statements on the path of socialism in Czechoslovakia prior to the invasion is a significant event. The compiler contends that the four texts he has chosen provide a "blueprint for the further development of a Socialist political order." Ello provides each document with an introduction and an analysis based on the speech itself.

SR, 29:3:538-39.

1281. Golan, Galia. **The Czechoslovak Reform Movement: Communism in Crisis, 1962-1968.** Cambridge: Cambridge University Press, 1971. 349p. $16.50.

The author lists and interprets even such obscure phenomena of the liberalization battle as the "Standpoint of the Party Organization on the District of Usti and Orlici Concerning the Situation on the Cultural and Artistic Front of 1965." Her book renders very well the tragedy of Czechoslovakia between 1962 and 1968.

CSP, 16:2:308-9; Choice, 9(1972):1189.

1282. Golan, Galia. **Reform Rule in Czechoslovakia: The Dubček Era, 1968-1969.** Cambridge: Cambridge University Press, 1973. 327p. $18.50.

Reading the story of the proposed reforms and their shattering collapse, one is impressed by their completeness, consistency, and imaginativeness, as well as puzzled by the relative ease with which brutal force relegated them to the archives of history. The author presents the case in its entirety, giving the reader a concise picture and inviting him to ask questions on prospects for and methods of change in a Communist society.

SR, 33:4:799-800; AHR, 78:5:1496.

1283. Kennan, George F. **From Prague after Munich: Diplomatic Papers, 1938-1940.** Princeton, NJ: Princeton University Press, 1968. 266p. $6.50.

Kennan has included documents and materials containing explanations of the conflicts between the Czechs and Slovaks. The greatest value of the book, however, is Kennan's perception of the climate of opinion at the time of writing his confidential letters from his post in Prague (and later Berlin) to the State Department.

SR, 29:1:119-20; CH, 56(1969):230.

1284. Krystufek, Zdenek. **The Soviet Regime in Czechoslovakia.** Boulder, CO: *East European Quarterly,* 1981. vii, 340p. $21.00. Distributed by Columbia University Press, New York. (East European Monographs, no. 81.)

This volume contains an excellent portrait of the most appalling aspects of the process of Russification and Sovietization of Czechoslovakia, which was imposed on the country by Stalin and the Czech and Slovak Communists after the February 1948 coup. The author maintains that the imposition of Russian institutions, practices, and values was so brutal that it destroyed a once highly developed national culture and democratic institutions. The best sections of the study deal with the reform movement generated under Dubček in 1968, in which he himself was involved.

NP, 11:1:125-26; Choice, 19(1982):1134.

1285. Kusin, Vladimir V. **From Dubček to Charter 77: A Study of "Normalization" in Czechoslovakia, 1968-1978.** Edinburgh, England: Q Press, 1978. x, 353p. £8.50.

Kusin distinguishes four stages in the process of normalization: the first, from the aftermath of the invasion until April 1969; the second, lasting until May 1971; the third, which involves the political equilibrium of normalization; and the final one, from the end of 1976, which deals with the issue of human rights. The author makes intelligent use of colorless Communist party statements by emphasizing their most ambivalent sentences.

   SEER, 58:3:467-68.

1286. Loebl, Eugen. **Stalinism in Prague: The Loebl Story.** Translated by Maurice Michael. American edition edited and with an introduction by Herman Starobin. New York: Grove Press, 1970. 330p. $8.95.

Eugen Loebl, former deputy foreign trade minister, is one of three Communist defendants of the Slansky trial to survive. Here he unveils the decisive role of the Soviet advisers in the preparation of the trial and describes the techniques of interrogation, consisting of a "combination of continual hunger, repeated interruption of sleep, and of having to walk or stand in small, hard leather slippers throughout the day."

   SR, 37:2:323-25.

1287. Mlynar, Zdenek. **Night Frost in Prague: The End of Humane Socialism.** London: C. Hurst & Co., 1980. 300p. £9.50.

This detailed and vivid eyewitness account of what happened at the meeting of the Czechoslovak party presidium on the night of the Warsaw Pact invasion of Czechoslovakia in August 1968, and the negotiations between the Czechoslovak leaders and their counterparts in Moscow a few days later, presents the political memoirs of the author, who was a member of the Czechoslovak Communist establishment.

   SS, 33:4:619-22.

1288. Paul, David. W. **Czechoslovakia: Profile of a Socialist Republic at the Crossroads of Europe.** Boulder, CO: Westview Press, 1981. xiv, 196p. Figures. Map. Photographs. $18.50.

Paul has produced a profile that will soundly introduce socialist Czechoslovakia to those who lack a basic understanding. He discusses international relations, government and politics, the economy, the social and ethnic structures, and education and culture. The author displays familiarty with the conditions of daily life with the sensitivity of a frequent visitor to that country.

   SR, 39:2:338-39.

1289. Pelikan, Jiri, ed. **The Czechoslovak Political Trials, 1950-1954: The Suppressed Report of the Dubcek Government's Commission of Inquiry, 1968.** Stanford, CA: Stanford University Press, 1971. 360p. $10.95.

In April 1968, in its third attempt since 1955, the Communist party of Czechoslovakia set up a special commission to investigate the background of the show trials of the period 1949-54 under strict rules of secrecy. For the first time in the history of a Communist party in power, access was given to the secret party archives, including the minutes of the meetings of the highest party organs. This published text has the merit of being an authentic report.

   SR, 30:1:177; Choice, 8(1972):1633.

1290.   Piekalkiewicz, Jaroslaw A. **Public Opinion Polling in Czechoslovakia, 1968-1969: Results and Analysis of Surveys Conducted during the Dubček Era.** Foreword by Barry Bede. New York: Praeger Publishers, 1972. 357p. $18.50.

The author is concerned with the degree to which the regime and its policies were supported by the population between March 1968 and March 1969. In examining this problem, he relies on the data collected in some twenty public opinion polls conducted by him in Czechoslovakia during that year. Thirty-five thousand people were interviewed, selected largely at random.

SR, 32:4:837-38; Choice, 10(1973):684.

1291.   Remington, Robin Alison, ed. **Winter in Prague: Documents on Czechoslovak Communism in Crisis.** With an introduction by William E. Griffith. Czech and Slovak translation revised by Michael Berman. Cambridge, MA: MIT Press, 1969. 473p. $12.50.

The Remington work, like most documentary collections, has a lasting value, and its importance is likely to increase if new evidence should come to light (for example, a report on the Dubček-Brezhnev conversations) that would enable us to reevaluate the events of 1968. The stated purpose of the collection is to document the experiment of Prague's attempt "to sweep the ashes of Stalinism from the Czechoslovak road to Socialism."

SR, 29:4:729-30; LJ, 95(1970):1849; Choice, 7(1970):448.

1292.   Skilling, Gordon H. **Charter 77 and Human Rights in Czechoslovakia.** London and Winchester, MA: George Allen & Unwin, 1981. xv, 363p. $37.50.

"Charter 77" refers not only to the document issued in January 1977, but to a human rights movement which Skilling considers "a significant phenomenon in the history of Czechoslovakia and of world Communism." The charter itself is a unique appeal to the government to obey its own laws and ratified international covenants. Not a single sentence of the charter has been quoted in the Czechoslovak mass media, yet thousands of citizens were forced to sign statements condemning something they were not permitted to read. The number of signatories of the charter exceeds one thousand.

NP, 11:2:318-19; SR, 41:4:743-44.

1293.   Valenta, Jiri. **Soviet Intervention in Czechoslovakia 1968: Anatomy of a Decision.** Baltimore, MD: Johns Hopkins University Press, 1979. xii, 208p. $12.00.

Valenta, who fled his native country in the wake of the 1968 upheavals, has produced a dispassionate account of the complex processes of decision-making in the Soviet Union that ultimately led to the fateful determination that military intervention in Czechoslovakia was unavoidable.

RR, 39:3:385-86; LJ, 104(1979):2459; Choice, 17(1980):278.

Communism, Communist Party

1294. Hruby, Peter. **Fools and Heroes: The Changing Role of Communist Intellectuals in Czechoslovakia.** New York and Toronto: Pergamon Press, 1980. xx, 265p. $30.00.

Many of the disappointed Czechoslovak Communist intellectuals who now wander throughout the Western world had enthusiastically helped to impose the Soviet regime on their homeland during and after the 1948 coup. The author depicts the gradual transformation of the political and moral principles of a group of well-known Czechoslovak intellectuals who in 1948 cast themselves in the role of saviors of the nation and its proletariat.

    CSP, 23:3:359-60; Choice, 18(1980):576.

1295. Korbel, Josef. **Communist Subversion of Czechoslovakia, 1938-1948: The Failure of Coexistence.** Princeton, NJ: Princeton University Press, 1959. 258p. $5.00.

A former member of the diplomatic service of Czechoslovakia describes the instruments of power seized by the Communist party, its clever propaganda designed to convince the people of the moderation of its policies, and the illusions to which the democrats fell victim. Korbel's firsthand experience adds to the study's importance.

    SEER, 39:92:277-78; LJ, 84(1959):3141.

1296. Suda, Zdenek L. **Zealots and Rebels: A History of the Communist Party of Czechoslovakia.** Stanford, CA: Hoover Institution Press, 1980. xi, 275p. $8.95.

Among the Communist parties that have had the opportunity to implement their own programs, the Communist party of Czechoslovakia occupies a very important place. Its experiences and that of the Czechoslovakian population over the past thirty years are of special significance because of several unique circumstances, the geopolitical location of the country, and Czechoslovakia's traditionally Western political culture.

    AHR, 86:3:883; Choice, 18(1981):1341.

1297. Taborsky, Edward. **Communism in Czechoslovakia 1948-1960.** Princeton, NJ: Princeton University Press, 1961. 628p. $12.00.

The author presents a penetrating view of the operation of a modern welfare-garrison state in which people still have not learned to like Communism; they have merely learned to survive under it. The book also portrays a unique aspect of people who are living under a totalitarian regime as "split personalities."

    SR, 21:3:558-59; LJ, 87(1962):1144.

1298. Zinner, Paul E. **Communist Strategy and Tactics in Czechoslovakia, 1918-1948.** New York and London: Praeger Publishers, 1963. 264p. $6.50.

The Communist seizure of Czechoslovakia still ranks high among the fateful events of the Cold War. This study adds to our understanding of why the Communists emerged victorious in a country that used to be regarded as a "bastion of democracy" in east-central Europe.

    SR, 23:2:352-53; LJ, 88(1963):3630.

Diplomacy, Foreign Relations

1299.   Bittman, Ladislav. **The Deception Game: Czechoslovak Intelligence in Soviet Political Warfare.** Syracuse, NY: Syracuse University Research Corporation, 1972. 246p. $9.95.
The author is fully qualified to impart his knowledge of Czechoslovak and Soviet intelligence work. He served in the Czechoslovak branch for fourteen years, part of them in a high position in D-Department (Department of Disinformation). All activities were closely supervised, and those of special importance were directed by the Soviet intelligence. Their network extended the world over. The book throws interesting light on the qualities and qualifications of Czechoslovak agents. Bittman was in Vienna during the Soviet invasion of Czechoslovakia in 1968 and escaped to the United States. The American reader is now the beneficiary of his deception-game experiences.
    SR, 32:3:642; BL, 69(Dec. 1972):317.

1300.   Campbell, Gregory F. **Confrontation in Central Europe: Weimar Germany and Czechoslovakia.** Chicago and London: University of Chicago Press, 1975. xvi, 383p. $15.00.
This is the first comprehensive and analytical study of Czechoslovak-German relations from 1918 to 1933. The author stresses almost exclusively the diplomatic aspects of the Czechoslovak-German relationship, places it in the context of European foreign relations, and reveals how it was affected by every important international crisis or conference from 1919 to 1933.
    SR, 37:9:326-27; Choice, 13(1976):263.

1301.   Kalvoda, Josef. **Czechoslovakia's Role in Soviet Strategy.** Washington, DC: University Press of America, 1978. x, 382p. $8.75 pa.
This book begins with the encounter of the Czecho-Slovak Legion with the Bolsheviks in Russia in 1918 and ends with the events revolving around the "Prague Spring" in 1968, including the description and analysis of the manifold activities of Czechoslovak nationals and the Prague-trained professional revolutionaries in Latin America and other countries. The study also includes details about Beneš's role in the process of Communist seizure of power in east-central Europe.
    NP, 7:2:240; AHR, 84:1:211.

1302.   Nowak, Chester Michael, comp. **Czechoslovak-Polish Relations, 1918-1939: A Selected and Annotated Bibliography.** Stanford, CA: Hoover Institution Press, 1976. xii, 219p. $12.95. (Hoover Institution Bibliographical Series, 55.)
This work contains 869 citations to bibliographies and published primary and secondary sources. Literature up to 1972 is included. All items are annotated and use of the book is facilitated by cross-references and an author index.

1303.   Smelser, Ronald M. **The Sudeten Problem, 1933-1938: Volkstumspolitik and the Formulation of Nazi Foreign Policy.** Middletown, CT: Wesleyan University Press, 1975. x, 324p. $16.00.
Smelser concludes that it was not only Hitler's aggressive foreign policy that led to Munich; equally important were the factional rivalries among the Sudeten Germans

themselves, which helped to mold Hitler's ambitions toward Czechoslovakia. The author shows how Nazi foreign policy worked in practice.

SEER, 59:1:125-26; AHR, 81:4:1152.

1304.   Ullmann, Walter. **The United States in Prague, 1945-1948.** Boulder, CO: *East European Quarterly*, 1978. x, 205p. $12.00. Distributed by Columbia University Press, New York. (East European Monographs, 36.)

This book is based primarily on State Department archives and deals with the Prague ambassadorship of Laurence Steinhardt. The author concludes that Steinhardt may have been adequate for a conventional station, but he was hardly a counterweight for the diplomatic efforts of the USSR. The ambassador's good wishes and hopes were not enough then, nor are they enough today.

SR, 38:3:517-18; Choice, 15(1978):1422.

Economics

1305.   Teichova, Alice. **An Economic Background to Munich: International Business and Czechoslovakia, 1918-1938.** New York: Cambridge University Press, 1974. 422p. $27.50.

This book presents a study of the available foreign capital in the interwar economy of Czechoslovakia. The financial links are extended to foreign interests. Important cartels are studied and analyzed and their influence on output, prices, and foreign trade of the central and southeast European states is shown. The study is complete with numerous tables, data, and statistics.

BHR, 49(Spring 1975):130; Choice, 11(1975):1819.

1306.   Wright, William E. **Serf, Seigneur, and Sovereign: Agrarian Reform in Eighteenth-Century Bohemia.** Minneapolis, MN: University of Minnesota Press, 1966. 216p. $6.00.

The volume concerns itself with empress Maria Theresa's and emperor Joseph II's agrarian reforms in Bohemia. In 1740 most Bohemian peasants enjoyed little personal freedom, and those who held land normally did so on very precarious tenures and in return for heavy labor dues. By 1790 all Bohemian peasants were personally free, and those on crown and ecclesiastical lands held hereditary leases to their property and owed practically no labor dues. Wright describes, step by step, how this came about.

SR, 26:4:679-80; Choice, 4(1967):742.

Society, Sociology

1307.   Kansky, Karel Joseph. **Urbanization under Socialism: The Case of Czechoslovakia.** New York: Praeger Publishers, 1976. xviii, 313p. Tables. Maps. Figures. $22.50.

This study proposes a general synthesis for socialist urbanization. The emphasis is on spatial aspects of city development through a geographic and demographic approach. The volume contains a mass of housing and population data. There is detailed information on everything from the inhabitable floor space per dwelling unit to the proportion of in-commuters by city size.

SR, 37:2:327-28; SRNB, 4(March 1977):68.

1308. Krejči, Jaroslav. **Social Change and Stratification in Postwar Czechoslovakia**. New York: Columbia University Press, 1972. 207p. $11.00. (Political and Social Processes in Eastern Europe Series.)

The author clearly demonstrates that social differences do exist in socialist societies and that the citizens of these societies are willing to recognize this fact. Communist rule facilitated the growth of a small, powerful concentration of political and economic power, which had been unknown in the Czechoslovakia of the interwar period.

SR, 32:4:838; Choice, 10(1973):812.

1309. Kusin, Vladimir V. **The Intellectual Origins of the Prague Spring: The Development of Reformist Ideas in Czechoslovakia, 1956-1967**. Cambridge: Cambridge University Press, 1971. 153p. $8.95.

The Czech concept of "socialism with a human face" did not fall from the sky. It had been elaborated upon for a decade by the efforts of hundreds of writers, politicians, and economists, and widely discussed since the early 1960s in many Czechoslovak journals and newspapers. The author suggests that the reform stream was so strong that the pre-January establishment was unable to suppress it.

CSP, 15:1-2:239-40; Choice, 9(1972):121.

1310. Rodnick, David. **The Strangled Democracy: Czechoslovakia, 1948-1969**. Lubbock, TX: Caprock Press, 1970. 214p. $7.95.

The general reader will find this book highly informative and educational. It offers an analysis of the Czechoslovak society since 1948 with emphasis on its ability to resist Communist indoctrination. The author, a native of Czechoslovakia, collected material for his study during visits to his homeland in 1948 and 1969.

National Minorities

1311. Jaksch, Wenzel. **Europe's Road to Potsdam**. Translated and edited by Kurt Glaser. New York and London: Praeger Publishers, 1963. xxiv, 468p.

This work by the leader of the Sudeten German Social Democratic party takes a long-range view of the history of Central Europe—an area of intermingled nationalities. Analyzing Czechoslovak government policies with respect to national minorities, the author shows how the road to Munich was followed by the road to Potsdam.

LJ, 88(1963):4369.

1312. Janics, Kalman. **Czechoslovak Policy and the Hungarian Minority, 1945-1948**. Introduction by Gyula Illyes. English version adapted from the Hungarian by Stephen Borsody. New York: Social Science Monographs. Distributed by Columbia University Press, 1982. 240p. $25.00.

This is a translation of a work written by a Hungarian medical doctor and sociologist living in retirement in one of Slovakia's still predominantly Hungarian regions. He writes from the Hungarian minority point of view about the treatment accorded the group during the years 1945-48.

Choice, 20(1983):753.

1313.   The Jews of Czechoslovakia: Historical Studies and Surveys. 2 vols.
        The Jewish Publication Society of America, Philadelphia. New York:
        Society for the History of Czechoslovak Jews. Vol. 1, 1968. xxiii, 583p.;
        Vol. 2, 1971. xxii, 707p.
Volume 1 offers essays dealing with the history of the Jews in the Czech historical
lands, Slovakia and Ruthenia before and after the establishment of the Czechoslovak state, their legal position, organizational life, religion, welfare, education, art,
and emigration. The articles in volume 2 are devoted to past leaders of the Jewish
movement in Czechoslovakia, Zionism, religious life and organization, the
economy, literature, the press, publishing houses, and music of Jews in
Czechoslovakia.

1314.   Magocsi, Paul Robert. The Shaping of a National Identity: Subcarpathian
        Rus', 1848-1948. Cambridge, MA: Harvard University Press, 1978. 640p.
        $25.00.
The theme of the book is that Subcarpathian Rusyns failed to develop into an
independent nationality because their intelligentsia suffered from a sense of
inferiority vis-à-vis other closely related nationalities. The study contributes to the
understanding of the national development of people who for centuries have lived
under foreign domination.
        NP, 7:2:221-22; AHR, 84:2:510; Choice, 15(1979):1713.

1315.   Muneles, Otto. Bibliographical Study of Jewish Prague: The Jewish
        Museum of Prague. Prague: Orbis, 1952. 562p.
This bibliography surveys principally the holdings of the Jewish Library of Prague.
The work discusses a variety of publications in many languages published over the
past four centuries on the history of the Jewish community in that city.

1316.   Wiskemann, Elizabeth. Czechs and Germans: A Study of the Struggle in
        the Historic Provinces of Bohemia and Moravia. London and New York:
        Oxford University Press, 1938; 2d ed., 1967. viii, 299p. Maps.
This is a study of the 1919 settlement concerning Czechoslovakia and the ensuing
problems and conflicts between the Czechs and Germans living in the historic
provinces (Bohemia, Moravia, and Austrian Silesia). It presents a historical background for the establishment of the Czechoslovak republic and the cultural developments in the two nations in the heart of Europe.

Language and Literature

1317.   Czech and Slovak Short Stories. Selected, translated, and with an intro-
        duction by Jeanne W. Nemcova. London: Oxford University Press, 1967.
        296p. $3.50.
This well-selected anthology presents more new stories than one would probably
expect; nearly half the narratives chosen are recent ones.

1318.   French, Alfred, comp. Anthology of Czech Poetry. Introduction by
        René Wellek. Ann Arbor, MI: Department of Slavic Languages and Litera-
        tures of the University of Michigan, and Czechoslovak Society of Arts and
        Sciences in America, 1973. 372p. $4.50 pa. (Michigan Slavic Translations,
        no. 2.)

This anthology of Czech poetry covers the six centuries between the emergence of poetry in the Czech language in the early fourteenth century and the foundation of the Czechoslovak republic in 1918. This being a bilingual anthology, the Czech prototypes are printed beside the English translations, which are the work of a whole team of translators.

SR, 30:4:915-16.

1319.   Kirschbaum, J. M. **Slovak Language and Literature:** Essays. Edited by J. B. Rudnyckyj. Winnipeg and Cleveland, OH: University of Manitoba, Department of Slavic Studies, 1975. xvi, 336p. Plates. (Readings in Slavic Literatures, 12.)

This book serves two very useful and important purposes (aside from the fact that it is the largest compilation on Slovak literature available in English): it emphasizes the fact that, in the course of their development, Slovak language, literature, and culture were much more independent of Czech influences than many Westerners, including Czechs, have been wont to think; and it emphasizes the importance of standard Slovak.

SR, 36:1:160-61.

1320.   Konus, Jozef J. **Slovak-English Phraseological Dictionary**. Passaic, NJ: Slovak Catholic Sokol, 1969. 1664p.

This is not only a very comprehensive Slovak-English dictionary, it also includes thousands of the most common Slovak phrases and expressions, synthesis, as well as the newest political, social, and scientific terminology.

1321.   Novak, Arne. **Czech Literature**. Translated from the Czech by Peter Kussi. Edited and with a supplement by William E. Harkins. Ann Arbor, MI: Michigan Slavic Publications, 1976. x, 375p. $8.00.

Although Czech is the oldest of Slavic literatures, few works have received recognition outside Czechoslovakia, and those that have been noticed are recognized through the strength of their ideas, not artistic qualities.

SR, 36:4:723-24; WLT, 51(Spring 1977):300.

1322.   Poldauf, Ivan. **Anglicko-Český a česko anglický Slovník** (English-Czech and Czech-English Dictionary). Prague: Státni Pedagogické Nakl., 1971. 1223p.

This bilateral dictionary, with over thirty thousand words in each part, is useful for general translations. Special attention is paid to English and American colloquial phrases, terms, and expressions.

1323.   Selver, Paul, comp. and trans. **An Anthology of Czechoslovak Literature**. New York: Kraus Reprint, 1969 (1929). 301p. $12.00.

This representative anthology of Czechoslovak literature offers insight into the development of Czech and, to a lesser degree, Slovak literature.

1324.   Šimko, Ján. **Anglicko-slovenský slovník** (English-Slovak Dictionary). Bratislava: Slovenské Pedagogicke Nakl., 1968. 1443p.

The dictionary contains over seventy-five thousand words of British and American modern lexicography and can be used by translators and also for educational purposes.

1325. Trensky, Paul I. **Czech Drama since World War II.** Introduction by William
E. Harkins. White Plains, NY: M. E. Sharpe, 1978. xii, 250p. $20.00.
(Columbia Slavic Studies.)

This book contains the most comprehensive treatment of the subject and is a work
that will be of great value to anyone interested in modern drama. It is a vivid and
inspired account of one of the most captivating epochs (1960s) in the history of
the Czech stage.

SR, 39:1:167-68; LJ, 104(1979):418; Choice, 16(1979):231.

HUNGARY

Reference Works

1326.   Bako, Elemer. **Guides to Hungarian Studies**. 2 vols. Stanford, CA: Hoover
Institution Press, 1973. Vol. 1.: 636p.; Vol. 2: 639-1218pp. $35.00 set.
This large publication has been prepared as a source of information on Hungarian
history, society, culture, and economics. It lists books, journals, scholarly and
popular articles, reviews, reports, maps, and music—all published before 1965.
NP, 2:2:88-90.

1327.   Erdei, Ferenc, ed. **Information Hungary**. Oxford, England: Pergamon
Press, 1968. 1,144p. £12.10. (Countries of the World Information Series,
vol. 2.)
The contributors to this volume are all prominent Hungarian scholars, literati,
and public officials. Eleven major sections cover such topics as the country's
geography, history, governmental apparatus, economy, health education, science,
literature, the fine arts, and international activities. It contains maps and beautiful
illustrations of Hungarian paintings and folk art. Much of the interpretation reflects
official viewpoints.
SR, 29:2:362.

1328.   Tezla, Albert. **Hungarian Authors: A Bibliographical Handbook**. Cambridge, MA: Harvard University Press; Belknap Press, 1970. 792p. $25.00.
In this handbook emphasis is on individual authors and secondary studies that deal
specifically with them. It is a massive work containing 4,646 entries for 1,962
authors, from the beginning of Hungarian literature to today.
SR, 31:1:236-37; LQ, 41(1971):184; Choice, 7(1971):1496.

1329.   Tezla, Albert. **An Introductory Bibliography to the Study of Hungarian
Literature**. Cambridge, MA: Harvard University Press, 1964; London:
Oxford University Press, 1965. 290p.
Although this bibliography of 1,295 primary and secondary sources of Hungarian
literature is designed for beginning students and researchers in the United States, it
also serves as a most useful basic reference book on literature outside Hungary,
because each item includes information on the location of copies of the work in
major U.S. libraries.
SEER, 44:103:501.

Geography

1330.   Enyedi, György. **Hungary: An Economic Geography**. Translated by Elek
          Helvei. Revised and edited by Mary Völgyes. Boulder, CO: Westview
          Press, 1976. xi, 289p. $22.75.
This is the first economic geography of Hungary written by a Hungarian author for
English readers abroad. Innovative in structure as well as in topics, the book presents new material and ideas culled from recent geographic literature in Hungarian.
          CSP, 19:3:396-98; GJ, 143(Jul. 1977):297; Choice, 14(1977):424.

1331.   Pecsi, Marton, and Sarfalvi, Bela. **The Geography of Hungary**. London:
          Collet's, 1964. 299p. Maps. Photographs.
This volume discusses such topics as the evolution and present aspect of the relief,
mineral resources, climate, soils, population and settlement, industry, agriculture,
and forestry. Most valuable is the excellent regional discussion called "Landscape
Units of Hungary." It also presents changes in the demographic and economic
development of Hungary.
          EEQ, 1:4:401-3; GJ, 131(March 1965):106.

History

1332.   Barany, George. **Stephen Széchenyi and the Awakening of Hungarian
          Nationalism, 1791-1841**. Princeton, NJ: Princeton University Press, 1968.
          497p. $15.00.
Széchenyi was a rich aristocrat and cosmopolitan who remained unswervingly loyal
to the Habsburg dynasty, a man who till the age of thirty hardly knew Hungarian
and was scarcely familiar with his "fatherland." The book is more than a biography
of an outstanding person, for Széchenyi is skillfully placed within his age. Barany
finds that his subject's character and ability coincided with the needs of an age ripe
for reform, and he expertly interweaves the other figures and problems of the first
part of the Hungarian "Reform Age" with Széchenyi's activities and concerns.
          SR, 33:3:683-84; AHR, 75:2:543; LJ, 94(1969):1628.

1333.   Deak, Istvan. **The Lawful Revolution: Louis Kossuth and the Hungarians,
          1848-1949**. New York: Columbia University Press, 1979. xxi, 415p.
          $16.95.
The author focuses on the revolutionary leadership of the Hungarian nobility.
This nobility was unrivaled by other social classes to a greater degree than any
other in Europe. Deak marshals evidence to show Kossuth and the nobility as
stable and centrist in their ideology.
          NP, 9:2:252-53; AHR, 85:1:427; HRNB, 8(Nov. 1979):41.

1334.   Ignotus, Paul. **Hungary**. New York: Praeger Publishers, 1972. 333p.
          $11.50. (Nations of the Modern World Series.)
Although not a historical survey in the traditional sense, this is a book that should
be read by a broad readership. The author has produced a work that is enlightening
and refreshing. He is at his best when dealing with the impact of literature and the
literati on Hungarian history.
          SR, 33:3:575-76; JMH, 45:1:94.

1335.　Lacko, M. **Arrow-Cross Men, National Socialists: 1935-1944.** Budapest: Akadémiai Kiadó, 1969. 112p. $6.00.

The author, a Marxist, freely admits that the Arrow-Cross had a wide base, even among workers, and that at one point the Arrow-Cross miners almost brought the Hungarian economy to a standstill while vainly hoping for a German invasion of their country. The book swarms with Marxist statements on the collective behavior of various social groups.

　　　　SR, 30:1:185.

1336.　Lasky, Melvin J., ed. **The Hungarian Revolution: The Story of the October Uprising as Recorded in the Documents, Dispatches, Eye-Witness Accounts, and World-Wide Reactions.** New York: Praeger Publishers, 1957. 318p. $5.00.

This documentation of the Hungarian revolt is a successful attempt to "catch history on its wings." The collection is prefaced by a brilliant essay, "Hungary 1945-1956," by H. Seton-Watson. It shows a small nation, crushed by the East, and abandoned by the West, in its heroic struggle for freedom.

　　　　SR, 18:1:126-28.

1337.　Lomax, Bill, ed. **Eyewitness in Hungary: The Soviet Invasion of 1956.** Nottingham, England: Spokesman Books, 1980. 183p. £8.50.

This is a collection of accounts by people who were present in Hungary during the 1956 uprising—all were Communists and all were greatly shaken by the events they witnessed but nevertheless remained "committed communists or socialists."

1338.　Macartney, C. A. **Hungary: A Short History.** Chicago: Aldine Publishing Co., 1962. 262p. $4.50.

This brief survey succeeds admirably in recounting all that is relevant in the long history of Hungary: from Arpad, who led the Hungarians westward, to Janos Kadar, who led them, after their latest heroic bid for freedom in 1956, back to their prison of the East. This work is suitable for the lay reader.

1339.　Molnar, Miklos. **Budapest 1956: A History of the Hungarian Revolution.** Translated by Jennetta Ford. London: George Allen & Unwin, 1968. 303p. £4.95.

Molnar's study establishes the complete interdependence of events in the people's democracies and their dependence on the will of the USSR. The logic of the Hungarian revolution and the rhythm of its development are part of an interlinked chain of events ranging from the ferment in the Soviet Union after Stalin's death to that in other East European countries, including Hungary.

　　　　SR, 32:4:842.

1340.　Pastor, Peter. **Hungary between Wilson and Lenin: The Hungarian Revolution of 1918-1919 and the Big Three.** Boulder, CO: *East European Quarterly*, 1976. viii, 191p. $13.00. Distributed by Columbia University Press, New York. (East European Monographs, no. 20.)

Focusing on the relationship between victors and vanquished, this study tells of Hungary's attempt to evade the territorial consequences of a punitive peace during the five-odd months between the dissolution of the Habsburg Empire and the coming to power of Bela Kun. Magyar leaders of this period emerge as naive visionaries, who were out of touch with the aspirations of their national minorities and with the mood of the victorious Allies.

SR, 36:3:523-24; AHR, 82:4:1020; Choice, 14(1977):589.

1341. Sinor, Denis. **History of Hungary**. New York: Praeger Publishers, 1959. 310p. $6.00.

This is chiefly a political history of Hungary. Although highly condensed, the book reads well. The interpretations are stimulating though controversial in some instances. The author presents the Hungarian point of view on many issues of the past.

SR, 20:3:531-32.

1342. Tökés, Rudolf L. **Béla Kun and the Hungarian Soviet Republic: The Origins and Role of the Communist Party of Hungary in the Revolutions of 1918-1919**. New York: Praeger; London: Pall Mall Press, 1967. 292p. $7.50. (Hoover Institution Publications.)

The author discusses Bela Kun's role in the creation of the Hungarian Soviet Republic. He traces the development of Hungarian Communism from the extreme socialists of the Hungarian labor movement, and discusses the role of the Hungarian prisoners of war who became members of the Bolshevik faction and who first established the Communist party of Hungary in Russia during October-November 1918.

SR, 27:2:323; Choice, 4(1968):1308.

1343. Vali, Ferenc A. **Rift and Revolt in Hungary: Nationalism versus Communism**. Cambridge, MA: Harvard University Press, 1961. 590p. $9.75.

This analysis of the clash between nationalism and Communism turns out to be a concise history of the political, economic, and cultural-ideological changes caused by twelve years of Soviet and Communist domination in Hungary. This is an excellent source for the study of Communism through the example of an individual East European country following World War II.

SR, 21:2:353-54.

1344. Vardy, Steven Bela. **Modern Hungarian Historiography**. Boulder, CO: *East European Quarterly*, 1976. xii, 333p. $16.50. Distributed by Columbia University Press, New York. (East European Monographs, no. 17.)

Vardy analyzes the roots of the changing outlook of Hungarian historians in the vicissitudes of Hungarian society and in the shifting currents of European thought, pointing out the political implications of the position taken by Hungary's interwar historians.

SR, 37:1:155-56; AHR, 82:2:686; Choice, 13(1977):1645.

1345. Volgyes, Ivan, ed. **Hungary in Revolution, 1918-19: Nine Essays**. Lincoln, NE: University of Nebraska Press, 1971. 219p. $12.50.

Nine recognized experts express themselves on various aspects of the 1918-19 events in Hungary. The first three essays set the stage for the establishment of the

Hungarian Soviet Republic. Other contributors cover a great variety of topics dealing with the internal policies, nationality problem, and foreign relations.
SR, 32:2:645-46; Choice, 8(1972):1504.

1346. Zinner, Paul E. **Revolution in Hungary**. New York and London: Columbia University Press, 1962. 380p. $6.00.
This is an excellent treatment of the Hungarian thaw and revolution, replete with psychological and sociological insights. It should be read by all who are interested in the workings of Communism. The author has fully utilized the ten thousand pages of Columbia University's Hungarian refugee interview project material.
SR, 22:1:165-66; LJ, 87(1962):2547.

Government and Politics

1347. Kovrig, Bennett. **The Hungarian People's Republic**. Baltimore, MD: Johns Hopkins University Press, 1970. 206p. $7.50. (Integration and Community Building in Eastern Europe.)
Much of the book relies on evidence published in the West. In examining short-comings of the Hungarian People's Republic, Kovrig fails to give Hungary full credit for its economic achievements.
EEQ, 5:3:424-25; ASR, 36(1971):949.

1348. Shawcross, William. **Crime and Compromise: Janos Kadar and the Politics of Hungary since Revolution**. New York: Dutton, 1974. 311p. $10.00.
This is an account of the political career and private life of Janos Kadar, who emerged after 1956 "as a pragmatic politician who tries to win the cooperation of his countrymen, not through fear and terror, but by granting concessions and by raising the standard of living." This is the first coherent and well-documented Kadar biography, which should be of interest to libraries and to the general public.
TLS, Nov. 29, 1974:1348.

Communism, Communist Party

1349. Kovrig, Bennett. **Communism in Hungary: From Kun to Kadár**. Stanford, CA: Hoover Institution Press, 1979. xviii, 525p. $10.95. (Histories of Ruling Communist Parties, Hoover Institution Publication, no. 211.)
Kovrig takes the chronological approach and deals with Hungarian history from 1919 to the present. In the most interesting part of the book the author deals with the contemporary development of Kadar's policies and his attempts to modernize both Hungary and the apparatus necessary to rule the country.
AHR, 85:2:677-78; Choice 17(1980):283.

1350. Molnar, Miklos. **A Short History of the Hungarian Communist Party**. Boulder, CO: Westview Press; Folkenstone, England: Wm. Dawson & Sons, 1978. 168p. $16.50.
Molnar deals with the history of the Hungarian Communist party and its natural interrelatedness with Hungarian social history. Only a few months after it had come into being (November 1918), the Party assumed power over Hungarian society (March 1919), bringing an end to the parliamentary regime in the Western sense.

During the interwar period, the Party was insignificant, with membership ranging from a few dozen workers to several hundred, and it could in no way be considered a workers' party.

SEER, 58:3:459-60; HRNB, 7(Oct. 1978):6; Choice, 15(1978):1279.

Diplomacy, Foreign Relations

1351.   Dreisziger, Nador A. F. **Hungary's Way to World War II.** Astor Park, FL: Danubian Press, 1968. 239p. $5.00. (Problems Behind the Iron Curtain Series, no. 5.)

This history of Hungarian foreign policy is based on documentary collections recently published in Hungary. The author does away with many Western myths, such as the quasi-dictatorial rule of Admiral Horthy and Hungary's enthusiasm for armed collaboration with Hitler's Germany. He makes amply clear the dual aim of post-1933 Hungarian foreign policy: trying to resist the expansion of German influence and, at the same time, seeking to revise Hungary's frontiers.

AHA, 75:2:545.

1352.   Fenyo, Mario D. **Hitler, Horthy, and Hungary: German-Hungarian Relations, 1941-44.** New Haven, CT: Yale University Press, 1972. 279p. $10.00. (Yale Russian and East European Studies, no. 11.)

Fenyo deals with German-Hungarian relations between Hungary's entry into World War II and the fall of the Horthy regime in October 1944. The Hungarian internal scene is at the heart of the study: the politics of the Hungarian Nazi-sympathizers and those who opposed them.

EEQ, 8:2:242-44; Choice, 10(1973):517.

1353.   Juhasz, Gyula. **Hungarian Foreign Policy, 1919-1945.** Translated by Sandor Simon. Budapest: Akadémiai Kiadó, 1979. 356p. $29.00.

The author recognizes that not only internal factors but also external factors helped shape Hungarian foreign policy. He admits that the unwise peace settlement of 1919-20 created universal resentment in Hungary, and he acknowledges that the forces of the political left were very weak in interwar Hungary.

SR, 40:1:139.

1354.   Kertesz, Stephen D. **Diplomacy in a Whirlpool: Hungary between Nazi Germany and Soviet Russia.** Notre Dame, IN: University of Notre Dame Press, 1953. 273p. $4.75.

This very valuable volume treats the diplomatic history of Hungary during the last years of the Horthy regime and the turbulent time following World War II. As a former Hungarian diplomat, the author relates some of his personal experiences during that time.

LJ, 92(1967):2789.

1355.   Radvanyi, Janos. **Hungary and the Superpowers: The 1956 Revolution and Realpolitik.** Foreword by Zbigniew Brzezinski. Stanford, CA: Hoover Institution Press, 1972. 197p. $5.95.

The author was a member of the Hungarian foreign service for two decades and was Hungarian chargé d'affaires in Washington from 1962 to 1967. He was an inside observer of, or an active participant in, most events discussed in the volume. This story makes interesting reading for those who want to learn about the linkage between Communist party organs and the implementation of foreign policy.

SR, 32:3:647-48; Choice, 9(1972):1344.

1356. Sakmyster, Thomas L. **Hungary, the Great Powers and the Danubian Crisis 1936-1939.** Athens: University of Georgia Press, 1980. 284p. $20.00.

In this examination of interwar Hungarian politics the country emerges as being dominated by a conservative element that virtually went unchallenged. This was particularly true in the field of foreign policy, where it was generally agreed that caution, rather than reckless adventurism, would best serve Hungary's interest. This caution was cldearly shown in Hungary's behavior during the Munich crisis.

CSP, 23:1:111-12; HRNB, 9(Nov. 1980):54.

Economics

1357. Berend, Ivan T., and Ranki, Gyorgy. **Hungary: A Century of Economic Development.** Translated by Richard Allan. New York: Barnes & Noble; Newton Abbot, England: David & Charles, 1974. 263p. $18.50.

The authors conclude that the industrialization of the country was the logical outcome of an inevitable process, periodically marked by state intervention, which culminated in the socialist transformation of Hungary. The foundations for the industrialization of the country center around the years of the *Ausgleich.* At this time foreign banks and financial groups invested heavily in Hungary, providing the necessary capital accumulation for an economic takeoff.

EEQ, 9:2:247-49; Choice, 11(1974):1673.

1358. Fischer, Lewis A., and Uren, Philip E. **The New Hungarian Agriculture.** Montreal: McGill-Queen's University Press, 1974. 138p. $10.00.

The authors of this stimulating book have attempted to "examine the evolution of the Hungarian countryside since the advent of socialism," to trace "the main features of a socialist rural landscape and to draw some conclusions about its structure and functions." They have achieved their objective with admirable clarity. Much of the work is based on field studies carried out between 1966 and 1971 in Hungary.

CSP, 16:4:657-60; AAPSS-A, 420(July 1975):227.

1359. Held, Joseph, ed. **The Modernization of Agriculture: Rural Transformation in Hungary, 1848-1975.** Boulder, CO: *East European Quarterly,* 1980. 400p. $19.50. Distributed by Columbia University Press, New York. (East European Monographs, no. 67.)

This study analyzes the difficult process of rural modernization in Hungary, 1848-1975. It identifies the impediments to modernization, both cultural and technological, describes the process itself, and addresses the nature of the change that took place in the peasantry as a result.

SRNB, 8(Jan. 1981):38.

National Minorities

1360.   Braham, Randolph L., ed. **The Destruction of Hungarian Jewry: A Documentary Account.** 2 vols. New York: Pro Arte, for the World Federation of Hungarian Jews, 1963. Vol. 1: 416p.; Vol. 2: 555p.
This extensive documentary collection reproduces exact copies of German and other records dealing with the Jewish Holocaust. The first volume deals with the period from September 1940 through March 19, 1944, when the Germans officially occupied Hungary, while the second volume covers the period through April 4, 1945. It was during this latter period that most Hungarian Jews lost their lives.

1361.   Braham, Randolph L., ed. **Hungarian-Jewish Studies.** 2 vols. New York: World Federation of Hungarian Jews, 1966. 346p.; 300p. $60.00 set.
This collection of studies by experts on Hungary deals with the history of the Jews in Hungary, their extermination during the last years of World War II, and the present situation of the survivors.

1362.   Braham, Randolph L. **The Politics of Genocide: The Holocaust in Hungary.** 2 vols. New York: Columbia University Press, 1981. Vol. 1: xiii, 594p.; Vol. 2: xii, 674p. Figures. Maps. Photographs. $60.00 set.
At the time of the German occupation of Hungary on March 19, 1944, 825,000 Jews lived there. Within four months a relatively small band of Germans manipulated the Hungarian police and state administration into shipping almost half a million Jews to Auschwitz, where most were promptly killed. A quarter of a million Budapest Jews were largely saved from deportation by Regent Horthy early in July 1944. By the end of the war, 569,507 Hungarian Jews were gone.
      JMH, 54:3:631; JSS, 43(Summer 1981):336.

1363.   Lambert, Gilles. **Operation Hazalah.** Translated by Robert Bullen and Rosette Letellier. Indianapolis and New York: Bobbs-Merrill Co., 1974. xi, 235p. $6.95.
This book relates the story of the courageous and desperate Jewish resistance movement, organized in Budapest, Hungary, in 1944 by young Zionists, which helped save tens of thousands of Jewish lives in the face of the awesome and efficient death machine commanded by Adolf Eichmann. With forged documents, they released condemned Jews from prison or from trains heading for death camps, and guided escapees over borders.
      SR, 35:1:163-64.

1364.   Moskovits, Aron. **Jewish Education in Hungary (1848-1948).** New York: Block Publishing Company, n.d. 351p.
This survey traces the continual struggle to maintain a separate Jewish educational system and to keep Jewish religious and cultural traditions alive versus those who saw these institutions as barriers to a greater Jewish role in Magyar life. The author concludes that it was the divisions between the Orthodox and other Jewish groups that destroyed Hungarian Jewry's educational system.

1365.   Paikert, G. C. **The Danube Swabians: German Populations in Hungary,
         Rumania and Yugoslavia and Hitler's Impact on Their Patterns**. The
         Hague, The Netherlands: Martinus Nijhoff, 1967. 324p. (Studies in Social
         Life, X, edited by Günther Beyer.)
The author makes a point of stating that the past of the Swabians in the Danube
basin had been constructive and that only the decade from 1935 saw them making
two mistakes: "a negative position toward the state in which they lived; and an
enthusiastic, unscrupulous support of Nazism."

1366.   Paikert, G. C. **The German Exodus: A Selective Study on the Post-World-
         War-II Expulsion of German Populations and Its Effects**. The Hague, The
         Netherlands: Martinus Nijhoff, 1962. 97p. (Publications of the Research
         Group for European Problems, XII.)
This is a study of the motives for and circumstances of the expulsion of Germans
from east-central Europe, including Hungary.

1367.   Schieder, Theodor, ed. **The Fate of Germans in Hungary: A Selection
         and Translation**. Bonn: Federal Ministry for Expellees, Refugees and War
         Victims, 1961. 214p.
Detailed consideration is given to the expulsion and the fate of Germans in
Hungary. Nineteen eyewitness accounts and recollections illustrate the sufferings
of Hungarian Germans or the changes in their lives toward and after the end of
World War II.

1368.   Spira, Thomas. **German-Hungarian Relations and the Swabian Problem:
         From Károlyi to Gömbös 1919-1926**. Boulder, CO: *East European
         Quarterly*, 1977. 382p. $18.50. Distributed by Columbia University Press,
         New York. (East European Monographs, no. 25.)
The author has given more in this book than the title indicates since the three
introductory chapters cover "Hungary's Minority Policy before World War I,"
"Minorities 'Conciliated'—Education and Cultural Policy 1918-1919," and "The
Early Horthy Era: Swabians, Austrians and Germans—the Seeds of a Dilemma
(1919-1922)." The remaining chapters cover historical surveys of the difficulties
between the Magyars and the Swabians, the latter being the largest and most vocal
minority remaining in Trianon Hungary.
         NP, 6:1:89-90; AHR, 84:4:1093.

Language and Literature

1369.   Leader, Ninon A. M. **Hungarian Classical Ballads and Their Folklore**.
         Cambridge: Cambridge University Press, 1967. 367p. $12.50.
The excellent introduction provides a historical survey of Hungarian ballad
research, describes the chief collections, outlines regions of collections, and classifies Hungarian ballads into old and new. The author provides a description of the
main Hungarian classical ballads in the several versions, examines the characteristics,
recurrent themes, motifs, and underlying folk beliefs of Hungarian classical ballads,
and relates them to their international parallels.
         SR, 30:1:215-16; Choice, 4(1968):1522.

1370. Orszagh, Laszlo. **Magyar-Angol Szótár** (Hungarian-English Dictionary). 2 vols. 3d ed. Vol. 1: A-K, 1196p.; vol. 2: L-Z, 2159p. Budapest: Adakémiai Kiadó, 1969.
The dictionary comprises over eighty thousand words, terms, idiomatic phrases, and pronouncements. This is the most useful tool for translators in all subject matters.

1371. Reményi, Joseph. **Hungarian Writers and Literature: Modern Novelists, Critics, and Poets.** Edited with an introduction by August J. Molnar. New Brunswick, NJ: Rutgers University Press, 1964. 512p. $12.00.
The book contains two historical surveys, followed by essays on fifteen writers and poets of the nineteenth century. In the third part, twenty-seven novelists, poets, and critics of the twentieth century are presented, of whom seven are contemporary writers. Finally, three essays comment on Hungarian humor, on the tragic sense, and on English translations.
SR, 24:1:155-56; Choice, 1(1965):562.

1372. Riedl, Frederick. **A History of Hungarian Literature.** London: William Heinemann, 1906; Detroit: Gale Research, 1968. 293p. $14.50.
Riedl (1856-1921) was a well-known Hungarian literary historian. His approach is overwhelmingly nationalistic. "Hungarian literature," he writes, "is, in fact, the record of Hungarian patriotism. The ideas of nation, fatherland, and race are much more pronounced in it than in other literatures."
SR, 30:1:216-17.

1373. Vajda, Miklos, ed. and intro. **Modern Hungarian Poetry.** Foreword by William J. Smith. New York and Budapest: Columbia University Press and Corvina Press, 1977. xxxv, 289p. + 12pp. photographs. $11.95.
Vajda and his collaborators succeed in presenting a wide and attractive picture of contemporary Hungarian poetry or, at least, parts of it. The translators render the poems into vivid, colorful, and poetic English.
SR, 37:2:358-59; Choice, 14(1978):1506.

POLAND

Reference Works

1374.   Benes, Vaclav L., and Pounds, Norman J. G. **Poland**. New York: Praeger Publishers, 1970. 416p.
This handbook-study contains information on "History," "Land and the Resources," "The Polish Republic" (of interwar Poland), and "The People's Republic." This information is supplemented by maps and illustrations, and helpful appendixes, including one on place-name variations.
BL, 67(1971):681; TLS, (April 16, 1971):448.

1375.   Bromke, Adam, and Strong, John W., eds. **Gierek's Poland**. New York: Praeger Publishers, 1973. 220p.
This volume is unique in that of the seventeen contributors, eight are active in Polish society and politics. With the exception of military affairs, almost all major topics—domestic, politics, economic reform, agriculture, theater, religion, foreign policy—are touched upon.
Choice, 11(1974):160.

1376.   Davies, Norman, comp. **Poland, Past and Present: A Select Bibliography of Works in English**. Newton, MA: Oriental Research Partners, 1977. xxi, 185p. $13.00.
This bibliography contains almost eighteen hundred items dealing with all aspects of Polish history, culture, politics, ethnic groups (Jews), religion, immigration, architecture, law, economy, international relations, and East-West trade. It also contains a glossary of Polish historical terms, place names, and periodicals.
CSP, 19:4:548; SR, 38:3:702-3.

1377.   Hoskins, Janina W., comp. **Polish Books in English, 1945-1971**. Washington, DC: Government Printing Office, 1974. 163p.
This bibliography lists more than a thousand English-language books and pamphlets published in Poland or translated into English outside Poland from 1945 to 1971. It covers the social sciences and the humanities.

History

1378.   Ciechanowski, Jan M. **The Warsaw Rising of 1944**. New York: Cambridge
University Press, 1974. 332p. $19.50.
This revised version of the author's Polish edition (1971) is richly informative.
The author is preoccupied with why the Polish underground Home Army took it
upon itself to liberate Warsaw shortly before the Russians entered the capital, even
though it was so lacking in troops and ammunition. He examines the military background of the rising and traces Polish politics, strategy, and diplomacy during the
whole of World War II. The last three chapters discuss in detail insurrectionary
operations.
SR, 34:2:416-17; CH, 69(1975):142.

1379.   Cieplak, Tadeusz N., ed. **Poland since 1956**. New York: Twayne Publishers, 1972. 482p. $9.00.
The book is significant for several reasons, one of which is its correction of certain
preconceptions. Cieplak's collection of essays and readings, prefaced by his own
brief introductions to each section, helps to explain that "monumental" event of
1956.
Choice, 9(1973):1504.

1380.   Davies, Norman. **White Eagle, Red Star: The Polish-Soviet War, 1919-20**.
New York: St. Martin's Press, 1972. 318p. $10.00.
One of the main contributions of the monograph is the final destruction of the
myth that General Weygand had anything to do with the Battle of Warsaw. Weygand repeatedly and explicitly denied that he had contributed to the Polish victory.
Another merit of the book is that it views the war of 1920 not as an isolated and
exotic event but as part of a wider scene of action and as a crucial event which
determined the fate of Eastern Europe for some twenty years.
SR, 33:3:566; Choice, 10(1973):342.

1381.   Dziewanowski, M. K. **Poland in the Twentieth Century**. New York:
Columbia University Press, 1977. xvi, 309p. + 16pp. photographs. $14.95.
This survey of the modern history of Poland is written in a lively style and language
and is aimed at the student and general reader. It offers a balanced treatment of
politics, the economy, culture, education, and social issues. The author displays
a preference for empirical interpretation of history.
SR, 38:2:332-33; AHR, 83:1:225; Choice, 14(1977):1415.

1382.   Fitzgibbon, Louis. **Katyn**. Introduction by Constantine Fitzgibbon.
New York: Charles Scribner's Sons, 1971. 285p. $10.00.
This book on an already well-known subject consists mostly of extensive quota-
tions from the testimonies of the Polish prisoners of war and other documents.
It also contains twenty pages of most gruesome photographs and a list of the 4,143
victims identified at Katyn.
AHR, 77:5:1486-87; Choice, 8(1972):1501.

1383.   Gross, Jan Tomasz. **Polish Society under German Occupation: The Generalgouvernement, 1939-1944**. Princeton, NJ: Princeton University Press, 1979. xviii, 343p. $20.00.
This book represents an attempt at sociological synthesis of numerous works on German occupation of Poland.
  NP, 9:1:153-56; AHR, 85:1:168; Choice, 16(1979):1357.

1384.   Halecki, Oscar. **A History of Poland**. London: Dent, 1942. 359p. 2d enlarged ed., New York: Roy, 1955. 373p.
This one-volume history of Poland is recommended as the best survey presentation. The second edition was updated to 1955.

1385.   Hiscocks, Richard. **Poland: Bridge for the Abyss?: An Interpretation of Developments in Post-War Poland**. London, New York, and Toronto: Oxford University Press, 1963. 359p. $8.00.
This notable presentation of events in Poland after World War I gives an accurate picture of Polish Communism from its beginning to its successful seizure of power with the help of the Russian Red Army in 1944-45. The book as a whole serves to illuminate Polish history following World War II.
  SR, 23:4:771-73.

1386.   Kaplan, Herbert H. **The First Partition of Poland**. New York: Columbia University Press, 1962. 215p. $5.00.
This erudite work offers an unbiased discussion of the causes of the first partition of Poland. The subject is one that has divided Polish historians for over a century: Were the partitions the result of Poland's chaotic political system, or were they the result of her neighbor's rapacity and greed? Mr. Kaplan bridges both interpretations.
  SR, 22:4:764.

1387.   Karski, Jan. **The Story of a Secret State**. Boston, MA: Houghton Mifflin, 1944. 318p.
This is a firsthand account of the Polish political and military underground movement which challenged German occupation during World War II. It is an excellent report on the nature and function of the underground movement.

1388.   Korbonski, Stefan. **Fighting Warsaw**. New York: Funk & Wagnalls, 1967.; Minerva Press, 1968. 495p. $6.00.
Korbonski, the leader of the Polish underground movement during World War II, has written this history of the German occupation of Poland.
  LJ, 93(1968):2493.

1389.   Leslie, R. F., ed. **The History of Poland since 1863**. Cambridge: Cambridge University Press, 1980; 1983. 499p. £9.95.
The advent of Solidarity in Poland is best understood in the context of the historical development of Polish society. In this updated edition the authors supply a detailed background for the proper understanding of contemporary Poland. The book provides a great deal of information, with a mass of details clearly presented.

1390.   Polonsky, Antony, and Drukier, Boleslaw, eds. **The Beginnings of Communist Rule in Poland.** Boston, MA, and London: Routledge & Kegan Paul, 1980. viii, 464p. Maps. $37.50.
This is an important collection of documents related to the period December 1943 through June 1945. These previously unknown documents were delivered by Drukier, a former official attached to the Central Committee of the PZPR (PUWP). The documents are notes he made in the course of research in secret Party archives.
        HT, 31(Jan. 1981):58.

1391.   Pounds, Norman J. G. **Poland between East and West.** New York: Van Nostrand, 1964. 132p. (Van Nostrand Searchlight Book, no. 22.)
The theme of this highly readable book is that the periods of Poland's disappearance as an independent state were due not to Poland's exposed geographic location on the north European lowland plain with open frontiers to west and east, but rather to the weakness of its internal structure, both social and political.
        SR, 24:3:554-55.

1392.   Rothschild, Joseph. **Pilsudski's Coup d'Etat.** New York, London: Cambridge University Press, 1966. 435p. $10.00.
In simple, understandable terms the author records and explains the highly complex metamorphosis of Polish political life that produced Pilsudski's coup d'etat in 1926.
        SR, 27:1:143-45; Choice, 4(1967):338.

1393.   Rozek, Edward J. **Allied Wartime Diplomacy: A Pattern in Poland.** New York: Wiley, 1958. 481p. $8.50.
This volume traces the story of Poland from the "fourth partition" in 1939, through the uneasy Stalin-Sikorski agreement of July 1941, to the rupture of relations in March 1943; the discussions at Teheran and Yalta; the Soviet sponsorship of the Lublin Committee and the tortuous efforts at a lopsided compromise between the "Lublin" and "London" Poles; and finally the period of "national unity" government.
        SR, 18:2:265-66.

1394.   Staar, Richard F. **Poland, 1944-1962: The Sovietization of a Captive People.** Baton Rouge, LA: Louisiana State University Press, 1962. 300p. $7.50.
Among the captive nations, Poland has been attracting more interest than the other countries of Eastern Europe. This book deserves the attention of readers in search of factual information on Poland.
        SR, 22:3:556.

1395.   Terry, Sara Meiklejohn. **Poland's Place in Europe: General Sikorski and the Origin of the Oder-Neisse Line, 1939-1943.** Princeton, NJ: Princeton University Press, 1982. 400p. $40.00.
The Oder-Neisse line, the boundary between Poland and Germany since 1945, has long been viewed as the product of Communist making. Challenging this view, the author shows that the idea of shifting Polish boundaries westward was originally

proposed by General Sikorski, who saw gains in the north and west as a design for a postwar Europe that included a Central European federation.

LJ, 107(1982):2338.

1396.   Wandycz, Piotr S. **The Lands of Partitioned Poland, 1795-1918.** Seattle and London: University of Washington Press, 1974. xviii, 431p. Maps. $14.95. (A History of East Central Europe, vol. 7, edited by Peter F. Sugar and Donald W. Treadgold.)

This work surveys the partitions of Poland, with discussions of social, economic, and political conditions preceding each period discussed, followed by an outline of major political and social developments. Chapters on cultural trends and achievements conclude each major era.

SR, 36:3:518-19; HRNB, 4(Nov. 1975):30; Choice, 12(1975):1358.

1397.   Zawodny, Janusz K. **Death in the Forest: The Story of the Katyn Forest Massacre.** Notre Dame, IN: University of Notre Dame Press, 1962. 235p.

This volume documents the Soviet crime committed on thousands of Polish prisoners of war in the Katyn forest near Smolensk. At least forty-five hundred bodies were found.

SR, 23:1:153-55.

1398.   Zawodny, J. K. **Nothing but Honour: The Story of the Warsaw Uprising, 1944.** Stanford, CA, and London: Hoover Institution Press and Macmillan, 1978. 328p. + 8pp. plates. $12.95. (Hoover Institution Publications, 183.)

Zawodny concentrates on a two-month tragic segment of the six-year war, the Warsaw uprising of 1944. It is a most interestingly and assiduously documented book with a shattering logic of its own. It paints a picture of Western wartime leaders that is far from flattering. The book should be read by anyone who endeavors to understand the story of World War II.

NP, 8:1:101-15; SR, 38:3:701-2; Choice, 15(1978):1273.

Government and Politics

1399.   Bromke, Adam. **Poland's Politics: Idealism vs. Realism.** Cambridge, MA: Harvard University Press, 1967. 316p. $9.95.

The traditional gap between idealism and realism in Polish politics is the subject of this book. Bromke examines the program and policies of the Communist party and other political movements in order to achieve a better understanding of contemporary Polish political developments.

JP, 30(1968):246.

1400.   Groth, Alexander J. **People's Poland: Government and Politics.** San Francisco: Chandler Publishing Co., 1972. 155p. $3.95 pa.

The main objective of this useful little book is to serve as an introduction to Poland's politics, and it contains a comprehensive survey of political, economic, and social developments in that country from the Communist takeover in 1944 to Gierek's ascendancy to power in 1970. A good balance is maintained in describing political institutions and processes.

SR, 32:2:407-8.

1401.   Morrison, James F. **The Polish People's Republic**. Baltimore, MD: Johns
         Hopkins University Press, 1968. 160p. $2.95 pa.
This short survey contributes to social scientific analysis of Communist states.
Morrison quite correctly assesses Poland's future development as being determined
equally by its foreign relations and its domestic conditions.
         PR, 15:3:91-92; ASR, 34(1969):760.

1402.   Myant, Martin. **Poland: A Crisis for Socialism**. London: Lawrence and
         Wishart, 1982. xvii, 254p. $21.00. Distributed by Humanities Press,
         Atlantic Highlands, NJ.
The recent upheavals in Poland, culminating in the establishment and then the sus-
pension of the independent trade-union movement, Solidarity, and the imposition
of martial law in December 1981, pose crucial questions about the development of
socialism in Poland. This study sets events within the overall context of modern
Polish history from 1918 to the beginnings of a socialist Poland under Gomulka in
1945.
         Choice, 20(1983):1517.

1403.   Piekalkiewicz, Jaroslaw. **Communist Local Government: A Study of
         Poland**. Athens, OH: Ohio University Press, 1975. xiv, 282p. $10.00.
This book is guided by the proposition that "an understanding of communist
politics will never be complete without an investigation of the political process at
the local level." It contains factual material on how the councils function and
sheds light on the interplay of social groups and interests.
         SR, 35:3:558-59.

1404.   Polonsky, Antony. **Politics in Independent Poland 1921-1939: The Crisis
         of Constitutional Government**. Oxford, England: Clarendon Press, 1972.
         572p. $27.50.
The study documents the unsurprising thesis that Polish democracy worked poorly
in the early 1920s, and that Pilsudski's effort at guided democracy did no better,
Pilsudski himself emerges as a tragic figure illustrating the futility of moral
approaches to politics. Without greater industrialization, fuller employment, and
the diminution of rural poverty, political activity was inevitably restricted to an
élite.
         CSP, 15:4:595-96; SR, 33:3:566-68; Choice, 9(1973):1497.

1405.   Potel, Jean-Yves. **The Promise of Solidarity**. New York: Praeger Publishers,
         1982. 256p. $29.95.
Tracing the progress of the Polish Solidarity union from before the 1980 strikes at
the Lenin shipyards in Gdansk, the author examines all the major events that led
to the union's success in organizing 95 percent of the Polish industrial working
class. He also examines the parallel organizations of small farmers, intellectuals,
students, artisans, women, and other groups that have complemented the Solidarity
movement, as well as the role of the Catholic Church and the media in the formation of the union.
         Choice, 20(1983):800.

1406. Preibisz, Joanna M., ed. **Polish Dissident Publications: An Annotated Bibliography.** New York: Praeger Publishers, 1982. 416p. $38.95.
The bibliography lists publications by dissident groups during and leading up to the confrontation between workers and the Communist regime in Poland.

1407. Raina, Peter. **Independent Social Movements in Poland.** London: LSE, 1981. 632p. £15.00.
This volume documents the development of independent, dissident movements in Poland in the three years leading up to and including the birth of Solidarity. Raina does this by bringing together the most important primary—mostly *samizdat*—materials related to the 1978-80 period. The documents chosen cover the full range of ideas and activities that produced the political ferment of the late 1970s.
SS, 35:2:266-67.

1408. Wynot, Edward D., Jr. **Polish Politics in Transition: The Camp of National Unity and the Struggle for Power 1935-1939.** Athens, GA: University of Georgia Press, 1974. 294p. $12.50.
This study examines the political problems encountered by the men who governed Poland on the eve of World War II—problems complicated by the nation's difficult transition from a traditional agrarian to a modern industrial society in post-Pilsudski Poland.
CSP, 18:2:209; SR, 34:3:626-27; Choice, 11(1975):1830.

Communism, Communist Party

1409. Bethell, Nicholas. **Gomulka: His Poland, His Communism.** New York: Holt, Rinehart & Winston, 1969. 296p. $5.95.
Bethell concentrates on Gomulka's wartime and postwar activities and on his reemergence during the Polish "October" of 1956. Gomulka's very early socialization, why and how he came to identify with Communism, are, according to the author, too sparsely documented to permit thorough investigation.
SR, 30:1:182; LJ, 95(1970):657; Choice, 6(1970):1642.

1410. Dziewanowski, M. K. **The Communist Party of Poland: An Outline of History.** 2d ed. Cambridge, MA: Harvard University Press, 1976. 419p. $20.00.
The study traces the history of the Polish socialist and Communist movements and of the respective parties, from their beginning in the nineteenth century to the events of 1974. This is the best monographic study on the Polish Communist movement.
NP, 5:2:231-35; AHR, 82:3:687.

1411. Gibney, Frank. **The Frozen Revolution: A Study in Communist Decay.** New York: Farrar-Straus-Cudahy, 1959. 264p.
This book contains exceptionally successful journalistic research on events that took place in Poland in 1956. The author explains the situation of postwar Poland that led to the riots of 1956.
SR, 19:4:606-7.

Diplomacy, Foreign Relations

1412. Budurowycz, Bohdan. **Polish-Soviet Relations, 1932-1939.** New York: Columbia University Press, 1963. 229p. $6.00.
The author's account of the years preceding the Polish war disaster leaves no doubt that its rulers were extremely shortsighted men. The book conveys an objective picture of Polish-Soviet relations in these fateful years.
SEER, 63:100:245-47.

1413. Debicki, Roman. **Foreign Policy of Poland, 1919-1939: From the Rebirth of the Polish Republic to World War II.** Foreword by Oscar Halecki. New York: Praeger Publishers, 1962. 192p. $5.50.
This is a short and effective treatment of the complexity of Poland's foreign policy in the interwar period. The author's personal experience of Polish diplomatic activity conveys a deeper understanding of the matter.
SR, 24:2:339-40.

1414. Drzewieniecki, Walter M. **The German-Polish Frontier.** Chicago: Polish Western Association of America, 1959. 166p. $3.00.
This volume presents a study of German-Polish past and contemporary relations, outlining a historical background and focusing on the post-World War II situation between these two countries.
JMH, 32:4:434.

1415. Horak, Stephan. **Poland's International Affairs, 1919-1960: A Calendar.** Bloomington, IN: Indiana University Press, 1964. 248p. $6.50. (Russian and East European Series, vol. 31.)
This collection contains a listing of almost all bilateral treaties to which Poland was a signatory between 1919 and 1960, including selected multilateral treaties and documents related to Poland in the same period.
SEEJ, 9:3:356.

1416. Kacewicz, George V. **Great Britain, the Soviet Union and the Polish Government in Exile (1939-1945).** The Hague, The Netherlands: Martinus Nijhoff, 1979. 255p. $45.80. (Studies in Contemporary History, 3.)
This book offers an account of the political, constitutional, and legal questions that arose in the transfer to and operation of the Polish government in exile and its armed forces on foreign soil, with an analysis of the politics of the Grand Alliance that led to its decline. The turmoil within the Polish government and the struggle to reach a *modus vivendi* with Moscow and London are brought to light here.
AHR, 85:2:681.

1417. Komarnicki, Titus. **Rebirth of the Polish Republic: A Study in the Diplomatic History of Europe, 1914-1940.** Melbourne, London, and Toronto: Heinemann, 1957. 776p. $10.75.
This remarkable account describes in detail the aspects of the Polish problem against the background of European diplomacy. An interested reader will greatly benefit from this study of diplomatic activity that resulted in the rebirth of the Polish state.
SR, 17:2:247-49.

1418.   Korbel, Josef. **Poland between East and West: Soviet and German Diplo-**
macy toward Poland, 1919-1933. Princeton, NJ: Princeton University
Press, 1963. 321p. $6.95.
Poland found itself between two unfriendly and strong neighbors and this study
sheds light on the diplomatic efforts by Poland during the interwar period. The
book also elaborates on the shortsightedness of Polish policy in not exploiting
the German-Russian differences.
SR, 23:4:771-73.

1419.   Kulski, W. W. **Germany and Poland: From War to Peaceful Relations.**
Syracuse, NY: Syracuse University Press, 1976. xxii, 336p. $22.50.
Kulski, a member of the Polish diplomatic corps until 1945, surveys the relations
between Poland and West Germany since World War II. Ultimately, this is a study
of the territorial changes (and their consequences) between Germany and Poland
that resulted from the war. The author traces the history of the Oder-Neisse
boundary from its diplomatic origins up through Willy Brandt's *Ostpolitik* and the
Warsaw Treaty of 1972.
CSP, 19:4:521-22; AHR, 81:4:1156.

1420.   Newman, Simon. **March 1939, the British Guarantee to Poland: A Study**
in the Continuity of British Foreign Policy. Oxford: Clarendon Press,
1976. viii, 253p. $14.25.
Newman details the British guarantee to Poland, which was issued on March 31,
1939. The study is based on the newly opened materials in the British Public
Record Office, revising previously held interpretations of the reasons and circumstances that led to the guarantee. Newman contends that, in essence, World War
II was started by Lord Halifax and others in the Foreign Office who recognized
the risk and accepted the inevitability of war.
SR, 36:4:700-1; Choice, 14(1977):436; HRNB, 5(May 1977):166.

1421.   Polonsky, Antony, ed. **The Great Powers and the Polish Question, 1941-**
45: A Documentary Study in Cold War Origins. London: The London
School of Economics and Political Science, 1976. 282p. £5.00.
This collection of documentary source materials, mostly hitherto unpublished,
should stimulate further discussion of the topic, while simultaneously resolving
many unanswered questions and illuminating many unclear issues. The picture
that emerges is one of confusion and division within the British, American, and
Polish leadership circles over the proper approach to the Polish question.
SR, 36:2:236.

1422.   Riekhoff, Harald von. **German-Polish Relations, 1918-1933.** Baltimore,
MD: Johns Hopkins University Press, 1971. 421p. $15.00.
The author skillfully relates foreign affairs to domestic developments in each
country, thereby revealing the intimate connection between international relations
and internal political considerations. He frequently points out the role played by
German-Polish affairs in Soviet, British, and French diplomatic calculations.
SR, 31:4:917-18; JMH, 45:2:348.

1423.   Wandycz, Piotr S. **Soviet-Polish Relations, 1917-1921**. Cambridge, MA: Harvard University Press, 1969. 403p. $10.00. (Russian Research Center Studies, 59.)

Basing his work on much hitherto unpublished archival material, Polish, Russian, and to some extent British, as well as extensive published sources, Wandycz has produced the most significant study of his subject to date. He demonstrates that the Soviet version of self-determination was a farce—in reality an attempt at the federation and then unification with Soviet Russia of all her borderlands, including Poland. However, while Lenin succeeded in imposing his policy on the Communist leaders of Belorussia, Lithuania, and the Ukraine, Pilsudski failed to get strong backing for his aims from the Polish parliament and public opinion, which were dominated by the National Democratic party. It is hoped that this book will be read not only by historians of Eastern Europe but by historians of Western Europe as well.

SR, 29:3:533-34; AHR, 75:4:1103.

1424.   Wandycz, Piotr S. **The United States and Poland**. Cambridge, MA: Harvard University Press, 1980. 465p. $25.00.

This is a survey and synthesis of the political relations between the United States and Poland during the past two centuries. The American image of Poland was no more realistic than the Polish image of the United States. These distortions contributed to frustration and disappointment on both sides.

PR, 26:1:120-23; AHR, 86:3:815; HRNB, 9(April 1981):128.

Economics

1425.   Feiwel, George R. **Poland's Industrialization Policy: A Current Analysis: Sources of Economic Growth and Retrogression. Industrialization and Planning under Polish Socialism**. Vol. 1. 748p. $25.00.

Problems in Polish Economic Planning: Continuity, Change, and Prospects: Industrialization and Planning under Polish Socialism. Vol. 2. 454p. $20.00. New York: Praeger Publishers, 1971.

Feiwel presents an extensive study of Polish economic development since World War II. He analyzes the following aspects: the nature of the planning economy, dynamics of a centrally planned economy, shifts in patterns of resource allocation, all three five-year plans with their implications and problems, economic reforms in perspective, financing of investments, blueprints for 1971-75, changing the system for the 1970s, and optimism in planning.

1426.   Korbonski, Andrzej. **Politics of Socialist Agriculture in Poland, 1945-1960**. New York: Columbia University Press, 1965. 330p. $7.50. (East Central European Studies of Columbia University.)

Korbonski's unique contribution to scholarship is his explanation of the collapse of collectivization in Poland. Collectivization did not increase agricultural production and served merely to alienate the peasants, who hated the entire program. The policy was introduced under pressure from Moscow during Gomulka's imprisonment. Upon his return to the leadership of the Polish Communist party, Gomulka acknowledged the failure of socialist agricultural policy and permitted the immediate dissolution of the collectives.

JMH, 37:4:522-23; AHR, 71:2:624.

1427.   Podolski, T. M. **Socialist Banking and Monetary Control: The Experience of Poland.** New York: Cambridge University Press, 1973. 392p. $28.50.
In addition to the description of bank control over enterprise behavior, Podolski also suggests that the bank has little power to control the overall level of spending and thereby the rate of inflation through the use of traditional monetary policy tools. He argues that Polish enterprises have resorted to the use of illicit trade credit, that the velocity of money in Poland is quite variable and accommodates itself to the needs of the enterprise.
SR, 33:1:161; JEL, 12(1974):927.

1428.   Zielinski, Janusz G. **Economic Reforms in Polish Industry.** New York: Oxford University Press, for Institute of Soviet and East European Studies, University of Glasgow, 1973. 333p. $21.00. (Economic Reforms in East European Industry Series.)
Zielinski's analysis quite often transcends the narrower boundaries of economic reforms in Polish industry to deal with more general aspects of Communist planned economies and their uphill struggle to evolve more rational methods of planning and management. This book is a gold mine of statistical information on various aspects of the Polish economy.
SR, 33:4:795-96; Choice, 11(1974):1001.

Society, Sociology

1429.   Kruszewski, Anthony Z. **The Oder-Neisse Boundary and Poland's Modernization: The Socioeconomic and Political Impact.** Foreword by Morton Kaplan. New York: Praeger Publishers, 1972. 246p. $16.50. (Praeger Special Studies in International Politics and Public Affairs.)
The author tells how the seven million Poles, resettled into the former German territories, molded into the new society effected by the Communist party and the Catholic church.
SR, 33:1:159-60; JP, 35(1973):259.

1430.   Lane, David, and Kolankiewicz, George, eds. **Social Groups in Polish Society.** New York: Columbia University Press, 1973. 380p. $24.75.
This book, though basically a secondary analysis of earlier Polish research findings, presents a lucid and in-depth description of the main social groups in postwar Poland. The organization of the book follows the division of Poland's population into its most important social groups: the peasantry, the working class, and the intelligentsia, composed of writers and technicians. In addition, there is a part discussing the interaction of social groups in local communities. The volume is a most welcome addition to Szczepanski's *The Polish Society*, and it offers rich material for more comparative studies of social change.
CSP, 16:3:494-97; APSR, 68(1974):1364.

1431.   Matejko, Alexander. **Social Change and Stratification in Eastern Europe: An Interpretive Analysis of Poland and Her Neighbors.** New York: Praeger Publishers, 1974. 272p. $18.50.

The book was written by a Polish sociologist who has considerable practical knowledge of the problems he discusses. This is an objective and sober study of contemporary Polish society with focus on the impact of industrialization on the Polish structure and the resulting classes: the peasantry, the blue-collar workers, the managerial establishment, and the intelligentsia.

CSP, 17:4:679-80; SR, 34:3:617-18.

1432; Pirages, Dennis Clark. **Modernization and Political-Tension Management: A Socialist Society in Perspective: Case Study of Poland.** Foreword by Jan F. Triska. New York: Praeger Publishers, 1972. 261p. $16.50.

This informative and well-documented study of some of the major political, economic, and social institutions and problems of contemporary Poland deals with significant issues such as economic development, political stability, and the current techniques of governing a socialist society.

CSP, 15:4:598-99; SR, 32:4:639-41.

1433. Szczepanski, Jan. **Polish Society.** New York: Random House, 1970. 214p. $2.25 pa. (Studies in Modern Societies.)

"The main objective of this book," explains the author in the introduction, "is to show the process of the transformation of Polish society from a capitalist society in the interwar period into a socialist society." The book achieves this task and also accomplishes much more than this—it presents an informed picture of contemporary Poland set against the background of its past.

PR, 16:3:95-100; Choice, 8(1971):262.

National Minorities

1434. Ainsztein, Reuben. **The Warsaw Ghetto Revolt.** New York: Holocaust Library, 1979. 238p. Distributed by Schocken Books.

This book contains a detailed history of the background, evolution, and outbreak of the Jewish rebellion in the Warsaw ghetto in the spring of 1943. The author also goes into some detail on the impact of the uprising on Poland's remaining Jewish population.

1435. Banas, Josef. **The Scapegoats: The Exodus of the Remnants of Polish Jewry.** Translated by Tadeusz Safar. Edited by Lionel Kochan. London: Weidenfeld & Nicolson, 1979. 221p.

This is the history of official Polish anti-Semitism since 1948, and its impact on the exodus of Poland's remaining Jewish population over the next twenty years.

Choice, 17(1980):714.

1436. Bartoszewski, Wladyslaw, and Lewin, Zofia, eds. **Righteous among Nations: How Poles Helped the Jews, 1939-1945.** London: Earlscourt Publications, 1969. 834p. $7.50.

This volume is a compilation of documents describing, often in poignant terms, the assistance rendered by Poles from various walks of life and under the most difficult circumstances of the Nazi occupation to a doomed Jewish community. The documents, mostly narratives written by the rescued, are not intended to be exhaustive, but they reflect the heroism and humanism of those Polish rescuers whose exploits fill the pages of this work.

PR, 15:1:108-10; SR, 30:1:181.

1437.   Checinski, Michael. **Poland, Communism, Nationalism, Anti-Semitism.** Translated in part by Tadeusz Szafar. New York: Karz-Cohl Publishing, 1982. viii, 289p. $22.95.

The argument of this study is that anti-Semitism in its present form in Poland, like the current Polish government, is an import from the Soviet Union. The study collates much material on a frequently misunderstood subject.

SS, 35:3:425-26; CH, 81(1982):384; Choice, 20(1983):798.

1438.   Eisenstein, Miriam. **Jewish Schools in Poland, 1919-1939.** New York: King's Crown Press, 1950. 112p.

This is a brief study of the complexity of school systems for Polish Jews during the interwar period. For the most part, Jewish secular and religious education often followed the religious and political divisions of the Polish Jewish community as a whole. Therefore, the author centers the discussion around the educational thrust of two of the Jewish community's major organizations, the Bund and the Zionists.

1439.   Heller, Celia S. **On the Edge of Destruction: Jews of Poland between the World Wars.** New York: Schocken Books, 1980. 369p. $14.95.

This is a detailed history of Poland's Jewish community during the interwar period. It deals with the Jewish religious, community, and political organizations and their relationship to the Polish state. It also discusses anti-Semitism in Poland during this period and its relationship to the degenerative status of Jews in interbellum Poland.

AHR, 83:2:486-87; SR, 37:3:694-95.

1440.   Horak, Stephan. **Poland and Her National Minorities, 1919-1939.** New York: Vantage Press, 1961. 259p. $5.00.

The author illustrates how the Polish government treated the 30 percent non-Polish population of the reemerged Polish state, including such ethnic groups as the Belorussians, Germans, Jews, Lithuanians, and Ukrainians. The government employed severe educational, economic, and colonizing measures on these minorities.

JMH, 34:4:462-63.

1441.   Johnpoll, Bernard K. **The Politics of Futility: The General Jewish Workers Bund of Poland, 1917-1943.** Ithaca, NY: Cornell University Press, 1967. xix, 298p.

This valuable study deals with the history of the Polish Jewish Bund from its inception through the Holocaust. It provides a rare glimpse of Jewish domestic politics in Poland during this period, particularly the impact of Jewish religious and cultural differences on political issues.

APSR, 62(1968):667; Choice, 5(1968):114.

1442.   Katz, Alfred. **Poland's Ghettos at War.** New York: Twayne Publishers, 1970. 175p. $6.00.

The author's aim is to present a picture of Jewish life in wartime Poland, and to give special emphasis to Jewish resistance. He describes Jewish political parties and politics in prewar Poland, the establishment of ghettos in Poland, their internal organization, the resistance they offered to the Germans, and relations between Jews and Poles during the war.

SR, 31:2:447-49.

1443. Komjathy, Anthony, and Stockwell, Rebecca. **German Minorities and the Third Reich.** New York: Holmes & Meier, 1980. 217p.
This work includes a chapter on the Germans of Poland as part of an examination of how Germans throughout eastern Europe behaved toward their countries of residence in the face of the rise of Nazism in Germany and the emergence of Hitler's ambitions in eastern Europe. In the case of the Germans of Poland, the authors contend that they were as loyal as could reasonably be expected and do not deserve the "fifth-column" label commonly applied by Polish historians.

NP, 10:2:251-52; Choice, 18(1980):576.

1444. Magocsi, Paul Robert. **Galicia: A Historical Survey and Bibliographic Guide.** Toronto: University of Toronto Press, in association with the Canadian Institute of Ukrainian Studies, 1982. 300p. Maps. $19.50.
This book surveys the history of Ukrainian Galicia from earliest times to the present. A separate chapter is devoted to Galicia's minorities—Poles, Jews, Germans, and Armenians. The volume covers the extensive literature on archeological, political, social, economic, literary, ethnographic, linguistic, and artistic developments in Galicia.

1445. Mendelsohn, Ezra. **Zionism in Poland: The Formative Years, 1915-1926.** New Haven, CT: Yale University Press, 1981. 373p. $35.00.
This is a superb study of Polish Zionism from the early days of World War I through 1926. It emerged in the midst of the chaotic foundation of the new Polish state at the end of World War I. Its significance for Poland centered around its development among Poland's 2,853,318 Jews, Eastern Europe's largest Jewish community. The birth of the Polish state with its accompanying pogroms dashed any Jewish hopes that Polish independence would bring a better life to them.

NP, 11:1:114-16; AHR, 88:1:143; HRNB, 11(Jan. 1983):75.

1446. Rabinowicz, Harry M. **The Legacy of Polish Jewry: A History of Polish Jews in the Inter-War Years, 1919-1939.** New York: T. Yoseloff, 1965. 256p.
An informative study of the Jewish community of Poland between the two world wars. The author provides an interesting overview of Jewish life in Poland during this period.

TLS, (Dec. 16, 1965):1185.

1447. Revyuk, Emil, comp. **Polish Atrocities in Ukraine.** New York: United Ukrainian Organizations of the United States, 1932. 512p. Illustrated.
This is a collection of eyewitness accounts of the so-called pacification of the Ukrainians in eastern Galicia in the summer of 1930. The physical punishment of hundreds of Ukrainians and the destruction of Ukrainian cultural facilities and

cooperative economic installations are illustrated by numerous original photographs. The pacification was carried out by units of the Polish armed forces and the police.

1448. Weinryb, Bernard D. **The Jews of Poland: A Social and Economic History of the Jewish Community in Poland from 1100 to 1800.** Philadelphia: Jewish Publication Society of America, 1973. 424p. $10.00.
This remarkable survey of the Jewish saga in prepartitioned Poland relates the history of Poland to that of world Jewry and Polish Jewry. Weinryb covers seven centuries of what was to become by 1500 the largest single group in world Jewry. The author emphasizes the legal status of Polish Jewry, which was "that of freemen, apparently resembling that of the knights and gentry, and in certain respects that of the burghers."
SR, 34:1:169-71; Choice, 11(1974):500.

Language and Literature

1449. Birkenmayer, Sigmund S., and Krzyzanowski, Jerzy R., eds. **A Modern Polish Reader.** University Park, PA: Pennsylvania State University, 1970. 187p. $3.00.
This Polish reader presents a selection of Polish prose, a dictionary, and a set of exercises. The vocabularies that follow each reading are exhaustive. The readings selected are interesting and well chosen.
SEEJ, 16:1:119-20.

1450. Brooks, Maria Zagorska. **Polish Reference Grammar.** The Hague, The Netherlands: Mouton, 1975. xvi, 580p. 120.00. Dglds.
This volume contains rich material on all aspects of Polish grammar. It consists of two main sections—grammar and review exercises. The merit of this work lies in the somewhat novel methodological approach to Polish grammar.
CSP, 19:4:542-43.

1451. Bulas, Kazimierz, et al. **English-Polish,** vol. 1; **Polish-English,** vol. 2. New York: The Kosciuszko Foundation, 1962.
These two volumes are recommended as the best available dictionaries for translators and students of the Polish language.

1452. Gerould, Daniel, ed. **Twentieth Century Polish Avant-Garde Drama: Plays, Scenarios, Critical Documents.** Introduction by Daniel Gerould. Translated by Daniel Gerould in collaboration with Eleanor Gerould. Ithaca, NY: Cornell University Press, 1977. 287p. $15.00.
Gerould presents to the American audience the contemporary experimental drama of Poland. The anthology includes six selected playwrights, who are represented by some creative works and some theoretical pronouncements and personal confessions.
SR, 37:2:356-57; Choice, 14(1978):1506.

1453. Gillon, Adam, and Krzyzanowski, Ludwik, eds. **Introduction to Modern Polish Literature: An Anthology of Fiction and Poetry.** New York: Twayne Publishers, 1964. 480p. $6.95.

This anthology includes the works of forty-seven authors, divided between prose and poetry from the roster of acknowledged major Polish classics of the last century, with a sprinkling of contemporary authors. Among the latter are powerful stories; works of female writers are also included, as well as some psychological historical fiction.

SR, 28:2:360-61.

1454. Maciuszko, Jerzy J. **The Polish Short Story in English: A Guide and Critical Bibliography.** Detroit: Wayne State University Press, 1968. 473p.

This book covers the period from 1884 (first recorded translation) through 1960, listing some six hundred items painstakingly traced in obscure periodicals, out-of-print anthologies, and ephemeral publications.

Choice, 6(1969):1366.

1455. Milosz, Czeslaw, ed. **Postwar Polish Poetry: Anthology.** Selected and translated by C. Milosz. Garden City, NY: Doubleday, 1965. 149p. $4.95.

Milosz presents ninety poems by twenty-one poets. He stresses living poets and works written since 1956, although some of the older poets are included. The editor supplies biographical and partly critical remarks about the poets included.

SR, 28:2:359-61.

1456. Milosz, Czeslaw. **Selected Poems.** Introduction by Kenneth Rexroth. New York: Seabury Press, 1973. 128p. $5.95.

Milosz's poems represent his own autobiographical explanations and explorations, stressing his life in Poland until World War II and then in the United States. The translations capture a great deal of his Polish feeling and the form of the originals.

BL, 70(1973):315; Choice, 11(1974):608.

1457. Schenker, Alexander M. **Beginning Polish: Revised Edition.** Vol. 1: **Lessons, Polish-English Glossary.** Vol. 2: **Drills, Survey of Grammar, Index.** New Haven, CT: Yale University Press, 1973. 491p.; 452p. $10.00. (Yale Linguistic Series.)

This grammar is designed as a first-year introduction to the language, with twenty-five lessons in the first volume and twenty-five corresponding drills in the second. Tapes for materials in both volumes are available from the Yale University Language Laboratory.

SR, 33:3:616-17.

1458. Schenker, Alexander M., ed. **Fifteen Modern Polish Short Stories: An Annotated Reader and a Glossary.** New Haven, CT: Yale University Press, 1970. 186p. $8.50.

Schenker's selection of Polish short stories is intended as a supplement to his two-volume textbook, *Beginning Polish.* The book consists of fifteen short stories, each by a different author, published in the last fifteen years. All the stories are of good artistic quality and are representative of the main trends and attitudes in contemporary Polish prose.

CSP, 13:4:450-51; Choice, 8(1971):840.

1459.   Stanislawski, Jan. **Wielki slownik angielsko-polski** (the Great English-
          Polish Dictionary). Warsaw: Wyd. "Wiedza Powszechna," 1968. 1,175p.
The dictionary contains over a hundred thousand words, phrases, and expressions
commonly used in the English language of the nineteenth and twentieth centuries.
A considerable number of terms from technology, medicine, and science have also
been included.

1460.   Stanislawski, Jan. **Wielki slownik polsko-angielski z supplementem** (the
          Great Polish-English Dictionary Supplemented). 2 vols. Warsaw:
          Panstwowe Wyd. "Wiedza Powszechna," 1978. Vol. 1: 800p. A-Q; Vol. 2:
          928p., P-Z.
This dictionary supplements the *Great English-Polish Dictionary* published in 1968.
It comprises about 180,000 words, phrases, and expressions commonly used in the
Polish language. A considerable number of terms from technology, medicine, and
science have also been included, as well as dialectical, colloquial, and historical
terms and phrases.

ROMANIA

Reference Works

1461. Fischer-Galati, Stephen A. **Rumania: A Bibliographic Guide**. Washington, DC: Slavic and Central European Division, Reference Department, Library of Congress, 1963. 75p.
This guide incorporates a number of excellent features: a balanced coverage of the major categories of knowledge, a helpful cross-reference between its two major divisions, an evaluative survey and a detailed bibliography listing, and the critical comments of the author.
SR, 23:4:792-93.

1462. Fischer-Galati, Stephen A., ed. **Rumania**. New York: Published for the Mid-European Studies Center of the Free Europe Committee by Praeger Publishers, 1957. 399p. $8.95.
The handbook contains general reference material on Romania, the government, the Party, literature and the arts, economy, and history.
SR, 18:2:268.

1463. Matley, Ian M. **Romania: A Profile**. New York: Praeger Publishers, 1970. 292p. $8.50.
This is a handy and generally reliable book of data and insights on Romania's past and present. It contains comprehensive descriptions and evaluations of Romanian geography, culture, ethnic groups, and history. The general reader and undergraduate student will benefit from this lucid synopsis of Romanian affairs.
SR, 30:3:691; BL, 67(1971):928; Choice, 8(1971):132.

History

1464. Bobango, Gerald J. **The Emergence of the Romanian National State**. Boulder, CO: *East European Quarterly*, 1979. 307p. $17.00. Distributed by Columbia University Press, New York. (East European Monographs, no. 58.)
This book presents Romanian history from 1829 to 1866, with concentration on internal political events and on foreign reactions to the Romanian drive to achieve nationhood. The author discusses such aspects as the efforts toward international recognition of the country, internal social, economic, and political development, and church-state relations.
HRNB, 8(Sept. 1980):236; Choice, 16(1980):1633.

1465. Fischer-Galati, Stephen. **Twentieth Century Rumania**. New York: Columbia University Press, 1970. 248p. $7.95.
The author has chosen historical change and continuity as his main theme. His purpose is to examine the validity of the present regime's claim that the socialist republic of Romania represents the fulfillment of the Romanian people's age-old aspirations. The author confines himself mainly to political history. In describing Romania's development under Communism, the author gives particular attention to the national current in the Romanian Communist movement.
SR, 30:1:187-88; AHR, 76:3:801; CH, 60(1971):303.

1466. Georgescu, Vlad. **Political Ideas and the Enlightenment in the Romanian Principalities (1750-1831)**. Boulder, CO: *East European Quarterly,* 1971. 232p. $7.50. Distributed by Columbia University Press, New York. (East European Monographs, no. 1.)
The author, a researcher at the Institute of Southeast European Studies in Bucharest who has also taught at UCLA, aims to give a history of political ideas in the Rumanian principalities during the Enlightenment. By delineating the main coordinates of this political thought, he wishes to define the role it played in the history of Rumanian political ideology and development as well as to place it in the general movement of Enlightenment thought. The book's comprehensive analysis of the political ideas of the Phanariot era is both much needed and usefully done.
SR, 32:2:417-18; Choice, 9(1972):1030.

1467. Hitchins, Keith. **The Rumanian National Movement in Transylvania, 1780-1849**. Cambridge, MA: Harvard University Press, 1969. 316p. $8.00. (Harvard Historical Monographs, 61.)
This book is a survey of the evolution of the Romanian national movement in Transylvania from its inception until its arrest during the reaction of 1848.
SR, 29:2:318; AHR, 75:5:1490.

1468. Matei, Horia C., et al. **Chronological History of Romania**. 2d rev. and enl. ed. Bucharest: Editura Enciclopedica Romana, 1974 (1972). 608p. Lei 38.
This history is arranged by periods and dates, beginning with the Paleolithic age and ending with the year 1971. Under each date there is a short description of events.

1469. Seton-Watson, Robert W. **A History of the Rumanians from Roman Times to the Completion of Unity**. London, 1934; Hamden, CT: The Shoe String Press, 1963. 596p. $10.00.
Although dated, this standard work on the early periods of Romanian history is still very useful.

Government and Politics

1470.   Fischer-Galati, Stephen. **The New Rumania: From People's Democracy to Socialist Republic.** Cambridge, MA: MIT Press, 1967. 126p. $6.00. (Studies in International Communism, no. 10.)
The study traces Romania's evolution since 1944, with emphasis on the strategies and tactics adopted by the Communist party in the transformation of the country into a "people's democracy" and then into a full-fledged "socialist republic." The book contains many interesting interpretive insights into the dynamics of postwar Romanian society.
SR, 28:4:505-7; Choice, 5(1968):112.

1471.   Graham, Lawrence S. **Romania: A Developing Socialist State.** Boulder, CO: Westview Press, 1982. 136p. Map. Photographs. Tables. $17.00.
Graham discusses Romania not just as a Communist state in Eastern Europe but also as a developing system with a Latin heritage. The book is written for students and the general public. Over half of the volume is devoted to introducing the historical and institutional setting of Romanian Communism.
SR, 42:2:319-20; AAPSS-A, 465(1983):169.

1472.   Jowitt, Kenneth. **Revolutionary Breakthrough and National Development: The Case of Romania, 1944-1965.** Berkeley: University of California Press, 1971. 317p. $12.00.
The author approaches Romania through the medium of political science and presents a comparative analysis of the "process of nation building" and its application to the experience of Romania between 1944 and 1965.
SEER, 53:130:139-42; Choice, 9(1972):132.

Communism, Communist Party

1473.   Ionescu, Chita. **Communism in Rumania, 1944-1962.** London: Oxford University Press, 1964. 378p. $8.00.
This is a history of the Romanian Communist party since its inception in 1921 and of its postwar administration in particular. The author examines not only events but also the national interpretation of events when "the Party has become its own historian." Because of its chronological arrangement this book is easily understood by the student and lay reader.
SEER, 64:102:250-52.

1474.   King, Robert R. **History of the Romanian Communist Party.** Stanford, CA: Hoover Institution Press, 1980. 190p. $8.95.
This is the first history of the Rumanian Communist party to appear in any language. It will serve only as a point of departure for further extended investigations when access to Rumanian archives if far more possible than at present. There is, however, too much reliance on official Rumanian publications and materials, making some of the author's observations less convincing.
HRNB, 9(March 1981):122; Choice, 18(1981):1019.

Diplomacy, Foreign Relations

1475. Braun, Aurel. **Romanian Foreign Policy since 1965: The Political and Military Limits of Autonomy.** New York and London: Praeger Publishers, 1978. xvi, 217p. $20.00.
This book analyzes in some detail Romania's unorthodox foreign policy objectives. There are basic limitations within which Romania's leaders know they must live. They cannot allow much domestic dissent or criticism of the USSR or the Communist party. Nor can they quit Comecon or the Warsaw Pact outright, or make military alliances that would appear to threaten the integrity of the Soviet bloc.
SR, 39:2:344-45; Choice, 15(1979):1574.

1476. Jelavich, Barbara. **Russia and the Rumanian National Cause, 1858-1859.** Bloomington, IN: Indiana University Press, 1959. 169p. (Slavic and East European Series, vol. 17.)
This detailed and thoroughly documented monograph is primarily based on the private papers and official reports of Nikolai K. Giers, who served as the Russian consul general in Bucharest from 1859 to 1863. There is an excellent introductory chapter on Russia and the principalities from 1829 to 1858.
JMH, 32:3:299.

Economics

1477. Mitrany, David. **The Land and the Peasant in Rumania: The War and Agrarian Reform (1917-21).** New York: Greenwood Press, 1969. 627p.
The author presents a detailed account of the agrarian reform carried out in Romania after World War I. Against a broad historical background, Mitrany discusses the conditions of the Romanian peasantry and the new land reforms. The applications of the reforms and their effect on the Romanian economy are given much space.

1478. Montias, John Michael. **Economic Development in Communist Rumania.** Cambridge, MA: MIT Press, 1967. 327p. $15.00.
The picture that emerges from this study is that of a rapidly industrializing and modernizing economy. According to Montias, Romanian policy-makers and planners have been able to raise significantly the investment level, particularly in the late 1950s, and expand substantially the per capita outputs, especially for basic industrial products. The author has carefully gone through the official statistics with a fine-toothed comb to reach objective conclusions.
SR, 27:1:162-63; AAPSS-A, 377(1968):219.

1479. Roberts, Henry L. **Rumania: Political Problems of an Agrarian State.** New Haven, CT: Yale University Press, 1951. 414p.
This work offers a very thorough analysis of Romania's economic and political history during the past thirty years. The author's study of the Romanian peasantry's unsuccessful struggle is, in most of its findings, equally valid for other agricultural societies throughout East Europe. From that point of view this study maintains its importance, even today, in view of the similarity of conditions in Africa, South America, and Asia.
SR, 21:2:159-61.

1480.   Spigler, Iancu. **Economic Reform in Rumanian Industry**. Foreword by
        Michael Kaser. New York: Oxford University Press, for Institute of Soviet
        and East European Studies, University of Glasgow, 1973. 176p. Fold-out
        map. $12.50. (Economic Reforms in East European Industry Series.)
This study is crammed with information on the changes that have taken place
since mid-1967 in Romanian macro-, branch-, and micro-planning, the industrial
management mechanism, budgetary procedures, and banking. It is generally
assumed that the Romanian economy is the most conservatively Stalinist in the
Eastern bloc.
        SR, 33:4:813-14; Choice, 11(1974):1000.

National Minorities

1481.   Deak, Francis. **The Hungarian-Rumanian Land Dispute: A Study of
        Hungarian Property Rights in Transylvania under the Treaty of Trianon**.
        New York: Columbia University Press, 1928. 272p.
This work presents an excellent study of land reform in Transylvania. The author
analyzes the political and economic purposes and effects of the reform, which
worked to the detriment of the historic ruling class in Transylvania.

1482.   Illyes, Elemer. **National Minorities in Romania: Change in Transylvania**.
        Boulder, CO: *East European Quarterly*, 1982. 360p. $25.00. Distributed
        by Columbia University Press, New York. (East European Monographs,
        no. 112.)
This is a basic study of historic and contemporary problems related to the position
of all national minorities in Transylvania. The author discusses the process of force-
ful Romanianization of non-Romanians living in Transylvania.

Language and Literature

1483.   Augerot, James E., and Popescu, Florin D. **Modern Romanian**. Seattle:
        University of Washington Press, 1971. 329p. $12.00.
This is the best up-to-date Romanian textbook for English speakers. The book is
divided into two parts of sixteen lessons each. There is a useful appendix in two
parts—"Pronunciation" and "Inflection"—and a Romanian-English glossary.
        SR, 31:2:488-89.

1484.   Levitchi, Leon. **Dictionar Roman-Englez** (Romanian-English Dictionary).
        Bucharest: Editura Stiintifica, 1965. 600p.
The dictionary covers some fifty thousand words mainly within the social sciences
and humanities areas. Its usefulness is limited to students of the English language.

1485.   Steinberg, Jacob, ed. **Introduction to Rumanian Literature**. Foreword
        by Demostene Botez. New York: Twayne Publishers, 1966. 411p. $6.95.
The editor chose some of the most representative prose works of modern Romanian literature, and his anthology is a first step toward the understanding of an
original literary phenomenon. All the writers included in the anthology are pre-
eminent personalities in the Romanian literature of the past hundred years, and
their names are synonymous with the most important moments in the intellectual

history of Romania. The introductory notes to each short story draw convincing portraits of these writers, revealing the main characteristics of their work.

SR, 30:1:218-19; Choice, 4(1967):849.

YUGOSLAVIA

Reference Works

1486.   Byrnes, Robert F., ed. **Yugoslavia.** New York: Praeger Publishers, published for the Mid-European Studies Center of the Free Europe Committee, 1957. 488p. $8.50.
This useful reference aid on postwar Yugoslavia contains information on all aspects of that country.
   JMH, 30:4:402.

1487.   Eterovich, Francis H., and Spalatin, Christopher, eds. **Croatia: Land, People, Culture.** Toronto: University of Toronto Press, 1970. 568p. $7.50.
This volume, like the first one (1964), contains independent monographic studies on Croation history, language, literature, and culture, whose common denominator is the extended region of Croatia, including Bosnia and Hercegovina, as well as Croatians living abroad.
   JMH, 37:3:359-60.

1488.   Horton, John J. **Yugoslavia.** Oxford: Clio Press, 1977. xvi, 195p. $25.25. (World Bibliographic Series.)
The 617 items in this selective bibliography on Yugoslavia are primarily citations to books and articles in English. Each entry is annotated in detail.
   SR, 38:3:547.

History

1489.   Clissold, Stephen, ed. **A Short History of Yugoslavia: From Early Times to 1966.** New York: Cambridge University Press, 1966. 280p. $5.95.
The region-by-region approach results in good encyclopedic articles on each region. Useful political summaries and generally good maps characterize this valuable handbook.
   AHR, 72:4:1031-32; SR, 26:3:491.

1490.   Djilas, Milovan. **Wartime.** Translated by Michael B. Petrovich. New York and London: Harcourt Brace Jovanovich, 1977. x, 470p. Plates. $14.95.
The wartime memoirs of Djilas are of special importance because they come from a man who, while once prominent as a participant on one side of the conflict, is

no longer a blind protagonist of that side. This book is revealing in many respects. It gives us an intimate portrait of leading Partisan personalities, including Tito. Djilas describes the senseless brutality of the war—the hundreds of thousands of executions attributed more to the internal than to the external conflict.

SR, 37:3:491-94; AHR, 83:1:210.

1491. Djordjevic, Dimitrije, ed. **The Creation of Yugoslavia 1914-1918.** Santa Barbara, CA, and Oxford: ABC-Clio Press, 1980. xii, 228p. Maps. $24.50.

The authors base their work on the most recent scholarship and offer insights into the historiographical controversies underlying certain issues. The essays are brief and well documented. The major themes deal with the problems underlying Yugoslav unification.

SR, 40:4:672-73; HRNB, 9(Feb. 1981):108; Choice, 18(1980):575.

1492. Dragnich, Alex N. **The First Yugoslavia: Search for a Viable Political System.** Stanford, CA: Hoover Institution Press, 1983. 182p. $24.95.

The author examines the reasons for Yugoslavia's failure and analyzes the circumstances surrounding the ambitious unification project. Citing differences in religion, culture, and social values among the Serbs, Croats, and Slovenes as contributing to the decline of the "Kingdom," he also inspects the constitution drafted for the new state, the provisional parliament, and the provisional ministries for inherent weaknesses. To those interested in nation building, it is essential reading.

1493. Gazi, Stephen. **A History of Croatia.** New York: Philosophical Library, 1973. 362p. $11.95.

This survey takes the reader across the whole span of Croatian history, from the earliest times to the present. Gazi favors the concept of Croatian independence, but he has some critical comments to make about Croatia's first venture into independence, the period of the Ustasha regime during World War II. Gazi writes from a strongly pro-Croatian and anti-Serbian viewpoint, but tries to be restrained and to speak without anger.

CSP, 16:3:485-86; Choice, 11(1974):149.

1494. Heppell, Muriel, and Singleton, Frank B. **Yugoslavia.** New York: Praeger Publishers, 1961. 236p. $7.50.

This compendium provides a picture of Yugoslavia that is not thickly covered by national or ideological bias. The first part of the book treats the history of the Yugoslav lands up to the outbreak of World War I; the second part covers the history of Yugoslavia since 1918. The popular style of the book suits the general reader.

SR, 21:2:361-62.

1495. Hoptner, Jacob B. **Yugoslavia in Crisis: 1934-1941.** New York: Columbia University Press, 1962. 328p. $6.50.

The essence of the book is the author's stylistically impeccable description of the total political failure and military unpreparedness of the Western powers, the brutal conduct of the Axis partners, and the desperately difficult international and domestic situation of Yugoslavia.

SR, 24:2:332-33.

1496. Palmer, Alan W. **Yugoslavia**. New York: Oxford University Press, 1964. 127p. $1.25 pa.

This brief survey appraises Yugoslavia's past and present. This publication is especially suited for high school use and for the general reader.

1497. Petrovich, Michael Boro. **A History of Modern Serbia, 1804-1918**. 2 vols. New York and London: Harcourt Brace Jovanovich, 1976. Vol. 1: xxxiii, 359p. + 8pp. plates. Maps.; Vol. 2: xi, 372p. (360-731pp.) + 8pp. plates. Maps. $49.50 set.

Petrovich's interpretation of Serbian history is traditional, and this work has become the standard account of its subject in any Western language. He believes that the church preserved the memory of Serbia's medieval past during Turkish times, that the folk epics reinforced the resulting sense of national identity, and that local autonomy under the Turks prepared the Serbs for political democracy. He makes it clear that whereas the idea of Yugoslavism was always present among the Serbs, its fluctuating importance never rose to the level of the other goals.

SR, 36:4:707-9; AHR, 82:4:1014; BL, 73(1977):986.

1498. Prcela, John, and Guldescu, Stanko, eds. **Operation Slaughterhouse: Eyewitness Accounts of Postwar Massacres in Yugoslavia**. Philadelphia: Dorrance, 1970. 557p. $10.00.

This book purports to be a factual and documented account of the so-called Bleiburg massacres perpetrated by the Yugoslav Communists on Croat soldiers, who had surrendered to the British in Austria and were then handed over by the British to the Partisans to be abused, mistreated, and often killed. The liquidations were in part the result of deliberate policy, in part the expression of individual bestiality of Partisan commanders and certain units. The murders were motivated by ideological and national hatred.

SR, 30:2:413-15.

1499. Rogel, Carole. **The Slovenes and Yugoslavism, 1890-1914**. Boulder, CO: *East European Quarterly,* 1977. viii, 167p. $12.00. Distributed by Columbia University Press, New York. (East European Monographs, no. 24.)

Rogel traces the evolution of this small nation from its middle period from 1890 to 1914 with skill and considerable success. This account is meant to be an introductory study and, as such, it serves its purpose well.

SR, 38:1:147; AHR, 83:2:480.

1500. Tomasevich, Jozo. **War and Revolution in Yugoslavia, 1941-1945: The Chetniks**. Stanford, CA: Stanford University, 1975. x, 508p. $20.00.

This study is a most ambitious effort published as the first volume of a projected series *War and Revolution in Yugoslavia.* This work is primarily a political-diplomatic history of the Draza Mihailovich Chetnik movement. It deals as briefly as possible with the military aspects of the war and omits much consideration of its social background.

SR, 35:2:375-77; AHR, 81:3:897; CH, 70(1976):124.

1501.   Vucinich, Wayne S., ed. **Contemporary Yugoslavia: Twenty Years of Socialist Experiment.** Berkeley: University of California Press, 1969. 441p. $9.50.

This is a collection of eight papers attempting to place the twenty years of socialist experiment in perspective. The following topics are considered: Mihailovich-Tito conflict; establishment of a new political order; Tito's foreign policies; conflict of nationalities; economy and industrialization; and modernization of Yugoslav society.

SR, 30:2:415-16; Choice, 7(1970):449.

1502.   Wilson, Duncan. **Tito's Yugoslavia.** New York and London: Cambridge University Press, 1979. xvii, 269p. Map. $27.50.

The death of Tito marked the end of the most important phase so far in Yugoslavia's history. It is now possible to assess the impact of his career on the evolution of present-day Yugoslavia. Wilson's book, written and published before Tito died, makes an excellent start. The author served as a diplomat in Belgrade in the fifties and sixties and his account, which is addressed to the general reader, is full of information and specialized knowledge.

SEER, 59:1:130-31; CH, 78(1980):222; Choice, 18(1980):153.

Government and Politics

1503.   Chloros, A. G. **Yugoslav Civil Law: History, Family, Property.** Oxford: Clarendon Press, 1970. 285p. $9.75.

This excellent book does not attempt to treat the whole civil legal system of Yugoslavia. Three fields are chosen for discussion: the history of Yugoslav law, family law, and the law of property. The author's style is simple, and the book will be easily understood by persons having no legal background.

SR, 30:4:921-22.

1504.   Fisher, Jack C. **Yugoslavia—a Multinational State: Regional Difference and Administrative Response.** San Francisco: Chandler Publishing, 1966. 244p. $15.00.

The study explores the development of the Yugoslav state, the historical background of regional differences, regional variation of economic development, and housing policy and conditions; two chapters deal with the communal system. The author uses two approaches to present his study: descriptive and statistical analysis to express quantitatively the regional variation of socioeconomic characteristics.

SR, 27:2:343-35; EG, 44(1968):88.

1505.   Hondius, Frits W. **Yugoslav Community of Nations.** The Hague, The Netherlands: Mouton, 1968. 375p. 65 Dglds.

This book is a historically grounded analytic monograph that focuses on the federal aspect of the Yugoslav constitutional system. Although Hondius relies heavily on an industrial and legalistic database, he also locates this within a broader ecological context touching upon both ethnoregional and historical factors.

SR, 29:4:735.

1506.   Ra'anan, Gavriel D. **Yugoslavia after Tito: Scenarios and Implications.**
         Boulder, CO: Westview Press, 1977. xiv, 206p. $14.50.
This study treats the most difficult problem in political science, namely the prediction of future political behavior. The author concentrates on the internal politics of Yugoslavia and the international politics of Yugoslavia's special position, from both geopolitical and military points of view. He concludes that the country is vulnerable because of its many internal ethnic frictions, and Yugoslavia's internal and external brittleness might present the Soviets with an almost irresistible temptation to intervene.
         NP, 8:2:254-56; LJ, 103(1978):982; Choice, 15(1978):936.

1507.   Zukin, Sharon. **Beyond Marx and Tito: Theory and Practice in Yugoslav Socialism.** New York: Cambridge University Press, 1975. x, 302p. $15.50.
After observing participants in local meetings in Belgrade and interviewing ten Belgrade families, Zukin presents her interpretation of the reality of self-management and socialism. Between practice and theory, she discovers, there is an extraordinarily wide gap.
         CSP, 19:4:526; CH, 70(1976):124.

Communism, Communist Party

1508.   Avakumovic, Ivan. **History of the Communist Party of Yugoslavia.** Aberdeen, Scotland: Aberdeen University Press, 1967. 207p. 60s.
This study is instructive not only for the history of the Communist party of Yugoslavia but also for that of Communist parties elsewhere. The author has produced a most useful, readable, and enlightening work. The study is replete with unusually valuable social statistics.
         SR, 25:3:702-5; AHR, 71:1:254-55.

1509.   Dedijer, Vladimir. **The Battle Stalin Lost: Memoirs of Yugoslavia, 1948-1953.** New York: Viking Press, 1971. 341p. $8.50.
Dedijer, journalist, biographer of Tito, and erstwhile high Communist functionary, presents his lucid recollections of those dramatic days after Yugoslavia's expulsion from the bloc in June 1948, when many expected the Tito regime to fold under Stalin's relentless pressure. This important account of an influential insider reminds us of the often underestimated influence of small countries on world affairs.
         SR, 30:4:921; AHR, 77:4:1160.

1510.   Djilas, Milovan. **Anatomy of a Moral: The Political Essays of Milovan Djilas.** Edited by Abraham Rothberg. New York: Praeger Publishers, 1959. 181p.
This is the translation of the author's eighteen articles from *Borba* (1953-54) dealing with the Yugoslav establishment and Tito's Communism. The one-time devoted Communist became disillusioned with Communist practices. His experiences can be multiplied by many similar cases, giving particular significance to his "confession." Students are urged to study this case.
         SR, 19:2:305.

1511. Djilas, Milovan. **Memoir of a Revolutionary**. Translated by Drenka Willen. New York: Harcourt Brace Jovanovich, 1973. 402p. $12.00.

This is the second volume of Djilas's autobiography, recounting events of the thirties in Yugoslavia. Djilas rose from poverty to become one of the most powerful men in the successful European revolution since 1917. In this volume he describes personal relations and political disputes among Yugoslav Communists in the period before World War II.

SR, 33:3:595-96; AAPSS-A, 410(1973):194.

1512. Djilas, Milovan. **Tito: The Story from Inside**. Translated by Vasilije Kojić and Richard Hayes. New York: Harcourt Brace Jovanovich, 1980. 185p.

Few individuals were in a better position than Djilas to know Tito, and his opinion must therefore be taken seriously. In commenting on Tito's personal weaknesses and idiosyncracies, Djilas tells us that Tito was egotistical and conceited. He cultivated the impression of being a simple man dedicated exclusively to the good of his people, even though he loved to be surrounded by beautiful women and was vain and extravagant in clothes and habits.

CH, 80(1981):178; LJ, 106(1981):140.

1513. Hoffman, George W., and Neal, Fred W. **Yugoslavia and the New Communism**. New York: Twentieth Century Fund, 1962. 546p. $8.00.

This compendium deals with the main aspects of Yugoslav development under Tito's regime. The topics comprise the land of the South Slavs, Yugoslav Communism—Soviet style, the emergence of Titoism, Titoism as a system, and the impact and problems of Titoism.

SEEJ, 7:2:228-29.

1514. Johnson, A. Ross. **The Transformation of Communist Ideology: The Yugoslav Case, 1945-1953**. Cambridge, MA: MIT Press, 1972. 269p.

This important book offers the first systematic effort to analyze in detail the emergence and evolution of the ideological underpinnings of what is commonly known as "Titoism" or the "Yugoslav road to socialism." The author closely examines the six most important tenets of the post-1948 doctrine, which was to transform postwar Yugoslavia.

SR, 33:3:596-97; CH, 65(1973):178.

1515. McVicker, Charles Po. **Titoism: Pattern for International Communism**. New York: St. Martin's Press, 1957. 332p. $6.00.

This volume is the best available synthesis of the development of Titoism as pictured in major political and social reforms attempted since 1950. Titoism as a separate political philosophy claims to be a halfway house to freedom, a middle stage between Stalinist tyranny and democratic socialism.

JMH, 30:2:168-69.

1516. Reinhartz, Dennis. **Milovan Djilas: A Revolutionary as a Writer**. Boulder, CO: *East European Quarterly*, 1981. xii, 112p. $12.50. Distributed by Columbia University Press, New York. (East European Monographs, no. 89.)

This monograph contains a list of books and articles published by Djilas in English, a list of other sources, and a chronology of the life of Djilas. The author restricts his focus to "primarily a literary biography," but by necessity also shows some aspects of Djilas's political activities. This overview, aimed at the general reader, is quite satisfying and provides some interesting insight.

NP, 11:1:123-25; Choice, 19(1982):633.

Diplomacy, Foreign Relations

1517. Campbell, John C. **Tito's Separate Road: America and Yugoslavia in World Politics.** New York: Harper & Row, published for the Council on Foreign Relations, 1967. 180p. $3.95.

In this book the author reviews and assesses U.S. policy concerning Tito's Yugoslavia. Surprised by the Cominform action against Yugoslavia, the United States waited until the beginning of 1949 before concluding that it was in the U.S. interest to see the Yugoslav-Soviet break continue. The United States chose "a course of helping a Communist country to maintain its independence" of the Soviet bloc and ultimately to strengthen its ties with the West.

SR, 27:2:331-32; JP, 30(1968):593; Choice, 4(1968):1316.

1518. Clissold, Stephen, ed. **Yugoslavia and the Soviet Union, 1939-1973.** London: Oxford University Press, 1975. xxiii, 318p. $29.95.

This useful collection underscores the range and vitality of the Soviet-Yugoslav relationship during the past forty-odd years. Of the 238 documents or parts thereof printed here, about 30 relate to Soviet relations with either the prewar Yugoslav government or the government in exile. Many of the rest are communications between Tito and the Comintern, Stalin, or the Soviet government.

CSP, 20:3:430-31; CH, 70(1976):124; Choice, 13(1976):124.

1519. Larson, David L. **United States Foreign Policy toward Yugoslavia, 1943-1963.** Washington, DC: University Press of America, 1979. viii, 380p. $11.75.

This book provides a detailed and mainly chronological survey of American-Yugoslav relations between 1943 and 1963, including the difficulties Americans had in reconciling themselves to having any such relations at all. It quotes extensively from a number of official statements and speeches and cites many English-language sources.

SR, 39:3:521; HRNB, 8(Jan. 1980):56.

1520. Lederer, Ivo J. **Yugoslavia at the Paris Peace Conference: A Study in Frontiermaking.** New Haven, CT: Yale University Press, 1963. 351p. $8.50.

This is a systematic study of the Yugoslav question at the Paris Peace Conference, the first in a Western language. This work largely completes the story of peace-making in the mid-Danube area after World War I.

AHR, 69:3:768-69; SR, 23:2:353.

1521.   Roberts, Walter R. **Tito, Mihailovič and the Allies, 1941-1945.** New
         Brunswick, NJ: Rutgers University Press, 1973. 406p. $15.00.
The author compiled many facts relevant to the Mihailovič-Tito question, based
on a wide range of sources, both official and unofficial. He had available the
Kasche-Ribbentrop correspondence of March 1943, but he was not able, at the time
of writing, to go through the British Public Record Office to include documents
from the British side.
         SEER, 53:130:135-36; SR, 38:2:343-44.

1522.   Rubinstein, Alvin Z. **Yugoslavia and the Nonaligned World.** Princeton,
         NJ: Princeton University Press, 1970. 353p. $11.00.
The author argues that Yugoslav leaders first initiated a policy that aimed at the
creation of a group of nonaligned states for pragmatic reasons: to break out of their
diplomatic isolation, to find markets for Yugoslavia's goods, and to develop a
policy that appealed to various factions within the Yugoslav Communist party.
Rubinstein has skillfully analyzed both the role of personalities in Yugoslavia's
foreign policy and the ways in which the instruments of twentieth-century
diplomacy have been fashioned and employed to achieve foreign policy goals. This
valuable study appeals to a wide audience.
         SR, 30:2:416-17; CH, 60(1971):48.

Economics

1523.   Bicanic, Rudolf. **Economic Policy in Socialist Yugoslavia.** London: Cam-
         bridge University Press, 1973. 254p. $11.50.
Bicanic demonstrates that the manner of political formation of a country profoundly affects the pattern of socialization. Thus the political security of the
regime determines the speed and direction of socialization. The author goes on to
describe the models of Yugoslav planning: the centralized, decentralized, and
polycentric, and then to trace the evolution of the administrative bureaucracy
that controls the planning mechanism. Other parts of this book deal with patterns
of industrialization, income policy, economic growth, and foreign trade.
         EEQ, 8:4:515-16; JEL, 12(1974):105.

1524.   Dimitrijević, Dimitrije, and Marcesich, George. **Money and Finance in
         Contemporary Yugoslavia.** New York: Praeger, 1972. 261p. $17.50.
The authors set out to test a monetarist hypothesis in Yugoslavia. This is of interest
because of the unique conditions of the Yugoslav economy. The study is broken
into four parts in which the authors examine the financial system, its institutional
background, basic questions of monetary theory in Yugoslavia, monetary policy
and policy formation and implementation, and make concluding observations
concerning future developments in Yugoslav monetary policy.
         EEQ, 9:1:120-21.

1525.   Dirlam, Joel, and Plummer, James L. **An Introduction to the Yugoslav
         Economy.** Columbus, OH: Charles E. Merrill, 1973. 259p. $5.50 pa.
         (Merrill's Economics Systems Series.)

The authors conduct their well-organized inquiry, relying on personal interviews and the Yugoslav press more than traditional academic sources. There are frequent parallels and contrasts between the U.S. and Yugoslav economies. The reader will appreciate the authors' perception of the increasingly important role that regional conflicts have played in the Yugoslav economy.

SR, 33:3:597-98.

1526. Farkas, Richard P. **Yugoslav Economic Development and Political Change: The Relationship between Economic Managers and Policy-Making Elites.** New York: Praeger Publishers, 1975. xii, 133p. $13.50.

Farkas focuses on enterprise "directors" as a key to understanding the interrelationships between the political and economic systems in Yugoslavia. Also, the implications of Yugoslavia's external economic relations for domestic policy are considered. In fact, the business elites have become most influential in the myriad micropolitico-economic decisions that shape everyday life.

SR, 35:1:169.

1527. Hamilton, F. E. Ian. **Yugoslavia: Patterns of Economic Activity.** New York: Praeger Publishers, 1968. 384p. $8.00.

The prime object of the study "is to present the aims and methods of planning in this socialist state, and to assess its achievements in the distribution and location of economic activity." Hamilton achieves this task by first describing the historical, demographic, and physical environment of Yugoslavia, and then analyzing the economic policy and development of Yugoslavia since 1945. The material is treated in a way that makes clear the relations between such factors as resources, population, transportation, and industrial and agricultural progress.

SR, 29:1:129-30; GJ, 135(1969):87; Choice, 6(1969):402.

1528. Milenkovitch, Deborah D. **Plan and Market in Yugoslav Economic Thought.** New Haven, CT: Yale University Press, 1971. 323p. $10.00.

This study contributes to the understanding of Yugoslavia's unique approach to economic organization. It is a review of the doctrinal debates in Yugoslavia that have accompanied the substitution of a market mechanism for the centrally planned, Soviet-style system adopted immediately after the war. It is not a study of the Yugoslav economy in operation.

CSP, 16:1:124-26; SR, 34:3:643-44.

1529. Moore, J. H. **Growth with Self-Management: Yugoslav Industrialization 1952-1975.** Stanford, CA: Hoover Institution Press, 1980. xvi, 334p. $17.95.

According to Moore, industrial policy in Yugoslavia has "amounted to a Yugoslav version of forced-draft industrialization." The implementation of self-management has been illusory because of the dominance of the director in enterprise decision-making and the continued control over the banking system by the central authorities.

SS, 33:4:628-29; Choice, 18(1980):567.

1530. Pejovich, Svetozar. **The Market-planned Economy of Yugoslavia.** Minneapolis: University of Minnesota Press, 1966. 160p. $5.75.

The author describes and analyzes the system in regard to both the overall economy and individual enterprises. He discusses the economic theories of socialism and applies these to the Yugoslav experiment. The book is clearly written and well documented.

SR, 27:3:672-73; CH, 54(1967):241; Choice, 4(1967):323.

1531.   Sirc, Ljubo. **The Yugoslav Economy under Self-Management**. London: Macmillan, 1979. xix, 270p. Tables. £15.00.

Sirc's aim is "to show the Yugoslav economy under self-management as it appears to Yugoslavs who have to live with it, so as to help outside observers to comprehend better what is happening there." The study contains a large number of interesting insights.

SEER, 59:3:469-70; Choice, 17(1980):433.

Education and Church

1532.   Alexander, Stella. **Church and State in Yugoslavia since 1945**. Cambridge: Cambridge University Press, 1979. xxii, 351p. £15.00.

Alexander takes the story of the Catholic church's relations with state and party in Yugoslavia down to 1966 (the signature of the protocol between the Vatican and the Yugoslav government). The relations of the Orthodox church with state and party are covered to 1967 (the breakaway of the Macedonian dioceses from the Serbian patriarchate). The author treats the pressures on state and party in the early postwar period and the resulting pressures on the churches.

SEER, 58:4:629-30; HRNB, 8(Feb. 1980):87; Choice, 16(1980):1598.

1533.   Pervan, Ralph. **Tito and the Students: The University and the University Student in Self-managing Yugoslavia**. Nedlands, Australia: University of Western Australia Press, 1978. xvi, 239p. $19.95. Distributed by International Scholarly Book Services, Forest Grove, Oregon.

This study provides a sociopolitical analysis of the 1968 student disorders at Belgrade University. The author pays particular attention to the inadequacies of self-management as practiced at Belgrade University, the problems resulting from the unprecedented and uncontrollable growth in the university system, the deteriorating material situation of students, and the failure of youth organizations to articulate students' needs or to channel their energies.

SR, 39:1:151: Choice, 16(1979):431.

Society, Sociology

1534.   Barton, Allen H.; Denitch, Bogdan; and Kadushin, Charles, eds. **Opinion-making Elites in Yugoslavia**. New York: Praeger Publishers, 1973. 344p. $18.50.

These articles on opinion-making elites in Yugoslavia, written by four Yugoslavs, four Americans, and one Yugoslav-American, make a number of positive reflections on the state of social science research both in and on contemporary Yugoslavia. The interdisciplinary composition of the research team has ensured a well-rounded research effort on an exciting and important topic of inquiry. For the most part, the contributors show a firm methodological grounding and approach without losing sight of the sensitive human and social dimensions underlying the problem they study.

EEQ. 9:1:115-17; AJS, 80(1974):571.

1535.   Doder, Dusko. **The Yugoslavs.** New York and Toronto: Random House, 1978. xiv, 256p. $10.00.

Doder, reporter for the Washington *Post*, lived for three years in the 1970s in Yugoslavia while covering Eastern Europe. The book deals with several of the crucial issues facing this unique land—national identity and the "ethnic key," socialist ideals and private goals, modernity and tradition, breadwinners abroad and dependents in Yugoslavia, political dictatorship, and other issues. Doder presents the true state of the country through references to individual human situations.

SR, 38:4:708-9; Choice, 15(1978):1270.

1536.   Halpern, Joel M. **A Serbian Village.** Illustrated by Barbara Kerewsky Halpern. Rev. ed. New York: Harper & Row, 1967. 359p. $2.75 pa.

The greater part of the book, which was first published in 1958, is based on field research in 1953-54 in the village of Orašac in central Serbia. The author had remarkable success in gathering data and he shows that he established meaningful contacts and rapport with the village residents.

SR, 28:3:514-16; Choice, 5(1968):272.

1537.   Hammel, Eugene A. **Alternative Social Structures and Ritual Relations in the Balkans.** Englewood Cliffs, NJ: Prentice-Hall, 1968. 110p. $6.95.

In this study of marriage, baptismal, and haircutting sponsorship in southwestern and eastern Yugoslavia, Hammel develops the thesis that the ritual, affinal, and agnatic institutions of this region are, in fact, part of a more general system of exchange or communication of goods, services, women, information, and values.

SR, 28:3:513-14; Choice, 6(1970):1840.

1538.   Winner, Irene. **A Slovenian Village: Žerovnica.** Providence, RI: Brown University Press, 1971. 267p. $14.00.

This is the first professional ethnographic account of a Slovenian community in the English language. It is also a beautifully produced book, with good photographs and charming drawings. Most of the book is about peasant economics and the relationship between social organization, everyday interaction, and economic factors. It is particularly helpful in its emphasis on the internal stratification of a peasant community.

SR, 31:3:724-25; Choice, 9(1972):445.

National Minorities and Dissent

1539.   Eventov, Y. **A History of Yugoslav Jews.** Edited by C. Rotem. Tel-Aviv: Copyright Hitahdut Olej Yugoslavia, 1971. 432p.

This is a broad historical account of Yugoslavian Jewry. Eventov studies the Sephardic Jews of Bosnia and Serbia as well as groups in Slovenia and Croatia.

1540.   Freidenreich, Harriet Pass. **The Jews of Yugoslavia: A Quest for Community**. Philadelphia: Jewish Publication Society of America, 1979. xiv, 323p. $14.95.

On the whole, Yugoslav nationalism facilitated the acceptance of the Jews as a nationality, but it also made it more difficult for them to integrate into the mainstream of Yugoslav society. Zionism and Communism emerged as alternatives. About 80 percent of Yugoslavia's Jews perished in the Holocaust, and the majority of the survivors emigrated to Israel, leading to the present situation where the Yugoslav Jewish community is gradually becoming extinct.

Choice, 18(1980):148.

1541.   Sher, Gerson S. **Praxis: Marxist Criticism and Dissent in Socialist Yugoslavia**. Bloomington, IN, and London: Indiana University Press, 1977. xx, 360p. $15.00.

The author presents a sympathetic and thorough treatment of the dissenting Yugoslav Marxist intellectuals who came together around the journal *Praxis* during its short, precarious existence in 1964-75. These philosophers and social scientists engaged in ideological combat with the state and party in an effort to further humanize Yugoslav socialism.

SR, 38:3:524; CH, 64(1978):180; Choice, 15(1978):288.

1542.   Shoup, Paul. **Communism and the Yugoslav National Question**. New York: Columbia University Press, 1968. 308p. $9.50.

Shoup surveys the positions of the Communist party of Yugoslavia on the nationalities question from 1919 through 1966, making a side trip into domestic and international politics known as the Macedonian question. He considers the important relationship between economics and the central goal, namely, national unity.

SR, 29:1:128-29; AHR, 74:5:1662; CH, 56(1969):232; Choice, 6(1969): 1486.

Language and Literature

1543.   Benson, Morton, with Biljana Šljivić-Šimšić. **Serbocroatian-English Dictionary**. Philadelphia: University of Pennsylvania Press; Belgrade: Prosveta, 1971. 807p. $27.50.

This book represents the first attempt to compile a dictionary in which American rather than British English is considered as well as both variants of standard Serbo-Croatian.

SEEJ, 16:3:370-75; Choice, 9(1972):623.

1544.   Benson, Morton. **An English-Serbocroatian Dictionary**. Philadelphia: University of Pennsylvania Press, 1979. 669p.

The dictionary was compiled to satisfy the acute need for an up-to-date English-Serbo-Croatian lexicon. Although American English is the dominant standard described in the dictionary, considerable attention is paid to British English. This is a companion volume to the author's *Serbocroatian-English Dictionary* published in 1971.

Choice, 17(1980):47.

1545. Grad, Anton; Škerlij, Ružena; and Vitorovič, Nada. **Angeleško-slovenski slovar** (English-Slovene Dictionary). Ljubljana: Državna Založba Slovenije, 1967. 1120p.
This is the only comprehensive dictionary for the Slovenian language and comprises over fifty thousand words. Useful for the study of the Slovenian language.

1546. Johnson, Bernard, ed. **New Writing in Yugoslavia**. Baltimore, MD: Penguin Books, 1970. 342p. $2.95 pa.
This collection of Yugoslav prose and poetry of the past two decades contains works by Slovenian and Macedonian writers as well as by Croats and Serbs. The editor has provided an interesting and informative introduction that sketches the cultural and political background against which current Yugoslav literature has developed and explains the scope and structure of the anthology. A set of biobibliographic notes on the authors is appended.
CSP, 14:4:724-27; Choice, 8(1971):840.

1547. Kadić, Ante. **Contemporary Serbian Literature**. The Hague, The Netherlands: Mouton, 1964. 105p. 12.50 Dglds.
In the absence of a full study of Serbian literature between the two world wars and also of any definitive history of Serbian literature in English, this book is, of necessity, interesting. The period covered is from 1903 to the present day. If, as the author tells us, it is only the precursor of a larger and more carefully prepared monograph, then we may look forward to its successor as a very welcome contribution to the study of Serbian literature.
SEER, 44:102:215-16.

1548. Kadić, Ante. **From Croatian Renaissance to Yugoslav Socialism: Essays**. The Hague, The Netherlands: Mouton, 1969. 301p. 48 Dglds. (Slavistic Printings and Reprintings, no. 90.)
Among the most interesting of historical pieces in this collection of the author's articles is the study on Croatian renaissance. He also examines the development of a South Slavic language. Kadić provides insights into Yugoslav culture and history for a better understanding of literature in Yugoslavia, particularly in Croatia, since the sixteenth century.
SR, 30:2:412.

1549. Kotnik, Janko. **Slovensko-angleški slovar** (Slovene-English Dictionary). Rev. 4th ed. Ljubljana: Državna Založba Slovenije, 1959. 762p.
Together with the *English-Slovene Dictionary* (see #1545) this volume can be well used for translation as well as for the study of the Slovenian languages.

1550. Magner, Thomas F. **Introduction to the Croatian and Serbian Language**. State College, PA: Singidunum Press, 1972. 351p.
This book is a thoroughly revised version of the author's work published in 1956. The Croatian and Serbian versions of the dialogues are separated right from the start and given in that order throughout. The glossary contains a large number of additional words usable for other purposes as well.

1551. Magner, Thomas F. **The Student's Dictionary of Serbo-Croatian: Serbo-Croatian-English, English-Serbo-Croatian**. State College, PA: Singidunum Press, 1970. 201p. $5.50.
This enlarged version of the glossary to the author's *Introduction to the Serbo-Croatian Language* contains about seven thousand entries in each of its two sections.
     SEEJ, 15:2:245.

1552. Mihailovich, Vasa D., ed. **Contemporary Yugoslav Poetry**. Iowa City: University of Iowa Press, 1977. xlviii, 242p. $12.50.
In addition to 237 pages of poems translated from Macedonian, Serbo-Croatian, and Slovenian and brief notes on forty-three contemporary Yugoslav authors, this collection contains an introduction entitled "The Poetry of Postwar Yugoslavia." There are 215 poems translated by thirty-one translators in this compendium.
     CSP, 20:3:436-37; BL, 74(1978):1534; LJ, 103(1978):1178.

1553. Mikasinovich, Branko, et al., eds. **Introduction to Yugoslav Literature: An Anthology of Fiction and Poetry**. New York: Twayne Publishers, 1973. 647p. $8.95.
This book contains samples from the works of important Serbian, Croatian, Slovenian, and Macedonian authors since the beginning of each modern literature. The introductions to the volume's four sections periodize and characterize the respective national literatures. They are, on the whole, factual and informative. The anthology provides a general view of the literary history of the peoples of Yugoslavia.
     SEEJ, 17:3:346-47; RSR, 1(1973):31.

1554. Mikasinovich, Branko, ed. **Five Modern Yugoslav Plays**. New York: Cyrco Press, 1977. xii, 339p. $15.00.
This book provides English-speaking readers with five representative samples of Yugoslav plays, representing Serbian, Croatian, Slovenian, and Macedonian ethnic backgrounds. In his introduction, the editor presents a survey of the history and development of Yugoslav drama from its beginnings until the present. Each play is preceded by a short biography of its author.
     SR, 37:4:721-22.

1555. Vidov, Bozidar. **Croatian Grammar**. Toronto: Canada Multicultural Program, 1975. 119p.
This textbook is divided into four parts: phonetics, morphology, syntax, and orthography. At the end of the book, a small Croatian-English dictionary has been appended explaining the words used in the *Grammar*.
     CSP, 20:3:439-40.

AUTHOR/SHORT TITLE INDEX